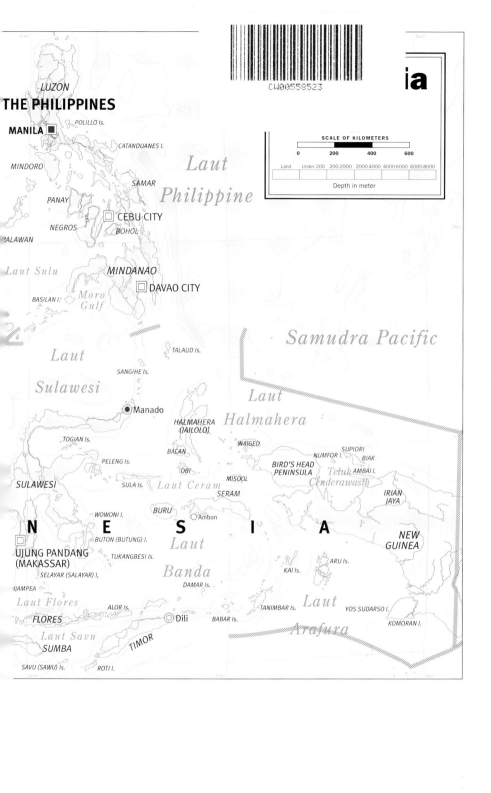

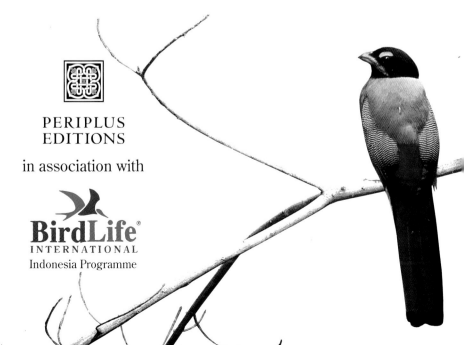

Birding
Indonesia

A Bird-watcher's Guide to the World's Largest Archipelago

Main contributor:
Paul Jepson

Editors: Paul Jepson
and Rosie Ounsted

PERIPLUS
EDITIONS

in association with

BirdLife®
INTERNATIONAL
Indonesia Programme

Published by Periplus Edition (HK) Ltd

Copyright © 1997 Periplus Editions (HK) Ltd
ALL RIGHTS RESERVED
ISBN 962-593-071-X
Printed in Singapore

Publisher: Eric Oey
Concept: Paul Jepson
Editor: Kim Inglis
Designer: Momentum Design Pte Ltd
Practicalities compilation: Rosie Ounsted
Production: Mary Chia
Cartography: Violet Wong, Ray Wiesling

Distributors

Belgium: Uitgeverij Lannoo NV, Kasteelstraat 97, B08700 Tielt

Germany: Brettschneider Fernreisebedarf, Feldkirchner Strasse 2, D-85551 Heimstetten

Hong Kong & Taiwan: Asia Publishers Services Ltd., 16/F, Wing Fat Commercial Building, 218 Aberdeen Main Road, Aberdeen, Hong Kong

Indonesia: C. V. Java Books, Jl. Kelapa Gading Kirana, Blok A-14 No. 17, Jakarta 14240

Japan: Tuttle Shokai Ltd., 21-13, Seki 1-Chome, Tama-ku, Kawasaki, Kanagawa 214

Singapore & Malaysia: Berkeley Books Pte. Ltd., 5 Little Road, #08-01 Singapore 536983

Thailand: Asia Books Co. Ltd., 5 Sukhumvit Soi 61, Bangkok 10110

The Netherlands: Nilsson & Lamm B.V., Postbus 195, 1380 AD Weesp

UK: GeoCentre U.K. Ltd., The Viables Centre, Harrow Way, Basingstoke, Hampshire RG22 4BJ

USA (Action Guides only): Fielding Worldwide, Inc., 308 South Catalina Ave, Redondo Beach, CA 90277

USA (Adventure Guides only): NTC Publishing Group, 4255 West Touhy Avenue, Lincolnwood (Chicago), IL 60646-1975

USA (All other titles): Charles E. Tuttle Co. Inc., RRI Box 231-5, North Clarendon, VT 05759-9700

Cover: A female Red-knobbed Hornbill rests quietly in the middle of the day. *Photo by Margaret Kinnaird.*

Pages 4–5: Birders out early in the day—sunrise is the best time on any bird-watcher's itinerary. *Photo by Alain Compost.*

Pages 6–7: Black-crested Bulbul, a common sight on Java. *Photo by Alain Compost.*

Page 8: Intrepid birders beneath tree-ferns! *Photo by Alain Compost.*

Page 9: Top left: Little Egret. *Photo by Alain Compost.* Bottom right: Scarlet-rumped Trogon. *Photo by David Tipling.*

CONTENTS

Photo by
Margaret Kinnaird.

Stalking an elusive species.

Birds of Indonesia

Diversity at the Crossroads of the Orient and Australasia

Indonesia holds 17% of the world's bird species, so becoming familiar with them might seem more like a post-graduate study than a fun vacation. In reality it is not nearly as daunting as it might seem: the 1,539 species are the sum of more manageable numbers occurring in distinct regions, islands and habitats. Narrowing the field by knowing what to expect is the key to bird identification.

A picture of the bio-geographic patterns in Indonesia's bird distribution is essential to understanding its bird mega-biodiversity, and also to planning a birding itinerary (*see pp 18–19*). The world has five major groupings of bird families and Indonesia straddles two of these, the Oriental and Australasian faunal realms. Wallace's famous line, which runs between Kalimantan and Sulawesi, then down between Bali and Lombok, marks the boundary between the two, or rather the point of "faunal balance". Biogeographers Lydeker and Weber also attempted to define these lines, but thankfully the modern approach is to dispense with academic arguments over lines, think of the central part of Indonesia as a transitional zone, and call it Wallacea.

Australians will feel at home in eastern Indonesia among the parrots, honeyeaters, white-eyes and monarchs; likewise, birders from Europe and Asia will find plenty of familiar families in western Indonesia's pheasants, woodpeckers, pigeons, flycatchers and thrushes. But Americans will face the bewildering and exciting challenge of totally new species—something that awaits us all in Irian Jaya, which, though part of the Australasian realm, has a bird fauna all of its own.

Bird Regions

Within this broad framework—west, transitional and east—biologists have divided Indonesia into seven biological regions based on distinct groupings of unique bird (and animal) species. So, for instance, Sulawesi has 96 bird species not shared with other regions, and the Lesser Sunda region has 72. This guide is structured on these biological regions, except for Maluku, where the provincial boundary—which encompasses the Moluccas and parts of the Lesser Sundas, and Irian Jaya—has been used for practical travel reasons. Sumatra and Irian Jaya are the regions with the greatest numbers of bird species—605 and 647 respectively; Sulawesi and Nusa Tenggara, with 379 and 398, have the smallest. By focusing on one of these regions it is quite possible to come away from a 2- or 3-week birding holiday feeling that you know the birds well. Conversely, if your goal is to see as many species as possible, the advice is to choose an itinerary that includes sites in two or more of these regions.

Endemic Species

The great attraction of birding in Indonesia is the large number of

Opposite: Using a microphone to record bird calls is common practice. *Photo by Paul Jepson.*

species found nowhere else on Earth: 381, or 4% of all bird species. Every serious "world lister" must come to Indonesia some time. For the purpose of targeting scarce conservation resources, BirdLife International has identified areas of the globe with concentrations of unique species. They are termed Endemic Bird Areas (EBAs) and Indonesia, with 24, has more EBAs than any other nation (*see pp 22–23*). They are located mainly in Wallacea, where the colonization of numerous oceanic islands from east and west has promoted the rapid evolution of new species through isolation, and in Irian Jaya, where the distinct vegetation types and secluded valleys have similarly led to rapid speciation. For those interested in finding new species, Endemic Bird Areas are not to be missed, but to catch up with all Indonesia's endemic species will entail several visits, or many weeks travelling around the islands of Wallacea.

Field Guides

A pair of binoculars, a field guide and a notebook are essential for identifying birds. There is no single field guide for Indonesia. *A Field Guide to the Birds of Borneo, Sumatra, Java and Bali* by John MacKinnon and Karen Phillipps and *A Field Guide to the Birds of New Guinea* by Bruce Beehler both clearly illustrate and describe all the species of these regions, but neither is available in Indonesia. Wallacea (Sulawesi, Nusa Tenggara and Maluku) has the frustrating distinction of being one of the last regions on Earth without a field guide. One is close to completion and the pocket guide *Birds of Sulawesi* by Derek Holmes illustrates a selection of species, but, for the moment, serious birders still have to rely on "White & Bruce": *The Birds of Wallacea*, an impressive work of taxonomic scholarship but a challenge to use for field identification. To overcome this problem, many birders come armed with notes and sketches of species from difficult or diverse families made from the excellent series of books dealing with individual families (see Further Reading).

In Sulawesi, bird identification is difficult without a comprehensive field guide, but it is surprising how far you can get armed only with island checklists in Nusa Tenggara and Maluku. Most islands support under a hundred forest species, with only a few representatives of each family. If you already know, for instance, the difference between a fruit-dove, a green pigeon, a cuckoo-dove and an imperial pigeon, faced with an unfamiliar pigeon there are probably only two or three options, and the species name will give you the last clue to identification. Island lists can be found in *The Ecology of Nusa Tenggara and Maluku* by Kathryn Monk *et al* or on the BirdLife

Below: Virtually anywhere can be reached by public transport; where four wheels stop, the *ojeks* or motorcycle taxis take over. *Photo by Alain Compost.*

Indonesia Programme's homepage on the World Wide Web. A checklist, which shows regional distribution, is included in the Practicalities.

The Birding Travel Experience

Putting a name to the bird is essential for many birders, but of course it is only one part of the enjoyment of bird-watching: the form, colours, calls, behaviour and ecology of birds is what makes the hobby so absorbing. The opportunity to see new and fascinating facets of these is the great draw of the tropics, and Indonesia is packed with the beautiful, evocative, unexpected and sometimes downright bizarre aspects of birds. From the manic laugh of the Helmeted Hornbill and splendid colours of pittas to the unique nesting behaviour of the megapodes and gorgeous displays of the birds-of-paradise, Indonesia is a delight whatever your particular birdwatching preference.

Add to this the sheer fun and wonder of travelling in this archipelago of diverse cultures and landscapes and Indonesia is sure to be a place you will want to return to time and time again. Most of the sites introduced in this guide are now easily accessible by car thanks to the country's rapidly improving infrastructure, but birders with a taste for adventure will find travelling to remoter sites a memorable and exciting montage of gazing out of airplane windows at awesome volcanic landscapes, bumping down awful roads in packed minibuses, chugging across sparkling seas on inter-island ferries, and careering along on the back of motorbike taxis (*ojeks*).

The energy-sapping heat and humidity are the biggest problems facing birders, especially when newly arrived. Whether searching for pheasants on Mt Kerinci, wader watching on the Brantas delta or enjoying birds-of-paradise in Irian Jaya, the chances are that you will be sweating copiously. Other discomforts are relatively minor or controllable (see the Travel Advisory for advice on how to keep fit and healthy) and you can wander around pretty much anywhere without fear of violence and attack. Indeed, if it were not for the accident risk on poorly maintained and

Above: Comparing notes and checking species lists in a watch-tower. *Photo by Alain Compost.*

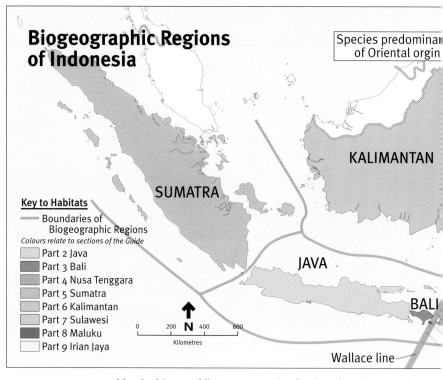

Biogeographic Regions of Indonesia

Species predominan of Oriental orgin

KALIMANTAN

SUMATRA

JAVA

BALI

Key to Habitats

Boundaries of Biogeographic Regions
Colours relate to sections of the Guide

Part 2 Java
Part 3 Bali
Part 4 Nusa Tenggara
Part 5 Sumatra
Part 6 Kalimantan
Part 7 Sulawesi
Part 8 Maluku
Part 9 Irian Jaya

0   200   **N** 400   600
Kilometres

Wallace line

recklessly driven public transport, Indonesia would rank as one of the safest countries in Asia for tourists.

Bird Families

The following section gives a brief introduction to some of the main bird families and groups found in Indonesia (for a full checklist see Practicalities); like all field guides and lists, it is ordered in taxonomic sequence. The purpose of this sequence is broadly to highlight evolutionary relationships: it starts with the bird families that are the oldest in evolutionary terms and ends with the most "modern".

Below: An Oriental Darter shows off its beautiful silver scapular feathers as it dries its wings. *Photo by David Tipling.*

Casuariidae— cassowaries: These very large, 1-m tall, flight- less birds inhabit the forests of Irian Jaya. The Southern Cassowary

is also found on Seram, where it was presumably introduced long ago. (3 species).

Procellariidae/Hydrobatidae —petrels and shearwaters: Indonesia is generally poor in seabirds and no good sea-watching sites are known, although the Sunda Strait, between Sumatra and Java, has potential in the autumn. Wedge-tailed Shearwater, Bulwer's Petrel and Matsudaira's Storm-petrel are the species most often seen from inter-island ferries. (15 species).

Phaethontidae—tropicbirds: These beautiful, white seabirds, with their long, central tail stream-ers, breed in small numbers on sea cliffs along the south coasts of Java and Bali and also in eastern Indonesia. They are rarely seen at sea in Indonesia. (2 species).

Fregatidae—frigatebirds: Common along the coasts of the archipelago, frigatebirds are unmis-takable: large, with black body, long-bowed, pointed wings and forked tail. The Lesser is the com-monest species, but identification of

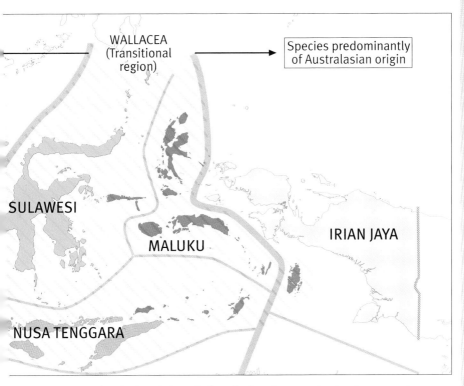

WALLACEA
(Transitional
region)

Species predominantly
of Australasian origin

SULAWESI

IRIAN JAYA

MALUKU

NUSA TENGGARA

immatures is a headache—bring notes from specialist seabird guides if you want to be sure. (3 species).

Phalacrocoracidae/Anhingidae—cormorants and darters: Wherever there are expanses of water—lakes, swamps and bays—you are likely to find these long-necked fish eaters. (6 species).

Sulidae—boobies: These are the gannets of tropical seas. The Brown Booby is quite common; the other three species are much rarer, unless you visit the remote seabird islands in the Banda Sea (or Christmas Island). (4 species).

Pelecanidae—pelicans: The Great-white Pelican is only a vagrant, and the Spot-billed now a very rare resident of coastal swamps in Sumatra. The Australian Pelican migrates to Maluku and Nusa Tenggara; the sight of a flock loafing on a sand bar is unforgettable. (3 species).

Ardeidae—herons, egrets and allies: White egrets and herons are still a familiar sight on Indonesia's marshes and coasts. The smaller bitterns are largely migrants to

Indonesia, but they are shy, hard-to-find inhabitants of dense marsh vegetation which is in itself becoming harder to find. Look out for the rare Great-billed Heron on coral flats. (22 species).

Ciconiidae—storks: Storks are confined mainly to western Indonesia and all species are now very rare. However, the two rarest, Milky and Storm's Storks, can be seen quite easily at Pulau Rambut (Jakarta Bay) and Way Kambas (Sumatra) respectively. (3 species).

Accipitridae/Falconidae—hawks, eagles and falcons: Raptor enthusiasts will find Indonesia a treat. Raptor populations have drastically diminished on Java (probably due to excessive pesticide use) but are still strong elsewhere. The magnificent White-bellied Sea-eagle is a characteristic sight along coasts, but a sighting of Javan Hawk-eagle, Sulawesi Hawk-eagle or Gurney's Eagle (in Halmahera or Irian Jaya) will be a highlight. In September and October large numbers of honey-buzzards and sparrowhawks migrate through Indonesia; Bali

Above: Blue-winged Pitta—venerated by birders on account of its glorious plumage and shy habits. Indonesia is home to half of the world's 25 pitta species. *Photo by Alain Compost.*

Barat is a good place to watch them. Field identification marks of resident goshawks and sparrowhawks are poorly understood. (65 species).

Anatidae—ducks, geese and swans: The resident duck population is swelled by migrants from the northern winter, but accessible wetlands are few. The Sunda Teal, easily recognised by its bulbous forehead, is still common in western Indonesia. One of Indonesia's top birding attractions is the near certainty of seeing the elusive and globally threatened White-winged Duck at Way Kambas in south Sumatra; in eastern Indonesia the stately White-headed Shelduck fills a similar niche along forested rivers, but is much more catholic in its choice of wetlands. (19 species).

Megapodiidae—megapodes: Indonesia supports all but five of the world's 22 species. These extraordinary birds, which bury massive eggs in sand or large mounds of rotting vegetation, from which free-flying chicks emerge, are one of Indonesia's greatest birding highlights. The black-and-white Maleo of Sulawesi is the most famous; the Orange-footed Scrubfowl of Nusa Tenggara and Dusky Scrubfowl of

North Maluku are among the easiest to see strolling around the forest floor. (17 species).

Phasianidae/Turnicidae: pheasants, quails and button-quails: Birders in Sumatra and Kalimantan invest considerable effort in catching up with the superb forest pheasants. Red Jungle-fowl, the ancestor of the domestic chicken, is locally common in Sumatra and Java, and the Green Peafowl's range extends from Java into Nusa Tenggara. Only the button-quails' range extends east of the Wallace line. (28 species).

Rallidae—rails, moorhens, and coots: Rails are long-legged, mostly drably coloured birds that skulk around the margins of forest pools or marshes. They are favourites with birders, probably because they are a challenge to see, although, with a few notable exceptions such as the Invisible Rail of Halmahera, they are easy to find in Indonesia compared with other countries in the region. (27 species).

Charadriiformes—waders: Indonesia is a good place to catch up with eastern palearctic species on their wintering grounds: they include Asian Dowitcher, Great

Knot, Grey-tailed Tattler, Oriental Plover, and Sharp-tailed and Terek Sandpipers. The largest concentrations of shorebirds are found on the river deltas of west Sumatra and north Java, but many birds are scattered in small groups along the eastern Indonesian coasts. Flocks of Red-necked Phalarope are a common sight on the seas of Maluku and Nusa Tenggara. (63 species).

Stercorariidae/Laridae—skuas, gulls, terns and noddies: The almost total absence of gulls is a striking feature of Indonesian bird life. Great Crested and Bridled Terns are the typical inshore species, but Black-naped Terns are quite common around rocky coasts. In the northern winter flocks of Common Terns, mixed with Brown Noddies and often with a couple of skuas in attendance, feed in the mangrove-fringed bays of the eastern islands. Whiskered and White-winged Terns are common over freshwater swamps. (26 species).

Columbidae—pigeons and doves: Indonesia's amazing variety of pigeons—flocking green

Extinct Species

In historic times only one species, the Javan Lapwing, is known to have become extinct in Indonesia. This handsome brown lapwing, with its black hood and striking yellow wattle, formerly inhabited grassy patches among the marshes of northwest Java and river deltas of the southeast, where it was last seen in the 1940s.

The Caerulean Paradise-flycatcher, a stocky blue member of the monarch family confined to forests on remote Sanghie Island in North Sulawesi, was widely feared extinct until a single bird was seen by a British/Indonesian ornithological expedition in 1995; with luck, further surveys will find a viable population still surviving.

The Bali Starling is Indonesia's best-known endangered bird. About 35 wild birds remain in Bali Barat National Park; their survival depends on the skill of the park authorities. Less well known, but perhaps equally threatened, are Kalimantan's White-shouldered Ibis and Bornean Peacock-pheasant. Their riverine forest habitat is under great threat because rivers form the roads in this developing province.

Although species on the very edge of extinction inevitably catch the headlines, birders resident in Indonesia are becoming increasingly alarmed at the population declines and local extinctions of once-common species. The situation is particularly acute on Java. The Brahminy Kite, so commonly seen on Asia's coastlines, is virtually extinct; typical farmland birds such as Spotted Kestrel, Red-breasted Parakeet, Black-winged Starling and Java Sparrow have disappeared from many of their former haunts, and a flock of Asian Glossy Starlings or egrets is now unheard of. Similar trends are beginning in Sumatra, Kalimantan and Sulawesi, but as yet no studies have been made on the extent of the declines or their root causes. It can be guessed, however, that these are a combination of agricultural intensification—in particular, heavy pesticide use—and widespread persecution by a burgeoning human population.

–Paul Jepson

Below: Artist's impression of Javan Lapwing—the only species known to have become extinct in Indonesia. *Drawing by Su TC.*

pigeons; delicate, long-tailed, warm brown and rufous coloured cuckoo-doves; magnificent imperial pigeons, whose deep calls reverberate through the island forests and mangroves of eastern Indonesia; gorgeously coloured fruit-doves; and the dainty ground-doves and famous crowned pigeons of Irian Jaya—will leave you with new depths of appreciation of this familiar bird family. (91 species).

Psittacidae—parrots, lories and allies: East of Wallace's line the forests resound with the screeches of parrots: Indonesia boasts no fewer than 30 endemic species. Most parrots are conspicuous and easy to identify, and the sight of a flock of cockatoos assembling for roost, red lories scorching over the forest canopy, or the exquisite, turquoise wings of a Great-billed Parrot catching the evening sun are some of the most enduring memories of a birding trip to Indonesia. (72 species).

Cuculidae—cuckoos, koels and coucals: This is another mega-diverse family in Indonesia,

comprising typical migrant and Asian species, with several island endemics. The Javan Coucal has the distinction of being one of Indonesia's most endangered birds, and the Plaintive and Brush Cuckoos the most maddening, because of their persistent, annoying, ascending whistles and the difficulty of getting good views to tell them apart. (53 species).

Caprimulgiformes—owls, frogmouths, owlet-nightjars and nightjars: If you want to make a name for yourself in birding circles, this is the group to focus on. The boobooks and scopsowls readily speciate on islands, as yet undescribed forms have been seen by birders on Timor and Sumba, and almost nothing is known about the Taliabu and Lesser Masked Owls of Maluku. (66 species).

Apodiformes—swiftlets, swifts and tree-swifts: The 12 species of swiftlet are among Indonesia's commonest birds but are so difficult to identify that most birders do not bother. Tree-swifts are larger, with long, scythe-shaped

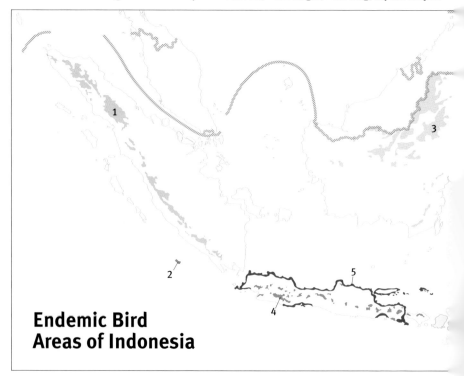

Endemic Bird
Areas of Indonesia

wings and forked tails; they sit around on exposed branches of forest trees. (24 species).

Trogonidae—trogons: These beautiful and unobtrusive forest birds, with their black hoods, red or orange bellies and exquisitely vermiculated wing feathers, are quite common in lowland forests of Sumatra, Kalimantan and Java. The Blue-tailed Trogon is an exception: it is a montane forest specialist with blue-and-yellow plumage. (8 species).

Alcedinidae—kingfishers and kookaburras: The great variety of kingfishers is one of the real joys of birding in Indonesia, and their diversity in North Sulawesi and Halmahera is a major factor in the increasing popularity of this region. Kingfishers range in size from the huge Black-billed Kingfisher of Sulawesi and Shovel-billed Kingfisher of Irian Jaya to the diminutive dwarf kingfishers of western Indonesia and Sulawesi. (45 species).

Meropidae/Coraciidae—bee-eaters and rollers: The distinctive, triangular wings and chirping calls of bee-eaters grace most open-country habitats in Indonesia. Rollers and dollarbirds are larger species and have spectacular display flights. The endemic Purple-bearded Bee-eater and Purple-winged Roller are top attractions of Sulawesi. (9 species).

Bucerotidae—hornbills: These massive birds are an unmistakable and unforgettable feature of Indonesia's forests. Diversity is highest in Sumatra and Kalimantan, where up to seven species can be seen at one site. Two species occur in Sulawesi, and Blyth's Hornbill is the eastern representative of the group in North Maluku and Irian Jaya. Hornbills are absent from Nusa Tenggara and South Maluku, except Sumba, which has an endemic of its own. (15 species).

Piciformes—barbets, woodpeckers and piculets: The Piciformes are a western Indonesian family, with only two species, both woodpeckers, crossing Wallace's line into Sulawesi. The monotonous *tonk-tonk* of barbets is a characteristic rainforest sound, though

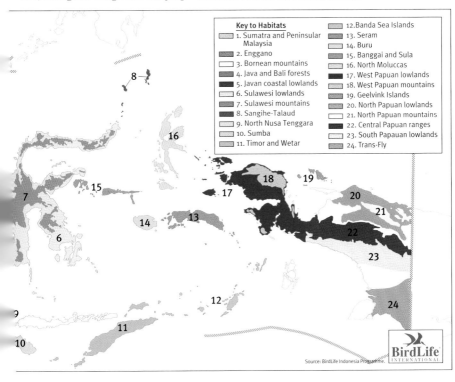

Key to Habitats
1. Sumatra and Peninsular Malaysia
2. Enggano
3. Bornean mountains
4. Java and Bali forests
5. Javan coastal lowlands
6. Sulawesi lowlands
7. Sulawesi mountains
8. Sangihe-Talaud
9. North Nusa Tenggara
10. Sumba
11. Timor and Wetar
12. Banda Sea Islands
13. Seram
14. Buru
15. Banggai and Sula
16. North Moluccas
17. West Papuan lowlands
18. West Papuan mountains
19. Geelvink Islands
20. North Papuan lowlands
21. North Papuan mountains
22. Central Papuan ranges
23. South Papuan lowlands
24. Trans-Fly

Source: BirdLife Indonesia Programme.

BirdLife INTERNATIONAL

Above: A White-bellied Woodpecker calls from its nest hole. *Photo by Alain Compost.*

getting views of these colourful, stocky birds can be neck-breaking. Some woodpeckers—the Crimson-winged and other Yellownapes—are equally gaudy. (41 species).

Eurylaimidea—broadbills: These boldly patterned and coloured birds, with their distinctive round heads and broad gapes, are confined to the rain forest of western Indonesia. They can be difficult to see, but the effort is well worthwhile. (8 species).

Pittidae—pittas: Pittas are quail- or partridge-sized ground birds of forest and secondary growth. The group most sought-after by birders, they have it all: beauty of form and colour and an ability to wind you up into a frenzy of anticipation before they finally reveal themselves. Half the world's species occur in Indonesia and four are endemic. (16 species).

Campephagidae—cuckoo-shrikes, cicadabirds, trillers and minivets: Another diverse group heaving with endemics, but, with the exception of the striking red-and-black or yellow-and-black (female) minivets, they are rather boring grey or pied birds. Field identification is difficult, mainly because they are hard to get worked up about and no one has yet sorted out the various species in detail. (46 species).

Pycnonotidae—bulbuls: These are thrush-sized birds with greatest diversity in western Indonesia. The Sooty-headed Bul-

bul, or *kutilang*, is one of Indonesia best-known birds and the Straw-headed Bulbul its best songster. Generally bulbuls do not hold a great deal of interest for birders because many are very drab. However, a few of the forest species are surprisingly attractive. (28 species).

Turdidae—thrushes, robins, chats and babblers: This is a large and diverse family and another great favourite with birders. In the forests of Sumatra and Kalimantan, you will be kept busy identifying the small groups of babblers foraging in the canopy and under-storey. In Nusa Tenggara and Maluku, the island-endemic thrushes are the attraction, and in Irian Jaya the jewel-babblers steal the show. (121 species).

Sylviidae—Old World warblers: Although many species have been recorded in Indonesia, these small, insectivorous birds do not form such a large proportion of the avifauna as they do, for example, in Europe or on the Indian sub-continent. The group includes a few highly prized species: two species of the diminutive, apparently tail-less tesias—Javan and Russet-capped, endemic *Phylloscopus* warblers on Sulawesi and Timor, and migrant Gray's Warbler (an extremely rare vagrant to western Europe), which is quite common in the beach forests of the eastern isles. (44 species).

Muscicapidae—Old World flycatchers: Typical Southeast Asian genera, the drab rhinomyias and blue *Ficedula* flycatchers are common in the forests of western Indonesia and several have colonized Nusa Tenggara and Maluku, where they have evolved into distinct species. In the northern winter, the resident flycatcher species are boosted by migrants: Narcissus, Yellow-rumped and Mugimaki Flycatchers are possible. (44 species).

Maluridae: fairy wrens: These striking, iridescent, cocked-tailed warblers are confined to New Guinea and Australia. (6 species).

Acanthizidae—scrub-wrens, thornbill, Australian warblers

and allies: Australian birders will feel at home with this family, which is mostly confined to eastern Indonesia. The gerygones are particularly well represented with 11 species, two of which are endemic. (24 species).

Monarchidae—monarchs: This is another family with Asian origins; 23 of the 36 species occur in Irian Jaya. Monarchs look and act like Old World flycatchers, but are a little stockier. They have spread across the islands of Indonesia, and many island groups have their own species. (36 species).

Rhipiduridae—fantails and allies: The broad, white-tipped tail, which is constantly fanned, renders this flycatcher family unmistakable. Fantails are found throughout Indonesia, but species diversity is highest in Irian Jaya. The islands of east Nusa Tenggara and south Maluku support several endemic species. (28 species).

Petroicidae: Australian robins: In Indonesia this family is found only in Irian Jaya, where it replaces the Old World robins and chats. (19 species).

Pachycephalidae—whistlers, pitohuis and allies: These are small, stocky birds that glean insects from foliage. Most have distinctive calls and some, such as the Common Golden Whistler, are strikingly coloured. They are found mainly in eastern Indonesia; just three species cross Wallace's line to the west. (31 species).

Dicaeidae/Nectariniidae— flowerpeckers, sunbirds and spiderhunters: Flowerpeckers are tiny, stumpy and normally brightly coloured birds that dash between flowering trees, calling with a "ticking" sound. Sunbirds are slightly larger with thin, down-curved bills and iridescent plumage patches. Both groups are familiar forest and garden birds seen throughout Indonesia. Spiderhunters are a specialized sunbird with extended, decurved bills; they are found only in western Indonesia. (54 species: Dicaeidae—32 species; Nectariniidae—22 species).

Zosteropidae—white-eyes: Although 20 of the species are endemic, many to single islands, it is rare to hear a birder enthusing about them, probably because they vary little from the basic design of white eye-ring, olive upperparts, and white or yellow belly with yellow breast and flanks. (31 species).

Meliphagidae—honeyeaters and friarbirds: Most honeyeaters are equally monotonous (bright-red myzomelas are the exception), except that these olive or green birds with their stocky, down-curved bills have quite cheery songs. Friarbirds are definitely Indonesia's ugliest birds: they have grubby, grey-and-brown plumage, a scruffy, dark, sometimes bare head and knobs on the top of their bills. However, they make up for their looks with loud and reasonably tuneful duetting. (70 species).

Below: Crimson Sunbird—the iridescent plumages of sunbirds light up the forest. *Photo by Alain Compost*
Far Below: Fantails, such as this White-throated Fantail, are typical members of mixed bird flocks. *Photo by Morten Strange.*

Above: The turkey-sized Victoria Crowned Pigeon of Irian Jaya is the world's largest pigeon. *Photo by Alain Compost.*

Estrildidae/Ploceidae—finches and sparrows: The 20 munia species make up the bulk of this group. These small finches, variously patterned with black, white, chestnut and brown, are serious pests to rice crops in some parts of Indonesia. The four species of parrot-finch are all quite rare: finding one of these will be a highlight in any day's birding. (38 species).

Sturnidae—starlings and mynas: The endemic starlings and mynas are one of Indonesia's, and particularly Sulawesi's, big birding attractions. The Bali Starling, with a population of fewer than 40, rates as one of the world's rarest birds. (25 species).

Oriolidae—orioles and figbirds: The western Indonesian oriole species share the typical yellow, green and black coloration of the family, but the endemic species in Maluku and Nusa Tenggara have lost this colour to become drab, brown friarbird mimics. (14 species).

Dicruridae—drongos: These black birds with forked, and—in the case of racquet-tailed drongos—long, spatula-tipped, wire tails are one of the most familiar birds of Indonesia's forests. They make an extra-ordinary range of sounds: you soon tire of checking out interesting calls only to find that they belong to yet another drongo. (12 species).

Ptilonorhynchidae—bowerbirds: In Indonesia bowerbirds are found only in Irian Jaya. The building of the large, intricately decorated bowers (and their tending of them) by these plump, thrush-like birds is one of the miracles of evolution. (8 species).

Paradisaeidae—birds-of-paradise: These are surely the world's most exciting birds: just about every birder dreams of seeing them in the wild. The good news is that, if you get to Irian Jaya, they are quite common and not too difficult to see, although you will need local information to experience the thrill of seeing dawn displays. If you cannot afford Irian Jaya, Wallace's Standard-wing can be seen on Halmahera, just a short flight from North Sulawesi. (32 species).

Corvidae—crows and jays: Although this family is rather thin on the ground in Indonesia, the green magpies and Crested Jay of western Indonesia are definitely worth searching out. (17 species).

—Paul Jepson

Discovering New Species

Two new bird species have been discovered in Indonesia in the past 25 years: the Tanimbar Bush-warbler, an inconspicuous inhabitant of forest undergrowth, was found on Yamdena as recently as 1985, and the Flores Monarch was discovered in the mountains of west Flores in 1971.

Although several 19th-century explorers did a remarkable job in collecting and describing many of Indonesia's birds, there are almost certainly a few more species still awaiting discovery. The Lesser Sunda chain of islands—Lombok through to Timor—must rate as one of the most promising areas: in addition to the two discoveries mentioned above, there have been recent sightings of unknown boobook owls on Timor and Roti and a scopsowl on Sumba, all of which may well turn out to be species new to science.

If finding a new species is your ambition, the best advice is to study Indonesian biogeography and the history of ornithological exploration in order to identify places that have been isolated at some period in their distant history—either by sea-level fluctuations or climatic changes affecting vegetation—but which have so far been poorly studied. Mt Mekongga in Sulawesi fits this bill better than anywhere, but a 1995 expedition from the UK found that getting into the mountain range required serious logistical planning.

However, it is likely that museum studies rather than heroic field surveys will provide the new additions to Indonesia's already impressive tally of unique species. Experts estimate that, if Indonesia's complex species groups were studied with the same rigour afforded to American or European bird taxonomy, 100 or more sub-species might be elevated to the status of full species. So, whilst in Indonesia, do make sure you see the unique island forms of the wider ranging species. Then, in the future, you may have the satisfaction of seeing your world list grow from the comfort of your armchair! –*Paul Jepson*

Above: Birders use tape play back to draw out an elusive species. *Photo by Alain Compost.*

Left: The Flores Monarch was discovered as recently as 1971. *Photo by S Buchart/BirdLife.*

Early Explorers

A brief History of Indonesian Ornithology

The literature of Indonesian ornithology is full of enthralling tales of great naturalists and adventurers who braved disease and hostile tribesmen, trekked into uncharted forests, and survived arduous sea journeys in pursuit of new discoveries and the fame and fortune that these brought among the educated elite of their homelands. The great era of exploration lasted a little over a century, up to World War II.

It is sobering, even humbling, to compare the achievements and standards of scholarship of this era with those of today. Although the early explorers lacked the advantages of the modern world—transport and communications, political stability and the conquering of disease—they did have the benefit of time: on long sea voyages there was little else to do but study catalogues and collections, and lonely colonial officers found the study of natural history a welcome intellectual distraction. Moreover, in those days it was easier to finance extended travels, either through the benevolence of wealthy patrons or by shipping back collections to European museums, which paid handsomely for new specimens.

Earliest Records

Technically, the written documentation of Indonesian birds (indeed of all wild birds) started with mention of a "speaking grackle" (the Hill Myna) from Sumatra in ancient Chinese texts of the T'ang dynasty (618–906 AD), but the first person to study Indonesian natural history seriously was G E Rumpf (Rumphius), who was resident in Ambon from 1657–1702 and described species brought to him from Ambon, Seram and Buru. Modern naturalists who find themselves stressed with the frustrations of field work in Indonesia can take solace that their travails pale into insignificance compared with those of Rumphius, who lost his wife and daughter when an earthquake destroyed their house, had his monumental collections and drawings destroyed in a fire, twice lost his manuscripts at sea, went blind from disease at the age of 42, and yet still completed a master work—the *Herbarium Ambonensis*, published in 1743, 40 years after his death.

It was in the 18th century that the study of natural history really got under way with the so called "voyages of discovery"—nautical survey expeditions that wandered around the "eastern archipelago" charting the seas and searching for sources of spices or anything else that might arouse the curiosity and imagination of a Europe hungry for exotica.

Most ships carried a surgeon who doubled up as a naturalist and the names of the vessels, *L'Etoile* (1766–8), *Le Géographe* and *Le Naturaliste* (1801 and 1803), *L'Astrolabe* and *Experiment*, *La Coquille* (1817–40) are still associated with historic ornithological discoveries in Sulawesi, Nusa Tenggara, Maluku and Irian Jaya. The published accounts of their voyages provide fascinating insights into the travel and natural history of the times (see Further Reading).

19th-century Exploration in West Indonesia

While these ships were wandering the eastern islands, Dutch, British and German scientists were busy documenting the birds of west Indonesia. Baron Friedrich van Wurmb, chief secretary of the Batavia (Jakarta) Hospital from 1779–82, has the distinction of having described the first ten birds from Java, but it was Thomas Horsfield who laid the foundations of Javan ornithology with his *Systematic arrangement and description of Birds of Java*, which described no fewer than 71 birds new to science in his collections between 1802–19.

Horsfield and other famous collectors, such as Vieillot and Diard, owed their success to the support given by Sir Stamford Raffles, Governor of Java during the brief period of British rule from 1811 to 1816. Raffles's work stimulated the Dutch authorities to take an interest in the science of the "colonies" after they regained control, and as a result the Natuurkundige Commissie vor Nederlansch Indie (Committee for the Natural History of the Dutch East Indies) was established in 1820. Temminck, Europe's greatest taxonomist of the time, was charged with organising a series of expeditions to areas of Java, Sumatra and Borneo. Temminck attracted the best young ornitho-

Below: Old print showing the first Dutch fleet leaving Holland for the Indies in 1596. Long sea voyages provided ample time for the study of catalogues, and, in the centuries following, Indonesian natural history began to be documented.

logical talent of the day. Kuhl, van Hasselt, Boie, Machlot, Müller, De Vries and Junghuhn are some of the names associated with this era. Only Müller returned home; the others all died of disease within a few years of their arrival and in 1850 the committee was disbanded because of this high mortality rate.

Wallace and Forbes

Fortunately, the two great English explorers of the era, Alfred Russel Wallace and Henry Forbes (who was accompanied by his wife), were luckier and left two wonderful books, *The Malay Archipelago* (1869) and *A Naturalist's Wanderings in the Eastern Archipelago* (1885), which still constitute the basic texts on the natural history of the region.

Below:
Photographer Frank Hurley setting up his equipment on an expedition to New Guinea in 1922.
Photo courtesy of the American Museum of Natural History.

During his eight years in Indonesia, from 1854 to 1862, Wallace collected a staggering 125,660 specimens including 8,050 birds, but it was his talent for theorizing that has led the scientific community to view his work as epoch making. While recovering from a fever on Ternate, in early 1858, Wallace formulated, as he put it, "the long sought for law of nature that solved the problem of the origin of species".

He sent his article to Charles Darwin to ask for his opinion. Darwin, it is said, was thrown into anguish and remarked: "If Wallace had my manuscript written out in 1842, he could not have made a better short abstract." As Wallace was in Indonesia, Darwin presented their ideas jointly at a meeting of the Linnean Society in 1858 and, not surprisingly, quickly finished *On the Origin of Species*, which later made him world-famous.

Darwin's name has since become synonymous with the theory of evolution. Rather than return home to share in the accolades being bestowed on Darwin, Wallace preferred to continue his journeys of discovery.

Voyages of Discovery

The sensation of *On the Origin of Species* fuelled intense demand for specimens for the world's museums, and the period from 1860 up to the outbreak of World War II was the golden age of Indonesian ornithology, with a plethora of expeditions and individuals scouring the remote islands and mountains of the archipelago in search of new species. The famous English naturalist and eccentric, Lord Rothschild, funded Doherty, Everett and Waterstradt to collect for his enormous personal museum; German-financed expeditions brought the leading ornithologist of the early 20th century, Ernst Stresemann, to the region. The inter-war years witnessed elaborate expeditions into uncharted areas of

New Guinea, the most famous being the massively supplied Archbold Expedition from the American Museum of Natural History in 1930, which surveyed areas in the North-west, Fly River and Snow Mountains.

First Detailed Studies and up to the Present Day

The expedition's ornithologist, A L Rand, became the preeminent authority on New Guinea's birds. At the same time there were several gifted ornithologists among the resident expatriate community, people like Louis Coomans de Ruiter, who published the first detailed studies of birds in North Sulawesi, Max Bartels, who wrote a series of landmark articles on Javan birds between 1906 and 1930, and A G Vorderman, a medical doctor, who described important new bird collections from Sumatra, Lombok and the Moluccas as well as Java. From this group we see the first signs of modern ecological and conservation perspectives. Dammerman published the first conservation strategy in 1929, and Alexander Hoogerwerf, who lived in Java from 1938 to 1953, was the father of Indonesian bird ecology.

Compared with the colonial era, the decades since independence in 1945 have been a relatively quiet time in Indonesian ornithology. At the beginning of the 1980s, an extensive set of surveys funded by the United Nations Food and Agriculture Program for a National Conservation Plan marked a revival of field surveys.

Today a new era of biological exploration is underway: surveys and expeditions by government projects, international conservation agencies and university scientists are re-visiting the haunts of the early explorers. The authors of this guide are all part of this movement, but none would seriously liken themselves to the heros of the past. Binoculars have replaced the gun, and collecting urgently needed conservation-related data takes precedent over esoteric studies. Three centuries of exploration have barely scratched the surface of Indonesian ornithology; the future is bound to bring numerous new and fascinating discoveries.

–Paul Jepson

Above: Painting by J C Grieve Jr (1865–72) depicting a typical exploratory foray into the interior.

Bird Conservation

Outlook for Indonesia's Birds in a Changing Nation

The 1992 "Earth Summit" in Rio de Janeiro—the decade's great environmental jamboree, where the world's leaders lined up at a photo session to declare their nations' commitment to conserving global biological diversity—has resulted in a plethora of strategies that rank Indonesia as one of the top five countries for investment in conservation. Millions of dollars are flowing into the country for conservation-related projects and several of the main international conservation agencies now have in-country programmes. So can we feel optimistic about the future of Indonesia's birds? Can birders be confident that the sites they visit today will still be intact in 10 or 15 years' time?

The reply from conservation experts is *belum*—not yet. The optimists among them will point to the vast tracts of natural habitat still remaining, the solid portfolio of environmental policy and legislation put in place by the government, Indonesia's extensive network of terrestrial reserves covering 16 million hectares, and the fact that influential development agencies such as the World Bank and Asian Development bank have "mainstreamed" biodiversity in investment planning. But in private you will find few optimists among those who have worked for any length of time in Indonesian conservation. You will hear about the scale of the problem: an average 1.6% annual growth rate in a population that is already approaching 200 million, the overwhelming majority of whom view nature as something to be tamed and utilized, limitless and

with no value. And people will talk of the frustrations of generating any change in the operational wings of the massive and complex government bureaucracy.

Bird conservation issues in Indonesia are varied and complex, and raise many interesting dilemmas for the individuals and agencies, who—despite seemingly insuperable odds—are dedicated to finding solutions.

The Bird Trade

The best known threats facing birds in Indonesia are the bird trade and the destruction of the rain forests. Bird catching is certainly rife—over 250 species have been recorded for sale in Javan bird markets alone—and may be a significant factor in the worrying declines of common bird populations. However, of the 104 Indonesian species classified by BirdLife International (an international conservation agency that is the leading authority on the status of the world's birds) as globally threatened with extinction, in the case of only four species is trade the principal cause of their plight.

The most famous of these is the Bali Starling, which, despite being strictly protected, has been reduced to just 35 birds as a result of poaching in its last home in the Bali Barat National Park (*see pp 76–77*). Sadly, a similar fate is facing Indonesia's national bird, the Javan Hawk-eagle. As a rainforest specialist confined to Java, the Javan Hawk-eagle's numbers are already severely limited by available habitat and may total as few as 150 pairs. Because a pair can raise—at best—one eaglet every two years, the regular appearance of nestlings in bird markets is a major worry, especially as the government nature conservation agency currently lacks the resources to make any concerted effort to control the trade or prosecute offenders.

Naturally, most bird lovers would be happy to see an end to the bird trade, but pursuing this goal presents a number of dilemmas. The most acute is the sheer numbers of people who earn their livelihood from the trade, especially those in the lowest income groups. Their number has been put at more than a million. It is a hard-hearted conservationist who can tell a smallholder on Halmahera that he is wrong to catch Chattering Lories (which are still common) to pay for his children's education. Outright bans also run the risk of pushing the trade underground and, as already indicated, the government currently lacks the capacity to enforce protected wildlife legislation.

A pragmatic approach would be to manage the impact of trade by developing commercial breeding or sustainable harvesting programmes. Demand for the hugely popular Peaceful Dove is now satisfied by breeding farms in Thailand, with the result that there is little capture of wild birds. Export quotas for parrots are already set each year and strictly enforced internationally. Re-structuring the economics of this trade so that communities and local government received a far greater share of the retail value of parrots would give local incentives to conserve the birds' rainforest habitat and manage populations sustainably in the long term. For example, cockatoo catchers on Halmahera currently receive only US$14 for a White Cockatoo, which retails for US$1,500 in Germany.

Despite their potential, such approaches are unlikely to be tried in the near future: Western donor and conservation agencies are sen-

sitive to powerful animal welfare lobbies against any trade in wildlife, and the Indonesian authorities are sensitive to the Jakarta trader wildlife exporter lobby.

Above: Migratory Oriental Pratincoles fall prey to a bird trapper. *Photo by W Lawler/Wetlands.*

Air Rifles

The bird trade is something tangible on which to pin the blame for the lack of common birds, but other factors are also undoubtedly at play. The first is simple persecution: taking a pot-shot at a bird with a catapult or air rifle is still socially acceptable behaviour, and, with more than 200 boys per sq km in Java's intensively managed countryside, the pastime is sure to be having a serious impact. Following successful lobbying by the Bali Bird Club, in 1993 the Minister of Home Affairs issued a decree banning bird shooting with air rifles, but this has had

Above: Capturing local people's knowledge of cockatoo status in Sulawesi. *Photo by Y Cahyadin/BirdLife.*

extensive network of protected areas: 356 have been established to date, covering 16 million hectares. They include a number of wildernesses, such as Lorentz in Irian Jaya, Kayan-Mentarang in Kalimantan, and Mt Kerinci in Sumatra, each over a million hectares. If you add to this 30.3 million hectares of watershed protection forest, 24% of Indonesia's total land area is protected. It would seem that all is well. If only it were so simple!

Most reserves are just paper parks; only those classed as National Parks, which total 5,607,437 ha, have an annual management budget, the rest receive little if any direct management. Moreover there are some huge gaps in the geographic and habitat representativeness of the reserve network. One of the most important regions for birds is the province of Maluku, which has more endemic bird species than Peru but only one declared terrestrial reserve of any significant size—Seram's Manusela National Park. BirdLife International is assisting with the gazettal of new reserves on Halmahera, Buru and Tanimbar, which, together with Seram, would embrace the habitat of all but four of the province's 90 endemic species.

Another worry is that the greater proportion of protected forest is in the mountains. Lowland forests, which are some of the richest habitats in terms of bird species, are under the greatest pressure from alternative land uses: shifting cultivation, agriculture, plantations and commercial logging.

little effect because conservation agencies lack the resources to follow it up with education and awareness programmes.

Use of Pesticides

The second factor is the heavy use of pesticides, which were introduced in the 1970s during the country's drive for self-sufficiency in rice. The effect on birds has never been monitored, but it is widely assumed that populations of egrets, birds of prey and even seed-eaters such as the Java Sparrow crashed as a result.

However, pesticide use is an issue for which there is hope on the horizon: rice yields are falling as pests become resistant to the chemicals, and integrated pest management systems are now being introduced, particularly in Central Java. Under this system, natural predators—other insects and amphibians—are recognised and managed as pest controllers. These in turn are the food of birds, and, as long as persecution is not rife, bird populations will recover.

Parks and Reserves

Forest is home to over 80% of Indonesia's resident land birds and their fate is inextricably linked with the future of tropical forests. Indonesia has acted to establish an

The Forestry Industry

"Save the rain forests" is an environmentalist's rallying call, and many groups campaign to preserve the rain forest pristine and intact, fiercely opposing logging companies, the plantation industries and government development projects. This position appears increasingly naive and futile, and may ultimately be counterproductive to saving large tracts of rain forest. The rub is that the timber industry is just too rich and powerful to be seriously worried by western conservationist opinion. Take a hard-line, purist view and conservation may just end up with the commercially worthless forest in reserves. These include montane rain forests, which are full of birds, but in lowland areas they are usually forests on nutrient-poor soils, which, as anyone who has been to reserves such as Morowali in Central Sulawesi will testify, are relatively birdless.

Virtually all Indonesia's lowland forest is either covered by logging concessions or scheduled for conversion. Faced with this sobering reality, conservationists are starting to think about ways in which to maintain and enhance the wildlife value of managed forest ecosystems. Forestry accounts for 7% of GDP and 20% of exports, so there are compelling economic reasons for Indonesia to manage rain forest sustainably and in the best interests of future generations. Blocks of forest are cut only once every 35 years, so a well-managed forest will support a rich bird fauna probably not very different from the original.

A crucial point is that if rain forest can be maintained as a national economic asset it is less likely to be converted to other land uses. Surprising as it may seem, the next century may see conservation agencies and logging companies forging partnerships to promote both sustainable yields and conservation.

Wetlands

Indonesia's wetlands and their globally important populations of resident and migratory waterbirds face a much bleaker future. The once magnificent marshes along the north coast of Java are today real estate developments and shrimp ponds—and no-one knows what has happened to the thousands of rails, crakes, bitterns and reed-warblers that once migrated to these marshes from other parts of Asia. The same process of destruction is happening all over Indonesia: if it is not shrimp ponds and real estate, it is irrigation schemes or paddy fields that are replacing the marshes and swamps. Wetlands International, an agency dedicated to the sustainable

Below: Timber cut in remote regions is floated down rivers to sawmills. *Photo by Alain Compost.*

use of wetlands, promotes awareness of wetland values and sustainable-use regimes, and the government has set up a National Wetland Committee to try to address the problem. If this body can act with commitment and vision, there is a chance to save the most important wetlands.

Identifying Priorities

Almost everywhere you look in Indonesia there is a worthy conservation issue: these include over-harvesting of seabird colonies now that reliable outboard motors have made once remote islands accessible, scrub invasion of megapode nest grounds following breakdown of traditional management practices, and the dilemma caused by Javan songbirds, carried to Eastern Indonesia by transmigrants, escaping and out-competing native species. These are just some of the problems not being addressed because they are beyond the limits of scarce conservation resources. And the scarcity is in people and solutions as much as in funds.

To be effective, conservation organisations working in Indonesia must set their priorities and then stick to them. BirdLife International is one of the best at doing this. By identifying Endemic Bird Areas (*see pp 22–23*), BirdLife has drawn up a shortlist of proposals for protected areas that are crucial components of a national reserve network and is

Shorebirds

Drop in for a meal at a food stall in Cirebon or Indramayu along the north coast of west Java and you are likely to be offered *burung goreng*—fried bird! This is the fate of thousands of the marsh- and shorebirds that migrate to this wetland area during the months from September to April.

Villagers inhabiting the landscape of rice paddies, fishponds and saltpans that stretches as a 5–10 km wide band almost 60 km along the coast around Indramayu have been hunting waterbirds for generations; catching was first reported from the area in the 1930s. The main victims are migratory Yellow Bittern, various species of snipe, and Oriental Pratincole; Wetlands International estimates that 21% of all Oriental Pratincoles migrating through the area are caught. Resident species—rails and egrets and, until very recently, Milky Stork—are also caught, and the total annual catch in this area is believed to be around 200,000 birds.

The peak catching season is from November to February; hunters employ locally-made mistnets and clapnets to catch the birds. Another technique is to go out on a dark night and dazzle now working with the government on surveys to prepare the areas for gazettal. As part of a global project to identify all areas of global importance for bird conservation by the year 2000, BirdLife's Indonesia Programme is now evaluating sites throughout the country against a set of objective criteria dealing with threatened and endemic species and species that concentrate to breed (eg seabirds) or migrate. The Important Bird Area project will provide bird conservation in Indonesia with a clear agenda for the new millennium.

Without people—without a movement of committed and professional conservationists—even the best conservation agendas will founder, and all the main international conservation agencies in Indonesia place heavy emphasis on training and human resource development. Again, there is reason to be optimistic: in Java alone a network of 42 local bird clubs is working with BirdLife to identify and conserve Important Bird Areas.

Bird-watchers travelling through Indonesia will be saddened by the sight of bird habitats being converted for development. But it is worth remembering a fundamental truth: that by far the most serious and insidious threat to birds and their habitats is poverty. National development is about alleviating poverty, and success in this area is essential for a future in which birds and people live in harmony.

–*Paul Jepson*

on the Menu

roosting birds with flashlights. Bags of waterbirds are carried back to the village where the villagers pluck the birds and then fry them in spices for sale to the food stalls, where they are then re-fried.

This traditional practice is having a serious impact on bird populations, but it contributes 40% of the income of families in the area. Wetlands International is working with local communities to provide them with alternative sources of income and to raise awareness of the wider consequences of their hunting activities. The programme chalked up an early success in making villagers aware of the fact that some of the birds they were killing were legally protected and, as a result, hunting of species such as Milky Stork, Whiskered Tern and egrets has stopped.

–*Yus Rusila Noor*

Left: A hunter transports home his catch of migratory watercocks. *Photo courtesy of Wetlands International.*
Right: Skinned and ready for frying in road-side food stalls. *Photo by W Lawler/Wetlands.*

Introducing Java

Unparalleled Geography

Access to site.

Main birding attractions.

Type of accommodation.

Habitat.

Weather conditions.

Degree of difficulty.

The island of Java, located just south of the equator, is the cultural, economic and population centre of the vast Indonesian archipelago. At 132,000 sq km, Java is slightly larger than New York State, a little longer in length than the United Kingdom and home to 120 million people; population densities in the rice producing heartland of central Java average 833 people per sq km, and in Jakarta, the world's ninth largest city, they reach a staggering 40,000 per sq km.

Unparalleled Geography

In 1881 the famous botanist A R Wallace remarked that Java was probably the finest and most interesting tropical island in the world and, despite the many and varied changes that have taken place on the island since Wallace's time, the same probably holds true today. Java is a great birding destination.

A comprehensive reserve network protects the last remaining tracts of lowland forest, and there is brilliant birding to be enjoyed in the forests cloaking the awesome volcanoes, the habitat of the majority of Java's 28 endemic bird species. Add to this the charming and friendly nature of the Javanese, the opportunity to take in a *wayang golek* puppet show or a *gamelan* orchestra performance along the way, and the sheer fascination of seeing at first hand the rapid social and infrastructural changes of an Asian tiger economy, and you are bound to conclude that Java still lives up to its reputation.

Java is the world's most volcanically active island: since 1600 no fewer than 33 of its volcanoes have erupted. Fertile soils and great scenery are the result, and a visit to the best of the volcanoes is a must on any Javan itinerary. The most famous is Krakatau, located 40 km off Java's west coast (actually now in Lampung Province, Sumatra, for administrative purposes). The eruption in 1883 was the biggest bang ever recorded on Earth, heard 4,600 km to the southwest on Rodriguez Island, in the Indian Ocean, and 3,500 km to the east in Alice Springs, Australia. The great tidal waves triggered by the collapse of the volcano's empty cone destroyed 165 villages and killed 36,000 people along the coasts of Java and Sumatra. Anak Krakatau (child of Krakatau), which rose

Previous page: Exhilarating dawn scenery from the summit of Mt Gede/Pangrango National Park.
Left: A common sight along the shores of Indonesia, the Brahminy Kite is Jakarta's faunal mascot.
Below: Banded Pitta, a common, though shy bird of secondary growth in Java. *All photos by Alain Compost.*

41

JAVA

INTRODUCING JAVA

from the ocean in 1928, is steadily growing and often belches smoke plumes and glowing rocks to entertain guests in the beach bars and cafés of the west coast resort of Carita. The best time of year to take a day boat trip out to the Krakatau group is from May to September. Rakata is the best of the islands for birding: Peregrine Falcons nest on the steep cliff face, Chestnut-capped Thrushes are quite common in the forest gullies and a pair of Beach Thick-knees patrols the shoreline.

Mt Tangkubanperahu, located close to Bandung, the capital town of west Java, is the closest thing to a drive-in volcano: a metalled road runs right up to the magnificent crater rim, which is surrounded by stunted elfin forest. This is the place to see the speciality birds of Java's mountain tops without having to climb: Volcano Swiftlet, Island Thrush and Mountain White-eye and, if you are lucky, Sunda Serin, are all present.

Merapi, on the outskirts of Yogyakarta, is the volcano currently giving people sleepless nights; since the mid-1980s it has been showing signs of a major eruption, which could damage the city and its cultural treasures such as the Borobudur temple. But for sheer breathtaking beauty the landscapes of Mt Bromo, in East Java, are unbeatable. Watching the sun rise over the active crater of Bromo and its sister peak of Semeru, both within in a vast, old crater, is one of the natural wonders of the world.

The lush rain forests cloaking the middle altitudes (700–1,400 m) of the mountains are home to the majority of the 28 bird species endemic to the island of Java, and the Gede/Pangrango National Park (*see pp 52–55*)—a 2-hr drive from Jakarta—is one of Asia's premier birding sites. The best time to visit is in the drier season from May to October; in West Java the wet season really is wet, and colossal afternoon rainfalls effectively rule out birding after 2 pm. Two species, Black-banded Barbet and White-breasted Babbler, are endemic to West Java, as is the distinctive sub-species of Chestnut-bellied

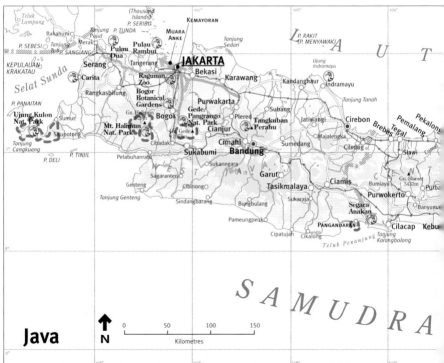

Java

Partridge. The partridge is a montane species, but the other two prefer lowland forest below 700 m, so birders head for Mt Halimun (Gede's sister park), Ujung Kulon National Park in the far southwest (*see pp 46–49*), and a little patch of forest behind the Carita beach resort to catch up with these and other lowland specialities such as Javan Frogmouth and Banded Pitta.

Disappearing Wetlands

The flat, alluvial plains of Java's north coast once boasted wonderful marshes, teeming with migratory shorebirds, crakes and herons. Sadly these wetlands have now been almost totally converted to rice paddies, shrimp ponds and industrial sites. The Javan Lapwing is already extinct and another wetland specialist, Javan Coucal, is in danger of suffering the same fate. The 27-ha remnant marsh at Muara Anke in Jakarta (*see p 44*) and the Brantas Delta near Surabaya provide an opportunity to enjoy these bird-rich habitats and add variety to Java's forest birding attractions.

Wayside Birds

Although Java's species list stands at 473, and the forests and reserves abound with birds, visiting birders are surprised at the lack of common or garden birds in Java's countryside. Nothing flies across the road, soars overhead or hops about in a hotel garden and, in contrast to most tropical countries, an evening wander around a village or kick about in a rough corner will produce very little in the way of birds. A combination of heavy pesticide use, the widespread persecution of birds and capture for the huge domestic bird trade have taken their toll.

But this is only one small drawback, more than compensated for by the exciting forest bird-watching and diverse cultural attractions that combine to make a visit to Java so memorable.

–Paul Jepson

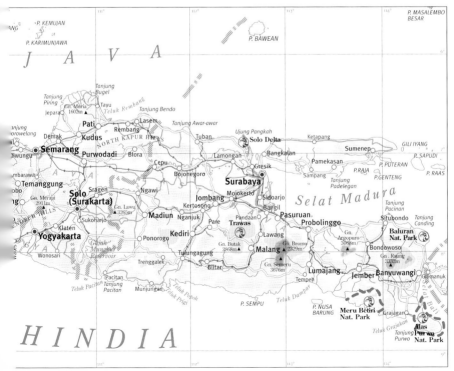

All sites easily accessible but traffic jams. Half-day trips.

Sunda Coucal at Muara Anke; nesting egrets at Pulau Rambut.

Every class of hotel available.

Relics of Jakarta's once great marsh.

Hot, humid and polluted—get up early. Afternoon thunderstorms Oct–May.

All sites are easy walking.

Birding Jakarta

Where Birds Survive in the Mega-city

Jakarta is the capital city of the world's fourth-largest nation, and a crowded, dynamic metropolis of nine million people. Nevertheless, birds survive in a few places of the tiny remnants of once-vast marsh that the city has engulfed. These oases are readily accessible and can be visited in 2- or 3-hr excursions or day trips.

One of the great pluses about arriving at Jakarta's Sukarno-Hatta airport is that the 14-km toll road into the city crosses a plain of flooded lagoons teeming with cormorants, darters, herons, egrets and terns. Unfortunately, stopping is forbidden on toll roads, so either get your taxi driver to drive slowly or sit on the left of the airport bus. All too soon, however, this delightful introduction is over and you enter a jumble of skyscrapers, construction sites, traffic jams and pollution where only a few species— including White-bellied Swiftlet, Savanna Nightjar, Tree Sparrow and feral pigeons—endure the diesel-filled air.

Muara Anke—Jakarta's Birding Hotspot

Jakarta's premier birding site is the 27-ha nature reserve of Muara Anke, on the seaward side of the wetlands along the airport toll road. As recently as 1993 the reserve was accessible only by boat, as it was surrounded by a marsh teeming with rails, gallinules and whistling ducks; the land around it now has been reclaimed for a new housing estate. Maybe because they have

nowhere else to go, birds crowd into this reserve, and they are easy to watch from the reserve's boardwalk and watchtower. Between November and February, when numbers are swelled by migrants, it is quite possible to see 50 species in a full day.

Surprisingly, this tiny urban reserve is the easiest place in the world to see Javan Coucal, a Javan endemic that ranks among Indonesia's most threatened birds. This large, black relative of the cuckoo clambers about in the reeds, and if you wait long enough up the watchtower one is sure to shoulder its way into view. But take care, the Javan black-backed race of the Lesser Coucal also occurs; its wings are all chestnut. In the Javan Coucal, only the primaries and bend of the wing are chestnut. While scanning the reeds for the coucal, you might well spot Black Bittern flying across, or Slaty-breasted Rail and White-browed Crake creeping out to the edge of the pool. Plaintive Cuckoo, Common Iora and, with luck, Racquet-tailed Treepie and Black-winged Starling may all appear at eye level in the trees around the tower.

Red-breasted Parakeets inhabit the trees bordering the western edge of the reserve, their incessant arguing demanding attention. Along the boardwalk, check out the Clamorous (or are they Oriental?) Reed-warblers. Somebody should put a net up and identify them conclusively one day. Here you will have your first views of the ubiquitous Bar-winged Prinia (a Javan endemic), Chestnut Munia and

Long-tailed Shrike. Keep an eye on the sky: Oriental Honey-buzzard, Black-winged Kite and Chinese Goshawk are all in the area; Lesser—and sometimes even Christmas—Frigatebirds glide overhead.

Depending on its state of repair, you can take the boardwalk out to the coastal mangroves and a new set of birds: Grey-capped Woodpecker, Pied Fantail, Mangrove Whistler and the superb Small Blue Kingfisher. Behind the mangroves, the trail leads west to the mouth of a large canal which was once a favoured feeding area for Milky Storks, but which is becoming less attractive as a maturing mangrove rehabilitation scheme reduces the area of mud.

Pulau Rambut

From the jetty at the bottom of the Muara Anke tower you can hire a wooden 20-seater outboard boat for the 2-hr journey to the waterbird breeding colony at Pulau Rambut. A quicker way to get there is to drive to Tanjung Pasir at the back of the airport, from where it is just a 15-minute crossing. Permits, which should be obtained in advance from PHPA (see Practicalities), are required to land on this nature reserve. The boat will drop you off at a jetty on the south side of the island from where you can take the 100-m walk north to a very tall watchtower that provides a panoramic view of the colony. Little Cormorant, Purple Heron, Great and Intermediate Egrets, Milky Stork, Glossy and Black-headed Ibises and Black-crowned Night-heron all breed here from May to July. After 5 pm from March to November, the sight of thousands of egrets and herons flying in to roost is dramatic.

City Sights

When sightseeing in Jakarta, take your binoculars along to the National Monument (Monas) in Medan Merdeka (Freedom Square) in the heart of the city. In this expansive, open park you will easily see Olive-backed and Brown-throated Sunbirds, Yellow-vented and Sooty-headed Bulbuls and Scarlet-headed Flowerpeckers. The view of Jakarta from the top of the 137-m monument is exhilarating; if you can, stay up there until dusk when thousands of White-bellied Swiftlets swarm in to roost.

Two km from downtown Jakarta in the north of the city, the wild bird sanctuary within Kemayoran urban park attracts cormorants, darters and herons. In South Jakarta the remoter corners of Ragunan Zoo harbour Javan Kingfisher, Red-breasted Parakeet, Black-winged Starling and Orange-headed Thrush. The migrant Chestnut-winged Cuckoo has also been seen here during the northern winter (see Practicalities).

Below: Close to Jakarta the heron colonies at Pulau Dua and Pulau Rambut make a memorable excursion. *Photo by Alain Compost.*

While in the south of the city, visit the bird park (Taman Burung) at Taman Mini Indah Indonesia, a 64-ha park exhibiting the architecture and cultures of the vast Indonesian archipelago. Two huge domes house a free-flying bird collection divided into species found in West and East Indonesia. This is an ideal place to familiarise yourself with Indonesian bird families, and even purist bird photographers will struggle to resist all the amazing birds posing in natural settings.

–*Daniel Philippe*

Ujung Kulon National Park

Java's Last Wilderness

6–7 hrs by road from Jakarta. 3 days stay, 5–7 if trekking.

Good range of lowland rainforest birds and shorebirds.

Good quality cabins on Peucang island. If trekking, camp or stay in basic shelters.

Diversity of rainforest and shore-line habitats.

Dry season May–Sep. Afternoon downpours frequent in other months.

Easy walking on Peucang. Trekking easy–moderate.

Lying on Java's southwest peninsula, the 120,000 ha Ujung Kulon National Park is one of the island's last wildernesses; it includes both terrestrial and marine conservation areas and several islands, two of which—Handeuleum and Peucang—offer visitor accommodation. However, the park's expansive forests are much less pristine than they appear at first sight. Much of the peninsula's vegetation was swept away by a huge tidal wave caused by the 1883 eruption of the massive Krakatau volcano, which lies 50 km north of the park in the Sunda Strait. Nowadays a mosaic of regenerating vegetation, tall forests, mangroves and man-made grazing fields offers the opportunity to find the full complement of Javanese open woodland, wetland and lowland rainforest birds in a single area.

There are countless ways to enjoy Ujung Kulon's wilderness: 1-week treks to explore the whole peninsula, 1-day walks from the park guesthouses and lodges or relaxed snorkelling and birding weekends on the islands.

Permits to enter the park are available from the National Park office at Labuan, where you can also arrange the 1 $^1/_2$–5 hr (depending on whether you take the new speedboat or a traditional wooden boat) journey along the coast to the accommodation on Handeuleum or Peucang Islands (see "Mouse Deer Island"). Alternatively, travel by road via Tamanjaya, where there is also an office. Tamanjaya is located at the foot of Mt Honje, the highest and least-visited part of the park. Adventurous birders who take an extra day to check it out will be rewarded with a long list of species including Javan Hawk-eagle.

Handeuleum Island— Mangrove Specialities

Handeuleum Island—named after a plant that is eaten raw with spicy *sambal* by the Sundanese—is a

Right: The Blue-winged Leafbird is a common bird of west Indonesian rain forests. *Photo by Alain Compost.*

great place to start a birding visit. A speciality of the island is the bizarre Nicobar Pigeon, easily recognized by its long, bottle-green "mane" and short, white tail: check out the forest by the guest-house. A morning spent birding in the mangroves that hug the shore and inshore islets of Handeuleum is a must, as this habitat supports two more specialized species. The blue-and-orange Mangrove Blue Flycatcher is located by its melodious, warbling song; apart from the female's pale nose patch, the sexes are identical. Another songster, the Mangrove Whistler, was called the "Javan Nightingale" in the colonial era because of its combination of dull plumage and swelling and varied song phrases, so reminiscent of the palearctic maestro. And it is magical to go out after dark on Handeuleum and listen for the loud, rolling *rrrrr* and hoot of the Spotted Wood-owl.

Peafowl and Rhino Tracks

On the mainland, just 15 min by motorboat from Handeuleum Island, is the Cigenter grazing ground—an area once cleared for cultivation but now scrubby, where beautiful Blue-throated Bee-eaters fill the sky with their aerobatics and chattering, and Green Peacocks show off their magnificent tails. From the mouth of the Cigenter river you can take an exciting, 1-hr canoe trip to its headwaters, then a 1-hr walk to a terraced waterfall. There's just a slim chance of seeing a crocodile or giant python in the water. The impressive footprints and huge, fibrous stools of the Javan Rhinoceros are common along the trail, but you will be lucky to see the beast itself. Large Green Pigeon is a possibility here, as are river specialists such as White-crowned Forktail and Blue-eared Kingfisher.

South Coast Trail

Along the south coast there is a beautiful trail starting from either Karang Ranjang or nearby Kalejetan (both 3–4 hrs from Tamanjaya on foot) to Cibunar, 20 km to the west. Birders should certainly allow plenty of time—two or three days—and camp at simple, palm-roofed shelters along the way.

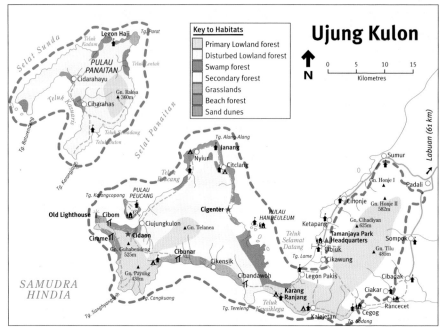

Ujung Kulon

Key to Habitats
- Primary Lowland forest
- Disturbed Lowland forest
- Swamp forest
- Secondary forest
- Grasslands
- Beach forest
- Sand dunes

From Karang Ranjang the first part of the trek is a magnificent, though rather strenuous, 7 $1/2$-hr walk over the loose sand of the glorious south coast beaches, interspersed with short stretches through shady, pandanus beach forest and rocky outcrops; it ends at the crystal-clear Cibunar river. These beaches are the best place in Java to find the Beach Thick-knee, and between August and April migratory shorebirds—in particular sand plovers and Sanderlings—run along the strands. The sight of massive White-bellied Sea-eagles picking up sea snakes from inshore waters is unforgettable. Along the way, keep your eyes open for the rare Grey-headed Fish-eagle.

Turning northwards along the Cibunar river, the trail gently rises through hilly, forested terrain full of birds. The energetic can make the 3 $1/2$-hr climb to the summit of Mt Payung. This is one of the areas of Ujung Kulon that was spared the Krakatau tidal waves, and its magnificent primary forest forms a wonderful setting to catch up with forest species you may otherwise miss. Try to call the beautiful Orange-breasted Trogon out from

the dense canopy: it responds surprisingly well to attempts to mimic its *chaw-chaw-chaw* call; and marvel at the extraordinary agility—despite their seemingly immobilizing, white tail streamers—of the exquisite male Asian Paradise-flycatchers. Listen for the *tooloong-toompook* of Black-banded Barbet, which is unique to Java, the *wook-wok* of Rhinoceros Hornbill, and the chicken-like cackle of its smaller cousin, Asian Pied Hornbill. Along the way an enjoyable diversion is to try to whistle out a Large Wren-babbler: the loud, clear phrases of its simple but varied song are easy to mimic, and this ground bird will probably venture out to investigate. If you walk quietly you may get views of perched forest raptors such as the Crested Goshawk and the long-crested, Javan race of the Oriental Honey-buzzard.

If you walk at a slow, bird-stalking pace, it will be about 3 $1/2$ hrs before the trail emerges at the Cidaon grazing ground opposite Peucang Island on the west coast. Green Peafowl, with their mewing and loud pairing calls, and Green Junglefowl, calling their Sundanese name *canghegar*, will announce your arrival; the swelling trills of Javan Owlet and plaintive whistles and trills of Javan Frogmouth soon join the forest concert.

There are no campsites on Peucang or near Cidaon, however there is a site at Cibom, 1 1/2 hrs to the west, and a camping area on the lovely Cirame beach about 45 min southwest of Cibom.

"Mouse Deer Island"

A 10-min boat ride from Cidaon brings you to Peucang (Mouse Deer) Island, famous for its white sand beaches and coral reefs. Three lodges look out over a lawn where Sambar Deer gather at night to forage, and rutting stags fight their mostly harmless battles. The island is covered with lush, tall trees; its open undergrowth and network of trails make birding a little easier. The migratory Malaysian Night-heron has its winter quarters here, as does the continuously bobbing Forest Wagtail.

Other highlights in the forest include a 45-min walk to look for nesting Black-naped Terns on Karangcopong, a rocky outcrop on the north coast. Search, too, for the eyrie of the White-bellied Sea-eagle pair in one of the huge *kepuh* trees.

Return to Labuan by boat from Peucang. At the weekends you should have little difficulty joining one of the package tour boats, but during the week it would be prudent to arrange your return boat before leaving Labuan. This is expensive, but the alternative is to retrace your steps and take another long walk through the jungle.

Carita Beach

Close to Labuan, the popular Carita Beach resort also has some first-class birding to offer. North of Labuan, 10 km along the road to Merak, a turnoff on the right through an entrance way leads to a "recreation forest". Towards the end of an asphalt road, a 1-hr walk along a trail through degraded forest brings you to a patch of semi-primary lowland forest and the Curug Gendang waterfalls. Lesser Forktail and Blue Whistling Thrush are common along the river; both species have loud, high-pitched calls, and are easy to hear over the noise of the water. Listen also for the machinegun-like rattle of Crested Jay, and the long, trilled whistle of White-breasted Babbler, Java's rarest babbler—a species you are more likely to see here than anywhere else in the world.

On a moonlit evening, a night walk in this forest is not to be missed (but inform the local forest guard, at his house on the asphalt road, beforehand.) No fewer than six nightflying species have been recorded, including Javan Frogmouth, Javan Owlet and Brown Boobook.

–B van Balan & M Clarbrough

Below: Normally confined to small remote islands, the Nicobar Pigeon is one of Ujung Kulon's highlights. *Photo by Alain Compost.*

1 hour by car or bus from Jakarta.

Night-heron roost, reasonable variety of commoner Javan birds.

Wide choice close to the gardens.

One of the world's best and oldest botanical gardens.

Torrential tropical downpours common Oct–Apr.

Gentle stroll.

Bogor's Kebun Raya

An Easy Introduction to Java's Birds

The Botanic Gardens or Kebun Raya—Bogor's heart and hallmark—is a delightful place to get acquainted with typical Javan town and woodland birds. Many birds take refuge in the shady, 180-year-old Botanic Gardens: Collared Kingfisher, Black-naped Oriole, Sooty-headed Bulbul and Magpie Robin abound, and this is the easiest place on Java to see Blue-eared Kingfisher, Grey-cheeked Green Pigeon and Black-naped Fruit-dove. With perseverance 30 or more species can be seen during a morning's stroll; the checklist stands at over 150 species, though this figure includes some escapees from local bird markets. Plan a midweek visit, as on weekends the gardens are packed with visitors from both Bogor and Jakarta.

After entering the main gate at Pasar Bogor, head first for the lake in front of the Istana Bogor, 100 m down the main avenue. The roost of Black-crowned Night-herons on the islet is a real spectacle; Rufous Night-herons also occasionally put in an appearance. A high-pitched call helpfully draws attention to the Blue-eared Kingfisher as it flashes across. With luck it will perch very visibly in the lower branches of one of the huge old trees on the edge of the lake. The avenue of tall trees that lines the road from the entrance to the palace is a favourite haunt of beautiful Black-naped Fruit-doves, the males with their striking plumage combination of grey, green and red, and Grey-cheeked Green Pigeons, recognized by their smart grey, green and maroon coloration. Their calls, a dull *oo-OO* and a peculiar "yammering", will help you locate them.

Paying Homage to Two 19th-century Birders

At the far end of the avenue, on the corner where the road turns to the left in front of the palace, take the cobbled path into a grove of tall bamboos surrounding an old Dutch cemetery. Here Horsfield's Babbler, a noisy though nondescript and stealthy bird, utters its characteristic rising whistle from the bushes. Violin-like notes identify the Hill Blue Flycatcher—very much in its element in this mosquito-infested

50

Kebun Raya Bogor

0   0.1   0.2   0.3
Kilometres

Tourist Information
Palace Grounds
JL. MUSLIHAT

Bhinneka Garden & Holy Banyan tree
medicinal plants

gate
Palace wall
Orchid House
JL. G. GEDE

Presidential Palace
climbers
JL. ASTRID
CIHARUM

⑨
⑩
⑤ palms
④
Sunday Gate
JL. PALEDANG
rattan
tropical rainforest
JL. IR. H. JUANDA
③
flying Foxes
oil palms
⑧
water lilies
Ciliwung
CIHARUM
water plants
cacti
ferns
⑦
shrubs
wild corner

⑥
②
⑪
Pasar Bogor
JL. EMPANG
JL. SURYA KENCANA
JL. RAYA PAJAJARAN

↑ N

To JI. Tol & Bus Station ↓

— Birding Route
① Main gate
② PHPA
③ Night-heron roost
④ Main avenue
⑤ Cemetery/ bamboo grove
⑥ Guesthouse
⑦ Fern garden
⑧ Café Botanicus
⑨ Bibliotheca Bogoriensis
⑩ Ornithology dept
⑪ Zoological Museum

little grove. Birders should pay homage at the tombs of two 19th-century ornithologists, Joh. Coenraad van Hasselt and Heinrich Kuhl, who succumbed to disease in 1821, just three years after their arrival in Java. Their names used to be commemorated in the English names of the two sunbirds that they discovered: Kuhl's and van Hasselt's, but nowadays field-guide writers prefer to use the names, White-flanked and Copper-throated.

From the cemetery, either retrace your steps or walk back towards the entrance on a longer, curving route—roughly parallel to the main avenue—past the Guesthouse, and look back at the wall of trees that surrounds the Guesthouse lawn. When they catch the sun, these trees attract several typical garden species such as Scarlet-backed White-eye, Olive-backed Sunbird and Javan Munia.

Birding in Solitude

Next head for the fern garden—a 15-min walk from the south end of the lake. Take any of the paths down to the river, pausing on the way to admire the gigantic leaves of the *Victoria amazonica* waterlilies on the round pond and the roost of Flying Fox fruit bats high in the trees in the clearing below. Cross the river and turn right along the metalled road to the far southeast corner of the gardens. This wild area of dense herbs and fern ground-cover on a small hill above a smelly stream (another good place to see the kingfisher) is the best area to find Orange-headed Thrush, a favourite with birder and birdkeeper alike because of its beautiful orange body, grey wings with white epaulettes and varied song. Another great songster, the White-rumped Shama, is also found here very occasionally.

By this time you will probably be in need of refreshment. Continue on the road round to the Café Botanicus, which overlooks a vast lawn—the main feature in the south of the gardens. The café is the best place to watch for Javan Hanging Parrots, flying high over the lawn, so there is no need to feel guilty about dawdling over a cold drink. Plain Flowerpeckers are common in the trees bordering the lawn.

–Bas van Balen & Paul Jepson

Above: The world-famous landscapes of Bogor's Kebun Raya provide a delightful setting for getting acquainted with Java's commoner birds. *Photo by Alain Compost.*

Searching for Java's Mountain Endemics

Gede/Pangrango and Cibodas

2 hrs by road from Jakarta; 1 hr from Bogor. 2 or 3 day visit rec.

25 Javan endemics including Javan Cochoa. Migrant Siberian thrushes.

Basic *losmen* by park entrance. Many good quality hotels in the *puncak* area.

Montane rain forest, giant edelweiss meadows around the summit.

Afternoon rain any season. Frequent and heavy between Oct and Mar.

Moderately hard uphill walking. 6–7 hours to the summit.

Birding in the lush mountain forests of West Java, home to all but three of Java's 28 endemic bird species, is a delight. Amongst the stately, epiphyte-cloaked *rasamala* trees and elegant tree ferns of the mid-altitude forests, shortwings, wren babblers and tesias give forth with their strident or plaintive whistles from the trail-side vegetation; roaming flocks of babblers flit tantalisingly into view; and occasionally a bird party crosses the path and the trees burst into life with drongos, fulvettas, woodpeckers, sibias, shrike-babblers and warblers. At higher altitudes, beautiful moss forest is the habitat of such specialities as Island Thrush. Higher still, giant edelweiss studs a barren landscape of volcanic calderas.

This is Asian birding at its best, and it is easy to enjoy during two or three days in the popular Gede/Pangrango National Park, located 2 hrs by road south of Jakarta. For those with time, or in search of greater solitude, the sister national park of Mt Halimun, offers an exciting extension to the trip.

Gede/Pangrango National Park, and the Cibodas Botanic Gardens adjoining its eastern boundary, are reached via the Puncak Pass. After the end of the Jagowari toll road, the road to the pass winds up though scenic tea estates; just before the summit, the tiny Telaga Warna (Coloured Lake) reserve makes a pleasant break in the journey. This large pond, tucked below a steep escarpment, is reached by a 500-m track on the left of the road, 50 m below the Rindu Alam Restaurant. Along the track, look out for Striated Grassbirds performing song-flights over the tea bushes. The narrow, slippery trail encircling the lake provides an introduction to the commoner mountain birds: Lesser Forktail on the lakeside boulders, Mountain Leaf-warbler and White-rumped Warbler in the foliage, and Javan Fulvetta on the escarpments.

Cibodas Botanic Gardens

Back on the highway, the road crosses the pass and winds down to Pacet, 7 km beyond the summit. Here, a large red signpost to Cibodas Golf Park identifies the turning on the right up to the National Park and Cibodas Botanic Gardens (4 km). The side-road is lined with colourful plant nurseries and ends in a large, open-air market at the entrance to the Botanic Gardens.

The Botanic Gardens were established in 1852 as a 60-ha annex to the Bogor Botanic Gardens (*see pp 50–51*) for plants adapted to cooler mountain

climates. At weekends and holidays it teems with people. In order to be "on the spot", most birders choose to stay in this area, either at Fredy's Homestay (where a bird log is kept), the Youth Hostel or the Botanic Gardens' guest-house. The gardens themselves (which open at 8am) are the natural choice for the first birding excursion: this is the easiest place to encounter a flock of Pygmy Tit which enjoys the distinction of being Java's smallest bird and the only representative of its family in the Greater Sundas.

The open, semi-formal landscape of the gardens provides a first opportunity to get acquainted with the commoner forest birds: Grey-throated Dark-eye and White-flanked Sunbird flit amongst the shrubs, and a stroll along the upper boundary and scan of the forest edge may well reward you with your first views of Indigo Flycatcher, Black-winged Flycatcher-shrike and Blood-breasted Flowerpecker. Perhaps the best birding, though, is along a narrow trail in the gulley of vegetation bordering the fast-flowing stream that bisects the gardens. Listen here for the pleasant *poop-poop-poop* of the Crescent-chested

Babbler and the descending, three-note whistle of the Pygmy Wren-babbler. Look out for the striking black and white-banded tails of Lesser and White-crowned Fork-tails on boulders in the stream. You might also see the beautiful, dark-blue Sunda Whistling-thrush.

The Trail to Cibeureum Waterfall

The entrance to the 15,000 ha Gede/Pangrango National Park is reached via a paved drive running alongside the golf course. The trek to the summit of Mt Gede (2,958 m) is a stiff, 5- to 6-hr walk; numbered posts along the well-defined trail, which starts at the park entrance, mark points of interest explained in the park guidebook. Birders usually opt to spend a night or two on the mountain, camping or staying in one of the very basic shelters. Drinking water is available, but food needs to be carried. It gets bitterly cold at night, and afternoon downpours are the norm; warm clothes, a sleeping bag, torch and waterproofs are essentials for over-nighting on the mountain.

Left: The National park is a stronghold for Indonesia's national bird—the endangered Javan Hawk-eagle. *Photo by Alain Compost.*
Above: Magical moss forest near the summit of Mt Gede. *Photo by Alain Compost.*

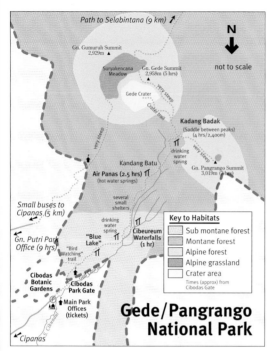

Path to Selabintana (9 km) ↗

Gn. Gumuruh Summit
2,929m ▲

N
↓

Suryakencana
Meadow

Gn. Gede Summit
2,958m (5 hrs) ▲

not to scale

Gede Crater

very steep

Crater trail

Kadang Badak
(Saddle between peaks)
(4 hrs/2,400m)

Kandang Batu

very steep

drinking
water
spring

Gn. Pangrango Summit
3,019m (2 hrs)

Air Panas (2.5 hrs)
(hot water springs)

very steep

several
small
shelters

Small buses to
Cipanas (5 km)

drinking
water
spring

Cibeureum
Waterfalls
(1 hr)

Gn. Putri Park
Office (9 hrs)

"Blue
Lake"

"Bird
Watching"
trail

Key to Habitats

☐ Sub montane forest
☐ Montane forest
☐ Alpine forest
☐ Alpine grassland
☐ Crater area
Times (approx) from
Cibodas Gate

Cibodas
Botanic
Gardens

Cibodas
Park Gate

Main Park
Offices
(tickets)

**Gede/Pangrango
National Park**

Cipanas

S. Cibeureum

Bodja trail

After the bustle of the entrance area you may be tempted to head quickly up the trail, but several species are commoner at lower altitudes and the first 500 m of the trail is the best area to look for Sunda Blue Robin, Orange-headed Thrush, the endemic White-bellied Fantail, and two real rarities, Sunda Thrush and Javan Scopsowl. Being on this trail at first light will dramatically increase your chances of seeing the thrushes; the best way to find the little-known scopsowl is to listen for the wheezy whistle of a hungry juvenile at dusk.

About 600 m up the trail a sign indicates a bird-watching trail leading off to the left. Actually, it leads nowhere special; keeping a steady pace up the main trail will bring better rewards. However, it is well worth stopping at Telaga Biru ("Blue Lake"), a small pond on the left, 1 1/2 km up the trail. If the trees on the opposite hillside are fruiting, great views of Brown-throated and Orange-fronted Barbets and the Pink-headed Fruit-dove are possible.

Ten minutes further on, the trail opens into a forest clearing with head-high grass. This is the only place along the path from where, clouds permitting, you have a clear view of the summit of Mt Pangrango. Flocks of the eye-catching White-bibbed Babbler are often encountered here, and it is a good spot to see Crimson-winged Yellow-nape and Spotted Crocia. The secretive Sunda Bush-warbler hides in the dense grass, but you will need a tape of its call—or be able to "pish"—to lure it into view.

Two hundred metres beyond this clearing you will see a stone hut that sleeps six or eight people and has drinking water piped from a stream. Here, the summit trail branches left off the path to Cibeureum waterfalls, the destination of the majority of visitors. The 200-m path to the falls is an excellent place to see two of the keen birder's favourites: White-browed Shortwing, whose gloriously lusty song commences slowly, with high and low notes, and gets faster and faster, and the Eye-browed Wren Babbler which has beautiful, pearly drops on its chocolate-brown back. These small birds are denizens of dense undergrowth and it requires patience and skill to see them clearly. The spectacular waterfalls used to be home to a colony of Waterfall Swifts; the occasional bird is still seen at dusk, when Salvadori's Nightjar also appears and hawks insects from the cliffs.

The Final Ascent

Taking the summit trail, Air Panas, a hot stream at 2,150 m that tumbles across the trail into a steaming gulley, is the next landmark and a straight, 1 1/2-hr walk from the waterfall junction. This is a section of the trail worth lingering over, for here you will find some of the mountain's really spectacular birds: Blue-tailed Trogon, Javan Cochoa, Blue Nuthatch, Siberian Thrush (in the northern winter), Scaly Thrush and Chestnut-backed Scimitar-babbler. A non-bird highlight is the sighting of Javan Gibbon: the first km of this trail passes through a home range of this endangered primate. If you keep quiet, and avoid sudden movements, you should get a good look at them.

The dilapidated shelter at Air Panas is a favourite base for a day at the higher altitudes; your visit may be enlivened by a Malay Ferret-badger, sneaking around after scraps. This is the best area to try for Horsfield's Woodcock, and being first up the trail in the morning increases your chances of seeing the shy Chestnut-bellied Partridge—a quite superb species with which to start a day's birding.

The scruffy campsite at Kadang Badak is reached after another hour or so. This signifies the start of the moss forest and the final stretch of the trek to the summit. From here it is a gruelling 1 $^1/_2$-hr ascent, and it makes sense to leave birding for the return trip. The crater is awesome, and the spectacular view of the surrounding mountains is as memorable as the birding. Of the alpine specialities, Volcano Swiftlet and Island Thrush are quite easy to find, but Sunda Serin is much more difficult, and the best area for it is Suryakencana meadow, over the summit. It is the floor of an older caldera between the ancient crater rim of Gumuruh and the more recent Gede crater.

Descents from the Meadow

From Suryakencana meadow there are three options for descending the mountain. The easiest way is to return by the main trail, but the adventurous can choose one of two other routes: either follow a steep, 9-km trail from the southern edge of the meadow to Selabintana, near Sukabumi on the south of the mountain, or make an almost circular walk to Gunung Putri. The trail to Gunung Putri also starts from the south corner of the meadow and takes about 4 hrs. The first 2 hrs to the park boundary are very steep. Both these routes are poorly maintained, but the birds are confiding and the solitude is refreshing. If your legs are still up to it, Cibodas is a 2-hr walk through fields and gardens from Gunung Putri.

Mt Halimun National Park

Twenty-five km across the Cicurug valley, Gede/Pangrango's sister park, Mt Halimun, covers a sprawling massif of several peaks. The

forest in the 36,000-ha park extends down to 500 m above sea level. Facilities are not yet developed, but two days' birding in the surrounding forests can produce several mid-altitude or lowland species rare or absent from Gede/Pangrango, including Sunda Pin-tailed Pigeon, Dark-backed Imperial Pigeon, Crested Jay and Short-tailed Green Magpie.

—*Paul Jepson*

Below: Plaintive whistles betray the presence of the diminutive Pygmy Wren-babbler along the trail. *Photo by Morten Strange.*

Above: A view of an Orange-headed Thrush is the highlight of any day's birding. *Photo by Alain Compost.*

6–7 hrs by road from Bogor. 1–2 days recommended.

Selection of lowland birds. Storks, egrets and kingfishers on Cilacap backwaters.

Wide choice of moderately priced *losmen*.

Remnant of coastal lowland forest; extensive marshes around Cilacap.

Warm and sunny; afternoon rain Oct–Mar.

Easy walking.

Pangandaran and Cilacap

A Stopover on the Road East

Like a droplet suspended from West Java's south coast, the tiny Pangandaran peninsula offers a wide range of birding habitats against the beautiful backdrop of the Indian Ocean. A popular tourist resort occupies the narrow isthmus leading to the delightful, 457-ha Pangandaran National Park. For those travelling from west to central Java with two or three days to spare, the area makes a welcome birding stopover, especially if combined with the 4-hr trip through the mangroves of Segara Anakan.

above the sea. The forest is rather dry and not very species-rich, nevertheless there are some interesting birds: Oriental Dwarf Kingfishers flash across the trail, Asian Pied Hornbills cackle overhead and Scaly-crowned Babblers protest noisily. From the shadows, the White-rumped Shama adds its beautiful, sonorous song.

Pangandaran is the place to see the huge flowers of *Rafflesia patma*. It flowers erratically, so if you

Pangandaran Jungle Walk

The reserve entrance, where permits are obtained, is at the south end of the road down the isthmus. An easy, 2-hr circular trail leads first to a watchtower, then along a small stream through dry forest before winding its way back to the entrance.

If you are quiet enough on the path to the watchtower, you may be rewarded with views of an exquisite Banded Pitta hopping over the forest floor—they are quite common in this area. From the tower, which overlooks a grazing ground, a few semi-wild Banteng can still be seen, but unfortunately the bulk of the herd was wiped out by ashfall from an eruption of nearby Mt Galunggung in the early 1980s. This is a pleasant place to sit and watch Green Junglefowl walking out from the forest edge.

After the tower the trail enters the reserve proper: it wanders beside small streams and tiny rapids, and climbs rocky paths high chance upon one while stalking a bird you are sure to give up birding for a while to wonder at the huge fleshy flower that gives off a stench of rotting meat to attract pollinating flies. Check at the park office to see if they know of one in bloom.

The coastal zone is well worth exploring, as the rare Great-billed Heron can sometimes be seen, and the first (and only) Chinese Egret recorded in Java was spotted here in April 1988. Scanning the sea may reveal distant Christmas Frigate-birds and Abbott's Boobies.

Disappearing Mangroves

If you are travelling on to Yogyakarta—or just looking for a pleasant day out from Pangandaran —the backwater trip from Kalipu-cang to Cilacap (see Practicalities) is full of interest. The ferry passes the Segara Anakan—a huge man-grove and estuarine area, home to Javan Coucal, Lesser Adjutant and Milky Stork, and numerous herons, egrets and terns. Along the way, Stork-billed Kingfisher, easily recognized by its huge, red bill, is common; indeed, the presence of no fewer than six species of kingfisher is the real attraction here. However, the area's ecology is in crisis due to the thousands of tons of topsoil deposited each year by the Citanduy river—the result of upstream erosion. The future of this wonderful mangrove system is in real jeopardy.

The backwater trip cuts behind the densely forested, and infamous, prison island of Nusa Kambangan, where there are two small reserves that offer new and as yet unexplored additions to Pangandaran's birding sites. Ask at the Pangandaran tourist office for up-to-date details.

–Bas van Balen

VIFTLET NESTS

Birds' nest soup, a traditional Chinese delicacy and reputed aphrodisiac, is big business in Indonesia. Not the eating of, but the export each year of over 60 tons of nests of the Edible-nest Swiftlet to China and Taiwan. The glutinous nests, created from the swiftlets' spittle, are collected from the walls of limestone caves with great daring and regular loss of life.

Since 1990 there has been a price explosion and today one kilo—about 60–70—of the best quality nests commands an export price of US$3,000. For the rare red nests, believed to contain the blood of the swiftlet, but more likely to contain either ferrous oxides or insect keratin, the price may be as much as $5,000.

The biggest cave complexes are in Central Kalimantan, and they are patrolled by armed guards. Here whole village economies are based on the trade, the men collecting and the women painstakingly removing feather and grass fragments from the nests with tweezers. It takes several hours to clean each nest. In other parts of the range, such as Nusa Tenggara, nesting caves are rarer and smaller and usually the possession of a single, lucky family.

In Java, the shortage of caves is being overcome by the construction of swiftlet houses, architecturally unattractive concrete blocks with ledges inside. These are not naturally to the liking of Edible-nest Swiftlets but are readily colonised by the abundant White-bellied Swiftlet, which has a worthless nest. The swiftlet housekeepers develop an artificial colony by getting White-bellied Swiftlets to foster Edible-nest Swiftlet eggs; the Edible-nest Swiftlet nestlings later return as adults to their place of hatching and build their valuable nests. Needless to say, with such high prices the precise techniques are closely guarded secrets.

–Paul Jepson

Left: Swiftlet nests displayed for sale in Kuta, Bali. *Photo by Alain Compost.*

Javan Bird Markets

A Bird in a Cage

A horse, house, a spouse, a *kris* and a bird in a cage—these are the five symbols of a good Javanese. The horse, house and spouse are self-explanatory; the *kris* is the ceremonial dagger; and the bird in the cage symbolizes the need for a hobby in a well-balanced life.

In today's climate of concern for animal welfare and the environment, it is hardly surprising that tourists often find bird markets distressing places. The Manuk bird market in Yogyakarta is typical: a cacophony of noise, and the smell of mild putrefaction emanating from narrow alleys of open-fronted shops crammed with bamboo cages full of birds. It may not appeal over much, but a visit will enlighten you about the Javanese appreciation of birds.

A Fine Appreciation of Song

Central to this passion for birds is a refined appreciation of their song. The domed cages hanging over shop entrances house *perkici*, (Zebra or Peaceful Dove), a dainty dove with delicate barring on its neck and belly. Though drably coloured, the *perkici* is venerated for its soft, melodious, rolling *croo-croo, croo-croo, croo-croo*, which in the harsh, midday heat suffuses every *kampung* and neighbourhood with a sense of tranquility. So revered is this bird that a winner in a national song-contest may be valued at US$10,000.

Within the dim shop interiors, the jumble of cages harbours a selection of the more strident songbirds. Traditional favourites are the White-rumped Shama, Black-winged Starling and, arguably Indonesia's most enchanting songster, the Straw-headed Bulbul. A combination of trapping and destruction of its favoured riverside forest habitat, has caused this thrush-sized, streaky-green bird to become exceedingly scarce in the wild. As a consequence, it is now also quite rare in bird markets because, unlike the *perkici*, it is not yet bred commercially.

Laughing Thrushes, hectically jumping around their cages, have become popular in recent years because of their rich, liquid songs. Being Chinese imports, they are not covered by Indonesian legislation, which bans song-contests only between wild-caught, native birds; this, in combination with their affordability (US$20–25), lends them their appeal.

Like Buying Cut Flowers

The expert birder will recognize several species quite lacking in song, and on occasions a bird of prey is discreetly produced from a cage at the back of the shop. These birds appeal to collectors or, in the case of eagles, to people who believe that owning a protected species will heighten their status. Many of these species are quite unsuited to captivity and die within a few weeks; buying these birds can be likened to buying cut flowers.

However, if you come across a beautiful woodpecker with a gold back, you will have found one of the few birds on the market that is sold to be eaten, for in Central Java the consumption of *pelatuk bawang* is still believed to guard against disease.

Singing and Fighting Cocks

But before the unsavoury side of these bird markets gets you down, head into the chicken section. The cockerel you spy under the cage could be one of any number of breeds. If it has a large, floppy comb and long, muscular legs it is *ayam pelung* and we are back to song, for *pelung* are known as the "singing cocks of Cianjur". The very best cockerels, known as *jangkar*, have a three-part crow: a low, clear crow, followed by a slow melody, termed *lenggang-lenggang*, and a *kwung* or *kecubung* as a finale. Each year, enthusiasts meet in Cianjur in west Java for the contest of the *jankar*, where the cockerel with the perfect crow (known as *kukundur* or *kukulur*) is selected.

Fighting cocks can still be found in the market. Once the pastime of nobility, cockfighting is now illegal but, carefully concealed from the authorities, it survives as an illicit Sunday afternoon entertainment in many regions of Indonesia. Since the 1970s the massive, long-legged *ayam Bangkok* has been the champion breed. It has replaced *ayam kinantan*, the "Sumatran cock", which, although renowned for its intelligence and speed of movement, is no match for the powerful challenger from Thailand.

The smaller, pink-and-purple-combed cockerel will be a *bekasi*, which is appreciated for its colour and form. This chicken is a particular obsession in East Java: when, in 1992, the Environment Minister decreed that all provinces should select a wild fauna mascot, East Java chose the *bekasi*. The province successfully argued that the *bekasi* qualified because it was a cross between a wild Green Junglefowl cock and a village chicken.

Many birders rate the sight of a Green Junglefowl in its native habitat as one of their great birding experiences. Here in the market, they will find common ground with the aviculturists in their appreciation of the humble chicken.

You will undoubtedly leave the market wondering about the conservation impact of this trade. Actually, the shops do not display the businesses's full stock: many employ a band of peddlers carrying 25 or more birds in cages swinging from a bamboo pole on their shoulders. The store owner loans these *tukang bikul burung* money to buy birds from him, so that they themselves take the risk if any birds die. In an average month a street peddler may sell up to 30 birds, and bring in a relatively meagre income of US$100–150. Surprisingly, neither the effect of this trade on wild bird populations nor the number of people it employs have yet been objectively evaluated.

–*Paul Jepson*

Below: Java's bird markets hold a morbid fascination for birders. *Photo by Margaret Kinnaird.*

Around Surabaya

Herons and Dowitchers on the Solo Delta

2 hr by road from Surabaya to Ujung Pangkah.

Passage Asian Dowitchers/other shorebirds; Milky Stork and Sunda Coucal.

None, stay with villagers or camp.

Fish ponds, mangroves and mudflats.

Exposed, so hot in mid-day sun.

Easy walking; hire a boat to explore estuary.

60

JAVA

AROUND SURABAYA

At first glance the industrialized region of Surabaya may not seem very promising for birding, but marvelling at spectacular heronries, watching Asian Dowitchers on the Solo Delta, or relaxing at the hill retreat of Trawas are just some of the highlights this area has to offer.

Sadly, the abundant egrets and herons that once enlivened Java's rice fields are becoming a sight of the past: pesticides, persecution and the destruction of suitable nesting trees have all taken their toll. Today, heronries are generally restricted to remote reserves and off-shore islands, but nesting herons also find safe havens in some of Java's big cities. In Surabaya, a large colony of night-herons has taken up residence in the zoo, where their droppings try the patience of zoo-keepers and visitors alike.

Ujung Pangkah's Herons

Java's largest heronry, however, is found in the more natural setting of the Ujung Pangkah area on the delta of the Bengawan Solo: this huge river, popular in nostalgic Javan songs, is just a 2-hr drive from Surabaya's hustle and bustle. An entrepreneurial local fishpond keeper decided to protect the colony as it produced a cheap source of fertiliser which he used to raise Javan tilapia (a cichlid fish) in his pond. A careful scan through the breeding colony will reveal 13 waterbird species, including Oriental Darter, Black-headed Ibis and the odd Rufous Night-heron. This colony of 25,000 or more birds has become a popular destination for day trippers and has earned the pond-keeper the prestigious *kalpataru* award, presented by the government to individuals who have worked to benefit the environment.

Ujung Pangkah offers a glimpse of how the whole of Java's north coast used to look; today it has largely been converted to sterile shrimp ponds. The patchwork of ponds, avenues of trees, swamps, mangrove bushes and undisturbed shores here, however, support a full complement of the island's water- and shorebirds.

After enjoying the heronry, walk around the fish ponds and to the nearby estuaries for more good birding. The neat, yellow Javan White-eye and the endangered Javan Coucal, which reveals its presence with a loud "booping" call, are two speciality species that inhabit the bushes and trees edging the ponds. Swampy areas along the coast are good for Sunda Teal—easily recognized by its strange, bulging forehead, the rare Bronze-winged Jacana and flocks of Asian Golden Weaver.

Out to the Mud-flats

In the wet months between October and March, a boat journey down to the mud-flats at the mouth of the Kali Lemahan is a must. The pond owners will assist you to hire a small motorised *prau* (canoe) for the 45-min journey. Seeing the thousands of wintering or passage waders here is one of Java's great

birding experiences. These mud-flats are famous for the large numbers (up to 1,000) of rare Asian Dowitchers that spend the northern winter here. Indeed, the flats are a wader-watcher's delight: 18 or more species can be found by carefully scanning the flocks with a telescope. Other highlights are Australian Pelicans, swimming out at sea, and another endangered species, Milky Stork; although often seen on the mud-flats, the latter has yet to be recorded breeding in this part of Java.

Trawas's Centre for Environmental Education

The Centre for Environmental Education (PPLH Seloliman) above Trawas, a 1 $^1/_2$-hr drive inland from Surabaya, is a great place to combine fruitful birding with a comfortable stay in the hills. You can see rare Thick-billed Flowerpeckers and Violet Cuckoos in the forest on the hill above the Centre, and during the wet season, listen for the chirruping calls of Forest Wagtails. The Centre is planted with nectar-rich Calliandra shrubs, which attract numerous flowerpeckers and sunbirds. It is delightful to watch splendid Javan, endemic Violet-tailed and Purple-throated Sunbirds from the breakfast table.

The walk below the Centre to where tall forest drapes the river banks makes a pleasant 2-hr excursion, especially if you have so far missed Javan Kingfisher, Blue Whistling-thrush or the distinct Javan race of Greater Goldenback, all of which are quite common here. Some authorities consider the latter a full species on account of the female's having a yellowish crown rather than the normal white-on-black pattern. In any event, walk the short distance from the Centre's entrance to the main road, and at this junction follow a path leading down to the river, to check them out.

The more adventurous may wish to climb to Mt Penanggungan (1,653 m), where there are good vantage points for eagle watching (Javan Hawk-eagle has been recorded here) and rewarding views of the surrounding area. The trail for the 3 $^1/_2$-hr climb starts from the Hindu temple a 15-min walk uphill (on the right) from the Centre.

–*Bas van Balen*

Above: Groups of endangered Milky Storks are a regular sight on the Solo Delta. *Photo by Alain Compost.*

5 hrs by road from Surabaya, 1 hr from west Bali.

Easiest site for Green Peafowl and Green Junglefowl.

Basic PHPA guest-houses; plantation guest-house at Meru Betiri.

Mixed dry forest and savannah at Baluran. Lowland rain forest at Alas Puro and Meru Betiri.

Hot, generally dry.

Easy walking.

Eastern Parks

Peacocks and Wild Cattle in Sun-baked Savannah

If you thought that bird-watching in Indonesia was all about peering up into the forest canopy, trying to identify an elusive leafbird or patiently stalking a ventriloquial songster, the 250-sq-km Baluran National Park will come as a pleasant surprise. Although only a short journey from the lush greenery of Bali, Baluran—with its sun-baked savannahs, flat-topped acacia trees and large herds of grazing mammals—is more like East Africa than tropical Southeast Asia.

The low stature and relative openness of much of the vegetation provides good viewing conditions, and wildlife photography is probably easier in Baluran than in many of Indonesia's other national parks. In addition to these attractions, it is probably the best place in Java to see Green Peafowl and Green Junglefowl.

The park is easily accessible: the entrance at Batangan is on the main road between Banyuwangi and Surabaya and is only 35 km from the ferry terminal at Ketapang (the jumping-off point for Bali). From Batangan a rather poor, narrow, paved road runs for 12 km through the secondary monsoon forest, which covers much of the southeastern part of the park, to the guest-houses and park ranger centre at Bekol. From Bekol the road continues for another 3 km to the coast at Bama, where there are additional guest-houses.

The Eastern Part of the Park and Coastal Forest

Both Bekol and Bama are well situated for exploring the eastern side of the park, and interesting birding is possible without venturing very far from either area. Indeed, you are likely to see Green Peafowls within a few minutes of arriving, and, during the height of their breeding season (November/December) the cocks may be seen accompanying hens every 200 m, their tail feathers fanned out almost to the width of the road. Both Green and Red Junglefowls can also be seen along the Batangan—Bama road: the Green Junglefowl prefer the more open sections and the Red Junglefowl tend to occupy the forested areas.

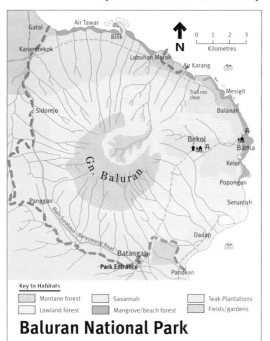

Baluran National Park

Key to Habitats

Montane forest	Savannah	Teak Plantations
Lowland forest	Mangrove/beach forest	Fields/gardens

Birders making only a short visit to the park are best advised to stay at Bama for the night and then explore the surrounding coastal forest in the early morning and late afternoon, perhaps moving to Bekol for a second night in order to explore the forest and scrub along the riverbeds close to the Batangan road. From Bama a footpath runs south through the forest for almost 1 1/2 km to a broken pier, and north for much the same distance to a small fishing hamlet; there is also a large pool with a watchtower, 200 m north of the guest-houses.

White-bellied Woodpecker, Great Slaty Woodpecker, Banded Pitta, Grey-cheeked Tit-babbler, Great-billed Heron, Asian Pied Hornbill, Lesser Adjutant and Spotted Wood-owl are all seen and/or heard frequently in this area. To improve your chance of seeing these, as well as the numerous monitor lizards (some almost 2 m long), explore the area between the southern track and the mangroves rather than following the track itself, which misses some of the more interesting pools.

There is also good, easy birding to be had along the road from Bekol to Batangan. Two especially good areas are in the so-called "Evergreen Forest" section, which starts about 2 km from Bekol, and in the usually dry riverbed that runs roughly parallel to the road until it meets a larger riverbed at the bridge, 2 km southwest of Bekol. (Enter the riverbed by walking NW from the road between the Km 110 and 116 marker posts close to the Bekol guard post.) Banded Pitta, Black-naped Oriole, Ruddy Cuckoo-dove, Green Imperial Pigeon, Emerald Dove, Black-naped Monarch, Racquet-tailed Treepie, Large-tailed Nightjar and various woodpeckers are all seen fairly frequently in this area. During the wet season (December–March) Javan Kingfisher, White-breasted Waterhen and Sunda Teal are attracted to the seasonal pools that form close to the Batangan road, 1 1/2–2 km from Bekol.

The watchtower on the hill at Bekol affords a panoramic view of the surrounding woodland, and in the evening Green Peafowls can usually be seen flying in to roost in nearby *gebang* palms or in the elegant, white-limbed *pilang* trees. For those with telescopes, Black-

Below: Displaying Green Peafowl— one of Asia's great birding spectacles. *Photo by Alain Compost.*

Above: A pristine cove with rain forest in Meru Betiri National Park.
Right: The impressive White-bellied Sea Eagle is a common sight along rocky shorelines throughout Indonesia.
Photos by Alain Compost.

winged Starlings and Black Drongos can often be seen riding on the backs of Javan Deer, Banteng (endangered wild cattle) and feral Water Buffaloes—the starlings and drongos take advantage of the insects attracted to the animals. Java Sparrows sometimes forage in the trees around the tower but, sadly, they are not all that common nowadays.

Exploring the remote Eastern Regions

If you have time to spare, the rest of the eastern side of the park has much to offer, especially in the wet season when the Banteng, deer and Water Buffaloes form sizeable herds on the Lempuyang grasslands. These lie east-northeast from the Talpat spring in the lower foothills of Mt Baluran. A day trek, starting in the early morning, to Lempuyang and then perhaps to the hills and low cliffs in the Balanan area (on the east coast) provides an opportunity to see munias and weavers (in the wet season), minivets, parakeets, eagles, bee-eaters, many swallows, swifts

and swiftlets as well as the ubiquitous Green Peafowls. You will need to hire a guide as there are no marked trails.

From the hills south of the village of Balanan several small valleys lead down to the coast, where small but interesting patches of evergreen forest often dominated by fig trees provide a respite from the heat of the more open woodland and savannah. Again there are no trails, but for the adventurous, fruiting fig trees in this area can provide a striking spectacle: hornbills, pigeons, barbets and monkeys feast in the trees, and wild pigs and Barking Deer search for fallen fruit below. These coastal forest patches are also good places to see leafbirds, malkohas, woodpeckers, kingfishers and Banded Pitta. From the coastline itself one can sometimes see shearwaters and frigatebirds out at sea.

Baluran's Future

Several things detract from Baluran's charm: at weekends hordes of noisy tourists descend upon Bama and Bekol; there is little visitor information; few rangers speak English and not many are willing to spend long hours patiently looking for birds, so if you wander far from the road or coastal tracks take a compass.

Most seriously, though, Baluran is sadly a case of "catch it while you can". The park is full of bird poachers, and the grasslands are rapidly being encroached by thorny scrub. The latter, an exotic which was introduced as a fire-break, has since run rampant and is depriving seed-eating birds of suitable habitat as well as making the wildlife more difficult to see.

Alas Purwo and Meru Betiri—Not to be missed

About 80 km south of Baluran, but still easy to reach, is the little-known Alas Purwo National Park. This 43,420-ha reserve offers good birding, as well as probably the best chance of seeing the Asiatic Wild Dog or *ajag* in Java. Much of the peninsula on which it is sited is rather inaccessible, so it is probably best to concentrate on Sadengan Feeding Ground (see Practicalities), a beautifully situated clearing with forest-clad limestone cliffs rising to one side, several meandering river channels to provide additional scenic (and birding) interest and a well-positioned observation tower.

Both Green Peafowl and Green Junglefowl are readily seen here, although in smaller numbers than in Baluran. Javan Kingfisher, however, is much more common, and Sadengan is a good place to see raptors including Peregrine Falcon and White-bellied Fish-eagle. Javan Hawk-eagle is said to occur, and Banded Pitta is frequently seen in the teak forest around Sandengan.

For those with more time available, the Segara Anak backwater, which lies to the north of the Marengan peninsula, is a good place to see waders and other water birds, whilst the peninsula itself is used as a nesting site by four species of turtle.

Probably most famous for being the last refuge of the now almost certainly extinct Javan Tiger, the 43,420-ha Meru Betiri National Park offers the more adventurous birder the chance to explore one of the few remaining areas of lowland rain forest on Java. Birders usually base themselves at the friendly guest-house of the Sukamade coffee plantation in the southeast corner of the park, which is served by a daily truck-bus service from Pasanggaran. The last 18 km from the village of Raja Wisi, on the edge of the park, passes through excellent forest and it is worth walking if your pack is not too heavy. Another less-used trail runs from Raja Wisi to the beach and the PHPA guest-house 5 km south of Sukamade, where five species of turtle nest.

West behind Sukamade two trails lead up a hill from almost the same point. The first leads over a ridge to a beach, a full day's hike there and back. Wreathed Hornbill is common and Crimson-winged and Checker-throated Yellownapes and Banded Woodpeckers are quite easy to find. The second comes to a dead end after 1 $^1/_2$ km, but it is good for pigeons. Another recommended $^1/_2$-day excursion is to walk the track through the plantations up the Sukamade river valley; Violet Cuckoo is regularly seen in the plantations. At the end, a trail leads through a bamboo grove, where there is a good chance of catching up with Pin-tailed Parrot-finch, and follows the river for a kilometre through disturbed forest to an old watchtower, a good place to see Black-crested Bulbul.

–*Simon Hedges*

Introducing Bali

In Search of the "Real" Bali

There are so many fascinating aspects to Bali that birders might be tempted to hang up their binoculars for a few days and immerse themselves solely in culture, be this the island's colourful Hindu ceremonies and exquisite temples or the vibrant modern beach life of Kuta and Sanur. But birding and culture are wonderfully compatible. Go birding on Bali and you will find yourself searching for forest birds around the Pura Luhur temple in the beautiful scenery of Mt Batukau, scanning the cliffs below the Uluwatu temple for tropicbirds, joining the diving crowd on a trip to Serangan or Nusa Penida islands, exploring the back roads through Bali's famous vivid green rice terraces and wandering around villages and gardens. Indeed, go birding and you may get close to discovering the "real Bali", which half the tourists on the island seem to be searching for anyway.

Although small (5,315 sq km) Bali is geographically diverse and very rich in birds: 317 species have been recorded on the island. The central mountains, dominated by the sacred Mt Agung (3,143 m), and its neighbours to the west, where 8 species unique to the mountains of Java and Bali can be seen, are cloaked with rain forest. In the far west a remnant of the dry, savannah-like forests that once covered the lowlands of west and north Bali survives in the Bali Barat National Park, the last refuge of the Bali Starling, the island's only endemic bird species. The south coast is a glorious mixture of sandy beaches, steep limestone cliffs where Red-tailed Tropicbirds breed in May and June, and—normally shunned by tourists—muddy bays fringed with mangroves where hundreds of shorebirds stop over on migration.

The southern slopes of Bali's central volcanoes are heavily cultivated and rice terraces extend high up the mountain sides. This area is the cradle of Bali's rich and ancient civilisation. It is virtually the only region of Indonesia that remains Hindu today, left to go its own way during the wave of Islamization that swept through the archipelago in the 15th century. When the Dutch finally colonised the island at the turn of the 20th century, they were so fascinated by what they found that they made a concerted effort to conserve and foster Bali's traditional culture.

As traditional Balinese art commonly features birds, a painting would seem to make the ideal souvenir. It is quite a challenge, however to find a piece depicting only native species: American Cardinals, Australian Rossellas and South American toucans regularly pop up among the lotus pools and nymphs—just one example of the ease with which Balinese culture accepts new and foreign elements. Perhaps the growing popularity of bird-watching will help the Balinese to appreciate the beauty and variety of their own native birds.

Nowhere matches Bali for such a fusion of birds, landscapes and cultures—for birders with eclectic interests it is an island not to be missed.

–Paul Jepson

Previous page: Could it be a Ruddy-breasted Crake? Birding in the Balinese countryside. *Photo courtesy of Soebek expeditions.* **Opposite:** On the brink of extinction, a tiny population of the Bali Starling survives in Bali Barat National Park. *Photo by Alain Compost.*

Access to site.

Main birding attractions.

Type of accommodation.

Habitat.

Weather conditions.

Degree of difficulty.

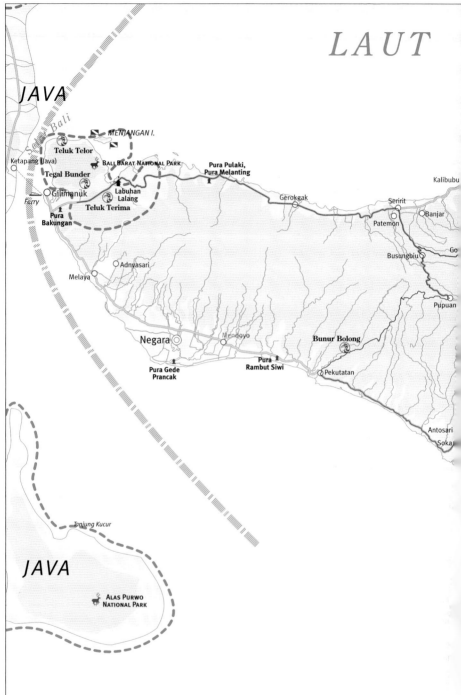

LAUT

JAVA

Selat Bali

MENJANGAN I.

Teluk Telor

Ketapang (Java)

BALI BARAT NATIONAL PARK

Pura Pulaki,
Pura Melanting

Kalibubu

Tegal Bunder

Gilimanuk

Labuhan
Lalang

Gerokgak

Seririt

Banjar

Ferry

Pura
Bakungan

Teluk Terima

Patemon

Busungbiu

Go

Adnyasari

Pupuan

Melaya

Mendoyo

Negara

Bunur Bolong

Pura Gede
Prancak

Pura
Rambut Siwi

Pekutatan

Tanjung Kucur

JAVA

ALAS PURWO
NATIONAL PARK

Antosari

Soka

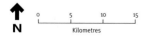

SAMUDRA

N

0   5   10   15
Kilometres

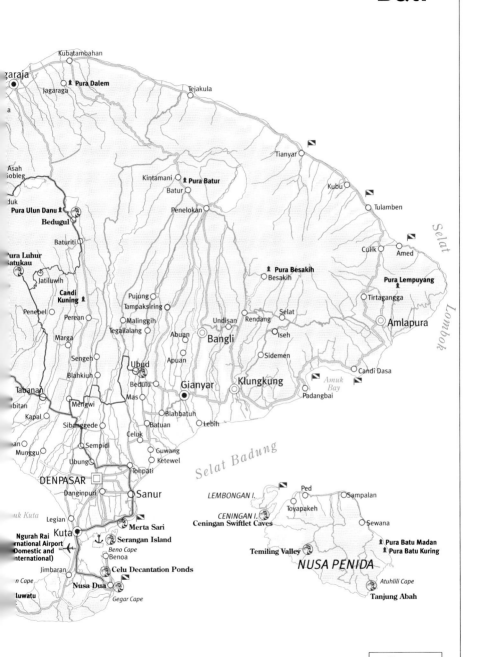

BALI

Bali

Kubatambahan

garaja
Jagaraga 🏛 **Pura Dalem**
Tejakula

Tianyar

Asah
ioblek

Kintamani 🏛 **Pura Batur**
Batur

Kubu

Tulamben

uk

Pura Ulun Danu 🏛
Bedugul

Penelokan

Selat

ura Luhur
iatukau

Baturiti

Culik
Amed

Jatiluwih

Pura Besakih 🏛
Besakih

Pura Lempuyang

**Candi
Kuning** 🏛

Pujung
Tampaksiring
Malinggih
Tegallalang

Tirtagangga

Penebel

Perean

Selat

Amlapura

Marga

Undisan
Rendang

Abuan

Bangli

Iseh

Lombok

Sengeh

Apuan

Blahkiuh

Ubud

Sidemen

Candi Dasa

Tabanan

Bedulu

Mas

Gianyar

Klungkung

Amuk
Bay

bitan

Mengwi

Blahbatuh

Padangbai

Kapal

Sibanggede

Batuan

Lebih

Celuk

an
Munggu

Sempidi

Guwang

Ubung

Ketewel

Selat Badung

Tohpati

DENPASAR

Danginpuri

LEMBONGAN I.

Ped

Sampalan

Sanur

Toyapakeh

Sewana

uk Kuta

Legian

CENINGAN I.
Ceningan Swiftlet Caves

Kuta

Merta Sari

🏛 **Pura Batu Madan**
🏛 **Pura Batu Kuring**

Ngurah Rai
rnational Airport
(Domestic and
nternational)

Serangan Island

Beno Cape

Temiling Valley

Benoa

NUSA PENIDA

Jimbaran

Celu Decantation Ponds

n Cape

Atuhlili Cape

luwatu

Nusa Dua

Tanjung Abah

Gegar Cape

Key
— Bali Bird Tour
🏴 Dive Sites

HINDIA

Bali Bird Tour

An unforgettable Fusion of Birds, Culture and Landscape

Bali's diverse attractions—tropical beaches, vibrant Hindu culture, scenic rice terraces and beach resorts—have made the island one of the world's premier tourist destinations. However, the island has much to offer the bird-watcher too: a wide range of birds and many other attractions can be enjoyed in a fabulous 5- to 7-day tour starting in the south, and going up over the mountains to the unspoilt north-west coast.

There is no need to attempt the whole tour in one fell swoop. It can be done piecemeal, with one or more stages as side-trips, or mostly in reverse if you arrive at Gilimanuk on the ferry from Ketapang in East Java. Ideally, to make the most of your time and allow the greatest degree of flexibility, it is best to have your own wheels, but all destinations are attainable by public transport.

 4 day car tour starting at the south coast resorts.

 Bali Starling at Bali Barat National Park.

 Wide choice of reasonably priced and quality *losmen* and hotels.

Rice terraces, forested volcanoes, dry forest in the west.

Usually dry, sunny and hot. Rains Oct–Mar.

 Easy walking at all sites on the tour.

A Day around the Resorts

A great many visitors choose to stay in the tourist resort of Nusa Dua, so here our tour begins bright and early one weekday morning. It is always better to avoid travelling at the weekend as there is more traffic. Most people tend to shun sewage farms, but to bird-watchers they are a veritable Mecca, and the one in Nusa Dua is no exception. The decantation ponds are situated in Celu, and the main entrance is exactly opposite the northern entrance to the hotel complex containing Club Med. Usually the gate is open and you can drive right in,

but it is better to park and walk. Here, on a series of large ponds dotted with heavily vegetated islands, is one of the most impressive arrays of large waterbirds to be seen in Bali. October to March (during the wet season) is a particularly good time to visit, as many species are nesting then.

The raised embankments dividing the ponds are now gated to reduce disturbance, but good views of the birds can be enjoyed from a wander round the perimeter. Note the huge population of herons, especially breeding Purple and Black-crowned Night-herons. Also breeding are Little Pied Cormorant, and suspected Oriental Darter and Glossy Ibis. A pair of Lesser Adjutants may also be taking up permanent residence.

Both Black-throated and Red-throated Little Grebes have been spotted here, and, although of the ducks only Sunda Teal is always present, both Lesser and Wandering Whistling-ducks, Pacific Black Duck and even Palaearctic migrants may be expected. In the encircling mangroves, look out for Small Blue Kingfisher and White-shouldered Triller. Sightings of Yellow-crested Cockatoos have been reported on several occasions, so they may be trying to establish a feral population. Given proper protection of this oasis, almost anything might choose to make its home here.

Whilst still in Nusa Dua, be sure to check out the reef between the two peninsulas for a good selection of waders; also both white-phase and black-phase Reef Egret.

On the main "island" is a healthy population of Striated Grassbirds and Common Pipits; Long-tailed Shrikes abound.

Our next stop is Sanur, where you go directly to the district known as Merta Sari, just south of the hotel called Travelodge. Park under the magnificent *suar* (white oak) trees adjacent to the exquisite coral temple. If the tide is out, a vast expanse of sand-flats stretches almost to the horizon. Invariably you will see an excellent selection of waders just off-shore. If the tide is in, walk 200 m north of the temple through the coconut plantation to the as yet unspoilt southern end of Sanur Beach. Then head south along the beach and, before the mangrove begins, check out the fishponds for roosting waders and Small Blue Kingfisher. Inside the mangrove, you will find Island Collared Dove, Sacred and Collared Kingfishers, Sunda Woodpecker, Blue-tailed Bee-eater, Golden-bellied Gerygone, Pied Fantail and Streaked Weaver.

Above: Rice terraces stretch as far as the eye can see. The sophistication of Balinese culture is even evident in their agriculture. *Photo by Alain Compost.*

Up into the Hills

Now it is time to head for our first night's destination, Bedugul in the central highlands—a mere 1 to 1 ½ hours' drive. An alternative more leisurely option is to make a whole day of the next stage of the journey with a detour via the amazing jungle temple, Pura Luhur, on the southern slopes of Mt Batukau. This will take you through the most spectacular landscape on the island—weather permitting.

Taking the Jl Ngurah Rai bypass road, go straight across the crossroads in Tohpati and come out north of Denpasar on the road to Tabanan. In Tabanan pay heed to the one-way system, taking a right turn after the market and doubling back so as to reach the road leading north to Penebel. Half way to Penebel, take a left turn to Yehpanas (hot springs), continuing north to the Pura Luhur. At Tengkudak pause briefly to visit the

astonishing church—a brick, syncretic folly elaborated with Balinese sculpted angels and demons—before proceeding to Wangagadegé (Wangaye for short), where the jungle begins. The road climbs more steeply now, and it is worth stopping to examine one or more of the vast, wayside fig trees for imperial and green pigeons, fruit-doves, minivets and barbets. The distribution of the latter in Bali, their last oriental outpost, is strange: here, in central Bali, Orange-fronted, Blue-eared and Coppersmith Barbets can be seen together in the same tree.

Some doubtless well-intentioned "improvements" to the temple precincts have recently been made and the old rustic spirit of the sanctuary has to some extent now been lost. Even the lake has been cleaned up. But no matter, there are still birds in abundance. Mugimaki, Little Pied and Grey-headed

Flycatchers, Black-naped Monarchs, White-rumped Warblers, Black-winged Hemipus, and Orange-bellied and Blood-breasted Flowerpeckers will all be found here. You are almost bound to see the striking, pied White-crowned Forktail. Look for it in the feeder streams to the shrines and pond or, failing there, in the tumbling river-bed, which may be gained by taking the forest path on the left before the temple.

After a bathe in the river, which is icy and so clean that you can drink from it, it is time to return to Wangaye, from where you turn left on to the pot-holed road to Jatiluwih. Drive slowly along this road, not because it is bad, but so as not to miss the wonderful landscape. There are various contenders for the most scenic route in Bali, but this one surely takes the prize. Pied Bushchats and Javan Kingfishers are everywhere—and keep an eye to the heavens for Black Eagle. Break the journey at Jatiluwih (the name means "lovely view") and over a picnic lunch gaze in awe at the unfolding panorama of rolling rice terraces... and go on gazing. And on at length to the hamlet which is liltingly called

Sengananankanginan, then left on a slightly better road which joins the main road to Bedugul at Pacung.

If you do not take a packed lunch, the Restaurant Mutiara Sari in Baturiti has a fine bill of fare and, amazingly, fresh milk from the local dairy herd. If it is a nice day, sit out in the ornamental garden; the view here is also grand. What is that peculiar liquid twitter, followed by a shushing sound? Here are the first Brown Honeyeaters of the tour.

Bedugul—Mountain Birds and Cool Vistas

Winding up and over the pass, we reach the area known as Bedugul, and a few hundred metres beyond the summit is the colourful fruit and flower market at Candikuning. A little further down the hill, on the left just before the lakeside, is a sign announcing Lila Graha. A steep driveway leads up the hill to this government-run pension, where we shall spend the night. Two nights, perhaps.

Make the most of the two hours' or so daylight remaining with a short excursion to the lake.

Below: Buffy Fish Owl—with skill or luck, a bird to be seen in Bali Barat National Park. *Photo by Alain Compost.*

Opposite the Lila Graha is the entrance to the Ashram Guest House. Cut through the Ashram's garden to the Balinese gate and continue by the lakeside, where a wonderful array of Painted Lady butterflies sun themselves on the paved pathway. The trail leads up into the tall trees and comes out in the gardens of the Hotel Bedugul. This little pocket of forest is full of birds, and is probably the best place anywhere to pick up the elusive Lesser Shortwing, whose tantalising crescendo is one of the most prevalent jungle sounds. At each bend in the trail, carefully check the way ahead. Here you will easily spot all three babblers—Horsfield's, the endemic Crescent-chested and Chestnut-backed Scimitar-babbler—and such little beauties as Yellow-bellied and Mountain Leaf-warblers, Mountain Tailorbird, Grey-headed Flycatcher, and all three White-eyes: Oriental, Mountain and Javan Grey-throated, the latter very common.

Early next morning visit the botanical gardens up the small road leading from the traffic island next to the market-place. Dawn is good for thrushes—Sunda and Orange-headed at the edge of the lawn, 200 m into the grounds, and Scaly Thrush by the temple and sulphur fissure at the topmost point. Loads of Grey-cheeked Green Pigeons and Short-tailed Starlings, as well as Ashy Drongo, babblers, honeyeaters and Common Golden Whistler, will keep you busy until well into the morning.

Lake Bratan Environs

Once you have exhausted the gardens, the rest of the day can be devoted to exploring the ridge that rings Lake Bratan. Either drive to Hotel Bedugul or walk once more on the short trail from the Ashram. At the brow of the hill leading down to the lakeside and the water-sports centre, turn up the track by the guard post and drive to the end (not far) or, better, walk on the lakeside

embankment and mount to the higher level on the obvious ramp. The original trail leads up from what looks like a new car park past fields of cabbages, then forks left again at a lone, spiny coral-bean tree. Immediately you are back in babbler land and treeshrew territory. Watch out for the latter, which utter disconcertingly bird-like alarm calls.

The trail goes on and on, initially through scrub dominated by giant pandanus, then into everlasting moss forest, climbing gently to a marvellous look-out after about 3 km. A trail starting soon after the small temple enclave leads all the way to Pelaga and is well worth examining, but beware of leeches. Green and Dark-backed Imperial Pigeons are plentiful here, the latter's double note *hoo-whoo* being the commonest sound; and listen out for the ringing cries of both Lesser and Malaysian Cuckoo-shrikes. Yellow-throated Hanging-parrot is not uncommon but, like the barbets, is hard to see in the canopy. Siberian Thrush, a winter

Above: Black-naped Monarch—away from its nest a harsh chirping will alert you to its presence. *Photo by Margaret Kinnaird.*

visitor, is quite easy to spot on the ground. And watch out for wren-babblers which are certainly here, but not yet positively identified.

There are some other good forest tracks: one leads from the rough road skirting the south side of Lake Buyan, which has a barrier after about 3 km. Even though it is sometimes open, it is better to park here and walk. Continue always bearing right and climb over the ridge to Lake Tamblingan: the lovely, primary montane jungle affords good views of most species already mentioned, plus Red Junglefowl and Chestnut-breasted Malkoha. Many Long-tailed Macaques and Barking Deer are also in evidence here. Another track worth exploring is the path that leads from the approach road to Bali Handara Golf Club, near the artificial ponds and adjacent to Green 2. From a dry stream gully emerge on to the path adjacent to a large pipeline and look for thrushes and Sunda Bush-warbler skulking in dank thickets nearby. Lunch in the club is thoroughly recommended.

The North Coast

Leaving Bedugul there are two roads to the north coast to choose from: either due north to Singaraja or along the scenic road that runs along the crater rim skirting Lake Buyan and Tamblingan, with unforgettable late afternoon views across to the volcanoes of east Java, and thence down through clove plantations to Seririt.

If you opt for the former, beware that the descent down from the northern slopes to Bali's former capital town is precipitous, and may be irksome if you get stuck behind a tourist bus or benzine truck. However, Singaraja boasts some old colonial architecture and you may see *Bugis* schooners loading on the wharf. And there is no better restaurant in Bali than Segar, on the corner of Jl Erlangga near the seafront. From Singaraja it is a hard 3-hr drive via Seririt through

avenues of painted tamarind to the Bali Barat National Park. An option is to spend the night at one of the many hotels at Lovina beach, and take the magical, early morning outrigger ride to see dolphins, where there is a possibility of seeing terns and even the odd skua.

Bali Barat National Park

The problem in the national park is accommodation—or lack of it: in fact, there is none (see Practicalities). The best bet is Pondok Sari at Pemuteran on the fringe of the park, about 30 km from Gilimanuk, or, if you are not too fussy, Nusantara II in Gilimanuk itself. The advantage of the latter is that it is nearer to the action and offers access to the beach and a very pleasant walk along the bay to a wide expanse of grassland, where Chestnut-headed Bee-eater, Asian Pied and Black-winged Starlings, White-shouldered Triller and Striated Grassbird are all to be seen. Migrating Oriental Plover and Little Curlew can be spotted on the turf, while across the bay, up to nine Lesser Adjutants are usually visible evenly spaced along the beach.

But first you must get a permit in order to prowl around. Go to the National Park headquarters at Cekik, at the junction of the north and south coast-roads, or the office at Labuhan Lalang, 8 km back along the northern road. Labuhan Lalang is the departure point for snorkelling and diving tours on the fantastic reef surrounding Menjangan Island, which is also the best spot for Beach Thick-knee and Lemon-bellied White-eye.

To see the endangered Bali Starling, you will need the assistance of the wardens who will take you by boat to Teluk Telor ranger station on Prapat Agung Peninsula. An alternative is to walk—12 km in each direction—from the Pre-release Training Centre at Tegal Bunder, located 1 km down a track that leads off the main road at the village of Sumberklampok mid-way between Labuhan Lalang and the Park Headquarters. The Bali Starling is one of the world's rarest birds, with only 35 or so left in the wild, and as the issue of its probable extinction is so sensitive, the situation changes all the time. However, if a visit is possible, Tegal Bunder, with its varied habitats of acacia forest, scrub, savannah and mangrove swamp, yields species seldom seen elsewhere. Nightjars, hornbills, malkohas, pittas, rollers and treeswifts are all there, and look out especially for Black-thighed Falconet, Orange-breasted Green Pigeon and Lineated Barbet. The whole place is seething with Green Junglefowl.

For a most rewarding foray, climb the steps to the Jayaprana temple at Teluk Terima, then descend to the stream-bed behind the compound. Follow the stream back to the road, cutting across the longer, almost parallel, reaches. Marvel at the wildlife in general: large squirrels such as *Ratufa bicolor* and Docherty's Squirrel, Barking Deer, and huge, black Silvered Leaf Monkeys or Langurs. With luck you may catch up with owls— Brown Hawk, Buffy Fish and even Oriental Bay, which has recently been "rediscovered" here. Perhaps the greatest reward will be Rufous-backed Kingfisher. Look for Banded Pitta and Fulvous-chested Flycatcher in the scrubby forest near the road.

If you have decided to base yourself at Pondok Sari, a walk west along the beach (or on the track behind it) will take you to a rainwater catchment area that is teeming with birds. Both Large-tailed and Savanna Nightjars are readily flushed and the area is good for bee-eaters, trillers, drongos, woodswallows and starlings, too.

Bunot Bolong and the Return home

It is best to avoid the bustling southern coastal route on the way back home, and one final deviation is proposed. At Seririt, turn inland on the road to Pupuan, and drive through incredible mountain scenery. Bear right in Pupuan on the road signposted Negara, and the way becomes ever more spectacular. Rounding a bend, you will be surprised to find the road passing through the bole of an immense fig-tree. *Bunut Bolong* (fig-tree hole) is the name of the place. Stop here; from the edge of the road, a leisurely scan of the forested valley may produce sightings of hornbills, barbets, and even the forest kingfisher and Hill Myna.

At Pekutatan, it is no longer possible to avoid the coastal road and by the time you reach Tabanan you will probably be heartily sick of it. So why not hop up to Ubud via Mengwi? Here, you can round off the tour with a relaxing bird walk in the countryside and enjoy some common or garden birds.

–Victor Mason

Below: The last remnants of Bali's monsoon forest are protected in the Bali Barat National Park. *Photo by Alain Compost.*

A Bali Bird Walk

Birds of the Balinese Countryside with the Colourful Victor Mason

Below: Rainbow Bee-eaters, migrants from Australia grace the fields of east Indonesia. *Photo by Alain Compost.*

Nine o'clock? Bit late, surely? We all know that birds are generally at their most active and evident during the two hours or so following first light, or preceding dusk. But then we have to consider that pretty well all our guests are enjoying long vacations far from home. Many are suffering from jet-lag, "Bali Belly" or culture-shock, and since they cannot all be accommodated in the Ubud area—for that is where the bird walks are—many will have had an early call to drive for up to an hour by road to our retreat at the heart of Bali.

We meet, then, at 9 o'clock, or preferably a little earlier, so as to enjoy the view from the top deck of Beggar's Bush. Time to be introduced to the guides and other guests, have a drink and a chat, and even spot a few species before we set off. Practically guaranteed in the few available minutes are the elegant Striated Swallows, which have chosen to build their nests under the main road bridge situated directly below. Then there are the Yellow-vented Bulbuls chortling away, a few plump Spotted Doves resting on palm fronds, Olive-backed Sunbirds rifling the hibiscus while their cousins, Brown-throated Sunbirds, busily inspect the sticky, flowering bracts of a coconut palm. Above us, milling about the crown of a giant banyan tree, we may see a host of White-bellied Swiftlets, which may surely count as the most abundant of all Bali's birds. There, we have six species under our belts already—and we haven't even begun!

 Start in Ubud, 35 km from south coast resorts.

 Typical birds of the Balinese countryside.

 Wide choice to suit all tastes and pockets.

 Rice fields, groves and gardens.

 Sunny and hot, changeable between Oct and Mar.

 Gentle two to three hour stroll.

A final few words from our guide, and a list of the birds we are likely to see if anyone wishes to "twitch". Has everyone got binoculars? Not essential, but recommended. Apparently no-one has brought their own binoculars this morning. Indeed, it soon transpires that hardly anyone has even held a pair before, unless it were to attend the race-track or opera! Ninety percent of our guests are not habitual bird-watchers: they merely wish to have a pleasant stroll in unaccustomed surroundings and a good, healthy dose of fresh air. And there are other things to see besides birds.

Such as? Swallowtail and birdwing butterflies, and giant spiders; massive trees and shrubs and vines; wild flowers, including orchids; original and hybrid strains of rice at every stage of growth, with planting, tilling and harvesting by ancient means sometimes being performed at once; and always the miracle of irrigation as ordered by the *subak* system; temples and relics of antiquity; stunning scenery; and, if we are lucky, a glimpse of the shy *alu*, or giant monitor lizard. No snakes? Well, occasionally one slithers from our path, disturbed by the approach of tramping feet.

Are we all present and correct, then? But let us not forget Harold, the dog who favours a watery habitat, and who is adept at flushing bitterns, rails and snipe—the odd button-quail in dry cultivation, too.

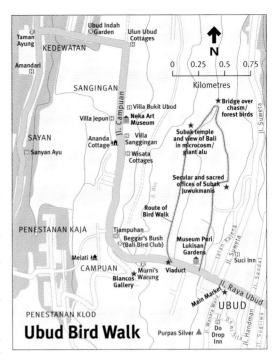

Ubud Bird Walk

At the Art Museum

Today we take the northern route, commencing with the gardens of the *Puri Lukisan* or Art Museum. For the most part well laid out and meticulously tended, the gardens nonetheless provide a haven for many small birds, and we are content to view these so easily in such picturesque surrounds. In rapid succession we pick up Common Iora (which is nesting on its tiny cup), Ashy Tailorbird and Bar-winged Prinia. The latter are found only in Bali, Java and south Sumatra. More sunbirds, with Brown-throated nesting in the Flame-of-the-Forest tree, and then, a brilliant flash of scarlet: a lovely view of the male Scarlet-headed Flowerpecker and his mate more drab with scarlet patch on rump only. A party of Oriental White-eyes peeping in the Champak tree. Several Eurasian Tree Sparrows—just like the ones in Europe—and here proliferating in pace with the increased incidence of building sites: this is one little bird that seems to benefit from the presence of man. And there on the gallery roof, an immaculate pair of Java Sparrows—grey with pink belly, black and white head, and massive pink bill—with their less colourful brood.

Thirteen species now; we are doing well. We could spend all day admiring these ornate gardens, but it is time to get into open territory. Behind the museum the rice fields stretch as far as the eye can see, bordered on either side by a screen of palms, acacia, coral-bean and bamboo. Our first Javan Kingfisher sits before us, atop a shrine—just as it says in the book—surrounded by newly-planted paddy. Has everyone got it? A collective gasp of astonishment ensues. How could any bird be so brilliant? On terraces beyond, white egrets forage—Little Egrets rather jerkily, Intermediate more sedately. There are Cattle Egrets too, noticeably less elegant, and some still bearing buffy traces of their nuptial plumes.

Proceeding on the grassy path between verges aglow with blue Snake-weed, white Stars of Bethlehem and yellow Ox-eye Daisies, we are suddenly alerted to a high-pitched, sibilant piping—Wood Sandpiper. Several flutter down to join a scattered flock in the low, green growth: these are the only migrant waders that venture far inland in significant numbers.

A little further on we come to a patch of slightly more advanced growth, not yet knee-high but ideal cover for larger waterbirds. Harold is in his element and goes about his duty. And, sure enough, not a minute passes before a brown form erupts on flailing wings and, wheeling, flies above the path in front of us, to alight in a flurry 100 m away. Cinnamon Bittern—well done,

Below: Javan Kingfisher—one common countryside bird you won't bore of. *Photo by Margaret Kinnaird.*

Harold! And a moment later, three plump, long-billed snipe whirr away, with a nasal rasp, in rapid flight. Probably Pintail rather than Swinhoe's, judging by experience, though it is practically impossible to identify them out of the hand. Harold has really excelled himself today.

Our tally already amounts to 20. What a day! Another Javan Kingfisher, emitting a staccato cackle, draws everyone's attention as it flies low over the fields, displaying white wing patches. Presently we arrive at a fairly substantial whitewashed building and some thatched sheds, adjacent to a spacious courtyard in the shade of a huge fruiting fig tree. These are the offices and temple of the local *subak*, the guild of land-owners who manage the water-supply system, and a good spot to pause for refreshment.

The discourse is punctuated by the mournful call of the Plaintive Cuckoo perched somewhere near at hand, but there is no sign of it. And so we continue through a grove of clove trees, then peering up succeeding bunds between the rice clumps, we are at last rewarded with the sight of a brownish lump—Ruddy-breasted Crake,

whispers the guide, as it suddenly comes to life and melts into the crop. The fields hereabouts are teeming with crake, but how often does one actually see them? Luckily, three of us saw this one.

A strip of dry cultivation now looms: sweet corn and sweet potatoes. Ploughing through a plot of the latter, Harold succeeds in putting up not one but two button-quail: Barred Button-quail. He shall be well rewarded! From above comes the prolonged, sweet-trilled refrain of a Singing Bush-lark, and at last, someone manages to get a good sighting of it.

Butterflies and Babblers

Time for a change of habitat. A mighty coral-bean, festooned with epiphytes and parasites including a mass of perfumed dog-orchids, stands at the entrance to a ribbon of relict forest which invades a deep ravine. Here we may see butterflies, if not birds. The poignant notes of Fulvous-chested Flycatcher and the hoarse bickerings of Horsfield's Babbler emanate from the jungle habitat, but the authors remain invisible. We move on to a bush of lilac White-weed smothered in *Danaid* butterflies and—wonder of wonders!—*Troides*, the golden Helena birdwing, sweeps by. Such luck! Lost in admiration we almost fail to hear the raucous outcry from the gorge: a pair of puff-throated Grey-cheeked Bulbuls... and everybody gets a decent look for once.

Next we head into fields of cream and golden Bali rice where harvesting is in progress. There are birds everywhere: Zitting and Golden-headed Cisticolas and all three munias—Javan, Scaly-breasted and the white-headed Chestnut. There is a further pause for refreshment on the banks of a stream—young coconuts garnered by a farmer—surveyed by a monstrous, black and yellow *Nephila* spider and surrounded by a host of bright, fox-red Malayan Lacewing butterflies.

Above: Ubud's sacred egret colony at Petulu. *Photo by Alain Compost.*

The first pangs of hunger begin to assai, but there are still a few birds to go. Final stop by a rustic *subak* temple to soak in the view of the majestic Campuan river valley. No sign of the *alu* today, though. A Greater Coucal only heard; but shrieking Collared Kingfisher seen by all. Pied Bushchat and Long-tailed Shrike perched openly, and a party of Blue-tailed Bee-eaters quilluping overhead. Both resident Pacific and visiting Barn Swallows swooping low; and both Asian Palm and Fork-tailed Swifts on high.

A White-breasted Waterhen breaks out of the bush and flutters across the Tjampuhan river under the main-road bridge. Ultimate lucky flush. Thirty-eight actually seen; four merely heard. Now, without further ado, let us sit down and have lunch. And Harold shall have a large bone.

–*Victor Mason*

Pulau Serangan

Shorebirds an Outrigger Ride from Sanur

Most people go to Turtle Island to see the important temple, Pura Sakenan, with its beautifully sculpted coral gates and shrines. During the ten days following the Galungan/Kuningan (All Saints/All Souls) festival, tens of thousands of pilgrims, together with their sacred icons, come here in resplendent procession. But for the bird-watcher, Pulau Serangan is the best site in Bali for shorebirds.

The nicest way to get there is by dug-out outrigger (*prau*) which may be hired by the hour from Sanur beach. A leisurely half-hour's sail along the lagoon should yield an assortment of terns—predominantly Common, Little and Great Crested—and the odd white-phase Reef Egret; and from about April to November, squadrons of mixed frigatebirds—Great and Lesser (but watch out for the odd Christmas Frigatebird, too)—cruise north above the coast. Note the extensive belt of protected mangrove, home to a profusion of herons, turtle-doves, kingfishers, bee-eaters, warblers, sunbirds, weavers and munias.

and sand-flat at the south end of the island that provides a feeding ground and a roost for migrating terns and waders as well as local herons. As you walk along the beach, observe parties of Sanderlings, pairs of small Malaysian Plovers and the odd Common Sandpiper. Rounding a bend in the beach and a shallow inlet, the extent of the flat becomes

Shorebirds on the Sand-flats

Ask the boatman to drop you half-way down the 1 $1/2$-km strand and walk the rest of the way. Or land at the usual disembarkation point, inspect the village and temple, and then take the clearly defined and well-shaded path that dissects the island north to south.

The main birding attraction is the vast expanse of exposed reef

Half hour out-rigger sail from Sanur.

Migratory shore-birds, herons and terns.

A day trip from south coast resorts.

Sand-flats and man-groves.

Hot, but sea breezes; take care with sunburn.

Easy walking, but muddy and wet out on the flats.

apparent, dotted with white egrets and an evenly-spaced line of dark, angular Purple Herons. Less obvious at first glance are the large numbers of Javan Pond Herons: whether in breeding or non-breeding plumage, they blend in with their background.

Even more difficult to see are the flocks of plovers and sandpipers, all brownish, which are collectively known as waders. The easiest of this group to spot are the Curlews, both Eurasian and Far Eastern—the former with white rumps like the numerous Whimbrels, obvious by their sheer size. Grey Plover are fairly plentiful and are easily distinguished by their black axillaries ("armpits") in flight. Not so the flocks of Golden Plover, which are almost impossible to detect against the mud. Calling for equally close scrutiny are the flocks of Mongolian Plover, interspersed with the odd Greater Sandplover, Grey-tailed Tattler, Rufousnecked Stint, and Sharp-tailed and Curlew Sandpipers. Redshanks are usually much in evidence, with a few Greenshanks and Ruddy Turnstones. And look out for some of Bali's more infrequent visitors, such as Black-tailed and Bar-tailed Godwits, Terek Sandpiper, Longbilled Dowitcher and Great Knot.

During the Spring and Autumn passage, thousands of birds congregate here (though it is a rewarding site at any time). Most numerous of all are the terns—great, pied swathes of them, comprising mainly Great Crested Terns with lesser numbers of Gull-billed, Common and Little. But now it is time to hurry back: the tide is getting low and the boatman becoming impatient....
  –Victor Mason

Below: Lesser Frigatebirds wheel over a fish shoal in the sparkling evening light. *Photo by Alain Compost.*

Nusa Penida
Island of Bandits

Opposite: The spectacular nesting cliffs of White-tailed Tropicbirds: south Nusa Penida. *Photo by Alain Compost.*

First known to Portuguese seafarers as Nusa Pendita, this island has always had an unsavoury reputation. Many sailing ships have been wrecked and plundered on its coasts, and still today the place is wild and inhospitable. Lacking any ground-water, it is unsuited to tourist development, and thus an excellent place for birds. It can be explored in a 2- or 3-day trip.

Accessible by charted outrigger (*jukung*) from Sanur or by a regular passenger service from Kusambe, what appears to be a solid formation is in fact three islands. The nearest, Lembongan, has been adopted by the surfing and pleasure-boating crowd. It could make a convenient base and is certainly worth a visit to see the peculiar man-made underground labyrinth at Jungutbatu. At low tide one can wander over to intervening Ceningan Island to see the spectacle of a host of cave-dwelling Edible-nest Swiftlets. The soup made from their mucus nests is a delicacy in Hong Kong and Taiwan, and the nests are harvested commercially here (*see p 57*).

Seabirds in the Strait

On the way over from Bali, keep an eye open for seabirds such as Wilson's Storm-petrel, Wedge-tailed Shearwater and Red-necked Phalarope. The main island, Nusa Penida, is now more or less ringed by road; whether exploring by push-bike, on foot or by public transport, be prepared for some discomfort. There is seldom any shade, and it is very hot.

On arrival at Toyapakeh or Sampalan, look out for at least two species which are common here but not seen on mainland Bali: Red-chested Flowerpecker and Black-faced Munia. Along the coast (and on high ground where there is some dry rice cultivation) you may be surprised to see White-faced Heron, a typically Australian bird at the very northern limit of its range.

Given limited time, two day-long excursions are recommended: the first to Batumadeg on the southern slopes of Bukit Mundi (Mundi hill), from where you may walk south to the remote Temiling Valley. This spectacular gorge, surrounded by the only jungle on the island, is home to many forest birds, notably imperial pigeons, drongos and flycatchers. The trail leads on to *kolam dedari*, the angels' pool—a wonderful spot to cool off. Inspect the nearby cliffside temple, *Pura Segara*, and see White-tailed Tropicbirds nesting in the 200-m chalk heads. Another route home starts with the rock-hewn staircase above the pool.

The second excursion is to Tanjung Abah (Abah cape), via the incredible Karangsari cave. From Sampalan take the east coast road to Suwana (from where it is a long, hard, scenic walk) or Karang (a short, rugged trail) to Tanjung Abah. White-bellied Sea-eagles still nest on the limestone stacks at Abah, and the view here is stunning. There is also a good chance of seeing Osprey and Peregrine Falcon—and if you see any other tourists, they are bound to be bird-watchers!

– *Victor Mason*

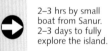

2–3 hrs by small boat from Sanur. 2–3 days to fully explore the island.

Swiftlet caves, tropicbirds, open country birding.

A few basic *losmen*, or stay with villagers.

Impressive cliffs, scrub and grass-lands.

Hot and dry.

Some long hot walks.

Introducing Nusa Tenggara

The "Dry Tropics" of Indonesia

Nusa Tenggara—the Lesser Sundas, as the area is known to biologists—encompasses the chains of islands that stretch 1,300 km eastwards from Lombok to Timor and beyond. This is the "dry tropics" of Indonesia, and the aridity of islands such as Sumba, Komodo, Timor and parts of Flores contrasts starkly with the lushness of the rest of the archipelago.

It is a fusion of diverse cultures and landscapes that really sets Nusa Tenggara apart as a travel destination. The three-coloured crater lakes of Keli Mutu on Flores are weirdly surreal. The 34-km wide, 300-m deep crater of Mt Tambora on Sumbawa is so awesome that it almost defies comprehension. The Komodo Islands are home to the world's largest lizard, the closest thing to a living dragon. Then there are the people. On Sumbawa they have turned ploughing rice fields into a spectator sport with thrilling buffalo races. On Sumba, hundreds of horsemen turn out once each year to intimidate each other with spear throwing at the ancient *pasola*, and on Lembata men still harpoon migrating whales by leaping onto their backs.

Lombok and Sumbawa are predominately Muslim, and the rest predominantly Christian. But visitors soon meet with traditional religious life based on animistic and ancestral beliefs and only thinly veiled by the great universal religions, especially in Christian areas. Rituals and ceremonies, clan groups and ancestral houses are still powerful forces in social organization in the region.

For birders Nusa Tenggara offers a delightful mixture. There is sunny, open country birding searching for quails, raptors and chats, as well as idyllic interludes watching for seabirds (*see p 92*) or whales from inter-island ferries. One can also scan for rare migrant waders on some of the myriad small estuaries, or venture into the forests in pursuit of the region's 57 endemic species.

To see all the endemics you will need to visit three of the larger islands. Flores, a 360-km long, rugged island, shares 13 endemic species with its large neighbour to the west, Sumbawa (15,600 sq km), and has four endemics of its own—including the enigmatic Wallace's Hanging-parrot and Flores Monarch. Sumba, slightly smaller at 11,150 sq km, has a landscape dominated by grassy plateaux, where an endemic button-quail is to be found. The island's other seven unique species, which include Nusa Tenggara's only hornbill and the beautiful Red-naped Fruit-dove, live in what is left of the forests along the south coast. Timor, at 33,615 sq km the largest of the three islands, is divided administratively into West and East Timor provinces. In birding circles Timor is best known as an island with no fewer than 21 endemic species, including such gems as Orange-banded Thrush and Black-banded Flycatcher

All this combined makes Nusa Tenggara Indonesia's hottest new destination. And in addition to the cultural attractions, there is plenty of pioneering birding to be done.

–Paul Jepson

Previous page: A landscape in Komodo National Park, typical of the dry tropical region of Nusa Tenggara. *Photo by Tui De Roy.* **Opposite:** Even when guiding birders, the men on Sumba always carry a spear used for hunting wild pig. *Photo by Margaret Kinnaird.*

Access to site.

Main birding attractions.

Type of accommodation.

Habitat.

Weather conditions.

Degree of difficulty

Komodo Island

After the Dragon—Clamorous Cockatoos

Birds are usually considered a second-rate show on this island of 3-m, 150-kg, drooling dragons rumoured to dismember unwary travellers. Against a backdrop of craggy peaks, the arid, inhospitable landscape of Komodo is the perfect stage for such a beast. But with every beast, we find a beauty: on Komodo Island, this is the chic Yellow-crested Cockatoo. Komodo is one of the last strongholds of these raucous, snow-white birds and, even during a short visit, you will be sure to encounter groups of 15 or more.

Dragon Viewing

Most of the 25,000 people who visit Komodo National Park each year arrive at its administrative headquarters at Loh Liang by the ferry that runs between Sape in Sumbawa and Labuhanbajo in Flores. They will then take the 2.8-km guided walk from Loh Liang to Banu Nggulung, commonly called Pondok Ora, where tethered, live goats were once offered to the lizards as gory snacks for tourists' amusement. Even without the bloody spectacle, dragon viewing is exciting as these reptilian leviathans approach the fenced area still dreaming of their once-free meal.

Visitors are strongly discouraged from veering off trails or leaving the confines of Pondok Ora. This is not without reason: Komodo is infamous for its abundance of highly poisonous snakes as well as its ill-mannered lizards. Despite

these limitations, there are numerous birds to see around the *pondok* (shelter) or in the open understorey through which the trails pass. With only around 80 species, bird numbers on Komodo are not terribly impressive compared with numbers on other islands in Nusa Tenggara. However, birds are abundant and easy to see, and even a casual look around as your group moves nervously along the trail to the viewing pen will reveal an interesting cross-section of this dry island's bird community.

The low, melodious coos of Spotted and Emerald Doves and imperial pigeons provide background music for the walk. Komodo's Orange-footed Scrubfowls are unusually bold and may be seen close to the trail, scraping through the leaf litter for tasty morsels; few other locations offer such great views of these big-footed mound-nesters. The dragons take advantage of the scrubfowls' industry and bury their own eggs in the ready-made compost heaps. Green Junglefowl perch on the backs of the abundant Timor Deer, a favourite Komodo dragon snack, as they pluck sumptuous ticks from their hosts' ears. In the distance, White-breasted Wood-swallows and Asian Palm-swifts swoop in and out of stiff borassas palm leaves while the white bodies of Yellow-crested Cockatoos flash in brilliant contrast to normally cloudless blue skies.

At Pondok Ora, the guides generally allow 20–30 minutes to take in the dragons and all else that abounds in the area. The dragons do come disturbingly close at

4–5 hrs by ferry from east Sumbawa or west Flores.

Yellow-crested cockatoo and Orange-footed Scrubfowl. And the "dragons"!

Stay at the national park guest-house.

Craggy peaks and lontar palm studded grasslands.

Dry sunny and hot, occasional rain Oct–Mar.

Easy walking to see the dragons. Longer treks to other parts.

times—close enough for you to watch cocky Richard's Pipits pick ticks from the deep, stiff wrinkles of their skin.

Also on view are Helmeted Friarbirds feeding on nectar in the waxy, red flowers of the enormous nearby *kapok hutan* tree. Black-naped Orioles sing their distinctive, melodious songs and Wallacean Drongos, distinguished by their metallic squawks, hunt from nearby trees. A ravine running parallel to the *pondok*, where the hapless goats were formerly sacrificed, is a great spot for viewing Barred and Emerald Doves and families of Green Junglefowl.

Nearby Walks

There are longer walks on the island, but you should not underestimate the birding potential around the park headquarters and along the beach: Black-naped and Sooty Terns may be sighted offshore, while White-bellied Sea-eagles and Brahminy Kites commonly cruise the strand.

Common Sandpipers shuffle at the water's edge and Reef Egrets forage from exposed rocks. Less than 500 m along the beach from the park headquarters is an interesting little inlet with a nice stand of mangroves that, although muddy, can be navigated during low tide for sightings of Whimbrel, Barn Swallow, Striated Heron and an occasional Collared Kingfisher.

Just in front of the headquarters, a line of *Erythrina* trees attracts Brown-throated and Olive-backed Sunbirds, Black-fronted Flowerpeckers, Lemon-bellied White-eyes and migrant Asian Brown Flycatchers. Large-billed Crows abound at the park's open-air restaurant, posing for photos and squabbling over the remains of a meal.

Even though Komodo makes for an interesting trip, beware of arriving during the peak tourist months from July to September when guides are busy and reluctant to assist you. A recommended alternative for those who desire more freedom to walk about in the land of the dragons is a trip to neighbouring Rinca Island. This is accessed from Labuhanbajo and is well worth the effort.

–Margaret Kinnaird

Below: Birding in the lontar-palm studded landscapes of Komodo. *Photo by Tui De Roy.*

SEABIRD MOVEMENTS

Situated on the boundary of the Pacific and Indian Oceans, Nusa Tenggara is an exciting region for seabird-watching. Migrants from both the northern and southern hemispheres pass through the straits and there is a chance of seeing some real rarities from the inter-island ferries.

Bulwer's Petrel, Streaked Shearwater, Matsudaira's Storm-petrel, Common, Little and White-winged Tern, all breeders from northern and central Asia or islands in the northern Pacific and north Atlantic, move south to equatorial seas in August and September. Our knowledge of most of these species' movements is scant, but it appears that Bulwer's Petrel and Matsudaira's Storm-petrel are migrating through Nusa Tenggara to spend their non-breeding season in the northern Indian Ocean. Other northern hemisphere breeders recorded as vagrants in Australia—Leach's Storm-petrel, Sabine's, Black-tailed and Black-headed Gulls and Asian Gull-billed Tern—must have passed through Nusa Tenggara on their way south.

Between September and April a highlight is the sight of flocks of the diminutive Red-necked Phalarope sitting on the water; ornithologists have recently realised that the seas of Nusa Tenggara and Maluku are the principal non-breeding area for this phalarope, which breeds on small, fresh-water lakes in the Arctic tundra.

During the southern winter, Wedge-tailed Shearwater, Australian Pelican and Bridled Tern move north into Nusa Tenggara from their southern hemisphere (Australasian region) breeding grounds. The best studied is the Bridled Tern: banding recoveries reveal that birds from colonies in Western Australia move north through Nusa Tenggara in April and May on passage to their non-breeding areas in the Celebes Sea and return in August, September and October.

As well as passage migrants there are plenty of resident seabirds—various species of terns, boobies and frigatebirds. Many of these make considerable local movements from breeding and roosting sites to areas with strong currents, deep-water upwellings and, especially, to the narrow straits between islands. Resident populations of Great and Lesser Frigatebirds, Red-footed Booby, and Crested and Sooty Terns are no doubt augmented by visitors from Christmas Island, the Cocos Keeling Islands and Ashmore Reef during their non-breeding seasons.

–Ron Johnstone

Top and below: Great Crested Terns wheel and soar from cliff tops. *Photos by Morten Strange and Alain Compost.*

Middle: Crested terns in flight on mud-flats. *Photo by Alain Compost.*

Sumba

Island Endemics and Megalithic Culture

Sumba is a truly special and memorable island. Eight endemics—including a hornbill, fruit-dove and button-quail—found nowhere else on Earth are the initial draw for birders, but few fail to be entranced by Sumba's ancient animistic culture and spectacular landscapes. In picturesque villages of megalithic tombstones and thatched *umas*, home of living and ancestral souls, women create exquisite *ikat* weaves. Men on horseback herd cattle across vast grasslands and show off their horsemanship at *pasolas*, symbolic battles held each year from February to April. In the wetter and remoter south of the island, stately forests form a backdrop to spectacular coastal scenery that is hard to better in Indonesia.

Sumba seems to inspire a "local patch" approach to birding. At 12,000 sq km, the island feels small enough to get to know intimately, and the reed-fringed, roadside pools, mangrove creeks and mud flats heave with such rarity potential that it is hard to resist the urge to kick around for a while and search for that new species for Sumba, Nusa Tenggara or even science: birders have already found a scops-owl on Sumba that has yet to be identified.

Sumba is still a wild, tribal land. Tourists are few and, away from the main cultural sites, it is essential to report to the village head and explain your purpose; if your Indonesian is limited, take a guide from either the local conservation office or one of the hotels.

Waingapu, the small capital town of east Sumba and main tourist entry point, is a base for a range of excellent day trips and the starting point for longer tours to the magnificent forests that survive along the south coast at Mt Wangameti, Terimbang, Langgiluru and Manupeu. For birders with limited time to spare and a world list at a premium, the island's endemic species can be seen in two or three days by flying directly from Bima in Sumbawa to West Sumba, and visiting the forest of Poronumbu, located just 14 km outside the district capital of Waikabubak.

Shorebirds and Parrots—Waingapu Side Trips

The morning flights from either Bali or Timor to Waingapu allow time for two pleasant birding excursions to occupy the rest of the day. Waingapu Bay, just a 15-min walk from the town centre, is a good place to watch shorebirds, particularly during migration seasons. Sitting out on the sandbars scanning through flocks of Whimbrel, Greater and

Below: The harsh *chek-chek-chek* call of White-collared Kingfisher is a familiar sound along the shores of Indonesia. *Photo by Morten Strange.*

1.5 hrs by air from Bali & Timor. Endemic species can be seen in 2-day visit.

Nine single island endemics including the threatened Sumba Hornbill.

Outside the two towns, camp or stay with villagers.

Grasslands, limestone plateaus and coastal scenery.

Hot, sunny and dry. Frequent rains Dec–Mar.

Charter a car to inaccessible sites.

Lesser Sand-plovers, and Rufous-necked Stints, with Brown Honey-eaters chirping happily from the stunted mangroves, to a backdrop of coastal terraces formed by ancient sea levels is refreshingly peaceful. With luck there should be a few Far Eastern Curlews and Terek Sandpipers among the commoner shorebirds.

The second excursion takes us west along the road to Waikabubak, which winds up the coastal terraces by the side of a deep river gorge. At Km Post 12 from Waingapu, a 50-m walk to the left brings you to the edge of an escarpment overlooking the valley. This is the place to spend the last hour of light, watching Great-billed Parrots, Rainbow Lorikeets and Green Imperial Pigeons flying along the valley below as the sun sets over Waingapu Bay. Look out for the bare tree in the valley bottom—it's a favoured roost of Sumba's unique and endangered citron-crested sub-species of the Yellow-crested Cockatoo.

A Day Trip to Luku Melolo

The nature reserve of Luku Melolo, 62 km and 2 hrs southeast by road from Waingapu, can be visited as an afternoon excursion, but it is better to take a full day and combine visits to the mangroves at Yumbu and the traditional village of Rende. Between Km Posts 16 and 17 from Waingapu, a track on the left leads to the back of the mangroves, where streams provide access to the coral flats on the seaward side. Yumbu is a pristine tropical scene: Collared Kingfishers dive out from the mangrove edge, Grey-tailed Tattlers, Greenshanks and Grey Plovers forage for crustaceans in the pools, while Great Crested Terns cruise the surf. Coral flats are a favoured habitat of the rare Great-billed Heron and at low tide the pools are worth investigating for marine life.

Sumba Button-quail

The sparse grasslands either side of the track from the road to the mangroves are "the site" for Sumba's endemic button-quail, for no better reason than that an expedition netted one here in 1989. Finding this bird is a matter of wandering around until you flush one, watching where it lands and hoping you get good views of it on the ground before it flushes again. And good views are needed, because only a heavy, grey bill distinguishes it from the widespread Red-backed Button-quail, which has a slimmer, yellow bill.

The turning inland to Luku Melolo is the first on the right after the bridge in Melolo village, but you may want to first look in at the traditional village of Rende, a famous centre of *ikat* weaving, just 7 km beyond Melolo.

Below: The Sumba race of the widespread Yellow-crested Cockatoo, has a beautiful citron coloured crest and ear patches and may soon be classed as a separate species. *Photo by Alain Compost.*

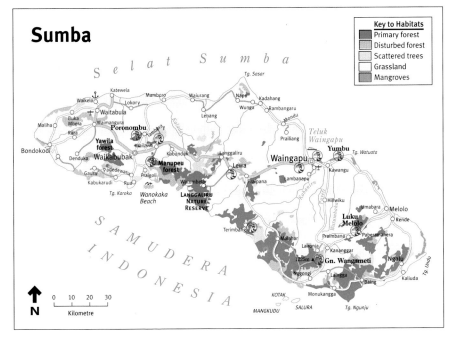

Sumba

Key to Habitats
- Primary forest
- Disturbed forest
- Scattered trees
- Grassland
- Mangroves

Scenic limestone escarpments have protected the gallery forests of Luku Melolo from the tradition of burning grasslands that has wreaked such havoc on Sumba's natural vegetation. The escarpments make spectacular vantage points for Short-toed Eagle, Peregrine Falcon or parrots flying over the forest canopy.

Spectacular Scenery and Unique Birds

For the fit, a steep trail leads down into the valley (25 mins) from Paberamanera village at Km Post 25, but the most productive birding is from the road that winds through a mosaic of forest and grassland along the top of the escarpment. Sumba Hornbill prefers the taller, forested areas, and the inconspicuous, brown Sumba Flycatcher inhabits the damp gulleys. In the more open forest look out for other endemic species: Sumba Green Pigeon, Red-headed Myzomela and Apricot-breasted Sunbird. This is also a good area to catch up with Elegant Pitta and Sumba Cicadabird (which, despite its name, is

also found on Sumbawa and Flores) and Sumba Brown Flycatcher, a resident race of the migratory Asian Brown Flycatcher, which some consider a separate species.

Sumba's South Coast

A 4–5 day tour of forests along Sumba's rugged south coast is the way to experience Sumba's wild and beautiful country and culture fully. The narrow, winding roads—sometimes just tracks—pass though sculptured limestone valleys, cross arid grasslands dotted with villages clustering on wooded knolls, and lead to waterfalls and beaches.

Red-naped Fruit-dove and Sumba Boobook, an owl, are the trickiest two endemics to find. The owl is not particularly rare, but skill is needed to track one down in a torch beam after dark. The fruit-dove is rare in lowland forest but quite common in the wet forests that cloak Mt Wangameti, the first destination on a south coast tour. Wangameti village is a 4-hr drive due south from Waingapu. Either camp or stay in the village and spend a full day exploring the forest along the multitude of trails used by collectors of *gaharu*—an aromatic resin found in the trunks of certain trees. A local guide is necessary if you intend to penetrate far into the forest or make the 4-hr ascent to the summit of Mt Wangameti.

Terimbang

Sumba's newest and arguably most idyllic birding site is the glorious cove of Terimbang, located between Wangameti and Sumba's other large forest, Langgaliru/Maupeu, and reached after an adventurous drive from Wangameti along the south coast route, or directly from Waingapu (see Practicalities). Most people choose to camp on the beach, which is home to a pair of Beach Thick-knees; ospreys fish in the cove and Orange-footed Scrubfowl are common in the km-wide band of beach forest that extends back to the village of Terimbang. The forested escarpments inland from the village are waiting to be explored by birders and will surely support endemic species such as Metallic Pigeon and Cinnamon-banded Kingfisher. To

find the kingfisher, track down the owner of the strident whistles emanating from the tops of forest trees in the early morning. Only recently has this whistle been linked to the kingfisher, which was once considered endangered but is now realized to be elusive, but common.

If you can bear to leave Terimbang, there are two more notable birding sites off the main road to Waikabubak. Over a small ridge on the left of the road at Km Post 51 (7 km before Lewa) is a small, degraded forest patch which is the site where twitchers have traditionally gone to see the island's endemics quickly, and found the still-unidentified "Sumba Scopsowl".

At Wailawa, 16 km before Waikabubak, a small side road leads 21 km south to the top of Manupeu valley, famed for the impressive Mata Yangu waterfall. Watching Sumba Hornbills cruising across this vista is one of Indonesia's best birding spectacles. As you wander back through the forest and fields, past villages and spear-wielding horsemen, you are bound to feel the revitalization that comes with a break from the 20th century.
—Paul Jepson

Below: Most of Sumba's rural population lives in traditional villages, like this one at Rende. *Photo by Alain Compost.*

Birding Flores

In Search of the Bare-throated Whistler

Long, rugged and volcanic, Flores is the most spectacularly scenic island in Nusa Tenggara. It also boasts some of the region's most intriguing and beautiful endemic birds. Few will stand at dawn in the high mountain pass above Ruteng, with folds of mountain ridges extending to the northern horizon, and fail to be enraptured by the ever-changing melodies of the Bare-throated Whistlers ringing out in the clean, mountain air. Memories of birding Flores's mountain trails are redolent with the music of this versatile songster, which sings with head thrown back, bill wide open, back puffed out, and bare, vibrating throat inflated and suffused with scarlet. Not for nothing has it been dubbed the "Flores Nightingale"!

The 14,000 sq km island of Flores shares 13 endemic species with Sumbawa and has a further four endemics of its own. It is a prime venue for the touring bird-watcher. You could find all the endemics during a week to ten days spent in Manggarai, in western Flores, the region with the highest mountains and most widespread evergreen forests; but why deny yourself the pleasure of spending a further week or two to explore the scenic treats and cultural interest of the rest of the island?

Labuhanbajo

The little west coast port of Labuhanbajo is the point of arrival for many visitors, and the Baju Beach Baru Hotel is an extremely pleasant out-of-town venue from which to relax and explore the local surroundings. Just a 10-min walk north of the town, scrubby hills and valleys support a nice selection of open country birds including Spotted Kestrel, Brown Quail, Barred Dove, Large-tailed Nightjar, Blue-tailed Bee-eater, Pied Bush-chat and Zebra Finch. Another good site for a half-day trip is a marshy area known locally as Dolat, which regularly holds substantial numbers of Wandering and Lesser Whistling-ducks, Sunda Teal and Pacific Black Duck, as well as other waterbirds and happily wallowing water buffalo. To reach Dolat, either charter a boat to take you down the coast to Memjaga and then walk 2 km inland, or wander along a 5-km trail leading off the road to Ruteng through dry paddy fields where Black-winged Kites and Rainbow Bee-eaters soar overhead (see Practicalities).

Mid-level Hills and the Flores Monarch

Some of the island's most intriguing species are to be found in the wetter, mid-elevation forest confined to the area of West Flores between Labuhanbajo and the Lembor Plains, half way to Ruteng. One of these is the Flores Monarch, which was discovered as recently as 1971 in the remote Tanjung Kerita Mese region of southwest Flores. In 1994 an expedition from Cambridge University found it to be quite common at this locality, together with another Flores endemic, the diminutive Wallace's Hanging-parrot.

1 hr by air from Bali or Timor. 1 week to visit the main sites.

 Rare endemics: Wallace's Hanging Parrot, Bare-throated Whistler and Flores Monarch.

 Simple *losmen* in all the main towns.

 Mosaic of dry forests and agriculture among volcanic scenery.

 Dry and hot Apr–Sep. Jan–Mar can be quite wet.

 All sites are close to the road; easy to moderate walking.

The adult Flores Monarch is black on the foreparts, black above with a bluish sheen, and white below, while the immature is grey and white with a suffusion of peach on the breast. It lives in the middle storey of the rainforest, in hills up to 1,000 m elevation, where it sometimes joins mixed feeding parties. Wallace's Hanging-parrot, like others of its genus, is most often seen zipping through the canopy, but flocks of up to 20 birds have been seen at fruiting fig trees, which never fail to provide an exciting venue for the forest bird-watcher.

Happily both these unique species can be seen close to the main road on the first day of an eastward tour. Just past Km Post 9 on the main road from Labuhanbajo to Ruteng, the new road to Terang on the north coast enters wonderful lowland forest after 2 km. Regular stops along the 11 km stretch to Pota Wangka village are guaranteed to pay dividends; and the locals know Wallace's Hanging-parrot well. Back on the main road, head for the Puarldo telecommunications

Below: Healthy populations of the Hill Myna, or "Talking Grackle" can still be found in east Flores. *Photo by Alain Compost.*

are the Chestnut-backed—a Lesser Sundas endemic—and the Chestnut-capped Thrush, which is at the eastern limit of a much wider range. Unlike their temperate counterparts, they are extreme skulkers and you have to be really alert to pick up their soft chuckling calls, let alone catch a glimpse, unless you have the fortune to chance upon a singing bird.

The Ruteng Mountains

Ruteng, 3 $^{1}/_{2}$ hrs of straight driving east, is situated at 1,200 m in the foothills of Flores's highest mountains, and there is easy access into good forest. Here you will find the mountain birds of Flores, including the Bare-throated Whistler and other endemics. Those familiar with the mountains of Java will recognize the songs of Oriental Cuckoo, White-browed Shortwing, Pygmy Wren-babbler and Mountain Tailorbird, while the common pigeon here is the Dark-backed Imperial Pigeon. There will be swift-flying parties of Rainbow Lorikeets (the Flores race is sometimes treated as an endemic species) and Short-tailed Starlings. In the forest and degraded forest margins you will need to concentrate on the smaller endemics, notably the three Darkeyes (Yellow-browed, Crested and Thick-billed, although the Crested prefers lower elevations), and the Scaly-crowned Honeyeater. In cultivated areas, seek out the uncommon Five-coloured Munia.

There are four recommended birding walks in the Ruteng area; check with the Ruteng Nature Recreation Park office on Jl Satar Tacik for full details. The first choice for birders may be the 1,600 m Golo Lusang pass between Mt Lika and Mt Watu Ndao, which offers spectacular views over the southern coast of Flores and an exquisite early morning symphony of bird song. The forest on the southern side of the pass is less disturbed; look out overhead for raptors and in the forest for Brown-

station, situated on the summit of the hills between the Nanga Nae valley and the Lembor plains, midway to Ruteng (33 km from Labuhanbajo). Both Flores Monarch and the hanging-parrot have been seen here regularly and without doubt this will become a standard stopping place for every birder.

Two other specialities to look for here are forest thrushes. These

Above: The magnificent view of Lewotobi volcano in East Flores. *Photo by Alain Compost.*

capped Woodpecker, Bare-throated Whistler, Brown-capped Fantail, Tricoloured Parrot-finch and Wallacean Drongo, among others. A second day-trip is the walk to Pong Toda, which starts at *Susteran* (nunnery) at Leda, 2 km from Ruteng. The trail brings you into a beautifully forested ravine with stands of old casuarina trees at the foot of Mt Golo Dukul. Along the way look out for the rather uncommon Five-coloured Munia as well as the ubiquitous cisticolas, friarbirds and bushchats; in the casuarinas Little Minivets are common, and other specialities are White-rumped Kingfisher, Scaly-crowned Honeyeater, Timor Leaf-warbler and Yellow-browed Darkeye.

Two other recommended walks are found east along the road to Mborong. Nine km from Ruteng, an 8-km long access road to an old Telecommunications Station on the 2,140 m summit of Mt Ranakah makes this one of the most accessible cloud forests on Sumba. This beautiful elfin forest, full of ferns and orchids, is home to Timor Leaf-warbler, Russet-capped Tesia, Yellow-browed Dark-eye and Scaly-

crowned Honeyeater. The second walk starts at the Km Post 22 mark on the Trans-Flores highway. Here a small path leads through healthy forest to Lake Rana Mese (1,200 m) which is being developed as the main visitor attraction of the Ruteng Nature Recreation Park. Pacific Black Duck, Garganey, Little Pied Cormorant and Common Moorhen all inhabit the lake.

Lowland Forests and the Flores Crow

The easiest venue for lowland forest birds is Kisol, near the south coast on the Ruteng-Bajawa highway. However, visitors to Riung, a peaceful marine reserve on the north coast with memorable snorkelling, will find an excellent area of monsoon forest on the escarpments behind the village. At both these sites there is a real chance of finding that other favourite endemic, the Flores Crow. The weird whistling calls of this curious, small crow with a pure purplish-black plumage recall the wails of a hungry baby.

From the little settlement of Kisol a rough road heads 12 km south to the coastal village of Nangarawa. To the west, forest covers the low peak of Mt Pacandeki and this is a good area to catch up with the Flores Green Pigeon, an unobtrusive bird that blends with the leaves in the canopy of the lowland forests and is most readily seen when feeding in small parties on fruiting figs. Other lowland species here are the Orange-footed Scrubfowl and Green Junglefowl, Common Golden Whistler (so colourful, yet so elusive), and the lovely Flame-breasted Sunbird. There is another chance of finding Chestnut-capped Thrush and, if there are any Yellow-crested Cockatoos now remaining on Flores, this will be the best site to look for them.

Down at Nangarawa, a few hours spent birding the mosaic of coastal scrub, gallery forests and grassland should be rewarded with a good mixture of species: Bonelli's Eagle and Changeable Hawk-eagle overhead, Golden-rumped and Black-fronted Flowerpeckers along the forest edge, and waders on the beach.

The next centre on the eastward trail is Bajawa, a 4-hr drive from Ruteng and often bypassed by bird-watchers. This high, cool town is located in a beautiful landscape of "mini-volcanoes" and valleys cultivated with mixed gardens of coffee, *kenari*, bamboo and maize. For a memorable cultural excursion a visit to the traditional villages of Bena and Langa is a highlight on anyone's itinerary, with birding stops in wooded parts of the magnificent range of volcanic scenery encountered on the way.

Into the Dry East

After Bajawa the landscape gets noticeably drier and the cone of Mt Ebulobo, which, with its massive fumarole splitting its side, looks as if it is about to explode at any minute, marks your passage into some of the best volcanic landscapes in Indonesia. Most birders, having seen all the specialities of Flores, opt to cross to Sumba or Timor at Ende, the next town east, reached after—yes! another 3–4 hour drive. But if you can spare 4 or 5 days more to let yourself be total-

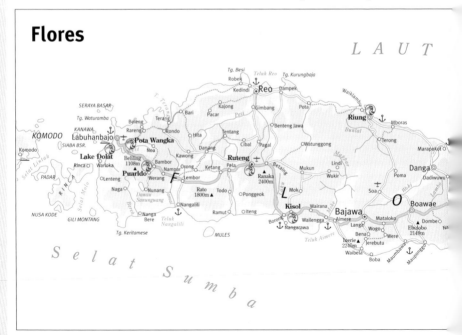

ly captivated by this remarkable island, head on east up through the breath-taking scenery of the Walowana gorge to Moni.

This acts as the base for a dawn excursion to Keli Mutu, a volcano with three differently-coloured crater lakes located at 1,690 m. These craters are widely regarded as the most spectacular natural wonder of Nusa Tenggara and are accessible by road. It's best to drive up to watch the dawn spectacle at the summit, then walk the 13 km back down to Moni. This gives the bird-watcher an easy opportunity for another go at the montane avifauna in the casuarina forest that cloaks the peak.

Virgin Birding Territory

The last leg of this trans-Flores tour will take you to ornithologically unexplored forests. Most tourists continue directly along the road to Maumere, but birders should take the northern coastal road via Deutusoko and Maurole. Seven kilometres west of Maurole a beautiful area of monsoon forest extends right down to the coast; Flores Crow has been seen here. For those interested in different forest types there is an opportunity to explore one of the last remnants of beach forest on the island.

Maumere is best known for the world class diving on the reefs surrounding the group of islands in the bay. A boat trip out to Pulau Besar, at 3,000 ha the largest in the group, is highly recommended. Apart from the chance of sea birds on the way, the island still has plenty of forest and is surprisingly rich in lowland birds. Look here for Flores Green Pigeon, perhaps Pink-headed Imperial Pigeon (together with the Green), Thick-billed and Black-fronted Flowerpeckers and Yellow-spectacled White-eye. An equally pleasant excursion is to Mt Egon-Ilimudu; a drivable track leads south off the Maumere–Larantuka road between Km Posts 23 and 24, and after 5 km enters eucalyptus savannah and then a rare area of pristine *Eucalyptus urophelia* forest. The birds of this forest type are very little known; adding to our limited knowledge of the birds of Flores would be a fitting way to end this journey of exploration.

–*Derek Holmes*

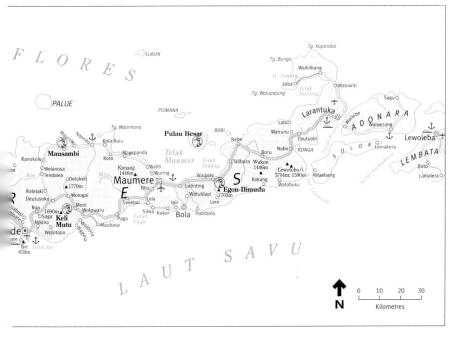

Timor Trips

Birding with an Australian Flavour

With half its resident birds of Asian origin and the other half Australian, Timor offers a brilliant introduction to Wallacea, with heaps of endemics from groups familiar to Australian birders as well as a generous sprinkling of widespread Asian species.

This 33,600 sq km island, the largest in Nusa Tenggara, has very pronounced wet and dry sesons and landscape reminiscent of the monsoonal (wet dry) tropics of northern Australia. The lowlands are a mosaic of tall palms and grasslands—bright green in the wet season and straw yellow in the dry season—and the lower hills are dotted with white-trunked eucalypt trees and pine-like casuarinas. But there is one big difference: Timor is mountainous, and its forests vary in form with altitude. Climbing a mountain you first enter a landscape with tall eucalypt forest, much like that of temperate Australia; higher up, the montane

rain forest, with its moss covered southern conifers, is reminiscent of Tasmania or the slopes of Gunung Leuser in North Sumatra.

Although just over an hour's flight (500 km) from Darwin in Australia's Northern Territory or 1 ½ hrs from Bali, bustling Kupang, the island and provincial capital, has an atmosphere and character all of its own. The *bemos* literally throb with techno rap rhythms and, like birds, are often first detected by sound rather than sight. Transport is no problem, either within the town or to the best birding localities. To catch up with all West Timor's birding highlights you will need 7–10 days, but the lowland sites can be visited as day trips out of Kupang. At the end of a hard day's birding, it is great to put your feet up at one of the seaside restaurants, such as Teddie's Bar, have a beer and watch the activities of local people in picturesque Kupang Bay,

Direct flights from Jakarta, Bali and Darwin.

Chance of all 21 species unique to Timor archipelago, in a 5-day tour.

Simple hotels in Kupang and Soe.

Mosaic of dry fields and forests. Beautiful Eucalyptus forests on Mt Mutis.

Hot, sunny and dry. Morning and afternoon rains Oct–Mar.

All sites close to the road, some longer walks and climbing.

with maybe a passing frigatebird for good measure.

Ashy-bellied White-eyes and Pied Bush Chats are practically street birds in Kupang, and even the pretty Flame-breasted Sunbird visits urban gardens. In dry grasslands on the outskirts of town flocks of finches may include Black-faced and Five-coloured Munias, as well as the distinctive Timor Sparrow.

Straight into the Birding

In terms of Nusa Tenggara endemics you cannot do any better than Timor, and the good news is that they are almost all accessible—indeed, mostly within an hour's drive of Kupang. If you are only passing through Kupang for a few hours before flying on, or just cannot wait till the morning, try Baumata, a 15 min, 6-km drive uphill from the airport entrance. Behind the swimming pool, a mixture of old forest trees, secondary growth and teak plantation sometimes crawls with honeyeaters—four of the five species found on Timor—and many of the other Timor endemics,

including the loud, but frustratingly timid Buff-banded Bushbird (look in scrubby lantana thickets), whose drab name belies its distinctive chestnut crown and ear streak, Timor Blue Flycatcher, Timor Leaf-warbler, Plain Gerygone, Fawn-breasted Whistler and, in the wet season between October and April, even Elegant Pitta. A sighting of this elusive, ground-dwelling species with its green upperparts, glittering light blue rump and wing coverts, and buff underside with crimson patch on the belly, will definitely have you celebrating.

On the other hand, if you are desperate for the beach, stop after 4 km, where the airport road meets the main road from Soe into Kupang, and walk down the short track to the seaside village of Oesapa. A walk northeast along the beach will produce terns and several species of wader, including Terek Sandpiper, Grey-tailed Tattler and—with luck—Far Eastern Curlew.

Bipolo and Camplong

If you have a couple of days, head out to the lowland forests of Bipolo

Above: The river at Bipolo, a rich birding area close to Kupang.
Left: Orange-banded Flycatcher, one of Timor's most striking endemics. *Photos by Richard Noske.*

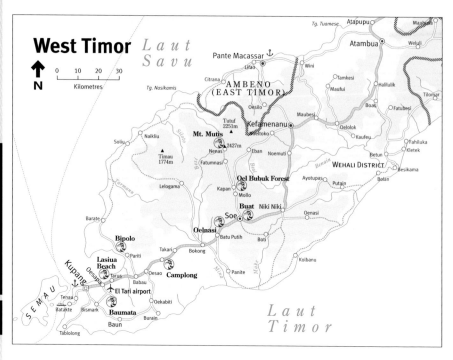

West Timor

N

0 10 20 30
Kilometres

Laut Savu

Tg. Tuamese Atapupu○ Maubesa

Pante Macassar Weluli

Lifao Atambua●

Wini

Citrana Tamkesi

AMBENO Maufui Halilulik

(EAST TIMOR) Tilomar

Tg. Nasikamis Oesilo Boas Fatubesi

Maubesi

Soliu Naikliu Tutuf 2251m Kefamenanu● Oelolok

Mt. Mutis Moeltoko Kaufeu Fahiluka

2427m Kletek

Timau 1774m Nenas Eban Noemuti Betun

Fatumnasi Besikama

WEHALI DISTRICT

Lelogama Oel Bubuk Forest Ayotupas Botan

Kapan Putain

Mollo

Barate Buat Niki Niki

Soe○ Oenasi

Oelnasi Batu Putih Boti

Bipolo Takari Bokong Kolbanu

Pariti

Lasiua Beach Oesao Camplong

Tarus Babau

Kupang Oesapa El Tari airport

Tenau Oekabiti

Batakte Bismark Baumata

SEMAU Baun

Tablolong Burain

Laut Timor

and Camplong, both about an hour's drive east of Kupang. Bipolo is just above sea level and is a rare example of tall, semi-evergreen forest with many large fig trees. Unfortunately these giants are being cut down, jeopardising the viability of this small forest remnant. Although only small, Bipolo is amazingly rich and there are plenty of birds. Look for fruiting fig trees, which often contain two or more of the following pigeon species: Rose-crowned and Black-backed Fruit-doves, Pink-headed Imperial Pigeon (more like dull pinkish buff headed!), Metallic Pigeon and—if you are lucky—Timor Black Pigeon or Timor Green Pigeon. The latter is one of the rarest of the region's endemics.

Parrots also abound: Red-cheeked and Olive-shouldered Parrots are abundant, noisy and easy to observe, while Rainbow and Olive-headed Lorikeets are usually glimpsed as they race over the tree tops. On the ground the diminutive Timor Stubtail pipes its monotonal, high-pitched whistle, and, if your luck is in, you may stumble upon Orange-banded Thrush. Meanwhile, whistlers, fantails, gerygones and leaf warblers can get on your nerves as you search high and low for the elusive Tricoloured Parrotfinch (try the road verges, forest edge and bamboo stands along the stony river) and Cinnamon-banded Kingfisher (listen for its sustained trill).

At Camplong (pronounced Chum-plong) the forest is somewhat drier, with more deciduous tree species. The birds are similar to those at Bipolo, but here you have a better chance of finding several "specials": for example, the demure Black-banded Flycatcher, with its neat attire and scarcely audible buzzing call, the White-bellied Bush-chat, which sings *ad nauseam*, often from a high perch, and the more elusive Spot-breasted Darkeye, often seen moving around in the lower canopy.

Soe—In Search of Mountain Gems

With a few more days available, venture farther along the main highway to Soe. As well as offering near pristine forests abounding in Orange-banded Thrushes and Black-banded Flycatchers very close to town, Soe is your launch pad for Oel Bubuk (near Kapan) and Mt Mutis to the north. *Bemos* will get you to the former, but to climb Mt Mutis you need 4 wheel drive, which is best organised from Kupang. Oel Bubuk forest, 13 ½ km north of Soe, is a tiny, wet-ever-green forest remnant at an altitude of about 1,000 m. It is the lower limit for some of the montane birds, such as the Chestnut-backed Thrush, Blood-breasted Flower-pecker and Mountain White-eye; Dusky Cuckoo-dove has occasionally been seen here. But you will need to drive higher, to Mt Mutis, to see the best birds. At about 1,500 m, in the *Eucalyptus urophylla*

forest canopy, you may see Yellow-eared Honeyeater, which is surprisingly brightly coloured for this generally drab family, while in the dingy rainforest understorey Island Thrush is overwhelmingly common.

Parking at the base of the summit, just below a meadow, you can now climb on foot through the mossy rain forests in search of the only montane endemic, the Timor Imperial Pigeon. Along the way you will see typically Asian montane birds, such as Yellow-breasted Warbler, Snowy-browed Flycatcher and Pygmy Wren-babbler. But the real jewel of these forests is the striking Chestnut-backed Thrush. Its coloration—bold black chest and flank spots, contrasting with a white belly and chestnut back—is just superb. For the fame seeking and brave hearted, try for Russet Bush-warbler. For taxonomic purposes, it is currently included with similar species scattered through Southeast Asia and the Philippines, and the Timor form, which has not been recorded since it was collected on Mutis in 1932, may well be a new species. Good luck!

–Richard Noske

Left: Orange-banded Thrush—the ultimate for thrush connoisseurs. *Photo by Richard Noske.*
Below: Timor's many beaches are always worth checking for shorebirds during migration times. Pictured here is a Mongolian Plover. *Photo by Morten Strange.*

Introducing Sumatra
Island of Diversity

Sumatra embodies all the wonders of the Asian tropics—lush rain forests supporting an astonishing diversity of life, impenetrable swamps and mangroves, towering volcanoes and a rich cultural heritage. Sumatra's forests are part of the once immense Sunda shelf rain forests, which covered Peninsular Malaysia, Borneo and Java. These are the richest habitats on Earth—605 bird species have been recorded on Sumatra.

Several of the world's most prized and sought after bird genera and families are well represented on Sumatra—pheasants, broadbills and pittas, to name but a few. Between 14 and 20 unique bird species (the number depends on which taxonomy you choose) and the chance of seeing Sumatran Tiger and Rhino, Orang-utan and the world's largest flower, the metre-wide, orange and white Rafflesia, significantly adds to the draw of the region.

Sumatra's topography is dominated by the Bukit Barisan range, a spine of rugged volcanic mountains running down the west coast. The two highest peaks, Mt Leuser (3,381 m) in the north and Mt Kerinci (3,800 m) in West Sumatra, give their names to two massive national parks, which are among Sumatra's top three birding destinations. The other is Way Kambas in the southeast, which, although an old logging area, is one of the easiest places to see the endangered White-winged Duck and Storm's Stork.

Birds apart, Sumatra has played a major role in the history of Indonesia, and the island's abundant natural resources—minerals and gas, timber and vast plantations of rubber, oil palm, cocoa and coffee—today account for over half of Indonesia's export income.

Lake Toba is Sumatra's premier tourist destination, and it can boast some pretty impressive statistics. It is Southeast Asia's largest lake and—at 450 m—the world's deepest; in the middle of the lake, Samosir Island (530 sq km) is the size of Singapore. The area was created 80,000 years ago by the greatest volcanic explosion the world has ever known. The resulting volcanic debris lay across Sumatra like a barrier and this is said to explain why the distribution of mammals such as Orang-utan and White-headed Gibbon is restricted to the north, and birds such as Sumatran Wren-babbler and Bronze-tailed Peacock-pheasant are found in the south.

After Toba, the Minang highlands of West Sumatra attract most tourists. Bukittinggi is refreshingly cool and makes an excellent base for walks through breathtaking countryside. This is the heartland of the Minang people, famous not only for their textiles and peaked wooden houses, but also for retaining a matrilineal kinship system that predates the arrival of Islam. Their other great claim to fame is Padang food, a distinctive cuisine of meats, fish and eggs covered in an extremely spicy sauce.

This compelling combination of rainforest birding, colourful peoples and stunning scenery all add up to the trip of a lifetime.

–*Paul Jepson*

Previous page: A pair of Weather Hornbills sail in to land on a massive emergent tree. *Photo by Alain Compost.*
Opposite: Watching the numerous pigeons, barbets and hornbills attracted to a fruiting fig is an exciting, if neck-breaking experience. *Photo by Margaret Kinnaird.*

Access to site.

Main birding attractions.

Type of accommodation.

Habitat.

Weather conditions.

Degree of difficulty.

SUMATRA

Gunung Leuser National Park

Classic Rainforest Birding

Below: Red-crowned Barbet. Sumatra's forests reverberate with the rhythmic calls of barbets, but the birds themselves can be difficult to see. *Photo by Alan Ow Yong.*

The 800,000-ha Gunung Leuser National Park is one of Sumatra's last rainforest wildernesses. It is home to at least 325 species of birds, and some 130 species of mammals, including orang-utans, rhinoceroses, elephants and tigers.

There are two recommended birding activities. The first is to explore the good trail system radiating out into the forest around the Gurah Recreation Centre, located 35 km north of Kutacane in the Alas valley. The second is to take a memorable 4-day rafting trip down the lower reaches of the Alas River, between Serakut and Soraya.

Around Gurah

Gurah's network of trails can be walked in 2–3 hrs, but birders will want to dawdle and walk them sev-eral times, searching for elusive babblers, partridges and pheasants. Along the stone path leading down to a beach on the bank of the Alas River, look carefully for Green Broadbills, whose colours blend in with the foliage.

On the opposite side of the gate a second trail leads to a hot spring in the upper reaches of the Gurah River a 4-km walk away. Along the way listen for the *chai-chai-chai-chai* of the Maroon Woodpecker, the *ku-wao ku-wao ku-wao* of the Great Argus in the hilly forest. Sightings of Cinnamom-rumped and Scarlet-rumped Trogons are frequent, and Chestnut-naped Forktails inhabit the small streams. In the lowland alluvial forest areas there are many *rambung* trees; if one is in fruit you will be sure to see a variety of bar-bets, including Brown, Yellow-crowned and Gold-whiskered,

 2 hrs by road from Medan.

 Over 300 species of rainforest birds.

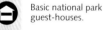 Basic national park guest-houses.

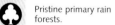 Pristine primary rain forests.

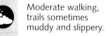 Moderate walking, trails sometimes muddy and slippery.

 Afternoon down-pours common especially Oct–Mar.

Rhinoceros Hornbills and Spectacled Spider-hunters—all attracted by the abundance of figs. After about 2 $^1/_2$ km, the trail reaches the 6-m wide river, which you will have to wade, before continuing on to the hot spring. Little Cuckoo-doves often bathe here, and sightings of some of the park's primates—Long-tailed Macaque, Thomas's Leaf Monkey, White-handed Gibbon, and Orang-utan—are all possible.

"River of Hornbills"

Between Serakut and Soraya, a good trail follows the Alas River. The abundance of Bushy-crested Hornbills (which always fly below the canopy), and Wreathed, Black, Asian Pied, Rhinoceros and Helmeted Hornbills, has led to this stretch being dubbed "the river of hornbills".

Soraya Rafting Camp

In the trees among the rafting cabins, it is easy to spot Rueck's Blue Flycatcher, which is endemic to Sumatra. Groups of Scaly-crowned Babblers and the occasional Short-tailed Babbler provide a prelude to the exciting lowland rainforest birding waiting in store along the trails beyond the Soraya research cabin.

A short 200-m trail leads west from the camp to a splendid, 34-m high waterfall (a good area for White-rumped Shama and Grey-bellied Bulbul) and then climbs steeply for a further 200 m to the research cabin. Here the forest atmosphere can certainly be felt, and the high canopy reverberates with the *tehoop-tehoop-tehoop* rhythms of Gold-whiskered Barbet.

These tall stature forests are among the most diverse habitats on Earth, but most have been logged over or converted to other land-uses. Here at Soraya, there is a rare opportunity to experience the joys (and frustrations!) of birding in pristine rain forest, along a well maintained trail system totalling 21 km in length.

There are several choices. The trail that heads north along the Alas River passes through hilly forest where there is a good chance of seeing Crested Partridge, Crestless Fireback or even Great Argus. Another option is to explore one of five 1 $^1/_2$-km long research trails heading north from the cabin, all of which join again at the trail to the Ruam River. Here you will find "classic" lowland forest birds: Black-and-yellow, Dusky and Green Broadbills, Maroon-breasted Philentoma, and the spectacular Crested Jay.

After several hours walking the Ruam River area, you reach a small tributary. White-crowned Forktail search for water insects along the muddy edges, and Red-bearded Bee-eater can be found along streams.

–Dolly Priatna

Top: Green Broadbill—one of Lesuer's most beautiful birds, though easily overlooked in the canopy. *Photo by Ray Tipper.*
Above: Gunung Leuser National Park protects some of the largest areas of primary lowland rain forest in Sumatra. *Photo by Alain Compost.*

Fabulous Pheasants

For centuries, pheasants have been esteemed both for sport and for ornament. The family includes the pheasants proper along with peacocks and junglefowl and, with the exception of one species in Africa, the 48 species are all found in Asia. Eleven species occur in Indonesia: the Great Argus, Crested Fireback, Green Peafowl and Green Junglefowl rate among the most spectacular, and the Bornean Peacock-pheasant and Hoogerwerf's among the rarest and least known. Not surprisingly, Indonesia is a Mecca for those hoping to see these fabulous birds in their native forest habitat.

The range of the Green Junglefowl extends from Java into Nusa Tenggara, but the remaining species are confined to west Indonesia: Sumatra with seven species (three endemic) and Kalimantan with five species are the richest pheasant regions. Observing these shy, ground-dwelling birds is no picnic: they stay mostly in the forest undergrowth and only rarely appear in clearings or on riverbanks. At the first hint of danger they run away—flight is saved for crossing water or explosive escapes from wild cats. Most sightings of pheasants occur when you surprise one on the trail, but these are invariably brief glimpses; the really memorable views come either by luck or quietly hanging round likely places, such as pools at midday.

Beautiful Displays

The Great Argus, whose males have enormously elongated secondary and tail feathers, is well-known to the people of Indonesia due to the male's far-carrying, clear *wow* calls. In fact, the Indonesian name is derived from this distinctive call that rings out from forested ridges in Sumatra and Kalimantan. The males create dancing grounds—clean circles cleared of all leaves and twigs—where they perform exquisite mating dances to attract females. During the dance the tail is lifted and wings spread to display the beautiful, green eye marks to their full advantage.

The Firebacks

The male Crested Fireback is Indonesia's most colourful pheasant and fairly common in lowland forest in Sumatra and Kalimantan. Like most pheasants the males are gaudy and the females drab (see photographs on right). Trekking through the forest of Way Kambas or Gunung Leuser National Park, you are quite likely to see a small group of Crested Firebacks crossing your path. The closely related Crestless Fireback is a rare bird, confined to primary lowland forests. It is easily distinguished from the Crested Fireback by its red facial wattles, lack of crest and blacker

plumage. Rare encounters are usually of a small party with only one adult male.

Forest Chickens

Few people realise that the wild ancestor of our domestic chicken is still alive and well: the Red Junglefowl is common throughout west Indonesia. In Java there is a zone of overlap with the Green Junglefowl, which, with its lilac-and-blue comb and metallic green, chestnut and yellow body plumes, is arguably the most exquisitely plumaged member of the pheasant family. Junglefowls prefer the forest edge and open, savannah-like woodlands, but they can even be found in timber plantations. Look out for them in Way Kambas and Bukit Barisan Selatan in Sumatra.

Peacock-pheasants

The Bronze-tailed Peacock-pheasant is endemic to Sumatra and locally common in hill forest at altitudes between 500 and 1,500 m. Its small size and overall brown colour make it difficult to spot in the dense forest. At close range, on a sunny day, the beautiful, iridescent, greenish-purple tail feathers become visible. A good place to encounter this little-known pheasant is the Kerinci-Seblat National Park in west Sumatra (*see pp 114–117*), where you will also find Salvadori's Pheasant, another Sumatran endemic.

In Kalimantan the species is the Bornean Peacock-pheasant, endemic to Borneo, as its name suggests. This pheasant is extremely rare, known from fewer than 30 specimens and observations, and may be critically endangered.

A Pheasant Mystery

Sumatra boasts probably the least-known pheasant on Earth. This is Hoogerwerf's Pheasant, described from two female specimens collected in the hills of Aceh province in 1937 and 1939. It is closely related to Salvadori's Pheasant, but the females are covered in fine dark vermiculations, a plumage character absent in female Salvadori's. This led the experts of the time to consider it a separate species. Then in the late 1970s, the conservationist Nico van Strien, working in the Mamas Valley in the Gunung Leuser area, saw a group of pheasants with a male that looked very like Salvadori's. Now the experts are wondering whether it is just a northern sub-species of Salvadori's Pheasant. Fifty years on from its discovery, we still do not know whether it is a full species or not—so if you chance upon a pheasant in the mountain forests of Gunung Leuser above 1,000 m make sure to take good notes of its appearance and you may be the person who solves the puzzle.

–*Resit Sözer*

Left, top: The comical looking Crested Partridge.
Far left: The Red Junglefowl is the ancestor of the domestic chicken.
Left: Malaysian Peacock-pheasant, a close relative of the Bornean Peacock-pheasant which has yet to be photographed.
Top left: A male Crested Fireback of the Bornean race. On Sumatra the males have a black belly.
Top right: Parties of three or four female Crested Firebacks accompanied by a single male are frequently met along trails through lowland forests.
All photos by Alain Compost.

Kerinci-Seblat National Park

Forest Trails in fabulous Scenery

Below: The Shiny Whistling Thrush, endemic to Sumatra is a common sight along the forest trails. *Photo by Alain Compost.*

Kerinci-Seblat is a truly beautiful birding landscape. Dominated by the formidable 3,800 m Mt Kerinci, ridges of forest-covered mountains descend into cinnamon and vegetable gardens and rich green rice paddies and tea plantations carpeting the large, fertile Kerinci valley. Comprising an area of 15,000 sq km, the park protects the largest remaining, continuous area of rain forest on Sumatra—a broad, 345-km long strip that envelops the populous Kerinci valley.

Kerinci caught the attention of birders in 1988 with the first sighting of Schneider's Pitta in 40 years. Since then, sightings of the hyper-elusive Sumatran Cochoa and Salvadori's Pheasant, the relative ease of finding a further 15 Sumatran endemics and the generally excellent birding have elevated Kerinci to the premier league of Asian birding destinations.

The favourite base for birders is Homestay Keluarga Subandi in Keresik Tua, a village by a tea plantation at the northern end of the Kerinci valley, and a scenic 5–6 hr drive from Padang through the Barisan range. The best two birding areas are the Mt Kerinci trail, a 50-min walk from Keresik Tua, and Mt Tujuh, a 14-km drive up the valley.

Pak Subandi (the owner of the homestay and part of the village ecotourism cooperative) will arrange transport (see Practicalities). A minimum of three (better five) days are required to see all the endemic species, but Kerinci is an area where you could happily spend a couple of weeks pioneering new trails, searching for tigers and tapirs and generally enjoying rainforest trekking. One area not to be missed is Mauro Sako, 49 km south of Keresik Tua on the Tapan road, where you will pick up a lot of the lower altitude species.

The Kerinci Summit Trail

A dilapidated entrance archway marks the start of the muddy trail to the summit of Mt Kerinci, a stiff 9 1/2-hr climb. Fortunately, all the best birds are in the lower forest and there is no need to punish your legs unless you want to experience the stunning summit views. Indeed, 20 minutes spent along the forest edge on either side of the arch should get your Kerinci list off to an excellent start with species such as Chestnut-capped Laughing Thrush, Silver-eared Mesia, Golden Babbler and White-throated Fantail.

Through the archway the trail enters a tunnel of dense scrub. Sunda Bush-warbler is easy to spot, and this is where everyone sooner or later meets a Bronze-tailed Peacock-pheasant on the trail. This is not one of the most spectacular pheasants, although the violet tail is attractive, but the

5 hrs by road from Padang.

Sumatra's legendary endemics: Schnieder's Pitta and Sumatran Cochoa.

Pleasant family homestays in Keresik Tuo.

Montane forest, tea and cinnamon plantations.

Best months Apr–Jul. Very wet Oct–Mar.

Moderately hard up-hill walking. Trails very muddy and slippery.

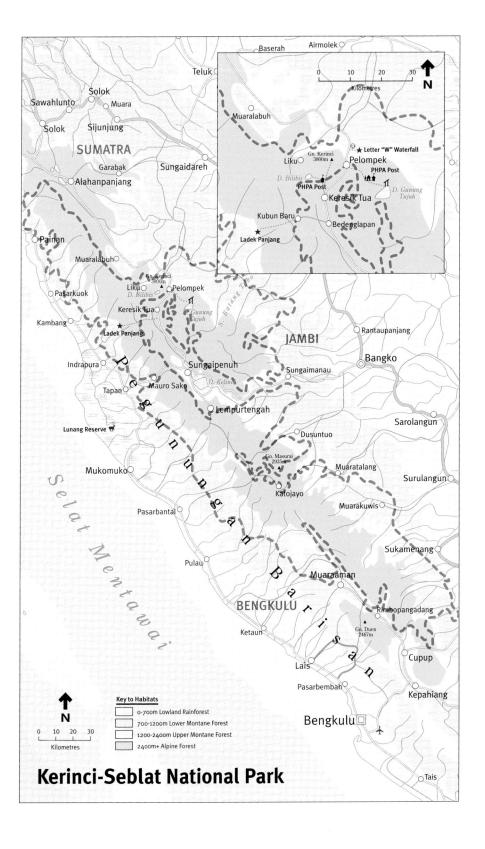

Kerinci-Seblat National Park

sight of a forest pheasant is always specially thrilling. The trail soon enters the forest and climbs gently to the base camp *pondok*; this takes about 40 minutes at a birding pace. This section and 200–300 metres beyond the *pondok* are prime Schneider's Pitta habitat. Naturally all your concentration will be on the ground layer, scanning intently among the lush, dripping herbs and moss-covered saplings for a movement, which—hope beyond hope—will reveal itself as a pitta. As a result you will see plenty of babblers and shortwings: minuscule Pygmy and Eye-browed Wren-babblers giving brief, tantalizing views as they hop among the dense brush, a pair of Spot-necked Babblers moving slowly through, a beautifully rotund Lesser Shortwing bouncing along a log. And the mechanical leaf flicking of the almost pitta-sized Rusty-breasted Wren-babbler will convert you into a fan of the exquisite charms of these "little brown jobs" if you are not one already!

Apart from these little gems, Shiny Whistling-thrush, Sunda Blue Robin and, all being well, close views of Common Green

Magpie and the endemic Sunda Treepie will keep the adrenaline levels high. However, sooner or later persistence is rewarded with a split-second glance of blue and rich rufous-orange on the trail, and that addictive sensation of panic mixed with relief that a first glimpse of a pitta brings. With luck the pitta will flush 5 m or so further on. With Schneider's Pitta under your belt, your new main goals are two more ground-dwelling species—the even more difficult Salvadori's Pheasant and strikingly patterned Red-billed Partridge. The pheasant is most frequently seen in this lower forest, but the partridge seems commonest above the first shelter at 2,400 m, a 2-hr climb beyond the *pondok*.

In the Canopy

Of course, your attention will regularly be drawn to the forest canopy. If it is not the attractive Banded Langur monkey crashing about, it will be the the Maroon Woodpecker with its sharp *chickik* call or a mixed species flock of startling black-and-red Sunda or Grey-chinned Minivets,

Below: Lake Tuju—Kerinci's montane forests harbour the enigmatic Schnieder's Pitta and Sumatran Cochoa. *Photo by Alain Compost.*

curious White-browed Shrike-babblers, Mountain Leaf-warblers and Scarlet Sunbirds. Keep your mind on woodpeckers for there are some fine specimens to be seen on this trail, notably the scarce Orange-backed and Grey-faced Woodpeckers and the Greater Yellownape.

The gaudy Fire-tufted Barbet, with its conspicuous grey throat and strange orange tuft of feathers at the base of its bill, is quite common and one of the best species to lead you to a fruiting tree. When you find such a tree, spend time watching it, for this is your best chance to see Pink-headed Fruit-dove and the enigmatic Sumatran Cochoa. This thrush-sized, navy-blue frugivore, with its stunning blue crown, primaries and tail base, has been seen only here and at Mt Tapan—and then very rarely.

Letter "W" Waterfall and Mt Tujuh

Two sites near the village of Pelompek, 10 km north of Keresik Tua, are recommended. The first is the popular Letter "W" waterfall, reached via a 200-m trail starting at a group of restaurants 4 km beyond Pelompek. The view of this magnificent waterfall, although blemished by collapsed and rusting national park shelters, is worth the trip alone, but some good birds have been seen in the small pocket of forest around the falls; this is the most reliable site for the endemic Blue-masked Leafbird, and Waterfall Swifts nest on the cliffs.

The other site is the scenic, 1,000-ha crater lake of Mt Tujuh at 1,950 m above sea level. The trail starts at the PHPA post, 2 km down a side turning on the right in Pelompek village. The first km leads through cinnamon and disturbed forest to a PHPA guest-house; behind the guest-house it enters the forest proper. It is a tough, 2-hr slog up a ridge high above the river to reach the lake. Birds are the same as on Mt Kerinci, although sightings of Wreathed Hornbill, Long-tailed Broadbill and Rufous-vented Niltava seem more frequent. What this area does have is the opportunity to camp at the shelter by the lake, watch a magnificent dawn and then slowly bird downhill in the early morning.

–Paul Jepson

Above: Green Magpie—a widespread Asian species but always a thrill to see. *Photo by Alan Ow Yong.*

Way Kambas National Park

White-winged Ducks & Frogmouths

Famed as the easiest locality in Sumatra to find White-winged Duck and Storm's Stork (both endangered and both very elusive), the 130,000-ha Way Kambas National Park is also an excellent place to see other lowland forest species. The availability of overnight accommodation at Way Kanan, a small forest clearing on the banks of the scenic Way Kambas river, 13 km inside the park, means that you are right on the spot to search at dawn and dusk for shy forest species such as pheasants and frogmouths.

Sadly, Way Kambas is not a place where the magnificence of pristine Sumatran rain forest can be experienced. The area was logged-out prior to its annexation for conservation in 1972 and the trees are still stunted in appearance. Luckily the birds and an impressively large number of animals have survived, and many of the 300 bird species can be seen during a 3–4 day visit. The park's accessibility—under 8 hrs by road and ferry from Jakarta and 1 1/2 hrs from Bandar Lampung airport—adds to its popularity.

Searching for White-winged Duck

With a world population of only about 250 individuals spread across India, Thailand, Laos, Cambodia, Vietnam and Sumatra, White-winged Ducks are decidedly thin on the ground. However, they are birds of lowland swamp forest, and a few of the 30 or so that live in Way Kambas are always to be found in the vicinity of Way Kanan. It is just a matter of catching up with them—something which is much easier during the dry season between June and November, when water levels recede, leaving a few small pools, and you do not have to wade through waterlogged forest.

Apribadi, a ranger at Way Kanan, will guide you expertly through the dense swamp forest to the duck's favourite haunts. Rawa Gajah (elephant swamp), a 20-min paddle up the river from Way Kanan, is usually the first place to try. On the river you will have no trouble getting acquainted with the impressive Stork-billed Kingfisher —unmistakable, thanks to its large size and yellow head—and you will probably also see Grey-headed Fish-eagle perched on an overhanging bough. Rawa Gajah is a wetland of about 1 ha that dries out to grass and mud at the height of the dry season (October) but which, when flooded, is a regular spot for the ducks as well as Lesser Adjutant.

Rawa Pasir (sand marsh) and the forest pond of Ulung-ulung Satu are also good areas for ducks: both are located 3–4 km from Way Kanan, along (for the first part) a well-maintained trail that starts behind the Tiger project building at Way Kanan. There are plenty of exciting birds to see on the way— so it is worth taking your lunch and making a day of it. The forest edge around Rawa Pasir can be particularly productive for leaf-birds, bulbuls, flowerpeckers and sunbirds.

The ducks are incredibly wary, so getting good views before they

1.5 hrs by road from Bandar Lampung, 8 from Jakarta.

Endangered White-winged Duck and Storm's Stork. Pheasants.

Basic park guest-house, take your own supplies.

Swamp forest and logged-over lowland rain forest.

Height of the dry season Aug & Sep best for the ducks.

Flat walking, but can be muddy, may need to wade.

fly away is something of an art. The problem lies in the abrupt juxtaposition of forest and water: scanning the whole of the river at Rawa Pasir or the large pond at Ulung-ulung Satu without stepping into full view is almost impossible. Moreover, many birders can tell of how, after assuring themselves that no ducks were present, they stepped out into the open only for a group of ducks to explode in a blaze of black-and-white wing flashes from behind a semi-submerged log.

Along the Look Trail

Storm's Stork is less wary than the duck, but more difficult to find. You may strike lucky at any of the above-mentioned sites. Apribadi considers Ulung-ulung Dua to be the most reliable area, but this swampy lake is only accessible (with a guide) in October when the water is at its lowest. Ironically, a small pool on the Look Trail, just a 10-min walk from the guest-house, is where most bird-watchers finally see this little-known stork, whose nest was first described for science as recently as 1987.

The 2-km, circular Look Trail enters the forest on the right, 150 m back along the track out of Way Kanan, and exits directly behind the guest-house. It passes through an area of stunted, secondary forest. The open undergrowth makes it a great place to get good views of galliformes, which are usually such difficult birds to see well. It is a real delight to watch a male Crested Fireback quietly scraping amongst the leaf litter, its blue eye-wattles, navy-blue, slightly iridescent body plumage and white outer tail feathers contrasting subtly with the browns and greens of the forest. With luck, a band of Crested Partridge will cross your path. Their spiky, red crests and energetic tramping give these little birds a rather wacky appearance. But the really memorable bird to be found along this trail is the Great Argus, a pheasant which, with its 75-cm long tail, is one of the world's more extraordinary birds. A few slow circuits of the trail may be required before you finally cross paths with this magnificent creature.

The main track leading out of Way Kanan is the most productive in terms of amassing a long list of

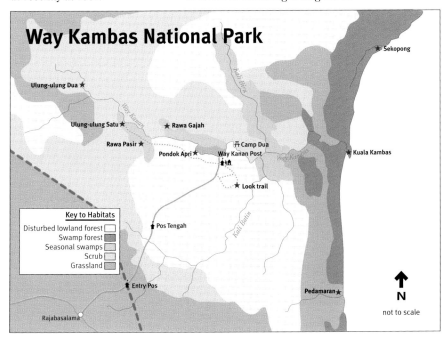

birds, including seven or eight species of woodpecker and up to ten species of babbler. Hill Myna frequently flies overhead, and two other common and distinctive birds are Black-bellied Malkoha and—a great favourite—Scarlet-rumped Trogon. Strangely enough, despite its intense scarlet-and-black body plumage, the trogon's blue eyelids are its really distinctive feature.

The Way Kanan clearing is a good place to watch at dawn or dusk for hornbills and pigeons flying over, and a Bat Hawk occasionally puts in an appearance.

Frogmouths

Below: A pair of the rare and endangered Storm's Stork feed peacefully on a forest pool. *Photo by Alain Compost.*

The main entrance track is also the place to find frogmouths: a particularly good stretch is 1 $\frac{1}{2}$–2 km from Way Kanan, where Gould's, Sunda

and Large Frogmouths regularly call after dusk. These close relatives of the nightjars specialize in picking off insects from foliage and the forest floor under the cover of darkness. Although quite common they are masters of camouflage, and only a very few birders have had the good fortune to notice that a dead branch is in fact a frogmouth. If you really want to see frogmouths, come armed with a tape recorder, recordings of their calls and a powerful torch. The peak calling periods are 8–9 pm and 5–6 am, and with luck you should be able to draw a bird in. Even without a tape,

the experience of spending a night at Way Kambas listening for the wheezy calls of Large Frogmouth or the clear, atmospheric, double whistle of Gould's Frogmouth is not to be missed.

A Peaceful Paddle

After the exertions of wading though swamps, dawn pheasant searches and late-evening frogmouth hunts, a gentle canoe trip down the Way Kanan river makes for a more peaceful excursion Although 45 km from the sea, the river is still tidal, so the technique is to leave on the falling tide and come back on the rising tide. Check tide times with the rangers at Way Kanan. Stork-billed and Blue-eared Kingfishers are constant companions along the river, and the diminutive Black-thighed Falconet is often seen perched on the top of dead trees.

After drifting along for about 45 minutes, you reach two watchtowers overlooking a large, scrub-covered clearing, which is the site of the old logging camp called Camp Dua. Green pigeons are common here, and a few Cinnamon-headed Green Pigeons can usually also be found among the commoner Orange-breasted. Be careful on the watchtowers: they have been cheaply built and will soon become unsafe.

For those whose budget stretches to the US$80 hire fee for the park's speedboat, a memorable bird-watching trip is to make the 2-hr journey to the sea and then continue south along the coast to Pedamaran, where there is a large breeding colony of Milky Storks, herons and egrets in an area of swamp forest located 250 m behind the beach. Spot-billed Pelican, another rare and endangered large waterbird, is occasionally seen in this area, and the sight of a group of pelicans roosting on a sand bar would make a fitting end to a trip to Way Kambas.

–Paul Jepson

G et a group of birders together, and talk naturally revolves around stories of magical moments—the first pitta, re-finding some lost species or a first record for a region. For birders of tropical forests the subject of "bird waves" is irresistible.

Invariably the talk is of a morning struggling to see a bird in the massive, three-dimensional rainforest structure, only to be overwhelmed suddenly by a deluge of birds moving through—the adrenaline rush as species after species pops into view. Some honest soul will admit to having panicked and, although maybe 100 birds of 15 or more species passed by, ended up identifying nothing. Then the discussion will focus on what to do: should you keep the binoculars on one bird until

Mixed Flocks

you identify it at the risk of missing something more interesting, or is it best to raise your "bins" only when something definitely looks new? And where in the flock are those rare species—at the front, end, bottom or top?

Mixed bird flocks are a feature of wet tropical forests, and the reason for this flocking behaviour causes similarly lively discussions among behavioural ecologists. Some argue that the primary purpose is to reduce the risk of predation—the old "two pairs of eyes are better than one" adage—and that a bird in a flock can spend more time searching for food and less looking out for danger. Other scientists are firmly in the foraging camp, and explain that rainforest insect fauna is incredibly diverse and that the birds' insect prey is either extremely well camouflaged or noxious tasting (or mimicking a nasty-tasting species). A flock of babblers or warblers moving through will disturb insects, and once an insect moves it loses its camouflage. Older birds will know which insects really are poisonous and which are mimics. Then there is the question of which species start a flock: are there "nuclear" species? Which species spend their whole day roaming through the forest with the flock and which just join it opportunistically? And what about woodpeckers? How can they be fitted into anti-predation or increased foraging efficiency theories? A discussion of these subjects could go on for hours!

–*Paul Jepson*

Top: Silver-eared Mesias travel in groups through dense scrub and undergrowth. *Photo by Morten Strange.*

Right: Flowerpeckers, such as this Crimson-breasted Flowerpecker, are frequently seen in mixed flocks. *Photo by Alan Ow Yong.*

Introducing Kalimantan

Bornean Birding at its Best

Access to site.

Main birding attractions.

Type of accommodation.

Habitat.

Weather conditions.

Degree of difficulty.

Kalimantan, the Indonesian territory of Borneo, and the world's third largest island, is well off the beaten track for the world bird-watcher. This is probably because most of the region's 480 recorded bird species and 20 endemics can be seen in the well-known and better established reserves in the northern (Malaysian) part of the island.

However, the birding in Kalimantan certainly rivals that of Sabah, and the possibility of finding White-shouldered Ibis, one of the world's rarest waterbirds, and better chances of seeing rare and unusual mammals such as Orangutan, Proboscis Monkey and Freshwater Dolphin might just give Kalimantan the edge.

Kalimantan—the name means river of diamonds—comprises 28% of Indonesia's total land area. At 549,032 sq km, it is twice the size of New Zealand, but home to just 5% (9.1 million) of Indonesia's population. Mighty rivers flow from the central mountains to the coast: the two largest are the Mahakam, which flows east to the Makassar Strait, and the Kapuas (Indonesia's longest river) which flows west to the sea at Pontianak. These are the highways of Kalimantan, plied by speedboats, longboats and some sizable ferries. Away from the coastal cities the road system is rudimentary so air travel is the only real alternative to riverboats.

Kalimantan still supports the largest remaining tracts of rain forest in Southeast Asia (excluding Irian Jaya), although large areas continue to be taken for agriculture, rice paddies and estate crops, and most lowland forest outside reserves is being logged. In 1987 just one province, East Kalimantan, accounted for 21% of Indonesia's export revenues. This is because the region is rich in reserves of oil, gas, coal and other minerals. Kalimantan is a key area for national development, but environmentalists question its sustainability: soils are thin and fragile, and each year fires set to clear new fields or stimulate new grazing nibble away at forest boundaries. In the drought years of 1982/83, fires damaged 3.6 million ha of forest, an area the size of Belgium.

For birders it is Kalimantan's network of extensive reserves, covering some 3.2 million ha, that catches the imagination. Unfortunately most of these are still in the early stages of establishment so exciting areas such as the Kayan Mentarang National Park on the Kalimantan/Sabah border and the Bukit Baka Bukit Raya National Park in West Kalimantan are unlikely to be geared up for tourism until next century. But not to worry: excellent rainforest birding is easily accessible in Kutai National Park, and a journey up the Mahakam river will be rewarded with rare waterbirds, as well as unforgettable encounters with the native Dayaks.

Another excellent birding area is Tanjung Puting reserve (famous for the rehabilitation of confiscated pet Orang-utans) on the south coast of Central Kalimantan province. If you take the plunge and leave the beaten track for a bird-watching trip to Kalimantan, you will definitely not be disappointed.

–Paul Jepson

Previous page: Dyak rattan collectors carefully cross a tributary river in the forests of west Kalimantan. *Photo by Alain Compost.* **Opposite:** Hudoq dance—stylised hornbill costumes are a feature of several ceremonial dances of the Dyaks. *Photo by Kal Muller.*

INTRODUCING KALIMANTAN

KALIMANTAN

125

2 hrs by road from Samarinda. A 3–4 day trip.

Lowland forest birds, hornbills, woodpeckers and the odd Bornean Bristlehead.

Basic park guesthouses. Take in your own supplies.

Lowland riverine forest, mangroves.

Hot and humid. Driest season Jul–Sep.

Flat jungle trails, some may be muddy.

Kutai National Park

The Sultans' Nature Reserve

In the coastal lowlands of East Kalimantan, just 2 hrs by road from Samarinda, the Kutai nature reserve, which was established by the Sultan of Kutai in 1936 to preserve populations of Two-horned (Sumatran) Rhinoceroses, Banteng, Orang-utans and Proboscis Monkeys, is an immense wilderness in the old Sultanate of Kutai. Although the rhinos have long since disappeared, and logging, mining, burning and farming have reduced the reserve to "only" 2,000 sq km, birds and other wildlife abound, and many species are easier to see in Kutai than anywhere else in Kalimantan.

A one-week trip is sufficient to see Kutai's impressive list of birds and explore the area's varied habitats. For bird-watching, the best bases are the Teluk Kaba and Mentoko field stations; the adventurous may choose to camp in the forest while exploring the park's network of old logging tracks.

Teluk Kaba

From Samarinda it takes the best part of a day to reach Teluk Kaba. First head north to Bontang, where the National Park office issues permits and advises on travel arrangements. It is a further 2 hrs up the coast by chartered motor boat (up to 5 passengers) from Bontang (Tanjung Limau) to Teluk Kaba.

The field station is located close to the Makassar Strait, in an open landscape of mangroves and degraded heath forest; good birding areas are relatively accessible and conditions are excellent.

Woodpeckers are abundant, due to the many dead trees left over from logging and the forest fires that raged here more than a decade ago. The always cheerfully chuckling Great Slaty, the no less impressive (and noisy!) White-bellied Woodpeckers and many of the smaller species are all easy to watch, searching for grubs in the decaying wood. At least three, and possibly six, species of hornbill are present: the Wrinkled Hornbill, which has suffered worrying declines in many parts of its range, is particularly noteworthy. The large, black-bodied, white-necked and tailed male is readily distinguished from the similar, commoner Wreathed Hornbill by its red casque and barking calls.

Mentoko

A varied and interesting day journey from Teluk Kaba brings you to the research station annex at Mentoko, on the northern fringe of the park. It starts with a sea crossing to Teluk Lombok, and continues northwest by road to the busy village of Sangatta on the river of the same name, where you change to a *ketinting* (motorised *prau*) for the 2 ½ hrs upriver to Mentoko. Along the way, take a close look at the untidy clumps of vegetation suspended from branches overhanging the water: they may be the nests of the Black-and-red Broadbill.

The Mentoko field station is situated on the bank of the Sangatta river, which marks the northern boundary of the park; behind it, an immense area of secondary and primary forest stretches far to the south and southwest.

The station's open vistas make this a good place to watch for raptors such as Rufous-bellied Eagle and the globally endangered Wallace's Hawk-eagle, which regularly perches in dead trees. But the real prize here is the extraordinary Bornean Bristlehead—a stocky, black bird with a bright, red-and-yellow head: it flies around in flocks, making strange, cat-like, mewing calls. Although closely related to the wood-swallows, it looks like no other bird on Earth.

Bird Studies

Several pioneering studies on tropical bird ecology have been conducted at Mentoko. In 1974, an American ornithologist, David Pearson, recorded no fewer than 142 bird species in a 30-ha block of primary forest. In the late 1970s, Mark Leighton made some of the first studies of the feeding ecology of seven species of hornbill.

These researchers established an intricate network of trails, some of which are still maintained. You can spend many enjoyable hours wandering around this maze, in the company of a local PHPA guide, and savouring the riches of Kalimantan's lowland bird fauna.

Forest Jewels

No birder should leave Mentoko before stalking Borneo's endemic and breathtakingly coloured Blue-headed Pitta and the no less splendid Garnet Pitta. A melancholy whistle alerts you to the Garnet Pitta (but beware—it is a clever ventriloquist!); the Blue-headed's call is a loud *ppor-or*. Getting views of these jewels of the forest floor demands the utmost patience. The overwhelming sense of anticipation when you know you are close, turning to knee-wobbling excitement at the first glimpse, and then, when— and if—you get a clear view, the

mixture of awe and relief, is one of the best birding experiences to be had in Asia.

Remember to re-visit the trails after nightfall to search for night-birds such as the Large Frogmouth, whose loud, rolling notes can sometimes even be heard from the bushes close to the Post.

No better Place to Wake up

A new day at Mentoko is heralded by the loud, bubbling duets of Straw-headed Bulbuls (Kalimantan's most accomplished songsters) and the peculiar, rasping grunts and booms of Large Green Pigeons, which haunt the towering canopy of trees. With yesterday's memories still fresh and the prospect of more joys to come, there can be few places a birder would prefer to wake.
–*Bas van Balen*

Below: Black-and-red Broadbill sports a remarkable blue-and-yellow waxy bill. *Photo by Alain Compost.*

HORNBILLS

ornbills are found throughout Africa, Asia and the Australasian region; a total of 54 species are recognized and Indonesia, with 13, is home to the most species. The variety is impressive—in size they range from the 400-g Tarictic Hornbill to the prodigious 3-kg Great Hornbill. Appearances vary from the uniformly dark Black Hornbill to the ornately decorated Rhinoceros Hornbill. However, scientists still know surprisingly little about the habits of forest hornbills.

The Casque: Function or Flirtation?

Hornbills are named after the casques that adorn their large, anvil-shaped bills. In the Helmeted Hornbill the casque is a solid block of bone or "hornbill ivory", whereas in all other species casques are formed from layers of keratin like our fingernails, and contain little or no bone. In several species, such as the Wreathed Hornbill, the casque is little

more than a raised ridge; in others, like the Rhinoceros Hornbill, it is enormous. Casques get bigger with age, and experts believe that these decorations have evolved to enable individuals to advertise their sex, age and dominance to other hornbills. The casque may also have an acoustic function, acting like a resonating chamber. All hornbills are extremely vocal, producing a variety of honks, croaks, squawks and barks, the loudest of which can be heard over a km away. Hornbills lack special underwing flight feathers, hence the jet-like swoosh they make as they fly over the forest canopy.

Nesting Niceties

Hornbills are famous for their unique breeding biology: all Asian species nest in tree cavities and seal the entrance, leaving a narrow slit through which the confined female and her chick receive food from the male. Usually the seal is composed of mud delivered by the male, and the female applies the finishing touches with her own excrement. The function of nest sealing is believed to be for protection against predators and other intruding hornbills in areas where nest sites are rare.

By enclosing the female the male must work hard to provide for her and their offspring. Two hornbills will maintain a monogamous relationship until one of the pair dies: this has led many societies to revere hornbills as a symbol of fidelity.

Feathered Foresters

Most hornbills are primarily fruit-eaters and especially relish figs, nutmegs and the oily fruits of wild avocados. Large, fruiting fig trees may attract flocks of more than 100 birds, but more typically hornbills forage in pairs or family groups. They will often carry fruit in their throat pouches many miles from a parent tree to eat and digest later. And because they regurgitate seeds unharmed, hornbills are natural farmers of the forest, aiding in the critical task of rainforest regeneration.

Cultures Old and New

The hornbill plays an active role in many of the cultures of Indonesia. To the Dyaks of Kalimantan hornbills are symbols of the "upper world", players in the creation of humanity and carriers of souls. They revere a mythological bird in the form of the Rhinoceros Hornbill called the Kenyalang. The special Kenyalang ceremony consists of dancing, drinking and parading elaborately carved effigies of hornbills around the longhouse. Men adorn themselves with headdresses of hornbill plumes and women don a fan of feathers on each hand during elegant dances.

In Sulawesi, casques and feathers of the Red-knobbed Hornbill traditionally decorated the drums that were beaten during the Cakalele, a feverish dance that prepared warriors for battle. The large, red knobs were believed to endow the warriors with power and ensure invincibility. In the past, the Cakalele signalled bloodshed; today it is a sign of peace.

Into the Future

As their cultural significance changes, so do the population figures of hornbills. In many regions of Indonesia, hornbill numbers have declined over the last decade, and some species, such as the Sumba Hornbill, are in danger of extinction. Hunting and loss of habitat lie behind the decline.

Logging, which supplies a major percentage of Indonesia's export revenues may destroy or degrade hornbill habitat. But more commonly it is clearance by a burgeoning human population satisfying their agricultural requirements that is the main cause of forest loss. For many species the future is increasingly uncertain: if Indonesia continues to lose forest at the present rate, soon the majestic call of hornbills over the canopy may become no more than an echo of a lost dream.
–M Kinnaird/T O'Brien

Far left: The Great Hornbill is largest of Asia's hornbills. *Photo by Alain Compost.*
Left: The loud *took* calls of the Helmeted Hornbill gain speed before climaxing in an amazing maniacal laugh. *Photo by Margaret Kinnaird.*
Top: A Dyak wall relief with hornbill motif. *Photo by Margaret Kinnaird.*
Right: A male Rhinoceros Hornbill brings food to its mate. *Photo by Morten Strange.*

Travel by riverboats. Allow 7–10 days to fully explore the area.

Fish-eagles, hornbills and rare White-shouldered Ibis.

Simple *losmen* in riverside villages.

River, lowland forest, lakes, swamps & cultivation.

Driest season Jul–Sep. Tropical downpours in other months.

Little walking required.

Birding the Mahakam

River Birding from a Longboat

Below: Forest and Nipa plam swamps on the Mahakam delta. *Photo by Alain Compost* .

From its headwaters in the Müller and Iban mountain ranges that form the border of the provinces of West, Central and East Kalimantan, the great Mahakam river flows east for 920 km to the Makassar Strait, just east of Samarinda. Although this is Kalimantan's busiest "highway" and the forests along its course have been heavily logged, the Mahakam offers some fine opportunities to see birds and some of Borneo's rarest animals, including Proboscis Monkeys, False Ghavial Crocodiles, monitor lizards, snakes, turtles and Freshwater Dolphins. Dayak longhouses are an additional attraction.

The starting point for this classic river journey is the dull town of Samarinda, but views of Brahminy Kites, locally called *Elang Mahakam* or "Mahakam Eagles", and White-

bellied Sea-eagles soaring over the river whet the appetite for what is to come. The first section of the journey takes you to Kota Bangun: the river here is about 400 m wide and the most frequently seen birds are Common Sandpiper, Slender-billed Crow, Reef Egret and Stork-billed Kingfisher.

The Mahakam Lakes

At Kota Bangun, break your journey for 3–4 days and hire a *ketinting* to visit the surrounding lakes, the largest of which are Jempang, Melintang and Semayang. The latter is the least well known and probably the best for birding. Pak Amir, a *ketinting* pilot in Kota Bangun, knows the area and birds. Look out

Mahakam River
and Kutai National Park

for Irrawaddy (freshwater) Dolphins as you enter the lake; the Kalaha tributary, which enters on the northern edge, is good for Long-tailed Macaques and Proboscis Monkeys. Typical birds on this shallow, swampy lake include Black-crowned Night-heron, Purple Heron, Little Egret, Oriental Darter, Lesser Adjutant, Purple Swamphen, Lesser Whistling-duck and Greater Coucal. The dry season (Aug–Sept) offers the chance to see Estuarine and False Ghavial Crocodiles.

If the Mahakam's non-feathered inhabitants fascinate you, stop at Muara Pahu, a village upriver of the entrance to Lake Jempang. Find a comfortable spot at the water's edge at the mouth of the River Kedang Pah and watch for Proboscis Monkeys and Malayan Water Monitors, which are quite common on the riverbanks.

For orchids and native culture, make Melak your next stop and take a car to the Kersik Luwai Orchid Forest to see, among others, the famous Black Orchid and pitcher plants. Afterwards, drive to the village of Eheng, where an authentic Benuaq longhouse remains. Emerald

Doves and Blue-rumped Parrots are easy to see round the village, but Hill Mynas, though quite common in the area, are more elusive. Travelling by road from Melak to Tering will give you a 6-hr headstart on the riverboat, so there is no need to wait another day before moving on.

A Rare Ibis

Upriver of Tering more trees line the riverbanks and you will quickly add new birds to your "trip list": Green Imperial Pigeon, Striated Heron and Asian Pied Hornbill (most visible at dawn and dusk), to name but a few. Around the village of Memahak Terbok, upriver of Long Iram, keep a sharp eye out for a large, blackish bird with long red legs and downward-curving bill foraging on gravel and sand banks in and along the river. This is the White-shouldered Ibis, the rarest member of its tribe, known only from a handful of records from Borneo and Vietnam; there have been several recent observations from this stretch of the Mahakam. It is possibile that the Bornean

Many of the Mahakam's tributaries offer excellent birding opportunities, but one of the best is probably the Ratah river, a southwestern tributary between Long Hubung and Laham. This tributary is particularly good because, after Ma'au, situated just 1 ¹/₂ hours from the Mahakam by boat, there are no more villages and you can travel upstream for two days without meeting too many people, for a change. Birding highlights along the Ratah are the sight of a rare Storm's Stork soaring high overhead on a midday thermal, Black-capped Kingfisher perched on an overhanging branch, the beautiful duetting of the Straw-headed Bulbul—sadly, a sound increasingly rarely heard due to over-collecting for Javan bird fanciers, the glimpse of the exquisite white tail plumes of an Asian Paradise-flycatcher dancing through the forest, Blue-throated Bee-eaters hawking from riverside trees, a Bat Hawk at dusk or a Crested Fireback wandering down to drink at the river's edge. At night you will hear the cry of the Great Argus, and at around five in the morning the calls of the gibbons will wake you for another memorable day in deepest Borneo.

The Upper Mahakam

Returning from the Ratah and continuing on to Long Bangun, the end of the line for the large boats, the river passes between limestone walls and beautiful scenery. Determined travellers who dare the rapids above Long Bangun will be rewarded with sightings of Lesser and Grey-headed Fish-eagles, and maybe even Blyth's Hawk-eagle. It is possible to cross the Kalimantan border into Sarawak at three places on the Upper Mahakam above these rapids, but do carry good shoes and plenty of cash; taking an airplane from Datah Dawai (Long Lunuk) back to Samarinda and then flying to Sarawak is a cheaper alternative, although less exciting.

–Resit Sözer

Far above: Stork-billed Kingfishers are a common sight along the Mahakam. *Photo by Alain Compost.*
Above: The Straw-headed Bulbul, a popular cage bird on account of its ringing, melodious song, has been trapped out in many areas, but still survives along quiet tributaries of the Mahakam. *Photo by Margaret Kinnaird.*
Opposite: Riverside forest along the upper reaches of the Mahakam. *Photo by Alain Compost.*

population may be a distinct species: compared with Vietnamese birds, they have whitish-blue rather than red bare parts on the head and back of the neck. The ibises are quite approachable—even when a noisy riverboat passes close by—but, if they do flush, look out for the diagnostic large, white, shoulder patches to verify your identification.

In the same area, you will start to notice large numbers of swiftlets. This is because the surrounding limestone hills and mountains are peppered with the caves that are the nesting places of these small but important birds. Two of the six species found in Kalimantan make edible nests—the essential ingredient of bird's-nest soup, which the Chinese believe has aphrodisiac qualities and helps to retain youth. Edible-nest Swiftlet nests are sold locally for as much as US$3,500 per kilo (*see p 57*).

Introducing Sulawesi

Dazzling Birds on an Island Rich in Culture

Access to site.

Main birding attractions.

Type of accommodation.

Habitat.

Weather conditions.

Degree of difficulty.

The odd shape of Sulawesi—once known as Celebes—has been variously likened to a drunken spider, a scarecrow in a hurricane, an amoeba and, more charmingly, the petals of a windblown orchid. This unusual shape is the result of tectonic movements: two islands colliding with each other 3 million years ago. The western island (today's south and north peninsulas), together with Sumatra and Borneo, broke off from the Gondwanaland mega continent 180 million years ago; the eastern island (now the east and southeast peninsulas) broke away from Antarctica along with Australia and New Guinea some 90 million years ago. This collision of islands carrying animals of quite different origins explains why Sulawesi is bursting with unique fauna.

Sulawesi has some really dazzling birds. Just a perusal of the names is enough to get the adrenalin going: Purple-bearded Bee-eater, Lilac-cheeked Kingfisher, Great Shortwing and Fiery-browed Myna. An assortment of unusual mammals—the strange Babirusa or "pig deer", the rarely seen Anoa (a dwarf buffalo) and four unique species of macaque—add to the excitement of being in the forest. World class snorkelling and diving are available whenever you need to cool off.

This 189,000 sq km island also boasts impressive landscapes and a fascinating range of cultures. Sulawesi is in essence a group of volcanoes and, if global warming were to raise the sea level just a few metres, it would become a cluster of islands separated by narrow straits, as the Philippines archipel-ago is today. Indeed, this was how Sulawesi appeared 4,000 years ago.

Ritual in Sulawesi, as elsewhere in the archipelago, is not only a rich part of the social calendar but also an arena to display and assure health and status. Best known are the death rites of the Toraja, a distinct ethnic group inhabiting the gloriously scenic Tana Toraja highlands in central Sulawesi. The Toraja are also famous for their beautifully carved "origin" houses, and effigy-guarded cliffside graves.

Birders will gravitate towards the northern peninsula and central Sulawesi, where the largest areas of rain forest are found, and in particular to the huge national parks of Lore Lindu, 50 km south of the provincial capital, Palu, Dumoga Bone, on the "northern neck", and the much smaller reserve of Tangkoko-DuaSudara, on the tip of the Minahasa peninsula. With 88 endemic species to go for, the birder will find Sulawesi a real Mecca. It is quite possible to see 80% of these endemics in a 3-week trip, with a little effort and planning.

For those wishing to get well off the beaten track, however, Sulawesi has a fascinating collection of satellite islands to explore. Muna and Buton, off the southeast corner, are the largest, but the most interesting for birders are the Banggai Islands—home to a unique megapode and crow—off the Eastern Peninsula, and Sangi-he and Talaud, which have the dubious distinction of supporting the highest concentration of threatened birds species in Indonesia.

–*Paul Jepson*

137

Previous page: A bird's eye view of Sulawesi's luxuriant forests. *Photo by Tui De Roy.*
Opposite: A female Red-knobbed Hornbill rests quietly in the middle of the day. *Photo by Margaret Kinnaird.*

Lake Tempe

Birds crowd at the Fishbowl

4 hrs from Ujung Pandang. Spend 2–3 days to explore all the lakes.

Thousands of waterbirds.

Simple *losmen* in Sengkang.

Shallow, swampy lakes.

Dry season Apr–Oct.

Explore the lakes by powered canoe.

Surrounded by the old kingdoms of Wajo, Soppeng and Sidenreng, Lake Tempe lies in the Buginese "heartland" of South Sulawesi. And a colourful land this is, with gaudily-painted boats, artistically-woven silks, and a natural panorama dominated by water, rice, fish and waterbirds. There are thousands of waterbirds of many species, all clamouring for fish and the shelter offered by the lake. Along the road to Sengkang, the largest town on the shores of the lake, the rhythmical click-clacking of the silk-weaving looms emanates from under brightly-painted houses, erected on poles so as to remain out of reach of the annual floods. In the distance,

between the houses, one can catch glimpses of the muddy, brown waters of Tempe. The bird spectacle at Lake Tempe can easily be seen in a 1 $^1/_2$-day *intermezzo*. For those who want to take in everything, a 2–3 day trip by local boat is another fine option.

Interconnected Lakes

Lake Tempe consists of three interconnected, shallow (1–5 $^1/_2$ m) lakes that coalesce into one 35,000 ha body of water during floods. Lake Buaya (Crocodile Lake) is the smallest of the three and has dark, peat-coloured waters and a somewhat eerie atmosphere. Lake Sidenreng, the next in size, is probably the least attractive of the lakes, as late afternoon winds always manage to churn up large waves, making it both muddy and dangerous; it is avoided by fishermen and birds alike. However, the sedge-swamps along the western shore teem seasonally with thousands of Glossy Ibis and Garganey duck. Lake Tempe proper is the largest, and generally the most interesting of the three lakes; some years it dries out, but its average size is about 13,000 ha. It is fed by the Bila River to the north, and drained by the Walanae River to the south east. During peak floods on the Walanae, the tributary connecting the river with Lake Tempe may reverse flow and, instead of draining it, debauche silt-rich waters into the lake.

The silt of the Bila and Walanae rivers is both a bane and a boon to Lake Tempe. It enriches the waters:

The Tempe Lake System

Bila
Jongkang
S. Bila
S. Tokaki
D. Sidenreng
D. Buaya
Belawa
Ajujawae
Awatu
S. Lasirara
Canranae
S. Tancae
Biloka
S. Walia
Cilelange
S. Biloka
Impakimpa
D. Tempe
Empagae
Balamalimpong
Tnjung
Sengkang
Tanetee
Bentengiampoe
Todadi
Lampowa
Ujungawe
S. Wenpka
S. Walanae
N
0 2 4 6
Kilometre
Tokare
Lopasaru

with about 800 kg of fish being harvested from each hectare of lake per year, Lake Tempe is Indonesia's most productive inland body of water. The floodwaters also leave a layer of fertile silt on the banks, which farmers hastily cultivate with corn and a variety of beans as waters recede from October to December. The downside is that, with a layer of 1–3 cm of mud being added annually, the lakes are rapidly silting up. Also, waters are so murky that it is beginning to affect fish and underwater plant life.

One of the first things that strikes you when boating on Lake Tempe are the many *bungka*—large ($\frac{1}{2}$–1ha), man-made circles of floating vegetation, held in place by bamboo tripods erected along the periphery. *Bungka* are elaborate fish traps, attracting fish in the wet season. The vegetation is harvested in the dry season. As water levels drop, a fine, split-bamboo fence is built around the *bungka* and all the floating vegetation and bamboo tripods are removed. This enclosure is made smaller and smaller until the waters are alive with fish; then they are just scooped out.

Bungka—especially old ones with taller, shrubby vegetation—are a haven for waterbirds. Drifting close to the edge of a *bungka*, you may see many species alongside each other: Little Grebe, Purple Swamphen, Common Moorhen, White-breasted Waterhen, Purple Heron, Javan Pond Heron, Little Egret, Comb-crested Jacana, Barred Rail, Yellow Bittern, Black Bittern and Cinnamon Bittern. Look out for Little Pied Cormorant, Darter, Purple and Great-billed Herons, Black-crowned and Nankeen Night-herons, Glossy Ibis, Brahminy Kite, Whiskered Tern, Blue-tailed Bee-eater, and occasionally Milky Stork, roosting on the bamboo poles.

It is the sheer numbers and the ease with which birds can be seen that makes this trip so memorable. From the relative comfort of a Buginese longboat you can drift close to the floating vegetation and

simply watch. Even resolute non-birders will enjoy the spectacle. Depending on the season, up to 5,000 or more Glossy Ibis, 10,000 or more Garganey and tens of thousands of reed-warblers can be seen. Or spot up to several dozen Comb-crested Jacanas in a circle of 50 m around your boat.

Above: The Lake Tempe river system floodwaters leave a rich silt good for cultivation. *Photo courtesy of Wetlands International.*

A three-day Odyssey

Lake Tempe's abundant bird life flourishes seemingly oblivious to the pretty but noisy Buginese boats, which are everywhere. For those who really want to take it all in, pottering about in a longboat for 2–3 days would be ideal. Only then can you, for instance, explore the streams connecting the lakes— watch out for a giant *Soa-soa* or Sailfin Lizard, resting on a branch above the water with its legs dangling on either side. The more adventurous can stay overnight in a Buginese house in one of the smaller villages around the lake, and enjoy eating wild duck or fresh fish for dinner. Hunting occurs, especially along Lake Sidenreng, where duck, swamphen, moorhen and Banded Rail are netted for food and appear on the menu of local restaurants. For the moment this seems to occur at sustainable levels, but both local government and conservation agencies are keeping a watchful eye.

–Wim Giesen

Endemics Galore

Lore Lindu National Park

Half to 1 day along a bad road from Palu. Allow 3–4 days in the park.

Premier birding site in Sulawesi with over 80% of the island's endemics.

Park guest-house at Kamarora.

Mid- and high-altitude rain forest.

Rain in all months, wettest Nov–Mar.

Long walks along quiet road.

Imagine quietly imbibing a beer while sitting on the veranda of a spacious bungalow on the edge of a clearing, surrounded by virtually pristine forests, listening to the calls of the Isabelline Bush-hen, while six Red-knobbed Hornbills fly overhead in their characteristic pterosaur-like flap-and-glide manner. This is no dream: this is Kamarora, the headquarters of Lore Lindu National Park in Central Sulawesi.

The largest of Sulawesi's national parks, Lore Lindu covers some 230,000 ha. It has an impressive altitudinal range from 300 m to a dizzy 2,610 m above sea level, and includes lowland, lower montane and upper montane (elfin) forests. There is probably nowhere better to see Sulawesi's unique avifauna: with 80% of the island's endemic species, this park has a well-deserved reputation for producing the goods, particularly the montane specialities. You will need at least one week to do the place justice; two weeks would be better.

Before entering Lore Lindu you need to obtain a permit from the PHPA office in Palu, the provincial capital of Central Sulawesi (see Practicalities). Rolex Lameanda, who works there, speaks excellent English and is a mine of information. You should base yourself at Kamarora, four hours from Palu.

Birding the Lower Areas

It is comforting to know that, barring an unforeseen volcanic eruption or the like, you simply cannot miss some of the most spectacular endemic birds that Sulawesi has to offer. Of course you will tremble uncontrollably when you first clap eyes on the awesome Red-knobbed Hornbill, but the effect soon wears off after you have seen your 29th flock! Far better, then, to catch sight of the rather comical-looking little Tarictic Hornbill, which travels in small groups, often well below the canopy. Situated at an altitude of 680 m, Kamarora offers an opportunity to see much of the Sulawesi lowland avifauna, although is perhaps not low enough for several of the endemic kingfishers. Behind the guest-houses at Kamarora, keep your ears and eyes open for the rarely seen Snoring and Bare-eyed Rails, both reported in this vicinity. White-breasted Waterhen, Barred Rail and Isabelline Bush-hen are more likely, however, and in the late afternoon the distinctive chatter of the latter is often heard from the grassy *alang-alang* clearings.

Unsurpassed Roadside Birding

The best birding is to be found along the park's only road, which climbs up to 1,620 m before descending to the Napu valley. From Kamarora, walk 4 km to the main road, then turn right, passing the park office check-point at Tongoa after 100 m. You can easily walk along this road up to about 900 m above sea level, then return to Kamarora (by truck or *bemo* if you are lucky) around midday. If you are fit, you could walk the 14 km from Tongoa to the shelter shed at

Km Post 57, a convenient camping spot and launching pad for upper montane gems to be found along the track to Anaso. This will take you through lowland jungle, palm forest and riverine forest with the massive endemic *Eucalyptus deglupta*, to lower montane forest, dominated by oaks and chestnuts, starting at around 1,500 m.

Working this road for several days in succession will keep rewarding you, as the forest is full of birds: noisy Caerulean Cuckooshrikes forage in the sub-canopy as Sulawesi Cicadabirds feed quietly higher up. Smaller birds include the Black-fronted White-eye, Black Sunbird, Black-naped Monarch, and the Citrine, Island and (oddly) Mangrove Blue Flycatchers. At ground level there are remarkably few birds: Sulawesi Babblers are the exception, but Maleo has also been seen along this stretch of road. After crossing the uncharacteristically well-built bridge over the river just below Dongi-Dongi mining camp, watch out for Ivory-backed Wood-swallows (a nice change from the common or garden White-breasted variety).

Mynas and Malkohas

Mynas are a special feature of Lore Lindu and you will see them *ad nauseam*. Noisy flocks of Finch-billed Mynas and pairs of fantastically long-tailed White-necked Mynas call harshly on every bend. The Short-crested Myna, with its awkward, mushroom-shaped head, is less conspicuous. About 2 hrs' walk from Kamarora (above 950 m) there are bands of yet another bizarre, endemic myna: the Fiery-browed. This is just the beginning. Flocks of piebald Piping Crows give their *wheeep* calls as they move through the forest canopy. Groups of fabulous Yellow-billed Malkohas, sometimes accompanied by a pair of Bay Coucals, travel through the middle and lower forest levels, often following a band of Tonkin Macaques. Many other stunners

are to be found on the forest edge: Purple-winged Rollers, hanging out on exposed tree limbs, and the large, pink-bellied, endemic Ashy Woodpecker, creeping up tree trunks.

Parrots, Pigeons and Raptors

Overhead, noisy flocks of Golden-mantled Racquet-tails, recognized by their oddly-shaped tail plumes and *keli-keli* calls, are regular sights. With luck you may flush Blue-backed Parrot from a roadside bush, but you are more likely to hear the harsh *kea* calls of this partly-nocturnal bird at night. The endemic Ornate Lorikeet can be seen in flowering trees around Kamarora, but the Yellow-and-green Lorikeet is found only at higher altitudes. Look out for the tiny Sulawesi Hanging-parrot in palms.

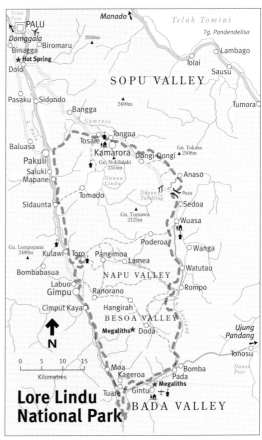

distinctive tail making identification simple. Other endemic goshawks are less obliging and difficult to identify, especially if in juvenile plumage: Sulawesi Goshawk, Small Sparrow-hawk and even Vinous-breasted Sparrow-hawk are all possible. Meanwhile there are almost always a few raptors circling overhead to distract you: Barred Honey-buzzard, Brahminy Kite and Lesser Fish-eagle are probably the most likely candidates.

An Extravaganza of Montane Endemics

With all these lowland "goodies" under your belt, you will now be ready for the mountains! About 14 km from the park check-point, 400 m up from Km Post 87, you will reach the pass at 1,620 m (where the road changes to asphalt). Just before this, take the now overgrown and, in places, deeply eroded track on the left towards the extinct mining camp at Anaso, where most of Sulawesi's montane birds can be found on a good day.

Far Above: Sightings of the endemic Yellow-billed Malkoha clambering through the canopy are a highlight of birding at Kamora.
Above: Yellow-sided Flowerpecker, one of Sulawesi's two endemic flowerpeckers.
Photos by Tui De Roy.

Pigeons include the Grey-cheeked Green Pigeon and Superb and Black-naped Fruit-doves, but commonest of all is the Slender-billed Cuckoo-dove, which you will continue to startle beside the road long after every other bird has disappeared. Grey-headed Imperial Pigeon gradually replaces the Green Imperial Pigeon (more typical of lowlands) at higher altitudes, but both species can be encountered in fruiting trees around Kamarora. However, the queen of pigeons must be the magnificent endemic White-bellied Imperial Pigeon, usually seen flying high overhead in ones or twos, or cooing from the top of a dead tree.

Lore Lindu is a marvellous place for raptor enthusiasts. The usual Oriental Hobbies and Spotted Kestrels perch on dead trees in the open, but do not be surprised to find the endemic Sulawesi Serpent-eagle or Sulawesi Hawk-eagle doing the same. Spot-tailed Goshawk perches low on the forest-edge, its

High above the moss and epiphyte-laden conifers and oaks, squadrons of lorikeets and Fiery-browed Mynas pass; watch out for the endemic montane Sombre Pigeon. The ubiquitous Mountain Tailorbird, which calls incessantly from track-side bushes, and flocks of the endemic Streak-headed Dark-eye, along with the less exciting Mountain White-eye, are among the most common montane birds here. Endemic Rusty-bellied Fantails flit about in the undergrowth, with Sulphur-bellied Whistlers clambering behind. With luck you may encounter the other endemic montane whistlers: Yellow-flanked and Maroon-backed Whistlers.

Colourful mistletoe flowers attract Scarlet Honeyeaters and one of the two special endemic honeyeaters, the White-eared Myza. With its blackish plumage and bluish eyeskin, the latter is quite different from the rather drab, so-called Dark-eared Myza of the lower montane forest. Feverish darting and careless chattering among the bushes in the understorey herald the arrival of one of Sulawesi's avian enigmas, the Malia, a bird that looks like a mix between a bulbul and a babbler. High in the tall trees, Crimson-crowned Flowerpeckers defy your best efforts to see any colour on them, and, if you are exceptionally lucky, a group of Sunda Serins will alight, rather than fly off, mockingly.

If you have spent a bitterly cold night in the shelter at Km Post 87, and set off uphill at 4.30 am with a torch, your expectations, like the altitude, will be high. If it is a cloudy day, the area can, at first glance, appear quite birdless. But eventually you should come across a mixed flock, containing such endemics as the large and strikingly patterned Red-eared Fruit-dove and graceful Pygmy Cuckoo-shrike foraging beside Sulawesi Leaf-warblers. The surprisingly wide-ranging Flyeater is also a possibility. Lower down in the same flock you may see Little Pied Flycatcher and the endemic Blue-fronted Blue Flycatcher, the female having a grey crown, face and throat instead of the usual brown head and orange throat and underside. But if all else fails, the gorgeous endemic Purple-bearded Bee-eater, perched on the edge of a clearing, casually swaying its orange-undersided tail, is guaranteed to lift your spirits.

Serious Twitching

For the ambitious twitcher, the real prizes are those rare, skulking thrushes of the mountain forest-floor: Sulawesi Thrush, Great Shortwing and the aberrant Geomalia. Unless you chance upon one of these crossing the track, you might try sitting quietly on a moss-covered log above a precipitous mountain slope (level ground is scarce hereabouts) and keep your eyes peeled.

Also, do not forget to watch and listen for the regionally-endemic Chestnut-backed Bush-warbler—and of course there is always the possibility of Sulawesi Woodcock! With all these attractions, and beautiful scenery to boot, it would be a stong person who could resist the lure of Lore Lindu!

–*Richard Noske*

Below: The icy stare of a Sulawesi Goshawk. *Photo by Margaret Kinnaird.*

Marvellous Mynas
of Sulawesi

An active Finch-billed Myna colony looks and sounds like a chaotic apartment building. Smoky-grey birds with red, waxy-feathered rumps nest by the hundreds in dead tree snags, using their strong, conical beaks to drill deep nest holes, where they raise two or three chicks. Hungry monitor lizards often cruise the ground floor, waiting to make a snack of any unfortunate chick that happens to fall. Highly gregarious birds, Finch-billed Mynas are rarely seen alone, even away from home. They wheel through the forest canopy in large, boisterous flocks, and you will seldom pass a day in Sulawesi's forests without encountering chattering hordes.

Mynas are members of the ubiquitous starling family: with four endemic mynas and one cosmopolitan starling, Sulawesi's collection is one of the most absorbing in Indonesia. The Finch-billed and Fiery-browed Mynas are so unlike other mynas that each is placed in its own separate genus. All the species are distributed throughout Sulawesi's sprawling peninsulas and most are catholic in habitat use; only the Fiery-browed Myna is restricted to higher elevations.

While the Finch-billed Myna may be the most flamboyant in behaviour, it is not the most smartly attired. All mynas wear basic black, but each is distinguished by a unique splash of colour. The White-necked Myna, a sleek, long-tailed bird with a startling white bib, has acquired the local name *Burung Pendeta*, or preacherbird. This vocal bird is found in pairs or small family groups along forest edges, and is often spotted in tree tops after it gives its characteristic "pop" and "whistle" calls. The rarest of Sulawesi's mynas is the retiring Short-crested Myna, with glossy plumage and contrasting white epaulettes; its most distinctive feature is its bristly head-dress worn low between the eyes. The lucky observer may spot Short-crested Mynas foraging in pairs high in the canopy or in mixed feeding flocks at popular fruit trees. The montane Fiery-browed Myna is the most stunning variant on the theme, with bold orange blazing across its brow.

Although 15-strong flocks have been recorded, these flashy birds are more often found in couples. The Asian Glossy Starling is the most modest of the group, but its green-black iridescence and startling red eyes lend a classy air. Like most starlings, it is rather common in open country, especially around human habitation.

Despite their conspicuousness, little is known about the natural history of Sulawesi's mynas. Most are believed to nest in tree holes, but only the Finch-billed Myna nests and roosts in large, raucous colonies. Mynas are important members of the fruit-eaters' society, although they include some insects in their diet. They are efficient harvesters and can easily clean out a large crop of ripe figs, one of their favourite foods, in several days. A stint spent watching these poorly known birds could very well lead to new discoveries about the secret lives of Sulawesi's mynas.

–Margaret Kinnaird & Tim O'Brien

Left: A Finch-billed Myna and her demanding offspring. *Photo by Margaret Kinnaird.* **Right:** Short-crested Myna, one of Sulawesi's least known endemic mynas. *Photo by Tui De Roy.*

Left: Nosily nesting colonies of Finch-billed Mynas in dead trees are a feature of lowland forests in Sulawesi. *Photo by Alain Compost.* **Below:** White-naped Myna, known locally as the preacherbird. *Photo by Tui De Roy.*

Birding the Northern Peninsula

Lowland Forest Birding

Tangkoko, 2 hrs by road from Manado.

Endemic kingfishers, Maleo and highest densities anywhere of Red-knobbed Hornbill.

Choice of pleasant *losmen* by the park entrance.

Full range of forest types from beach up to moss forest.

Wet season Nov–Mar, hornbills breeding in June.

Easy walking, some climbing required for higher altitude species.

Sulawesi's 500-km long, arching Northern Peninsula contains the majority of the island's remaining lowland forest. All its habitat types are found here: muddy mangrove flats, coastal forest, lowland rain forest, and elfin moss-forest high on the misty flanks of spectacular volcanoes and steep mountain ridges. Two of the most stunning yet accessible areas are the Tangkoko-DuaSudara Nature Reserve and Bogani Nani Wartabone National Park.

Tangkoko

The Tangkoko-DuaSudara Nature Reserve sits like a thumbnail on the tip of the peninsula. A 2+-hr drive from Manado, this 8,800-ha reserve is one of the most beautiful and accessible rain forests in Indonesia and, despite its modest size, offers opportunities for treks from beach forest through gently sloping lowland forest and on up to cloud forests that cling to the edges of volcanic calderas. The reserve's 3 volcanic peaks are the 1,109-m Mt Tangkoko, the ash cone of Bat-uangu (450 m), which resulted from an eruption in 1839, and the 1,351-m twin peaks of DuaSudara. Batuangu is almost bare of vegetation and has a new lava flow that extends to the sea, where a collapsed lava tunnel has formed a 400-m long cove with coral reefs and the only mangrove habitat in the reserve. The north coast is a series of crescent-shaped, sandy bays, separated by rocky headlands.

More than 150 of Sulawesi's 379 bird species have been recorded in Tangkoko, including 47 Sulawesi endemics. There are several good guides in the village who can be contacted via the PHPA post at the park entrance; with their knowledge of bird calls and the best areas, you should catch up with most of the park's specialities in a 3- or 4-day visit. In addition to endemic kingfishers and hornbills, Tangkoko boasts six endemic parrots: Green and Sulawesi Hanging-parrots, Red-spotted and Golden-mantled Racquet-tail, Blue-backed Parrot and Ornate Lorikeet. The cautious birder may also observe colourful Hooded and Blue-winged Pittas and Chestnut-backed Thrushes in the open forest understorey. Although Tangkoko

Opposite: Tangkoko's beach forest, fronted by black volcanic sand beaches. *Photo by Tui De Roy.*
Below: A rare photo of Green-backed Kingfisher. *Photo by Sunarto.*

was once famous for Maleos, their numbers have plummeted and better viewing is found elsewhere. Other highlights include friendly groups of Sulawesi Macaques, shadowed by mixed flocks of Yellow-billed Malkohas, Hair-crested Drongos and Spot-tailed Goshawks. Watching Tarsiers (one of the world's smallest primates) emerge from a daytime roost in a fig tree is a highlight at the end of any day.

Hornbill Highlights

Forest birds are notoriously difficult to see; their brilliant coloration and iridescent hues can provide effective camouflage in the darkness of the forest interior. The Red-knobbed Hornbill is an exception to the rule. It is among the flashiest forest inhabitants and impossible to miss, especially as, with an average of 51 birds per sq km, Tangkoko boasts the highest density of hornbills in the world. These gaudy birds, with their enormous, anvil-shaped bills, often weigh more than 2 kg and emit raucous barks as they soar above the canopy.

Red-knobbed Hornbill males have buff-coloured heads and sport the prominent, red casque from which they acquire their common name. Females have a glossy black head and neck and a smaller, yellow casque. Striking red chevrons decorate the base of the bill in both sexes. According to local lore, a new chevron is acquired with each year, which is why hornbills are called *Burung Tahun,* the Year Bird. Red-knobbed Hornbills normally move about in mated pairs, but flocks as large as 100 birds may be observed at fruiting fig trees. Sitting below one of these gatherings is like being in the waiting room of an international airport: the boisterous activity of feeding and squabbling over choice fruits is punctuated by swooshing departures and arrivals.

If you visit between July and December, you will be able to watch one of the 60 known Red-knobbed Hornbill nests. Every 2–3 hours, the male, his electric-blue throat pouch stretched to capacity, delivers food to his incarcerated female. Unlike other hornbills, the Red-knobbed Hornbill of Tangkoko does not use mud to make the nest door: the females have adapted to sandy, volcanic soils and a lack of mud by using a natural cement composed of digested figs and their own droppings.

Sulawesi's only other hornbill, the Tarictic Hornbill, is more of a challenge to find. This neat black and yellow bird is the smallest of the Asian hornbills. Unlike its larger cousin, the Tarictic has an inconspicuous casque, a less strident call and is much more thinly distrib-

Tangkoko-DuaSudara Reserve

Batuputih — Mama Roos' Tangkoko Homestay
Park entrance
Research Station
Tarsier fig ★
★ Beringin Lubong
Laut Sulawesi
Gn. Tangkoko 1109m
Gn. Batuangu 450m
Larva flow
Kasuari
Gn. DuaSudara 1351m
PULAU LEMBEH
Manado
Girian
Bitung
N
0 1 2 3
Kilometres

Key to Habitats

Moss forest	Lowland forest	Scrub
Montane forest	Casuarina forest	Coconut
	Disturbed Lowland forest	Grassland
	Beach forest	Mixed Cultivation

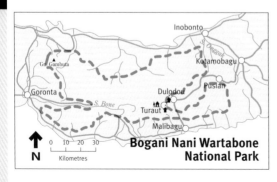

Inobonto
Gn. Gambuta
Kotamobagu
Goronta
Dulodou
Pusian
S. Bone
Turaut
Malibagu
Bogani Nani Wartabone National Park
N
0 10 20 30
Kilometres

uted. It does, however, have a more interesting family life: mid-canopy dwellers, Tarictic Hornbills live in kin groups that defend territories. During the April-July breeding season, the Tarictic male relies on the help of his older sons to provide food for his mate and new offspring.

Kingfisher Prizes

Darting with laser-like speed, Tangkoko's kingfishers pose an even greater test for the observer. They often leave no more than a blurred impression of shimmering blues, greens and purples as they dive for a grasshopper or perhaps a small fish. Ten of Sulawesi's 13 kingfisher species have been recorded in Tangkoko, and all of Sulawesi's seven endemic kingfishers inhabit its forests. A hunt for wily kingfishers covers a lot of ground, taking the explorer from mangroves to mountain-tops.

Sulawesi's kingfishers provide a textbook example of how several species with similar needs partition the environment. The Black-billed Kingfisher and the Sacred Kingfisher, an Australian migrant, are primarily coastal inhabitants, plying the beaches and mangroves for small fish, while the rare Scaly-breasted Kingfisher prefers montane forests, where it unobtrusively forages in the lower canopy for insects. Among kingfisher *aficionados*, the latter bird is the Holy Grail of a visit to Tangkoko. For those joining the search, the best bet is to head up the Puncak trail or try the area around Beringin Lubong.

Several more easily-spotted species, including the diminutive, purple Sulawesi Dwarf Kingfisher, the Green-backed Kingfisher and the more common Lilac-cheeked Kingfisher, live together in the lowland forest. Here, the forest is divided horizontally, with each species perching and foraging at a different height. Along the Batuputih stream, the Ruddy Kingfisher dominates but shares its watery feeding grounds with the Collared and

Above: Sulawesi Scopsowl, a possibility on the Northern Peninsula. *Photo by Alan Ow Yong.*

Common Kingfishers—all of which spear fish for slightly different-sized meals.

Although occasionally seen cruising the beachfront, the Black-billed Kingfisher is a muddy-boots bird; you will need to slosh through the black, sticky mud of a mangrove swamp to get a proper view. This is but one example of the challenges of getting to grips with North Sulawesi's elusive but beautiful birds.

Bogani Nani Wartabone National Park

Eight hours by car to the west of Tangkoko lies Bogani Nani Wartabone (formerly called Dumoga-Bone) National Park. At 285,000 ha, it is Sulawesi's largest protected area and a splendid birding destination. As you enter the park through

Above: A fallen tree creates a break in the canopy. *Photo by Tui De Roy.*
Below: The male Red-Knobbed Hornbill takes the prize as the wackiest of an already outrageous looking bird family. *Photo by Margaret Kinnaird.*

the Dumoga valley, it is easy to spot herons and egrets foraging in the rice paddies. Ducks, grebes and other water-loving birds wade, paddle and dive in the irrigation canals and ponds. In the past, a highlight of a trip to Bogani Nani Wartabone was a dawn visit to the Maleo nesting grounds on areas of thermal vents at Mt Ambang and Kosingolan. Unfortunately, the nest grounds have been allowed to become overgrown by scrub; as a consequence, bird numbers have dropped and it is difficult to get a clear view.

The main birding area is Turaut, where the Park Centre and accommodation is located by a river running along the edge of the forest. The swampy river and forest edge offer a good selection of birds, including Barred and Buff-banded Rails at dusk. A bridge by the Centre marks the start of the well-maintained loop trail, which gives access to some excellent forest birding. You may well see pigeons, including the attractive White-faced Cuckoo-dove and the impressive White-bellied Imperial Pigeon. It is also a promising place to scout out racquet-tailed parrots and hanging-parrots as well as Tarictic Hornbill and, at the other end of the size scale, Sulawesi Woodpecker and Sulawesi Kingfisher. Many trees on this trail are identified with placards, a bonus for the more ecologically-minded birder. However, unlike Tangkoko, the understorey of Bogani Nani Wartabone is heavily matted with rattan thickets that can make birding a frustrating experience. Once again, patience is the key.

—*Tim O'Brien & Margaret Kinnaird*

The Maleo and Other Indonesian Megapodes

Indonesia is home to 15 of the world's 22 species of megapode. They are found only to the east of Bali and nine of them occur in Irian Jaya. Unlike other birds, megapodes do not incubate their eggs by sitting on them but instead bury them in warm soil. Some species build mounds of leaves, where incubation heat is generated during the rotting process of the vegetable matter. Other species follow a seemingly less exhausting strategy by simply burying their eggs in a hole in the ground, where volcanic heating or the sun create suitable temperatures. After a long incubation period of 2–3 months, the chick hatches as deep as 1 m below ground; it takes days before it finishes its struggle to reach the surface. Once free, megapode chicks can fly immediately and, with no parents waiting for them, they have to be fully self-sufficient.

The Most Handsome of All

The most handsome of all megapodes is the endemic *Macrocephalon maleo* of Sulawesi. Its black-and-pink plumage, erect tail and grotesque helmet or cephalon (hence its scientific name) and characteristic rolling call make the Maleo a must for bird-watchers visiting Sulawesi. To incubate their large, 250 g eggs, Maleos dig holes in soils heated by hot springs, or in sun-exposed, coastal beaches. At dawn the birds descend from the trees where they have spent the night and both male and female start digging, an activity which can last all morning. Once they have reached a depth with a suitable temperature—about 34 degrees Celsius, which they measure with sensors inside their bills—the hen lays an egg. After filling the hole, the Maleos disappear into the forest, returning after about 8 days to lay again.

Some 85 so-called communal nesting grounds are known on Sulawesi, the majority in north Sulawesi. In the past these sites were visited by many pairs each day but, due to over-exploitation of their eggs, Maleo numbers have dwindled and some populations have disappeared entirely. Maleos can still be seen, though, at the nesting grounds of Tambun and Tumokang in the Dumoga Bone National Park, or at the beach at Bakiriang, just south of Luwuk in Central Sulawesi.

Other Species

In digging nest holes, the distinctive Maleo and the beautiful little Moluccan Megapode are exceptional: all the other species incubate their eggs in large mounds of rotting leaves and also lack distinctive plumage character.

The whole world population of the Moluccan Megapode is concentrated in North and Central Maluku, and they bury their eggs in just ten traditional nesting beaches. The two largest nesting beaches are on Haruku Island, just east of Ambon, and at Galela in North Halmahera. Unfortunately, because they visit the beaches by night, these mysterious birds are almost impossible to see.

–*Rene Dekker*

Above: A Maleo chick struggles to the surface.
Below: The black-and-white Maleo is the faunal mascot of North Sulawesi province. *Photos by Alain Compost.*

Introducing Maluku
The World's Forgotten Galapagos

Maluku—1,027 islands scattered across 151,000 sq km of ocean—is the world's forgotten Galapagos. It was on the famous "spice island" of Ternate in Maluku that Alfred Russel Wallace, simultaneously with Darwin, formulated the theory of evolution by natural selection, while recovering from fever in 1856. The main attraction for bird-watchers, however, is the region's 90 unique bird species. They are distributed into five distinct groups (Endemic Bird Areas) (*see pp 22–23*): The Halmahera group holds 24 unique species; the Sula Islands—8; Buru—10; Seram—21; and the island groups of the Banda Sea (Tanimbar and Kai) a further 16. So, to see them all you will need time and a penchant for adventure, jungle trekking and sea travel.

A journey in search of these specialities is definitely recommended: not only will you see some of the world's most unusual and least known birds—species such as the remarkable Wallace's Standard-wing and Invisible Rail on Halmahera, the gorgeous Salmon-crested Cockatoo and Purple naped-Lory on Seram, and the beach-nesting Moluccan Scrubfowl—but you are also sure to be captivated by a society oriented around the sea.

Previously known as the Moluccas or Spice Islands, some of the smallest islands, Ternate and Tidore—specks on the map next to Halmahera, Ambon—dwarfed by the bulk of Seram, and the tiny Banda Islands, have played a role in European history totally disproportionate to their size. The reason was spice: clove, the bud of an insignifi-

cant forest tree native to the Halmahera group, nutmeg and mace, the seed (and its waxy covering) of a rather splendid tree native to the islands of central Maluku. In past centuries, cloves and nutmeg were literally worth their weight in gold, not only to make badly preserved meat palatable but also as vital ingredients in medicines and magic potions.

Reminders of Maluku's trading past are everywhere. Portuguese, Spanish and Dutch forts are dotted throughout the islands. Some, like the old Dutch fortified trading house at Hitu on Ambon, have been lovingly restored; others—for example, Fort Oranje on Ternate—have been plastered in concrete, and scores more are just crumbling into the sea. Rusting wrecks in Kao Bay, Halmahera, a few amphibious landing craft on Morotai, and the Australian war cemetery at Tantui on Ambon are evidence of another cruel and bloody period in Maluku's history—the Japanese occupation from 1939–1945.

Today, Maluku is enjoying peace and growing economic prosperity as a result of government investment in agriculture, estate crops and transport infrastructure. The most visible manifestation of the people's improving fortunes is the church building boom currently sweeping the islands. The Moluccans are renowned for their beautiful voices and the uplifting sound of hymn singing bursting forth from packed churches is an abiding memory of this singular region.

–Paul Jepson

Previous page: A typical coastal village of Maluku in Buru. *Photo by Michael Poulsen/ BirdLife.*
Opposite: Parrots are popular pets throughout Maluku and the Purple-naped Lory is everyone's favourite. *Photo by Simon Badcock.*

Access to site.

Main birding attractions.

Type of accommodation.

Habitat.

Weather conditions.

Degree of difficulty.

Halmahera

Standardwings and Invisible Rails

Below: Anu calls out an Ivory-breasted Pitta at Tanah Batu Putih. *Photo by Morten Strange.*

Pulling into Sidangoli to the beat of *dangdut* blaring from the ferry's metre-high speakers, the view to the left is of a crane in the Barito Pacific log-pond, loading a barge destined for the plywood factory on Ambon. But to the right is a scene as pristine and beautiful as any you will find in Indonesia: a creek winds away through mangrove forest towards a backdrop of forested hills.

This is Halmahera, in shape a Sulawesi in miniature, with few people, few roads and vast forests, where logging has yet to make a significant impact. For birders it is home to 24 species of bird found nowhere else in the world, including the aptly named Invisible Rail

and Wallace's greatest find—the Standardwing bird-of-paradise. For decades an island so far off the beaten track that only one ornithologist ventured there between 1932 and 1986, Halmahera is now a surprisingly easy place to see some very special birds.

A Birder's Best Friend

This is due in part to the daily flights to Ternate, the famous neighbouring spice island, from Manado or Ambon, but it is mainly because the first adventurous birder chanced to meet Deminaus Bagadli (or Anu, as he is universally known), a farmer with a natural tal-

1 hr by ferry to Halmahera, 8 km further to Kali Batu Putih. 3–4 day visit.

Wallace's Standardwing, Invisible Rail and 22 more North Maluku endemics.

Basic accommodation in Anu's Birdwatchers' Home.

Lowland forest, sago swamps and mangroves.

Hot and humid, very wet Apr–Aug.

Easy to moderate walking along logging track and forest trails.

ent for birding, who has since become host, friend and ace guide to visiting birders.

Anu's "bird-watcher's home", a very basic *losmen*, is located in a dip to the right of the road at Tanah Batu Putih, 8 km along the road out of Sidangoli. Forested hills rise up behind the house, making it a great place to hang out and get into some serious birding. Finding it is simple: just climb into any of the *bemos* meeting the ferry and ask for Tempat Burung Bidadari (*bidadari*, or fairy bird, is the local name for the standardwing). Nowadays, Anu is often away working on conservation projects, so it is best first to call in at his brother's shop, *Toko Mandiri*, in Domato village, to make arrangements. If Anu is not around, his detailed birders' log will point you in the right direction.

Standardwing Leks and a Megapode Beach

The first morning's excursion at Tanah Batu Putih is the short pilgrimage to the Wallace's Standardwing lek. Just before dawn, Anu will guide you across the stream below his house and up a short, steep trail to a small clearing in the forest. Here, in the cool dawn, two or three male standardwings perform their display flights. Shadows at first, but, as the light improves, the iridescent breast spurs and four strange, white, elongated feathers become visible. What a bizarre bird!

Brilliant though it is, this standardwing lek is pitifully small. If you have three or four days and really want an unforgettable experience, ask Anu to take you to the lek tree of a hundred or more birds he discovered during the 1995 BirdLife International surveys. Getting there is a great journey, which starts with a 4-hr bus ride to Tobelo, followed by 2 1/2 hours by speedboat across the magnificent Kao bay to the village of Lel Lief. The display tree is just a 4-km trek away.

This trip is easily combined with a visit to another truly remark-

able bird phenomenon—the world's largest nesting beach of Wallacean Scrubfowl. The PHPA office in Tobelo will give permission to visit the 1.6-km long, black sand beach, which is pitted with the nest burrows of this extraordinary bird.

The beach owners harvest the eggs in an apparently sustainable manner. At least, for nearly a hundred years they have been collecting the eggs, and hundreds of scrubfowl still arrive each night to lay their single, massive egg.

Back at Tanah Batu Putih

But back to dawn at Tanah Batu Putih, where the next great bird identifies itself with a wolf whistle: the Ivory-breasted Pitta. Pittas are notoriously difficult to see but, with patience and stealth, you should be successful with this one. If you use

Far Above: The endemic Rufous-bellied Triller is common in secondary growth. **Above:** The remarkable Wallace's Standardwing. *Photos by Morten Strange.*

ging track, across the road from Anu's home, or along the road, where the greater openness makes it easier to spot Halmahera's other specialities. In the early morning or late afternoon, White Cockatoo, Chattering Lory and Blyth's Hornbill fly noisily overhead, and you will be rewarded with views of Blue-capped Fruit-dove, White-naped Monarch, Paradise Crow, Halmahera Cuckoo-shrike and Rufous-bellied Triller, to mention just a few of the endemics. Midday is the time to raptor-watch for Gurney's Eagle, backed by a magnificent panorama looking west to Ternate and Tidore, from a high-point 2 km up the main road.

Sago Swamps

No visit to Tanah Batu Putih is complete without at least an attempt to see the Invisible Rail. The species had not been seen for 35 years when Anu rediscovered it in 1995 in a sago swamp, a 30-minute hike inland from Sidangoli. You really will need luck to see this rarity, though Anu will undoubtedly be getting better at finding it, but, even if the rail remains invisible, the Great-billed Heron nest Anu can show you will certainly make the trip worthwhile.

By nightfall, you will be exhausted from a hard day's birding, but make the effort to return to the logging trail to search for Moluccan Owlet-nightjar. The sight of this strange bird, caught in a torch beam, will end a never-to-be-forgotten trip to Halmahera.

–*Paul Jepson*

Above: A parrot catcher, fully equipped with decoy birds, a coconut containing sticky resin and a back-pack cage. *Photo by Paul Jepson/BirdLife.*
Right: Buff-banded Rail, a common bird of wet grasslands and rice paddies throughout east Indonesia. *Photo by Michael Poulsen.*

tape-playback, seeing this splendid pitta, with its black head, cool white underparts and bright red vent, should not be difficult. If necessary, Anu will expertly whistle one into view for you!

During a 3–4 day visit the prospect of finding Nicobar Pigeon will draw you back to this fascinating hillside, but the favoured birding areas are along the log-

The Banda Islands

Seabirds and Imperial Pigeons in Maluku's Paradise Islands

The Bandas, a cluster of nine hilly islands rising out of the Banda Sea about 140 km southeast of Ambon, are Maluku's premier tourist destination. Breath-taking scenery, world class diving and snorkelling, crumbling and restored forts and Dutch villas—reminders of Banda's once inordinate importance in European history—along with the island's friendly, easy-going atmosphere are the draw. For birders, a small but interesting bird fauna is an added attraction.

Most people stay in Bandaneira on Banda and budget a minimum of three days to see the island's sites and speciality species. The two other main islands, Banda Besar and Gunung Api, are only 10–15 min away by speedboat.

Probably the first bird you will see is the beautiful turquoise-and-white Collared Kingfisher, whose ringing *kee-kee* calls follow you everywhere, or perhaps a Spotted Kestrel, hovering overhead. Several bird species difficult to see elsewhere in Maluku are common in and around Bandaneira. The hyperactive Rufous Fantail, flocks of bright yellow Lemon-bellied White-eyes and colourful Crimson Myzomela all visit the flowering bushes in hotel and homestay gardens, and Island Whistler can be found in scrub or clove and nutmeg plantations outside the village.

The best forest is found on the neighbouring island of Banda Besar: although little primary forest remains, good patches of closed forest survive on the slopes and hill-tops. The island can be walked end-to-end in half a day—on landing,

simply head inland on one of the many trails. Blue-tailed Imperial Pigeon is abundant and impossible to miss with its loud, continuous, booming calls. It feeds on large nutmeg fruits, digesting the meat and mace and passing the nut. Look also for two beautiful little fruit-doves, Wallace's and Rose-crowned. Both have bright orange bellies but the male Wallace's is recognised by its cool grey neck and breast and red crown. The neck of the Rose-crowned is washed with green and the rose colour is on the forehead only. Kai Cicadabird is another speciality of the island's forests.

The rocky, sandy and coral beaches surrounding the islands are good for waders on migration. Fifteen species have been recorded so far: Whimbrel, Grey-tailed Tattler and Common Sandpiper are the common species but look out also for rarities such as Little Curlew. Pied Herons and Australian Pelicans are regular visitors in small numbers from Australia.

Highlights of the sea journey to or from Banda are large flocks of Lesser Frigatebirds and Red-footed Boobies, which often associate with schools of hunting dolphins, but you should also see Wedge-tailed Shearwater, Greater Frigatebird, Brown Booby and Sooty Tern. Seabird enthusiasts can arrange a trip from Banda to Manuk Island, Indonesia's largest seabird colony, where thousands of frigatebirds and boobies nest, along with smaller numbers of Brown Noddies and Red-tailed Tropicbirds. The peak breeding months are April and May.
   –Michael Poulsen

Less the an hour by air from Ambon.

Imperial Pigeons, fruit doves, shore- and seabirds.

A lovely hotel and *losmen* in old colonial atmosphere.

Tiny islands covered in nutmeg groves, some forest.

Pleasant tropical climate. Rains Apr–Aug.

Plenty of short walks, some climbing.

Manusela National Park

In Search of Exquisite Parrots

Seram, the "mother island" from which the people of the region believe they all originate, dominates the map of central Maluku. Stretching 340 km from east to west, this 17,470 sq km island, three times the size of Bali, will end the 20th century as it began it—as a place of mystery and adventure with awesome mountains, endless forests and a forbidding interior.

For parrot enthusiasts, Seram is exceptional. Its 11 parrot species include two found only on Ambon and one on Ambon and Seram: two of these three must rate as among Indonesia's, if not the world's, most exquisite parrots. They are the subtle pink Salmon-crested Cockatoo and the intelligent, multicoloured Purple-naped Lory.

For birders with a penchant for tropical ecology, the 1,890 sq km Manusela National Park, which straddles the centre of the island, is fascinating; capped with the bare volcanic plug of Mt Binaya, which thrusts up through magnificent limestone peaks and escarpments, Manusela embraces an exceptional range of habitats, from mangroves and nipa palm swamps, through freshwater swamps and lowland forest, up into montane rain forest.

But Seram does not give up its treasures readily. Although made a national park in 1982 and the subject of a major Operation Raleigh scientific expedition in 1987, Manusela (the name means "bird of freedom") is still without many basic park facilities. To appreciate the area and find Seram's 21 endemic bird species, you will need time, a willingness to trek through forest—sometimes up to your knees in mud—to put up with rain and leeches and to survive for days on end on a diet of rice and noodles.

Trekking Routes

A number of trails cross the park from Wahai on the north coast to Mosso or Hatumete on the south. They can be tackled in either direction, but the climb out of Mosso is extremely strenuous: it is known locally as the "path of sorrow", a reference to a time in the colonial era when villagers were forced to move to the coast. So it is best to start from Wahai, which, in addition to the 5-day, cross-island trek, offers options for 5- or 6-day circular treks up to the Manusela valley inhabited by the indigenous Alifuru people, and back to the north coast via the Kobipoto ridge, or down the Isal river valley (see Practicalities).

Wahai

The pleasant coastal village of Wahai is a day's journey from Ambon. Early each morning direct buses leave Ambon's Merdeka bus terminal, cross to Seram by ferry and continue to Saka, a small collection of huts and a jetty nestling by the side of enormous cliffs on Seram's north coast. Public speedboats meet the buses in the late afternoon and whisk you off on an exhilarating, 2-hr dash along the coast to Wahai. As you pass the spectacular limestone cliffs—the end of a rugged ridge which still

A day by road and boat from Ambon. 8 days to trek up to the Manusela valley.

21 endemic species, including Salmon-crested Cockatoo.

Losmen in Wahai, in the park: villages, shelters and caves.

Mangrove and Neap swamps, flooded rainforest though up to high altitude elfin forest.

Hot and humid. Heavy rains Apr–Sep.

A tough jungle trek, only for the adventurous. Carry in food.

defies the road engineers—look out for flocks of migratory Australian Pelicans loafing on sandbanks.

Just 8 km to the east of Wahai is the boundary of a broad swathe of the National Park that sweeps down to the sea. A day spent birding along the road that runs through it to Pasahari provides a superb introduction to Seram's birds. Species to look for here include Gurney's Eagle, Oriental Hobby and Pacific Baza soaring over the forest edge, Lazuli Kingfisher in partially cleared areas, Metallic Pigeon, Claret-breasted Fruit-dove and Long-crested Myna in the swamp forest and Common Bush-hen in the grasslands. You will soon be over familiar with the ubiquitous, explosive *pprow* calls of Seram Friarbird, the island's most common endemic. It is so accurately mimicked by the Black-naped Oriole that most people leave Seram unsure whether they have really seen the oriole. With the help of the National Park rangers, a number of pleasant "off road" excursions can be arranged in this area: you can walk to the edge of the mangroves or through the swamp forest, or even float down the rivers to the sea on a bamboo raft.

Either on the way out or back (depending on the tides) check out the mangrove-lined mud-flats in Air Besar Bay, just 2 km east of Wahai. There are usually a few Australian Ibises around and a good range of shorebirds—and the possibility of Channel-billed Cuckoos—in the migration season. The small patch of forest behind the quay is good for Common Paradise-kingfisher.

Into the Interior

Park rangers will act as your guides for longer treks into the park; supplies can be bought in Wahai. The best birding route is a circular, 7–10 day trek from Wahai to Kanikeh and Selumena in the Manusela valley, returning to Wahai via the Kobipoto ridge and the Mual plains. However, many people like to trek

Above: A village elder of Manusela wearing a ceremonial head dress of Salmon-crested Cockatoo feathers. *Photo by Simon Badcock.*

across the island, continuing on from Selumena to Manusela and then crossing the Binaya ridge to Mosso on the south coast. A third option is to return from Selumena to Pasahari by a less interesting, 3-day hike down the Isal valley, which forms the eastern border of the park. The village of Kanikeh, at the entrance to the cultivated Manusela valley, is a 4-day walk from Wahai (3 days if you really move).

Spend the first two days on the trail that leads to the village of Roho; it passes through a logging concession where the forest is disturbed, but this does not detract from the birding. Raucous screeches will alert you to groups of Salmon-crested Cockatoos, either flying overhead or collecting in a roosting tree. Listen also for the strident call of the Lazuli Kingfisher, sitting high on an exposed vantage point. Other notable species on this

of the fabulous Purple-naped Lory, which feeds on flowering rattan or the red fruits of a climbing pandan.

The inhabitants of Kanikeh, a village of 60 houses on a ridge above the Wae Ule river, have supplemented their meagre incomes for at least 50 years by catching Purple-naped Lories and trading them on the coast. Using a decoy lory, villagers attract wild lories to nylon snares wrapped around exposed branches. A good decoy lory is a treasured family possession. Around Kanikeh look out for Drab Myzomela in the tree tops. Bicoloured Darkeye is common in the area and there is a good chance of Nicobar Pigeon, Cinnamon-chested Flycatcher and Black-fronted White-eye.

Searching for Mountain Specialities

The higher montane forest above 1,600 m is home to Seram's third endemic parrot species, the Blue-eared Lory, and such mountain specialities as Long-tailed Mountain-pigeon, Spectacled Honeyeater, Crimson Myzomela (between 700–1,400 m), Island Thrush and the little-known Moluccan Thrush (between 800–1,300 m) and Grey-hooded Darkeye. The trails over the Kobipolo and Binaya ridges both reach sufficient altitude for these, but only the trail to the summit of Mt Binaya climbs high enough to enter the alpine forest habitat of Seram's unique, white-headed race of Island Thrush.

Kanikeh is the base for the 4-day return trek to the summit of Mt Binaya (2,850 m), where spectacular views await the intrepid. It is essential that you take a local guide, warm clothes and a tent. Wae Hulu, a camp with water at 2,050 m, is reached after a 6–7 hr hike, and it is a further day to the camp just below the summit.

From Kanikeh it is an 8-hr, straight walk to Manusela; Selumena is about half way. After climbing out of the Kanikeh valley

Above: The Black Sunbird livens up gardens and forest edges throughout Maluku. *Photo by Morten Strange.*

part of the walk are likely to be Forsten's Megapode (recently split off from Orange-footed Scrubfowl as a separate species), Pale Cicadabird, Moluccan Cuckoo-shrike, Spectacled Monarch, Streak-breasted Fantail and Long-crested Myna.

After Roho, the trail enters uncut forest and steadily climbs a ridge. The forest here is stunted and bird densities are relatively low. However, views of Moluccan King Parrot, Blyth's Hornbill, White-bibbed Fruit-dove, Golden Bulbul and Rufous Fantail will maintain your interest until, after 3–4 hrs, the trail drops down to the Wasa Mata river and an overnight shelter.

If your time is limited you may wish to press on to Kanikeh, a further 4- to 5-hr walk. But this section of the trail passes through a beautiful mosaic of bamboo and mid-montane forest which is worth giving time to, especially as it is the habitat the trail drops into a wide, undulating valley and mostly follows the river through a mosaic of fruit gardens, sago palms, rattan and bamboo within secondary forest. The birding is excellent, so allow plenty of time or stay at the village of Selumena. After Selumena there are several rivers to be forded, but it is *extremely dangerous* to attempt this if they are in flood following a rainstorm, and there is no option but to camp and wait until morning.

The trail from Manusela to the south coast provides another opportunity to catch up with the mountain specialities; the fern zone at 2,000 m is reached after a hard, 3–4 hr, uphill climb. There is no water on these limestone ridges and you need to be fit and tough to make it over the top and down to Mosso in a day.

Even though there is a certain satisfaction in trekking across the island, it would be a pity to miss out on the great birding to be found on the trail back to Wahai via the Kobipolo ridge. The first night's camp, along an at times near vertical trail, is at a cave near the Mahala waterfall, up on the ridge at 1,220 m; the next day takes you down through pristine lowland forests into the swamp forest of the Mual plains. The large, mammal-like droppings of Southern Cassowary are everywhere. If you are lucky you may disturb a cassowary on the trail, but the birds can smell and hear you long before you approach. The best way to see one is to climb a tree that is dropping fruit, and wait patiently. The flightless cassowaries have been on Seram for thousands of years but, as it is an oceanic island, they must have been introduced by man from their native New Guinea.

During the 7-hour walk to Solealama, and the next day's walk to the village of Solea along the River Toloarang, try to find a tree in fruit where you can get good views of the canopy—perhaps at the edge of a river—and spend some time watching Superb and Claret-breasted Fruit-doves, which are some of the most wonderfully coloured and patterned pigeons in the world.

Wherever you finally return to civilisation, you will certainly be tired, filthy and dreaming of a *mandi* and good meal. But without doubt you will savour the memory of a remarkable birding adventure.

–Paul Jepson & Simon Badcock

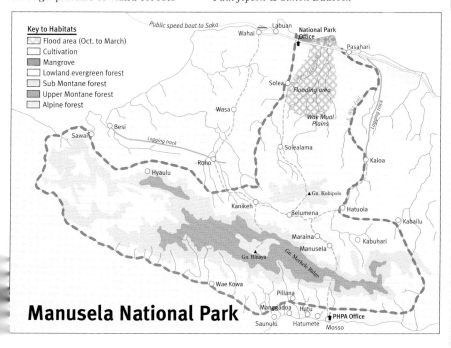

Key to Habitats
- Flood area (Oct. to March)
- Cultivation
- Mangrove
- Lowland evergreen forest
- Sub Montane forest
- Upper Montane forest
- Alpine forest

Public speed boat to Saka · Labuan
Wahai · National Park Office · Pasahari

Solea · Flooding area
Wasa · Wae Mual Plains
Besi · Sawai
Logging track
Hyaulu · Roho · Solealama · Kaloa
Kanikeh · ▲ Gn. Kobipolo
Selumena · Hatuola · Kabailu
Maraina · Kabuhari
Manusela
Wae Kowa · ▲ Gn. Binaya · Gn. Markeh Ridge
Pillana
Manggadoa · Hatu · PHPA Office
Saunulu · Hatumete · Mosso

Manusela National Park

Introducing Irian Jaya
Indonesia's Last Birding Frontier

The vast forests of New Guinea, the world's second largest island, are home to some of the most glorious birds on Earth. Bowerbirds, birds-of-paradise, crowned pigeons, cassowaries, palm cockatoos and vulturine parrots are the most famous, but even a cursory flick through the wonders depicted in Bruce Beehler's *Birds of New Guinea* will leave you wondering why birders are not flocking here in their thousands.

It may be because the region still conjures up an aura of mystery, and of stone age tribesmen inhabiting vast forests where only the most intrepid tourist would dare venture. Enticingly, the Indonesian province of Irian Jaya, which constitutes the western half of New Guinea, is rapidly gearing up for tourism, and a selection of the amazing birding to be found in the Arfak and Cyclops mountains, the Baliem Valley and the savannahs of Wasur is now accessible to any reasonably fit person with four weeks' holiday.

Irian Jaya is a massive and diverse region; its 421,981 sq km constitute 22% of Indonesia's total land area. New Guinea's most distinctive topographical feature, a 2,000 km long cordillera of mountains running down the centre of the island, is topped by Puncak Jaya in the Sudirman range, at 4,884 m the highest peak between the Himalayas and the Andes. The south-facing slopes of this range drop sharply to flat coastal swamps that reach 300 km inland. The northern slopes descend more gradually, with rolling foothills down to the vast Mamberamo Basin. In the west, the province is dominated by the distinctive Bird's Head Peninsula and Bintuni Bay, which has some of the world's most extensive mangrove swamps.

Complex patterns of bird distribution mirror this topography: of the 649 species recorded, 101 are endemic to New Guinea (Irian Jaya has 39 endemic species) and these are grouped into eight Endemic Bird Areas (*see pp 22–23*). Forest bird communities are notably different from elsewhere: they have an unusually high proportion of fruit and nectar eaters and ground birds, but no wood borers (woodpeckers).

Irian Jaya's ethnic diversity is no less remarkable; over 250 language groups are documented. The Dani are perhaps the best known. Another famous ethnic group is the Asmat, natives of the vast swamps along the south coast. Until quite recently, they were notorious for their fierce, headhunting culture, but nowadays it is their wood carving that catches attention.

Irian Jaya was the last territory to be relinquished by the Dutch—handed over to Indonesia by a UN transitional administration in 1967. Indonesianisation has not been totally smooth. The government's transmigration policy—whereby people are relocated from overpopulated Java—and environmental concerns associated with the massive Freeport copper mine are ongoing sources of tension. For the bird-watcher, however, Irian Jaya affords a chance not only to see wonderful birds but an opportunity to step into a world quite unlike anywhere else on Earth.

–Paul Jepson

Previous page: A group of Australian Pelicans fish peacefully on an Irianese back-water.
Opposite: Northern Cassowary—great skill is required to sight these remarkable birds in the forests of Irian Jaya. *Photos by Alain Compost.*

Access to site.

Main birding attractions.

Type of accommodation.

Habitat.

Weather conditions.

Degree of difficulty.

The Arfak Mountains
An Adventure Off-the-Beaten Track

Below: Bower of the Vogelkop Bowerbird.
Photo by Dr Magnus Aurivillius.

The isolated Arfak mountain range, in the far east of Irian Jaya's Vogelkop Peninsula, is home to nine bird species found on the peninsula and nowhere else on Earth. Some stunning and little-known birds, including nine birds-of-paradise, await the birder with three or more days to spend in the pristine forest.

The Arfaks rise to an elevation of 2,200 m and the best way to reach them is from the port of Manokwari by a 3-passenger plane chartered from the Missionary Aviation Fellowship. Any spare days waiting for a flight can be usefully spent birding the coastal forest near Manokwari: Maruni or Warkapi should offer plenty of sightings of lowland birds such as the striking Common Paradise and Hook-billed Kingfishers, Magnificent Riflebird

and King Bird-of-paradise. Rain permitting, two days or so around here, coupled with five days in the Arfaks, should produce more than 130 species.

Trekking along the Nggribou Ridge

The short hop over the ridge to the village of Mokwam in the heart of the mountains takes 15 minutes. Most of the region's specialities can be found a short distance into the mountains, but, as the walking is strenuous in the steep terrain, it is advisable to hire porters. A suggested walking route is along the Nggribou ridge, followed by a hard but straightforward 3-day trek back to the lowland road, from where it is a further 35 km to Manokwari.

Fly in by missionary plane from Manokwari, walk out. 4 days.

9 species of bird-of-paradise, torrent lark.

Camping on ridges, take food and porters.

Montane rain forests.

Warm and humid, cold at night. Wet season Nov–Apr.

Tough jungle trekking up and down steep valley sides.

At Mokwam the trek starts down the steeply sloping airstrip and along a path leading into the forest beyond the village. With luck you will soon see birds such as White-eared Bronze Cuckoo and Magnificent Bird-of-paradise before the trail drops steeply into the valley of the River Profi. It then follows the river for about 1 km, and here you can see the thrush-sized, black-and-white Torrent-lark, wagging its tail and flitting between rocks in the rapidly flowing water. The hardest part of the trek follows: a 4–5 hr, 1,000 m scramble up to the ridge between Mt Nggribou and Mt Umtjin—the first night's camping spot. The steep terrain and dense vegetation make birding quite difficult here.

Arfak Prizes

The biggest prizes on the ridge are the spectacular Black- and Buff-tailed Sicklebills and Arfak Astrapia, which are easiest to see early or late in the day. To see the shy Buff-tailed Sicklebill, you need to persevere with following up its repeated, whistling call.

Although much drabber, the endemic Vogelkop Bowerbird is renowned for its extraordinary, hut-like bower, decorated with separate piles of blue berries and red flowers. Several of its bowers can be found along the ridge trail, which is also home to an exceptional variety of robins, including Ashy, Smoky and Black-throated Robins, and the skulking Spotted Jewel-babbler and Lesser Ground Robin. Look and listen for a mixed-species flock, as they often contain gems such as Garnet Robin and Tit Berrypecker.

Finding the Long-tailed Paradigalla

A good place to spend the next night or two is in the large but basic hut at Binibei (1,500 m elevation), a comfortable day's walk along the ridge nearly as far as Mt Nggribou,

with a final steep descent of a few hundred metres. This is where to find the very rare Long-tailed Paradigalla, "rediscovered" in this region in 1989 and sometimes seen in the trees just below the hut.

Early morning can be a hive of activity with parotias, honeyeaters and difficult-to-find species such as Black Pitohui all in evidence here. It is possible to walk down to the road from here in a day, but better to take two days as some interesting birds, including the gaudy Flame Bowerbird, White-rumped and Green-backed Robins, Dwarf Whistler and Black-winged Monarch, are found only at lower elevations.

Pay off the porters when you reach the road at Tana Mera, near Warmare village; it should be easy to hitch a lift on a passing truck back to Manokwari.

–*Jon Hornbuckle*

Above: Artist's impression of Long-tailed Paradigalla. *Drawing by N Arlott.*

pressing against its flanks, this bird resembles an ornament dropped from the curls of a gouri and floating idly in the layer of air that encircles our planet's crust."

New Guinea is synonymous with birds-of-paradise. A few species extend to the northern rainforests of Australia and two species occur on Halmahera in Maluku, but the island of New Guinea supports 38 species, 30 of which may be encountered in Irian Jaya.

Wanderers f

❝They are wanderers from paradise", the people of Tidore evasively told the Portuguese sea captain, El Cano, in 1521, when he enquired as to the source of the exquisite feathers they showed him. The Tidoreans had no intention of revealing the source of these gorgeous feathers, the Vogelkop Peninsula of Irian Jaya, for they were worth more than gold.

Since the 14th century, when their plumes graced headdresses at Turkish courts, birds-of-paradise have surpassed all other bird groups in the imagination, superstition and scientific wonder they have aroused. Educated Europeans were tantalized by the accounts of early explorers such as Thomas Forrest, who wrote in his book *The Breadfruit Tree* (1784): "Birds of Paradise glisten like seldom glimpsed denizens of an Asiatic harem who are clad in gold of many hues and dipped with the purple of dawn". For centuries the myth survived that these birds were footless and lived only in the air; as late as 1760, the father of taxonomy, Carl Linnaeus, named the largest species *Paradisaea apoda*—"without foot"—a result of the Aru Islanders' method of preserving skins by cutting off the feet and wings.

These old accounts do not describe a bygone age: many bird-of-paradise species are still quite common and not difficult to see (although local knowledge is required to find the "courts" where males perform their spectacular displays). Replace "gun" with "camera" in this 1824 account by Rene P. Lesson, the first naturalist to observe birds-of-paradise in the wild; the same experience still awaits travellers in Irian Jaya. "The view of the first Bird of Paradise was overwhelming. The gun remained idle in my hand for I was too astonished to shoot. It was like a meteor whose body, cutting through the air, leaves a long trail of light. With the ornamental plumes

Diversity of Plumage and Displays

The Greater and Lesser Birds-of-paradise, with their long, fluffy, golden flank plumes and group displays, perhaps epitomize the popular image of the species. The family is actually quite varied: sicklebills, riflebirds, astrapias and manucodes are all birds-of-paradise. The sicklebills display singly, their pectoral shields of iridescent breast feathers spread upward like raised arms. The Black Sicklebill is the largest of the birds-of-paradise and its immense, 80-cm long tail is a traditional adornment on headdresses in the Wahagi valley.

Like sicklebills, riflebirds also possess curved bills, but they are stocky, short-tailed birds. During display, the iridescent, blue-green throat feathers of the black males are extended to a dazzling triangle and exhibited with a rhythmic jerking or whirring around on an exposed branch. The manucodes are thrush-sized birds with glossy purple, green or blue plumage; they lack the elaborate courtship displays and are probably close to the founding stock of starling or crow-like ancestors.

Around the turn of the century, bird-of-paradise plumes were New Guinea's most important resource; for more than 20 years, between 25,000 and 30,000 skins a year were exported from Merauke, and the total from New Guinea may have exceeded 80,000 in peak years.

And yet this formidable plume industry ceased at the onset of World War I, never to resume. Shocked by the sudden extinction of birds such as the Passenger Pigeon, public sentiment was easily aroused in the early years of the century. After a highly publicized campaign to halt the nauseous stripping of plumes from live egrets, conservationists quickly turned their attention to birds-of-paradise. Soon any woman wearing plumes was viewed with disdain and the lucrative trade went into a rapid decline.

The merchants, anxious to counter the conservationists' claims, asked the eminent New Guinea naturalist, A E Pratt, to draw up a report. He concluded that "so long as New Guinea remains underdeveloped, paradise birds will thrive, because the conditions under which they are killed preserve both the young males and the females". This biological assessment was right, but public sentiment won through: in 1924 the trade was banned and the local people returned to fishing and making sago, and collecting plumes only for traditional, ceremonial use. *–Paul Jepson*

m Paradise

Top left: Wilson's Bird-of-paradise is only found on the island of Batanta off the Vogelkop Peninsula.
Far left: The male King Bird-of-paradise performs its acrobatic displays.
Left: Male Lesser Bird-of-paradise display in leks of 40 or so birds.
Right: A King Bird-of-Paradise shows off its gorgeous iridescent throat feathers. *Photos by Alain Compost.*

The Plume Trade

No less remarkable than the birds is the story of their exploitation, which was brought to an abrupt end by one of the first public conservation campaigns. The birds' economic value was once very significant: in the 1880s a Blue Bird-of-paradise skin brought £20 in Port Moresby, and the skin of a Greater, £1. Income from bird-of-paradise plumes, in high demand from the millinery markets of Paris, Amsterdam and London, bridged the 7-year gap between the planting and harvesting of copra in the new colonies in New Guinea.

Lake Sentani and the Cyclops Mountains

Birding Outside Irian's Capital

The hot and steamy town of Jayapura, between the hills and sea, is the capital of Irian Jaya province. A week exploring inland from Jayapura—Lake Sentani and the lowland forests around the Cyclops Mountains—will be rewarded with birds such as Pesquet's Parrot, Palm Cockatoo and Lesser Bird-of-paradise.

After arriving at Sentani airport, about 40 km inland from Jayapura, you will need to go into Jayapura to get your permits—*surat jalan*—to visit other parts of the country.

Peaceful Lakeside Birding

Sentani Falls, on the northern side of the township, is an area of mixed lowland rainforest, re-growth and gardens. Birds to look for include

Irian's bird emblem, the spectacular Lesser Bird-of-paradise, with its gorgeous pale yellow plumes and velvety green throat. You may also see Blyth's Hornbill, easily located thanks to its honking call and noisy "whooshing" flight, as well as forest specialists like Rusty Mouse-warbler, Yellow-bellied Longbill, Variable Pitohui and Black-sided Robin.

The magnificent 9,600-ha, Lake Sentani is within a 15-min drive from the airport. Along the shoreline are picturesque houses on stilts built out over the water, and small swamps with pink waterlilies. Comb-crested Jacanas step carefully on the lily pads. White-browed Crake skulk in the swamps, revealing their presence by their squeaky calls. Here you will also find Buff-banded Rail, Black-throated Little Grebe, Black Bittern and a variety of ducks.

Towards the western end of the lake there is a good area of remnant vegetation and re-growth; search here for Black and Yellow-bellied Sunbirds, the rare black Jobi Manucode, Rusty Pitohui, Emperor and White-shouldered Fairy Wrens, Yellow-billed Kingfisher, Red-cheeked Parrot, cuckoo-doves, and Orange-fronted Fruit-dove.

At the extreme western end of the lake is a guardhouse barrier (show your *surat jalan* to pass). The 4–5 km stretch of road beyond is a treasure trove of birding highlights: the chance of seeing Pale-billed Sicklebill and other birds-of-paradise, the myriad parrots from tiny pygmy parrots to the giant Pesquet's Parrot, and the ease of seeing spectacular birds such as

Charter a vehicle for 4–5 days.

Bird-of-paradise, Victoria Crowned Pigeons, great diversity of other forest species.

Losmen at Lake Sentani, elsewhere camp.

Lowland forest and swamp forest.

Hot and humid. Driest months May–Sep.

Flat walking along forest trails, often muddy and flooded.

Golden Cuckoo-shrikes. A stroll along the road enjoying the evening flights of the majestic Palm Cockatoos and the numerous Blyth's Hornbills is one of life's great birding experiences.

Nimbokrang—Where the Birding Really Takes Off

Nimbokrang, a transmigration settlement just west of Genyem (65 km; 3 hrs west of Sentani), is a good base for exploring the bird-rich lowland alluvial forest at the base of the Cyclops Mountains. There are no tourist facilities in the area, so hire a car and driver in Sentani, and camp.

Along the drive to Genyem, stop at surviving patches of forest to look for Jobi Manucodes, and at the Deweruba Telecom Repeater Station (signposted) for a variety of common forest birds.

Nimbokrang I and II are the names of transmigration settlements. Although forest around Nimbokrang is being cleared for agriculture, huge areas remain intact and the roads and side paths provide access into the forest depths. In Nimbokrang I, find Jamil, an old bird-trapper and excellent guide, who will help you find those dream birds.

The roadside is mostly lined with pools and swamps with Yellow-billed Kingfishers, Shining Flycatchers, and Greater and Lesser Black Coucals. The forest edge along the road is superb for birds-of-paradise. Pale-billed Sicklebills, and Twelve-wired Birds-of-paradise—black and yellow with bright pink legs—perch conspicuously on snags above the canopy or feed inside the forest. Lesser Birds-of-paradise are very common, but you will find it is easier to hear the loud, ringing calls of Glossy-mantled Manucodes than to see the birds themselves.

Hunting has driven Victoria Crowned Pigeons, the largest pigeons in the world, deep into the forest and seeing them needs lots of time and the expert guidance of Jamil. The effort is worth it—as big as a turkey, these blue-grey pigeons have a maroon breast and an erect crown whose filamentous blue-grey feathers are tipped with white.

A Profusion of Parrots

Parrots are everywhere in these forests: look for Salvadori's Fig-parrot and Red-flanked Lorikeet. Red-cheeked and Eclectus Parrots are common. Flocks of Rainbow Lorikeets, Brown and Black-capped Lories and Sulphur-crested Cockatoos fly noisily through and feed in the canopy. Buff-faced Pygmy Parrots feed quietly on moss on tree trunks and Double-eyed Fig-parrots on fruits.

Two shy inhabitants of the forest interior are Northern Cassowary and Brown-collared Brush Turkey. Seeing a cassowary is mainly a matter of luck, but the brush turkey can be seen by patiently stalking a calling bird or waiting at an incubator mound.

–Margaret Cameron

Left: Pesquet's Parrot, is sometimes called the Vulturine Parrot on account of its unusual bill. *Photo by Alain Compost.* **Below:** The massive Palm Cockatoo surely rates as the most impressive of all parrots. *Photo by Margaret Kinnaird.*

IRIAN JAYA

The Baliem Valley

High-altitude Birding in Spectacular Scenery

Below: The discovery of the densely populated valley in 1938 by American explorer Richard Archbold caused an international sensation. *Photo by Alain Compost.*

2–3 flights a day from Jayapura to Wamena. 5–6 days for Habbema trek.

High altitude species ie, Snow Mountain Quail & MacGregor's Bird-of-paradise.

Camp in shelters along the trail.

Alpine swamp grasslands, moss forest, montane forest and cultivation.

Warm by day, cold at night. Wet months Nov–Apr.

Steep and slippery, but otherwise straightforward downhill trek.

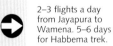
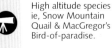

The Grand Baliem Valley in the central highlands of Irian Jaya, home of the Dani tribe, lies at about 1,600 m. It runs through the Snow Mountains, which are well-forested from about 1,800 m and 3,000 m and above which lie the alpine grasslands and ultimately the snow-capped peaks of Irian's highest mountains.

The forests and grasslands of the Baliem Valley hold some fabulous birds, including seven or eight birds-of-paradise. The best way to see them and enjoy the culture of the region is to make a 5+-day trek to or from Lake Habbema. There are potentially over 100 species to find here, but it will probably take at least a week to reach this target.

The trek can be made alone but the most pleasant way is to hire a guide and porters at Wamena airport. Then charter a jeep to Lake Habbema, a 90-minute drive up a new road that goes over a pass due west of the Baliem Valley. The lake lies in alpine grasslands, with a wonderful panorama of rugged, snow-capped mountains beyond. Salvadori's Teal and Spotless Crake are at the lake, while the grasslands hold the large Snow Mountain Quail, Alpine Pipit and Snow Mountain Munia. Spend a day in the grasslands, as the Quail is difficult to find, and you may be rewarded with other birds such asSwinhoe's Snipe and Eastern Marsh-harrier. A nocturnal foray, if it is not raining, could produce Eastern Grass-owl and the rarely recorded Horsfield's Woodcock.

The trail from Lake Habbema back east to the Baliem Valley crosses a 3,200 m high pass and then follows the Ibele Valley down to the village of Dyela. Flowering shrubs at the pass are good for Goldie's Lorikeet, Painted Tiger Parrot, New Guinea Thornbill and high-altitude honeyeaters such as Sooty and the endemic Orange-cheeked and Short-bearded. However, the star here is the almost

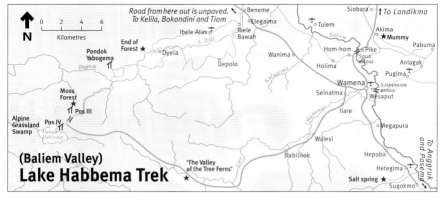

(Baliem Valley)
Lake Habbema Trek

mythical MacGregor's Bird-of-paradise, a striking black bird with brilliant gold primary feathers, difficult to see elsewhere in New Guinea. It is shy and retiring, but, with perseverance, can be found around here.

The Moss Forest

Beyond the pass, the trail passes initially through conifer dominated forest—where Lorenz's Whistler is possibly the commonest bird—before entering the stunted elfin forest, less than an hour's walk away. There is a very basic hut (at post 3) for sleeping, although camping is preferable. Key species here include the skulking Lesser Melampitta and Greater Ground Robin, the gaudy Crested Berrypecker, the tiny Alpine Robin and the wary and local Archbold's Bowerbird. The latter's bower, made of a mat of ferns, may be found a few hundred metres back down the trail. Mountain Nightjar is a possibility in flight at dusk or dawn, and Loria's Bird-of-paradise has been recorded.

The next day is a 3-hr walk to a forest hut below the trail at a clearing called Yabogema. A second night could be profitably spent here as birding can be exciting, with Chestnut Rail and a good selection of parrots including the handsome Papuan Lorikeet, usually of the melanistic phase, and both Brehm's and Modest Tiger-parrots.

From Yabogema the trail follows a narrow river, where you may have to wade, along a spectacular gorge to a ridge, before dropping down to the village of Dyela, a trek of some 4–6 hrs. This is the eerie world of the dripping moss forest, with trees covered in hanging lichens and creepers, the habitat of unusual birds such as Blue-capped Ifrita, Wattled Ploughbill, Brown Sicklebill and King of Saxony Bird-of-paradise. The large but secretive Sicklebill proclaims its presence by a staccato, machine-gun-like call, and the King of Saxony "sings" from a high bare branch, displaying its long, white head plumes.

It is worth having a full day at Dyela to bird the scrub and forest patches for lower-elevation species, such as the common Black-breasted Munia (an endemic), Common Golden Whistler and Superb Bird-of-paradise. Colourful parrot-finches—both Blue-faced and the scarce Papuan—occur here but great care is required to tell them apart.

Back to Wamena

The trail now leads through farmland, to Ibele bridge (3–4 hrs), where transport back to Wamena (1 $^1/_2$ hrs) can be arranged. The idea of returning to "civilisation" may be disappointing after such exciting birding, but will be well rewarded by a decent bed, a hot shower and good food! The building of new road towards Jayapura is inevitably leading to forest degradation so the next few years are likely to be the best time to explore this region.

–Jon Hornbuckle

Wasur

A Small Piece of Australia in Indonesia

As little as 10,000 years ago the southern coast of New Guinea was joined to Australia by the vast swamp area known as Lake Carpentaria—the largest lake ever known in the Australia and Torres Strait area. Rises in sea level at the end of the last ice age cut off this land bridge but the Merauke region in southeast Irian Jaya remains essentially a remnant of Australia in Indonesia. It is a distinct avifaunal region in New Guinea known as the Trans-Fly.

Wasur National Park

Just 20 mins drive from Merauke, the only town in the region, Wasur offers unparalleled, easy access to most of the habitats represented in the Trans-Fly. The park protects some 413,000 ha of vast, treeless plains, open savannah woodlands dominated by paperbark and eucalyptus trees, large swamps and denser forests on the river margins, which can all be visited in a 3–4 day trip. The park is best visited in the dry season (August–December) as neck-high water levels in the swamps in the wet season make access difficult unless you do not mind travelling in dug-out canoes surrounded by clouds of mosquitoes.

Paperbark Swamps and Grassy Plains

A 3-day circular trip starting at the park's coastal gateway at Ndalir, a 20-km drive (30 min) south of Merauke, is an excellent way to see most of the area's specialities.

There are good areas of beach forest interspersed with the ubiquitous coconut palms along the coast from Ndalir—where groups of Australian Pelicans congregate offshore—south to Tomer. A sandy track follows the coast here but it is also possible to walk along the beach—the intertidal mud-flats are good for a range of migrant waders and waterfowl from Australia (July–August) and Siberia (October–March). Blue-faced Honeyeaters favour the coconuts and Spangled Drongos are abundant dry season visitors from Australia in August to December. Pied Imperial Pigeon is also common.

From Tomer the track turns inland southeast to Tomerau, entering denser paperbark swamp. Small tidal creeks are bounded by mangroves, the favoured habitat of the New Guinea Flightless Rail. Palm Cockatoos are locally common. In patches of denser monsoon forest search for species typical of this habitat such as Little Friarbird, Noisy Pitta, and Rufous-bellied and Spangled Kookaburra. At Tomerau head northeast along a track in savannah woodland interspersed with monsoon forest that eventually leads out on to the plains at Ukra. Watch for Noisy Friarbird, Blue-winged Kookaburra, Papuan Frogmouth and flocks of Little Corella.

At Ukra spend a day birding in the plains and swamps that border the Fly River. Although not yet officially on the Indonesian list, Trans-Fly endemics such as Black Mannikin and Fly River Grassbird and the more widely distributed White-spotted and Grey-crowned

20 min drive from Merauke. 3–4 days.

Huge abundance of birds.

Stay with villagers.

Vast plains, swamps and savannah.

Dry season Aug–Dec. Flooding at other times.

Flat walking, in wet season travel by dug-out.

Mannikins have recently been sighted in the large expanses of reed-beds here. At the peak of the dry season (November–December) it is usually easy to find Southern Cassowary drinking at remaining water areas in the early morning. Vast numbers of Brolgas (cranes) and Magpie Geese congregate with commoner spoonbills, egrets, herons and ibises. Australian Bustards display during the heat of the day and the eerie cries of Bush Stone-curlew fill the air at night. This area is also good for raptors—Little and Wedge-tailed Eagles, Whistling Kite and Swamp Harrier.

Greater Bird-of-paradise

From Ukra continue northwards to Rawa Biru village and take the track to Yanggandur, where there is a guest-house. Some 200 m from the guest-house is a Greater Bird-of-paradise display tree (around August the birds still have their tail plumes). At dawn listen for the strident *wank wank wank* call and then stalk the birds, which are usually high in the canopy. From Yanggandur head back 8 km along a dirt road to the Trans-Irian Highway and return to Merauke—about 2 hr/50 km once you reach the road. If you have time, stop on the Highway at Wasur village to visit one of the nearby sago swamps (Mbur or Kumbi) where there are good chances of seeing Southern Crowned Pigeon.

The Maro River

It is possible to walk as far as the Maro River from Wasur, but it is a long hike. An alternative is to hire a local boat to take you up the meandering river. Lined by tall canopy monsoon and vine forest, the park side offers better viewing because there is less disturbance by settlement. Bythe's Hornbill and Great-billed Heron should be easily spotted. The real reason for the trip though, is the possibility of spotting the King Bird-of-paradise. Despite the brilliant ruby red colouring of the male, they are hard to spot, preferring to skulk in tangles of vines. But if you do see one, what could be a more fitting end to a visit to Wasur's birding bonanza?

–*Michele Bowe*

Below: Wasur's mosaic of swamps and paper-bark woodlands. *Photo by M Silvius/Wetlands.*

PERIPLUS TRAVEL MAPS
Detailed maps of the Asia Pacific region

This five-year program was launched in 1993 with the goal of producing accurate and up-to-date maps of every major city and country in the Asia Pacific region. About 12 new titles are published each year, along with numerous revised editions. Titles in **BOLDFACE** are already available (32 titles in mid-1996). Titles in *ITALICS* are scheduled for publication in 1997.

INDIVIDUAL COUNTRY TITLES
Australia	ISBN 962-593-150-3
Burma	ISBN 962-593-070-1
Cambodia	ISBN 0-945971-87-7
China	ISBN 962-593-107-4
Hong Kong	ISBN 0-945971-74-5
Indonesia	ISBN 962-593-042-6
Japan	ISBN 962-593-108-2
Malaysia	ISBN 962-593-043-4
Nepal	ISBN 962-593-062-0
New Zealand	ISBN 962-593-092-2
Singapore	ISBN 0-945971-41-9
Thailand	ISBN 962-593-044-2
Vietnam	ISBN 0-945971-72-9

AUSTRALIA REGIONAL MAPS
Brisbane	ISBN 962-593-049-3
Cairns	ISBN 962-593-048-5
Darwin	ISBN 962-593-089-2
Melbourne	ISBN 962-593-050-7
Perth	ISBN 962-593-088-4
Sydney	ISBN 962-593-087-6

CHINA REGIONAL MAPS
Beijing	ISBN 962-593-031-0
Shanghai	ISBN 962-593-032-9

INDONESIA REGIONAL MAPS
Bali	ISBN 0-945971-49-4
Bandung	ISBN 0-945971-43-5
Batam	ISBN 962-593-144-9
Bintan	ISBN 962-593-139-2
Jakarta	ISBN 0-945971-62-1
Java	ISBN 962-593-040-X
Lake Toba	ISBN 0-945971-71-0
Lombok	ISBN 0-945971-46-X
Medan	ISBN 0-945971-70-2
Sulawesi	ISBN 962-593-162-7
Sumatra	ISBN 0-945971-47-8
Surabaya	ISBN 0-945971-48-6

Tana Toraja	ISBN 0-945971-44-3
Ujung Pandang	ISBN 962-593-138-4
Yogyakarta	ISBN 0-945971-42-7

JAPAN REGIONAL MAPS
Kyoto	ISBN 962-593-143-0
Osaka	ISBN 962-593-110-4
Tokyo	ISBN 962-593-109-0

MALAYSIA REGIONAL MAPS
Kuala Lumpur	ISBN 0-945971-75-3
Malacca	ISBN 0-945971-77-X
Johor Bahru	ISBN 0-945971-98-2
Penang	ISBN 0-945971-76-1
West Malaysia	ISBN 962-593-129-5
Sabah	ISBN 0-945971-78-8
Sarawak	ISBN 0-945971-79-6

NEPAL REGIONAL MAP
Kathmandu	ISBN 962-593-063-9

THAILAND REGIONAL MAPS
Bangkok	ISBN 0-945971-81-8
Chiang Mai	ISBN 0-945971-88-5
Phuket	ISBN 0-945971-82-6
Ko Samui	ISBN 962-593-036-1

Distributed by:

Berkeley Books Pte. Ltd.
(Singapore & Malaysia)
5 Little Road, #08-01, Singapore 536983
Tel: (65) 280 3320 Fax: (65) 280 6290

C.v. Java Books (Indonesia)
Jl. Kelapa Gading Kirana
Blok A-14 No. 17, Jakarta 14240
Tel: (62-21) 451 5351 Fax: (62-21) 453 4987

MISS YOUR LOVED ONES BACK HOME?
PUT YOURSELF IN THE PICTURE WITH 001

When you're far away from home, nothing brings you closer to loved ones than a phone call. And it's so easy with 001. Indosat offers International Direct Dial to over 240 countries. Plus, you save 25% during discount hours on weekends*, and around the clock on national holidays and weekends. Call today, and share the good times!

IDD = **001** | COUNTRY CODE | AREA CODE | TELEPHONE NUMBER

From Hotel = HOTEL ACCESS CODE | **001** | COUNTRY CODE | AREA CODE | TELEPHONE NUMBER

001 IDD | **NUMBER ONE** 🌀 **INDOSAT**

* For information, call 102.

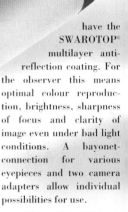

CONTENTS

PRACTICALITIES

Introduction, Area Practicalities, Appendix

The following Practicalities sections contain all the basic information you need for your journey.

We open with an **Introduction** that contains a **Travel Advisory**, which provides background information about travelling in Indonesia, a section entitled **Know Before You Go**, and a special chapter on **Birding-watching Tips**, as well as a language primer, with extra bird names in Indonesian.

The **Area Practicalities** sections focus on each destination and contain details on transport, accommodation and dining, along with plenty of general information relating to administration and National Park access. These sections are organized by area and correspond to the first half of the guide.

The **Appendix** contains a complete checklist of Indonesian birds and other relevant information compiled especially for birders.

Travel Advisory

Getting to Indonesia

In many ways, Indonesia is an easy place to get around. Indonesians are as a rule hospitable and good-humoured, and will always help a lost or confused traveller. The weather is warm, the pace of life relaxed, and the air is rich with the smells of clove cigarettes, the blessed durian and countless other wonders.

On the other hand, the nation's transportation infrastructure does not move with the kind of speed and efficiency that western travellers expect, which often leads to frustration. It is best to adjust your pace to local conditions. The golden rule is: things will sort themselves out. Be persistent, patient and good-humoured.

You can fly to Indonesia from just about anywhere. Most people travelling from Europe and the US arrive on direct flights to Jakarta, while those coming from Australia generally first go to Bali. The main international entry points are Soekarno-Hatta airport in Jakarta, Ngurah Rai airport in Bali and Polonia airport in Medan, North Sumatra. Singapore Airlines now flies direct from Singapore to Surabaya in East Java, and Mataram on Lombok. Manado in Sulawesi now has direct flights from Singapore and from Mindanao, in the Philippines. Several flights from the US stop at Biak in Irian Jaya, which has regular flights to Jayapura.

Direct flights connect Jakarta and Bali with many major cities in Asia and Europe. Air fares vary depending on the carrier, the season and the type of ticket purchased. A discount RT fare from the US or Europe costs from $850; about half that from Australia or East Asian capitals. Airport tax for departing passengers is Rp25,000 for international routes and Rp15,000 for domestic flights.

You can also enter Indonesia by ferry. From Malaysia and Singapore there are daily ferries to Belawan (near Medan) in North Sumatra. In 1997 a twice weekly ferry service is scheduled to start between Darwin in North Australia and Kupang in Timor.

Visas

Nationals of the following 46 countries do not need visas if they arrive at any major air- or seaport, and are granted visa-free entry for 60 days upon arrival (this is non-extendable). For other nationals, visas are required and must be obtained in advance from an Indonesian embassy or consulate.

Argentina, Australia, Austria, Belgium, Brazil, Brunei, Canada, Chile, Denmark, Egypt, Finland, France, Germany, Greece, Hungary, Kuwait, Iceland, Ireland, Italy, Japan, Liechtenstein, Luxemburg, Malaysia, Maldives, Malta, Mexico, Monaco, Morocco, the Netherlands, New Zealand, Norway, the Philippines, Saudi Arabia, Singapore, South Korea, Spain, Sweden, Switzerland, Taiwan, Thailand, Turkey, United Arab Emirates, United Kingdom, United States, Venezuela, Yugoslavia.

Before leaving for Indonesia check that your passport is valid for at least 6 months after your proposed date of arrival and has at least one empty page to be stamped.

Other Visas

The 2-month, non-extendable tourist pass is the only entry permit that comes without a great deal of paperwork. A visitor's visa, first valid for 4–5 weeks, can be extended for up to 6 months, but can only be obtained with a letter from a sponsoring agency in Indonesia. A business visa, valid for 30 days and extendable to 3 months, requires a letter from a company stating that you are performing a needed service for a company in Indonesia. This is not intended as an employment visa, but is for investors, consultants, or other business purposes.

If you want to conduct any sort of formal research, a research permit is required. This is obtained from the Indonesian Institute of Sciences (*see page 276*) and involves a great deal of paperwork. The process takes a minimum of 6 months and, even with the research permit, at least a week is required after arrival to complete the formalities—first in Jakarta and then in the research location.

Three other types of visas are available: government services visa (*visa dinas*), the temporary residence visa (KITAS) and permanent residence visa (KITAP). All are extremely hard to get.

Customs

Narcotics, firearms and ammunition are strictly prohibited. The standard duty-free allowance is: 2 litres of alcoholic beverages, 200 cigarettes, 50 cigars or 100 grams of tobacco. There is no restriction on import and export of foreign currencies in cash or travellers cheques, but there is an export limit of 50,000 Indonesian rupiah.

The use, sale or purchase of any narcotics will, once caught, result in long prison terms and huge fines. Several westerners are currently serving sentences as long as 30 years for possession of marijuana.

Keeping Your Cool

At government offices such as immigration or police, talking loudly and forcefully doesn't make things easier. Patience and politeness are virtues that open many doors in Indonesia. Good manners and neat dress are also to your advantage.

Getting Around

Within Indonesia, your travel choices will depend, as always, on time and money. Possibilities range from boats, trains, self-drive and chauffeur-driven cars, to both slow and fast buses. Hiring a car or minibus, with or without a driver, is a rewarding way of getting around, if you can afford it.

In fact, getting around in Indonesia is not for those used to efficient and punctual transportation. Bookings are often difficult to make and flights and reservations are sometimes mysteriously cancelled. However, what seems like nerve-wracking inefficiency is really so only if you are in a hurry. If you need to be somewhere on a particular day, allow plenty of time to get there. Check and double check your bookings. Otherwise, just go with the flow. You can't just turn off the archipelago's *jam karet* ("rubber time") when it's time to take an airplane and turn it on again when you want to relax. You will get there eventually.

Peak periods around holidays and during the July–August tourist season are the most difficult. It is imperative to book well in advance and reconfirm your bookings at every step along the way. Travel anywhere during the week of the Islamic Lebaran (Ramadan) holiday (1997 in mid-February, moving forward 11 days each year) is practically impossible. Find a nice spot and sit it out.

Domestic Air Travel

The cardinal rule is book early, confirm and reconfirm often. If you are told a flight is fully booked, go to the airport anyway and queue up. Garuda's booking system is computerized, but the other airlines' are not, and bookings evaporate at the last minute all the time.

Always keep the following points in mind:
☛ It's practically impossible to get a confirmed booking out of a city other than the one you're in. You can buy an OK ticket, but don't believe it until you reconfirm with the airline in the city of departure.
☛ Reconfirm bookings directly with the airline office in the city of departure between 24 and 72 hours before your flight. Your seat may be given away if you reconfirm either too early or too late (or not at all).
☛ Make bookings in person, not by phone.
☛ Get written evidence of bookings.
☛ Note the computer booking code. Concrete proof of your booking is essential.
☛ If your name isn't on the computer try looking under your first or middle names as these are frequently mistaken for surnames.
☛ If you are told a flight is full, go to the airport about two hours before departure and ask that your name be put on the waiting list. See that it is. Hang around the desk and be friendly and you will probably get on the flight. A tip will sometimes, but not always, help.
☛ Generally, students (12–26 years old) receive a discount of 10–25% (show an international student ID card) and children between the ages of 2–10 pay 50% of the regular fare. Infants not occupying a seat pay 10% of the regular fare. Ask the airlines or travel agent.

Garuda Indonesia's flagship airline has been in business for 46 years. It serves all major cities in Indonesia and at least 38 international destinations. They fly only jets, mainly wide-bodies, and the service is reasonably good. Offices in Jakarta are at BDN Building, Jl Thamrin 5, ☎ (021) 2300925; fax (021) 334430; Borobudur Hotel Intercontinental, Jl Lap. Banteng, ☎ (021) 2310023; fax (021) 3310448; Hotel Indonesia, Jl Thamrin, ☎ (021) 2300568; fax (021) 2300870; Wisma Dharmala Sakti, Jl Sudirman 32, ☎ (021) 2512286; fax (021) 3512276.

Ferry Routes (Pelni)

2000 PAX
1. Kerinci
2. Kambuna
3. Rinjani
4. Umsini
7. Tidar
11. Ciremai
12. Dobonsolo

1000 PAX
5. Kelimutu
6. Lawit
8. Tatamailau
9. Sirimau
10. Awu
13. Leuser
14. Binalya
15. Bukitraya
16. Tilongkabila

——— every 14 days
------- every 28 days

N

0   200   400   600
Kilometres

BABUYAN Is.

LUZON

MANILA

THE PHILIPPINES

POLILLO Is.

CATANDUANES I.

MINDORO

SAMAR

PANAY

NEGROS   BOHOL

CEBU CITY

LAWAN

MINDANAO

DAVAO CITY

BASILAN I.

Lirung

Kwandang
Gorontalo
Bitung
Ternate

Toli-toli

Luwuk   WAIGEO

Pantoloan

Kolonedale   MISOOL   Sorong   Manokwari   Biak

BIRD'S HEAD
PENINSULA   Serui   Sarmi

Parepare   SERAM   Fakfak

Kendari   Nabire   IRIAN
JAYA   Jayapura

E   S   Ambon   Kaimana   A

UJUNG
PANDANG   Raha   Banda   Timika   NEW
GUINEA

Baubau

Larantuka   Kalabahi   Dobo   Agats

L. Bajo   Tual

Maumere   Saumlaki   Merauke

Ende   Dili   Kisar

apu   TIMOR   Alternate Kelimutu route
(between Kupang and Dili)

SUMBA   Kupang

AUSTRALIA

Merpati A Garuda subsidiary, with a huge network of domestic flights serving more than 160 airports throughout Indonesia. Merpati (literally "pigeon") flies smaller jets (DC-9s and F-28s) as well as turbo-props (F-27s, Twin-Otters and locally-made CN 212s and 235s). Merpati has an awful reputation for its lack of punctuality, its lax service and ageing planes; however, it does at least connect remote towns and villages all across Indonesia. Baggage allowance is 20 kilos for economy class, but some of the smaller aircraft permit only 10 kilos (after which excess baggage charges of $1 per kilo apply). Main office: Jl Angkasa 2, Jakarta. ☎ (021) 4243608; fax (021) 4246616.

Sempati A privately-owned airline with quality service and a growing network inside and outside of Indonesia, it is the first choice of regular domestic travellers. Sempati flies new F-100s to several cities in Asia, such as Singapore, Kuala Lumpur, Bangkok, Hong Kong and Taipei. Domestically they fly between major cities such as Jakarta, Surabaya, Denpasar, Kupang, and Ambon. Head office: Ground floor terminal building, Halim Perdana Kusuma Airport, Jakarta. ☎ (021) 8094407; fax (021) 8094420.

Bouraq A small, private company, flying mainly older planes linking secondary cities in Java, as well as Bali, Kalimantan, Nusa Tenggara, Sulawesi, Maluku and other destinations. It is reasonably punctual and reliable. Main office: Jl Angkasa 1–3, Jakarta. ☎ (021) 6595364; fax 6008729.

Mandala Operates a more limited number of routes to Kalimantan, Sumatra and Sulawesi. Main office: Jl Garuda 76, Jakarta. ☎ (021) 4249360; fax 4249491.

Sea Travel

There is four times as much sea in Indonesia as land, and for many centuries transportation among the islands has been principally by boat. Tiny ports are scattered all over the archipelago, and the only way to reach many areas is by sea.

To travel by boat, you need plenty of time. Most ships are small, and are at the mercy of the sea and the seasons. Think of it as a romantic journey, and don't be in too much of a hurry.

Pelni Pelayaran Nasional Indonesia has ten modern German-built passenger ships criss-crossing the archipelago carrying up to 1,500 passengers. (See route map at back for destinations served). Fares are fixed, and

there are up to 5 classes; the first and second class cabins are comfortable.

Head office: 5th floor, Jl Gajah Mada 14, Jakarta 10130. ☎ (021) 3844342/3844366; fax (021) 3854130. Main ticket office: Jl Angkasa 18, Kemayoran. ☎ (021) 4211921. Open in the mornings.

In the eastern isles a fleet of old car ferries links the larger islands and ports. These can be cheap and efficient, especially as most sail overnight. The drawbacks are that most places only have a weekly or twice weekly service and outside the port it's virtually impossible to get reliable information on sailing days. Below deck tends to be noisy and crowded. Use your luggage to stake out a spot early, and bring a straw mat to lie on.

There are myriad other options. Wooden coastal steamers ply the eastern islands, stopping at coastal villages to pick up copra, seaweed and other cash crops and deliver commodities such as metal wares, fuel and the occasional outboard motor. You can book deck passage on one of these ships in just about any harbour, for very little money. If you do, stock up on food—you will quickly tire of the rice and salt fish that the crew eat. Bring a waterproof tarpaulin and a bag to protect your gear. You can often rent bunks from the crew to get a comfortable night's sleep.

In the eastern archipelago, larger villages not yet connected by road are generally served by public speedboats, which carry up to 20 passengers and connect with buses. These, or powered longboats, can usually be chartered to get to more out-of-the-way places, but charters are relatively expensive ($70 or more for a 1–2 hr journey) and the speedboats, especially, are over-powered and dangerous. If you have no other travel option, make sure you travel in the early morning when the sea is calm. Never go if the sea looks rough or the weather uncertain, and try to take a life-jacket.

Small *perahu* can be rented in many areas, by the hour or for the whole trip, for birding up rivers, in mangroves, around the coast or to neighbouring islands. Inspect any boat carefully before hiring it, as some craft are scarcely seaworthy. See if the boatman can rig up a canopy to block the blazing sun or the rain, and make sure camera and optical equipment is stowed in waterproof bags.

Travel Overland

Road conditions in Indonesia have improved dramatically over the past years, but traffic has also increased and driving is a slow and hazardous affair. Trucks and buses, minivans, swarms of motorcycles piled with goods or carrying a family of four, ox-drawn carts, bicycles and pedicabs *(becak)* and pedestrians of all ages compete in what is at times a crazy battle for tarmac, where the biggest and fastest rule. Rental cars and motorcycles are available in many major cities, and a number of buses run cheap and regular services.

Indonesia has only 8,000 km of railroad track, all of it on Java, Madura and Sumatra, and most of it dating from Dutch times. Only on Java is there a real system, running the length and breadth of the island.

Travelling by Air

Air transport is considerably more costly but also much faster than land or sea travel. From Jakarta to Surabaya takes an hour by plane, for example, while the fastest bus or train will take at least 12 hours. Travelling to Ambon in Maluku by the Pelni ferry from Jakarta will take three days, whereas a morning flight from Jakarta will have you in Ambon by the early afternoon. Obviously, if time is limited, this is the only way to travel—and, considering the distances, by international standards fares are quite reasonable. Flights from Jakarta to Bali cost $96 one way, but travelling further east is more expensive: return tickets from Jakarta to Kupang cost $380, to Manado $420, Ambon $450 and Jayapura $575.

The domestic network is organised around hubs: Jakarta, Bali and Ujung Pandang (Sulawesi) are the most important for birding itineraries. In the east it is difficult to fly directly between major cities (eg Kupang and Ambon) and you have to fly into a hub and then out again. As most flights leave these hubs in the morning and return in the afternoon, an overnight stay is often necessary when travelling cross-country by air.

The domestic airline, Merpati, operates "pioneer services" to smaller and more remote destinations. These are frequently cancelled and it is often not possible to book a return reservation, or even buy a return ticket. This leaves you open to the vagaries of the local Merpati agent at the destination (often the local hotel owner) and you may have to wait several days to get a seat out. In remote areas, you will have to take mission planes.

Travelling by Train

Train travel is a great way to see Java and can be very cheap, depending on which class

ticket you buy. First class trains travel at night; they are good, but first class tickets do not always guarantee a seat when you get on the train. Resort to 2nd and 3rd class only if your budget insists.

There are two basic rail routes across Java: a north coastal route running Jakarta–Cirebon–Semarang–Surabaya; and a southerly route Jakarta–Bandung–Yogyakarta–Surakarta–Surabaya. In addition, there are feeder lines running from the west coast to Jakarta, Semarang–Yogya and east of Surabaya (connecting with a ferry and bus to Bali at Banyuwangi).

Travelling by Bus

The preferred mode of transportation for Indonesians, the night express buses or *bis malam* operate only at night. They are available in a wide variety of classes: from the public *patas* air-conditioned with reclining seats (crowded, run by the army) to the ultra-luxurious "Big Top" buses that run from Jakarta (these have seats like business class airline seats).

The better buses have a toilet and arctic air-conditioning: the other reason you brought a sweater. The key to successful *bis malam* trips is sleep. Choose the best bus available, as the price difference is usually not very great and justifiable in that a good sleep is saving you a night's accommodation. There are also karaoke "sing-along" buses for masochists and anthropologists only.

Most buses are fitted with video screens and show movies whether you want to watch them or not. These are often followed by music. You are likely to be the only one who is annoyed by the volume, but a cheerful suggestion that the music be turned off *(dimatikan)* will at least get it turned down to the point where earplugs can block out the rest. The seats to avoid are in the very front and the very back. The back seats are raised up over the engine and don't recline, while front row seats give you too intimate a view of what the driver is doing.

Tickets are sold at the bus terminal, or by ticket agents. Usually there will be a number of different buses going your way. Shop around, check out the seats, or the photos if the buses are not there yet, to see what you are getting.

The other category of buses are the local buses. The major advantages of these rattling buses is that they are extremely cheap, run every few minutes between major towns, and can be picked up at the terminals or any point along their routes. This is also their biggest disadvantage: they stop constantly. They also have the annoying habit of touring round the town looking for customers and returning, sometimes two or more times, to the bus station before finally departing.

If you leave from a terminal, find a seat near a window that opens. Try not to share this breeze with passengers behind you; they are likely to have a strong aversion to wind for fear of *masuk angin* (the wind that enters the body and causes a cold).

Seats in the rear offer a more spine-jarring ride than the front. The seats are very small, both in terms of leg room and width. You and your bag may take up (and be charged for) two seats. This is fair. But be sure you're not being overcharged for not knowing any better. Ask someone what the proper fare is to your destination before getting on. A few words of Indonesian are indispensable to be able to ask for directions. People are generally very eager to help you.

Larger towns have city buses *(angot)* charging nominal fares, usually Rp350 (15c). Flag them down wherever you see them. The catch is knowing which one to take as there are seldom maps or guides.

Local Minivan (*Bemo/Colt*)

These non air-conditioned vans or *bemos* are the real workhorses of the transport network, going up and down small roads to deliver villagers and produce all over the island. Regular seats of *bemos* are supplemented by wooden benches, boosting the capacity of these sardine cans to 25. Take a seat up front with the driver whenever possible.

There are standard fares (Rp1,000–3,000 depending on distance), but these are flexible to account for how much room you and your bag are taking up. You can also charter one to most destinations. Just say "charter" and where you want to go, then bargain for the fare in advance.

In really out-of-the-way places, where road conditions are still appalling, trucks serve the function of *bemos*. Usually they have fixed benches, but sometimes just rough planks slung across the back or standing room only. As they are usually operated by a shop owner in the local town who transports supplies to local villages, you need to ask around the town to find who goes where and when. The truck back is invariably open to the sun, rain and wind, so be prepared with a hat, umbrella or tarpaulin.

Motorcycle Taxi (*Ojek*)

Where the *bemo* routes end the *ojek* takes over. These are local guys looking to earn a few extra rupiah, who will take you as a pillion passenger wherever you want to go, and save you that hot and tiring last few kilometre walk into a National Park or to the edge of a forest. Prices are negotiable: normally about Rp500 per kilometre, with a minimum charge of Rp1,000. Don't forget to arrange a date and time for your pick-up (but there's only a 50:50 chance they will turn up if you don't send a confirmation message with somebody going back). *Ojek* can also be hired by the day or half day. When negotiating a price, a good basis to work on is that the driver will be expecting to make Rp10–15,000 in a day on top of his fuel and food costs.

Chartering Vehicles

Chartering a car or minibus can be the best way to get around as you have the freedom to stop whenever you see something and the flexibility to check out interesting looking sites, but responsibility for the vehicle lies with the driver. If you are birding as a team, this is also a very economical way to get around. Prices vary and costs are higher on the outer islands, where vehicles, parts and fuel are more expensive. Asking around (start at your hotel or *losmen*) will quickly give you an idea of where to hire a driver and what the local rates are for a specific excursion or longer itinerary. A full days' driving one-way will cost from $50 to $80 and a 5-day trip around $300. Much of this is for gas, so distance travelled is a major factor and a less efficient vehicle like a jeep will cost more per day than a van. Most of the rest goes to the owner of the vehicle, with a tiny percentage left for the driver.

It is understood that you will pay for the driver's meals and accommodation both while he is with you and on his journey back home. A tip of Rp5,000 per day is appropriate.

The quality of both the driver and the vehicle will figure heavily in the enjoyment of your trip, so don't be shy about checking both out before striking a deal. The air-conditioning should work well enough to overcome the midday heat and the vehicle should be clean and comfortable. If the driver knows about the area you are visiting and can speak some English, so much the better. Travel agents can also arrange such charters for you. Stock up on water and snacks and head out early in the day.

Car Rentals

At first glance the unwritten driving rules of Indonesia seem like a maniacal free-for-all. It is only later that the subtle hierarchy (truck vs car: you lose) and finesse (2-cm tolerances) become evident. This is as good a reason as any that self-drive car rentals are expensive in Indonesia, with the exception of Bali, where car hire is abundant and relatively cheap. The most popular vehicles are Suzuki Jimnys, a small jeep that will seat two with luggage, four without (about $25 per day with insurance) and Toyota Kijangs, which can seat up to 9 without luggage, 5 with (about $30 per day inclusive). To drive in Indonesia you need a valid international driver's licence.

Motorbike Rental

Hiring a motorbike is an appealing proposition; it adds to the sense of fun and adventure and provides the freedom to check out forest areas, creeks, bays and mangroves accessible only via narrow tracks or paths. But this is only for experienced motor-cyclists, who should still think carefully about risks and safety before choosing this mode of transport. The roads are dangerous, and it's not just other traffic: potholes and ruts can be hard to determine, especially when you are wearing sunglasses, and on old roads patches of exposed bitumen heated by the sun have the same effect as hitting black ice. Indonesian crash helmets are virtually useless and there are no emergency services to speak of. Whatever your condition, you will be relying on a kindly truck driver to take you to the nearest hospital, which then will have only limited facilities. Except on Bali, it is virtually impossible to hire a motorcycle with insurance, so you will be responsible for paying if the bike is stolen or for any damage incurred.

Planning an Itinerary

The first thing to realize is that you can never cover the entire archipelago, even if you were to spend months or years here. Don't make yourself an impossibly tight schedule. Be aware that distances are great and travel slow. Better to spend more time in fewer places. You'll see more this way, not less.

Below are four 3–4 week and two overland birding itineraries that maximise both the range of species seen and time spent in the field.

1. **Sumatra and West Java:** In terms of getting a massive trip list with plenty of endemics, combining West Javan sites with Way Kambas and/or Kerinci, south and west Sumatra, is hard to better. There is a great itinerary, starting with a search for Javan Coucal in the tiny marsh reserve at Muara Angke in Jakarta, followed by a few days' cleaning-up on the montane forest endemics at Mt Gede/Pangrango National Park outside Bogor. Then head to the far west peninsula to see Green Peafowl and other lowland rainforest specialities at Ujung Kulon National Park before crossing to Sumatra to see highly prized species—Storm's Stork and White-winged Duck at Way Kambas and Schneider's Pitta and Sumatran Cochoa at Kerinci. Alternatively you can fly from Singapore to Padang in Sumatra and then, after visiting Kerinci, travel down to Way Kambas and across to Java.

2. **East Java:** There is a wonderful, circular 2–3 week itinerary commencing from Surabaya, Java's second largest city. The tour starts with a visit to the Brantas Delta to look for Asian Dowitchers and other waterbirds, then heads east along the north coast to Baluran National Park and its Green Peafowl, with a stopover to experience a sunrise over the awesome volcanic scenery of Mt Bromo/Tenggara. A short diversion can be made across to Bali Barat National Park from the ferry terminal at Banyuwangi, before swinging round south back on Java to the lowland reserves of Alas Purwo and Meru Betiri. Continuing west, the loop is completed after a relaxing sojourn at the peaceful environmental centre at Trawas, in the hills above Malang. Naturally, this can also be done as an add-on to Bali.

3. **Java Overland:** For those with more time available, the above two itineraries can be linked with birding stopovers on the overland journey from Bogor to Surabaya. In Bandung, three hours east of Bogor, a side trip to the active Tangkuban Prahu volcano is a must. You can drive right up to the magnificent crater rim, which is surrounded by stunted elfin forest, so this is a place to see the speciality birds of Java's mountain tops: the endemic Volcano Swiftlet, Island Thrush, Mountain White-eye and, if you're lucky, Sunda Serin, with minimal exertion.

Five hours southeast by road from Bandung is the popular south-coast resort of Pangandaran, where a small national park offers gentle lowland birding, an opportunity for a little sea-watching and the possibility of stumbling across a giant *Rafflesia* flower. In the same area the back-waters between Pangandaran and Cilacap have lots of unexplored potential for water and marshland birds, including such locally rare species as Racquet-tailed Treepie, Milky Stork and Ruddy Kingfisher. The route east continues to Yogyakarta, a full day—or more usually night—bus ride away. Yogya is the cultural centre of Java and famous for the large Buddhist temple of Borobudur. The Dieng Plateau, lying between Yogyakarta and Semarang, is popular with travellers on account of its evocative landscapes, but it features on few birders' itineraries, for the good reason that the birding is better elsewhere.

4. **Nusa Tenggara:** The way to see the most of the region's unique birds and varied cultures and landscapes is to make a 3–4 week circular tour taking in the main islands of Flores, Timor and Sumba. Using planes and ferries to hop between islands, the ideal would be to fly into Bima on Sumbawa and travel east to Sape. From there take the ferry to Labuhanbajo on Flores, breaking the journey for a stopover at Komodo, then drive along Flores to Ende or Maumere. Next fly or sail to Kupang on Timor and, after visiting the sites in West Timor, catch a plane to Waingapu on Sumba. Travel west across Sumba and fly from Waitabula back to Bima, thus completing the circuit. This itinerary will require a certain amount of forward planning if your time is tight, as Merpati flies between the smaller towns only two or three times a week. However, daily flights from Denpasar to Maumere (Flores), Kupang (Timor) and Waingapu (Sumba) mean that you can start the circuit at any of these places to suit flight schedules.

5. **North Sulawesi and Halmahera:** The chance to see 100 or more endemic species and specialities such as Maleo, Red-knobbed Hornbill and Wallace's Standardwing makes this probably Indonesia's most popular birding itinerary. Fly into Manado in North Sulawesi, direct from Singapore or the Philippines or via Bali or Jakarta. The Tangkoko reserve, brimming with endemic kingfishers and other goodies, is just 2 hours away by car. Afterwards a few days can be spent at Dumoga-Bone National Park, before catching a flight across to Ternate and the ferry across the narrow strait to Halmahera, where a new set of species awaits in the forest around Kali Batu Putih, just 8 km from the jetty.

6. **Sulawesi overland:** If you have plenty of time and really want to see and experience Sulawesi, its cultures and landscapes as well as wildlife, there is a classic overlander linking Ujung Pandang and Manado. Starting from Ujung Pandang in the south the route heads north, with birding stops at Lompobattang and Lake Tempe, into the fabulous mountain scenery and culture of Tana Toraja—one of Indonesia's premier tourist destinations. Continuing north on the Trans-Sulawesi Highway, the next stop is Lake Poso. Here birders will branch off the backpackers' route to take in the unforgettable birding in Lore Lindu National Park. Afterwards rejoin the usual route at Poso, to take the ferry across Tomini Bay to Gorontalo with a stopover on the Togian Islands, where endemic Golden-mantled Racquet-tails and Ashy Woodpeckers abound, and roosts of hundreds of Red-knobbed Hornbills are reported. This is also one of the easiest places to see Babirusa. Back on the road at Gorontalo, the next highlight is Maleos at Dumoga-Bone National Park before you end up on the northernmost tip of Sulawesi, at Tangkoko reserve, searching for Sulawesi's cracking kingfishers.

Trekking and local Guides

To trek in most areas in Indonesia it is necessary to be self-sufficient in food and to take a guide. As your guide will need to eat rice, and lightweight, pre-packaged food is not available, it is usually best to hire a couple of porters to carry provisions and equipment. The normal daily wage is Rp10,000 plus food. Few guides have their own trekking equipment and you will need to buy this before setting out. They will be adept at knocking up shelters (*pondok*) in the forest, so there's no need to worry about tents for them.

The usual pre-trek shopping list is: a large pot (for rice), a small pot (noodles and tea), plastic cups and plates, spoons, a ladle (for rice), small kerosene lamp, 1 litre jerrycan with kerosene (*minyak tanah*) and a piece of plastic sheeting and raffia. This will add up to about $40 in any general store and, unfortunately, unless you want to cart it around, you have to buy it again at each location. The essential food on the list is rice (plan on 1 kg/4 people/day), instant noodles (one or two packs/person/day), fish (either dried, or tinned sardines), chili sauce (*sambal*), cream-crackers, coffee, tea, sugar, tinned milk, cigarette lighter and cigarettes (for the guides, porters and anyone else you meet). You will quickly tire of rice and noodles for breakfast, lunch and dinner, so look for variety to liven up the diet. Good bets are *Beng-beng* (chocolate wafers), crispy crackers, egg-coated peanuts and boiled sweets. Ask the shop for rice sacks to put all this in. The porters will carry these, either slung from poles over their shoulders or in ingenious rucksacks rigged up from tree bark.

Almost everywhere you will be expected to take a local guide when entering a forest area, whether this is in or outside a National Park or reserve. In the reserves the guide will be a local PHPA ranger. They vary greatly in knowledge and enthusiasm, and the best are noted in each section's Practicalities. In rural areas the local village head *(kepala desa)* will feel responsible for your safety and will understandably be concerned if you try to wander about alone. Even if you are an old hand in tropical forests, it will be hard for them to believe it. So, even though it's a hassle, it is wiser to go with local wishes and to take someone with you from the village. Ask the *kepala desa* to recommend someone for you. You will be expected to pay Rp7,500–12,500 a day for their services. The trouble with local guides is that the concept of recreational bird-watching will be totally new and probably quite incomprehensible to them. Take the time to explain your needs carefully (see Birders' Language Primer).

Tours & Travel Agencies

Organized tours are a good way to travel if you don't want to bother arranging transport, lodgings and guides on your own. There are several specialist bird tour companies in the UK, US and Australia that offer 17–21 day itineraries, guided by a leading bird-watcher, to various regions of Indonesia.

Local tour agencies catering for the needs of bird-watchers are fewer, but the following all have some experience in this area:

– Sobek Bina Utama: Jl Tirta Ening No 9, By-pass Ngurah Rai, Sanur, Bali, Indonesia. ☎ (361) 287059; fax (361) 289448.
– PT Titawaka Indah Tour & Travel, Jl Monginsidi 7, Biak; PO Box 127, ☎ (0961) 21794; fax (0961) 22372.
– Ramayana Satrya Tours, Jl Bulukunyi 9A, Ujung Pandang; PO Box 107, ☎ (0411) 971791, 851114; fax (0411) 853665.
– PT Toranggo Buya, Jl G. Bulukunyi 9A, PO Box 107, Ujung Pandang 90131, Sulawesi Utara ☎ (0411) 858 836/851 114; fax (0411) 853 665.

Know Before You Go

What to Bring Along

When packing, keep in mind that you will be in the tropics, but that it gets cold in the mountains. What to bring depends on the region you are visiting, how you plan to travel and whether or not you intend to trek. Generally, you will want to dress light and wear natural fibres that absorb perspiration, but bring a warm sweatshirt and sturdy shoes.

Don't bring too much, as you'll be tempted by the great variety of inexpensive clothes and field gear available here. Most tourists find a Javanese batik cotton shirt more comfortable than western clothes. However, to visit a government office, men should wear long trousers, shoes and a shirt with collar. Women should wear a neat dress, covering knees and shoulders, and shoes.

Birders wishing to travel light should bring a couple of pairs of quick-drying, lightweight trousers and natural-fibre shirts. Long sleeves and trousers are recommended to protect against cuts, bites and sunstroke. Dull colours really make a difference when stalking birds. A hat is a good idea, particularly when out in the sun looking for shore- or marshbirds. Baseball-style caps can be bought anywhere in Indonesia, but for better protection bring a "foreign legion" cap with cloth down the back.

Shoes larger than size 9 (43) are difficult to buy in Indonesia, so bring all the shoes you are likely to need. For the field a pair of light-weight trail shoes, with good grip and made from a quick drying material, is the best option. Plastic sandals of the style with a strap round the back are ideal when birding on the shore, in mangroves and marshes, or when travelling by boat, and for use in the evening. These can be bought ($6–7) in most of the major tourist areas. Buy a sarong on arrival in Indonesia ($5–10); it is one of the most versatile items you could hope for. It serves as a wrap to get to the *mandi*, a beach towel, required dress for Balinese temples, pyjamas, bed sheet, fast drying towel, etc.

Waterproofs are another essential and the best choice is a poncho-style rain cape, which can cover rucksack and equipment and also double as a makeshift shelter. An umbrella is another invaluable item that can be purchased cheaply anywhere. Many birders find a photographer's waistcoat a practical alternative to a day-pack. The many pockets keep field-guides, notebooks, lens-cleaning gear and so on within easy reach; passport and money can be safely zipped away in the inside pockets and rain gear or umbrella stuffed down the back. These can be bought ($10) at branches of Alpina outdoor wear in most big Indonesian cities, but they are made from heavy cotton and you end up with an uncomfortably sweaty back, so it's probably best to get a good quality, lightweight version before you come.

If you are planning to spend time in the mountains, bring some warm clothes—several layers: a thick shirt and sweatshirt are the most practical options.

Indonesians are renowned for their ability to sleep any time, anywhere; so they are not likely to understand your desire for peace and quiet at night. Sponge rubber earplugs, available from pharmacies in the west, are great for aiding sleep on noisy journeys. A Swiss army knife always comes in handy, and tiny padlocks for use on luggage zippers are a handy deterrent to pilfering hands.

In most Indonesian department stores and supermarkets you can find western toiletries. Contact lens supplies for hard and soft lenses are available in major cities. Dental floss and tampons are available in western-style grocery stores like Gelael that are fast becoming common in larger Indonesian cities. Sanitary napkins are widely available.

Birdwatching Equipment

Binoculars are, of course, the single most essential item of equipment. A bewildering array of binoculars is available but relatively few models and brands meet the exacting needs of bird-watching. If you do not already own a pair, make sure you take advice from an experienced bird-watcher before buying, or buy from one of the specialist suppliers advertising in any bird-watching magazine.

As Indonesia involves a lot of forest birding, binoculars with a wide field of view and close focusing are what is needed: 8x32 or 8x40 are the best configuration. Prices can range from $150 to over $900. The top of the range brands use high quality glass, with minimal distortion and good light-gathering power. The difference can really be seen when looking up at birds against the light or at dawn or dusk, and good advice with binoculars is to buy the best quality you can afford. The humidity, which promotes fungal attacks to lens coatings and glues, is a real problem. Sealed binoculars are the best prevention, but only the top of the range manufacturers Leica and Swarovski currently manufacture such models.

Whether or not to bring a telescope and tripod is a matter of personal preference, but Indonesia is a country where you can usually manage without, and telescopes are little practical use in tropical forest. If you are a keen photographer, a lightweight tripod is worth bringing, because light levels inside the forests are so slow that film rated ASA400 or above is needed for hand-held shots. Bring a lens-cleaning brush and supplies of lens cleaning tissue and fluid with you.

A microphone and tape-recorder, for drawing birds out into view by playing back their calls, is a great help in Indonesia, but learning the techniques takes time and the equipment is not cheap. The microphone is the most important part and this needs to be a good quality, directional model. Sennheiser is the favoured brand among bird-watchers but is not cheap at around $700. The Hama Unidirectional Microphone at $80 is reputed to be good. Choosing a recorder depends on whether your purpose is simply to attract the birds or to get good quality recordings at the same time. For the former you can use any recording walkman with a built-in speaker (Sony TCM-59V and Sony TCM-77V are good first/budget machines at around $150); for the latter you need a semi-professional tape recorder. Probably the most reliable field tape recorder is the Sony TCM-500EV (*c.* $700), Sony WM-D6C Walkman Professional (*c.* $550) and Marantz CP430 (*c.* $800) are also good.

A powerful torch with spot-beam is

essential for observing owls and frogmouths; 3- or 4-cell Maglites are among the best, but they are heavy and expensive. Cheap torches are sold in general stores in the larger towns, and you should be able to find one which will suffice. Make sure to get one with a halogen bulb and which uses the large "A" cells, which are sold everywhere.

The risk of damage to your equipment in Indonesia from humidity, rain or accidental immersion can not be overstated. Come prepared with air-tight bags and silica gel to stow your equipment at night, during downpours or when crossing rivers. Buy silica gel of the type that changes colour when wet, and put it in bags made from nylon stockings. This can then be dried out anywhere in a wok over an open flame.

For details of field guides see "Further Reading". Pocket field notebooks can be bought in most shops stocking stationery; the Gunung Agung chain stocks an excellent notebook with a semi-waterproof, flexible cover. However, finding a good notebook is always a hassle and it's better to bring a supply of your favourite brand. Don't forget that ball-points will not write on damp paper so using a propelling pencil is a safer bet.

Camping gear cannot be hired in Indonesia, so if you plan to stay overnight in the forest you need to be self-sufficient. A carry-mat, particularly the foam, semi-inflatable type, is strongly recommended. A lightweight tent will come in useful, but this is extra weight. Most experienced bird-watchers in Indonesia choose instead to travel with a mosquito net and rig up their waterproof poncho with plastic raffia (available everywhere) as a shelter in case of rain. Plastic mosquito nets can be bought in most towns, but they are bulky. Several American and European outdoor suppliers market a small lightweight head and shoulder net (with supports like a small dome tent) designed for use with sleeping bags in mosquito-ridden northern forests. These are the best option, but you will need to modify them for use without a sleeping bag by sewing on an extra piece of mesh cloth so it covers your feet (which you can hold up with two bits of raffia). After your binoculars a mosquito net is the most important piece of equipment—for restful sleeps and keeping healthy—so do invest time in sorting this out before you come.

On your travels you will meet people who are kind and helpful, yet you may feel too embarrassed to give them money as a token or your appreciation. In this sort of situation a small gift (*kenang-kenangan*) is appropriate. Key rings, pens or stickers from your home town, bird club or favourite conservation agency will be appreciated. Birders will often find themselves staying with families or camping with guides and porters. Indonesians are very family oriented and photographs of your family are appreciated.

Climate

The climate in this archipelago on the equator is tropical. In the lowlands, temperatures average between 21°C and 33°C, but in the mountains can drop as low as 5°C. Humidity varies but is always high, hovering between 60% and 100%.

The rainy season is normally November to April, with a peak around January/February (except Maluku: May to September) when it rains for several hours each day. The rain is predictable, however, and always stops for a time, when the sun may come out. Before it rains, the air gets very sticky, but afterwards it is refreshingly cool.

The dry season, April to September, is a better time to come. June to August is the time to climb mountains or visit nature reserves, when wild bulls go in search of water and sea turtles more often lay their eggs.

Time Zones

Indonesia has three time zones. Sumatra, Java, West and Central Kalimantan are on West Indonesia Time (Greenwich Mean Time +7 hours). Bali, South and East Kalimantan, Sulawesi and Nusa Tenggara are on Central Indonesia Time (GMT +8 hours). Maluku and Irian Jaya are on East Indonesia Time (GMT +9 hours).

Money and Banking

Prices quoted in this book are intended as a general indication. Larger sums are quoted in US dollars because the rupiah is being allowed to devalue slowly, so prices stated in US dollars are more likely to remain accurate.

Standard currency is the Indonesian rupiah: Notes come in 100, 500, 1,000, 5,000, 10,000, 20,000 and 50,000 denominations. Coins come in denominations of 25, 50, 100, 500 and 1,000 rupiah. Unfortunately, some of the coins are similar in size, so look carefully.

Money changers and banks accepting foreign currency are found in most cities and towns. Banks are generally open 8.30 am to

PRACTICALITIES

INTRODUCTION

2.30 pm, Monday to Friday. Most are closed on Saturday; those that are open, close by 11 am. Gold shops usually bunch together in a specific area of town and change money at competitive rates when banks are closed. Money changers offer very similar rates to banks and are open longer hours. The bank counters at major airports offer competitive rates.

Get a supply of Rp1,000 and Rp500 notes when you change money, as taxi drivers and vendors often claim to have no change for big bills. Carrying cash (US$) can be a handy safety precaution as it is still exchangeable should you lose your passport, but it must be stored carefully and not crumpled: Indonesian banks only accept foreign currency that is crisp and clean.

Major credit cards are accepted in a wide variety of shops and hotels, but they often add a 3% surcharge for the privilege. Most cities have at least one bank at which cash advances can be made. Look for Bank Duta, BCA and Danamon. Visa and MasterCard are the best foreign credit cards in Java.

Officially you may not export more than Rp50,000, but excess rupiahs can be freely reconverted at the airport on departure.

Tax, Service and Tipping

Most larger hotels charge 21% tax and service on top of your bill. The same applies in big restaurants. Tipping is not a custom here, but it is of course appreciated for special services. Rp500 per bag is the appropriate tip for roomboys and porters (Rp1,000 per bag at Jakarta Airport). Taxi drivers will want to round up to the nearest Rp500 or Rp1,000. When tipping the driver of your rental car or a *pembantu* (housekeeper) of the house in which you've been a guest, fold the money and give it with the right hand only.

Office Hours

After a one-year trial period, the 5-day work week was deemed inefficient, so all government offices have now switched back to a 6-day work week: Mon–Thu 8 am–2 pm, Fri until 11 am, Sat until 1 pm.

The singular exception is in the capital of Jakarta, which runs on the 5-day work week, Mon–Fri 8 am–4 pm.

In big cities large shops are open from 9 am until 9 pm; small shops close for a siesta at 1 pm and re-open at 6 pm. However, there are regional variations.

Mail

Indonesia's postal service is reliable, if not terribly fast. Post Offices *(kantor pos)* are usually busy and it is tedious lining up at one window for weighing, another window for stamps, and so on. Hotels normally sell stamps and can post letters for you, or you can use private postal agents *(warpostel)* to avoid hassles. Domestic *kilat* express service is only slightly more expensive and much faster than normal mail. *Kilat khusus* (domestic special delivery) will get there overnight. International express delivers letters to the US and Europe within 7–10 days.

Telephone and Fax

Long distance phone calls, both within Indonesia and international, are handled by satellite. Domestic long distance calls can be dialled from most private phones, but only from public cardphones. To dial your own international calls, find an IDD phone, otherwise you must go via the operator which is far more expensive. Smaller hotels often don't allow you to make long distance calls, so you have to go to the main telephone office *(kantor telepon)* or use a private postal and telephone service *(warpostel)*.

International calls via MCI, Sprint, ATT, and the like can be made from IDD phones using the code for your calling card company. Recently, special telephones have been installed in airports with pre-programmed buttons to connect you via these companies to various countries. Faxes have become common, and can also be sent (or received) at *warpostel* offices which are available in every district town.

Access to e-mail can be made through the local server connected with the post office *(wasantara)*. Charges are minimal.

Electricity

Most of West Indonesia has converted to 220 volts and 50 cycles, though several areas in the east are still on the old 110 lines. If uncertain, ask before you plug in. Power failures are common in smaller cities and towns. Voltage can fluctuate considerably, so use a stabilizer for computers and similar equipment. Plugs are of the European two-pronged variety.

Tourist Information

The Directorate General of Tourism in Jakarta has brochures and maps on all Indonesian provinces: Jl Kramat Raya 81, Jakarta 10450. ☎ (021) 3103117/9; fax: (021) 3101146.

Local government tourism offices, Dinas Pariwisata, are generally only good for basic information. More useful assistance is often available from privately run (but government approved) Tourist Information Services. Be aware that many offices calling themselves "Tourist Information" are simply travel agents.

Overseas, you can obtain information from the Indonesian Embassy or Consulate, or one of the following **Indonesia Tourist Promotion Board** offices:

ASEAN & Southeast Asia, 10 Collyer Quay #15–07, Ocean Building, Singapore 049315. ☎ (65) 5342837, 5341795; fax (65) 5334287.

Australia and New Zealand, Level 10, 5 Elizabeth St, Sydney, NSW 2000. ☎ (61 2) 2333630; fax (61 2) 2333629,3573478.

Europe, Wiesenhuttenstrasse 17, D-6000 Frankfurt/Main, Germany. ☎ (49 169) 233677; fax (49 169) 230-840.

Japan and Korea, Sankaido Building, 2nd Floor, 1-9-13 Ahasaka, Minatoku, Tokyo 107. ☎ (81 3)35853588; fax (81 3) 35821397.

North America,3457 Wilshire Boulevard, Los Angeles, CA 90010-2203, USA. ☎ (213) 387-2078; fax (213) 380-4876.

UK, Ireland, Benelux and Scandinavia, 3–4 Hanover Street, London W1R 9HH, UK. ☎ (44 171) 493 0030; fax (44 171) 493 1747.

Etiquette

The people of Java, and especially the Central Javanese, consider themselves the most refined, polite and cultivated of people. In the areas frequented by Europeans, many are familiar with the strange ways of westerners but it is best to be aware of how certain aspects of your behaviour will be viewed.

You will not be able to count on them to set you straight when you commit a *faux pas*. They are much more likely to stay silent or even reply *tidak apa apa* (no problem) if you ask if you did something wrong. So here are some points to keep in mind:

☛ The left hand is considered unclean as it is used for cleaning oneself in the bathroom. It is inappropriate in Java to use the left hand to pass food into your mouth, or to give or receive anything with it. When you do accidentally use your left hand it is appropriate to say *"ma'af, tangan kiri"* (please excuse my left hand).

☛ Don't cross your legs exposing the bottom of your foot to anyone.

☛ Don't pat people on the back or head. Go for the elbow instead.

☛ Pointing with the index finger is impolite. You will see the Javanese using their thumbs instead.

☛ If you are having a cigarette, offer one to all the men around you.

☛ Alcohol is frowned upon in Islam, so take a look around you and consider taking it easy.

☛ Hands on hips is a sign of superiority or anger.

☛ It is appropriate to drop your right hand and shoulder when passing closely in front of others.

☛ Blowing your nose in public is likely to disgust everyone within hearing distance.

☛ Take off your shoes when you enter someone's house. Often the host will stop you, but you should go through the motions until he does.

☛ Don't drink or eat until invited to, even after food and drinks have been placed in front of you. Sip your drink and don't finish it completely. Never take the last morsels from a common plate.

☛ You will often be invited to eat with the words *makan, makan* ("eat, eat") if you pass somebody who is eating. This is not really an invitation, but simply means "Excuse me as I eat".

☛ If someone prepares a meal or drink for you it is most impolite to refuse.

Some things from the west filter through to Indonesia more effectively than others and stories of *"free sek"* (free sex) made a deep and lasting impression in Indonesia. Expect this topic to appear in lists of questions you will be asked in your cultural exchanges. It is best to explain how things have changed since the 1960s and how we now are practising *"saf sek"*.

Also remember that West Indonesia is predominantly Muslim and it is startling for the Javanese to see women dress immodestly. Exposed backs, thighs and shoulders can cause quite a stir.

Security

Indonesia is a relatively safe place to travel and violent crime against tourists is almost unheard of, but pay close attention to your belongings, especially in big cities. Be sure that the door and windows of your hotel room are locked at night. Use a small backpack or money-belt for valuables: shoulderbags can be snatched.

Big hotels have safety boxes for valuables. If your hotel does not have such a facility, it is better to carry all the documents along with you than leave them in your room. Make sure you have a photocopy of your passport, return plane ticket and traveller's cheque numbers and keep them separate from the originals. Be especially wary on crowded buses and trains; this is where pickpockets lurk and they are very clever at slitting bags and extracting valuables without your noticing anything.

Health

BEFORE YOU GO:
Check with your physician for the latest news on the need for malaria prophylaxis and recommended vaccinations before leaving home. Frequently considered vaccines are: Diphtheria, Pertussis and Tetanus (DPT); Measles, Mumps and Rubella (MMR); and oral Polio vaccine. Hepatitis A vaccination is recommended. For longer stays many doctors recommend vaccination to protect against Hepatitis B, requiring a series of shots over the course of 7 months. Vaccinations for smallpox and cholera are no longer required, except for visitors coming from infected areas. A cholera vaccination may be recommended but it is only 50% effective.

Find out the generic names for whatever prescription medications you are likely to need as most are available in Indonesia, but not under the same brand names as they are known at home. Get copies of doctors' prescriptions for the medications you bring into Indonesia to avoid questions at the customs desk. Those who wear spectacles should bring along prescriptions.

Check your health insurance before coming, to make sure you are covered. Travel agents should be able to direct you to sources of travel insurance. These typically include coverage of a medical evacuation, if necessary, and a 24-hour worldwide phone number as well as some extras like luggage loss and trip cancellation.

GENERAL:
Keeping your body's own defences strong is the surest way to avoid illness. Eat well and take plenty of rest. Taking a multi-vitamin and mineral tablet 3 times a week will also help. An excellent local brand sold throughout Indonesia is *Supratin*.

HYGIENE:
This is a problem throughout Indonesia, and

outside the main towns few places have running water or sewerage. Most water comes from wells, and raw sewerage goes right into the ground or into the rivers. Even treated tap water in the big cities is not potable and must be boiled.

Most cases of stomach complaints are attributable to your system not being used to the strange foods and stray bacteria. To make sure you do not get something more serious, take the following precautions:
☛ Don't drink unboiled water from a well, tap or *mandi* (bath tub). Brush your teeth with boiled or bottled water, not water from a tap or *mandi*.
☛ Plates, glasses and silverware are washed in unboiled water and need to be completely dry before use.
☛ Ice is not made from boiled water. It comes from water frozen in government regulated factories. Locals who are adamant about drinking only boiled water are, in general, not fearful of the purity of ice. However, we advise you to err on the side of caution and forego it.
☛ Fruits and vegetables without skins pose a higher risk of contamination. To avoid contamination by food handlers, buy fruits in the market and peel them yourself.

DIARRHOEA:
A likely travelling companion. In addition to the strange food and unfamiliar micro-fauna, diarrhoea is often the result of attempting to accomplish too much in one day. Taking it easy can be an effective prevention. Ask around before leaving home about what the latest and greatest of the many remedies are and bring some along. Imodium is locally available, as are activated carbon tablets that will absorb the toxins giving you grief.

When it hits, diarrhoea is usually self-limiting to two or three days. Relax, take it easy and drink lots of fluids, perhaps accompanied by rehydration salts such as Servidrat. Especially helpful is young coconut mik (*air kelapa muda*) or tea. The former is especially pure and full of nutrients to keep up your strength until you can get back to a regular diet. Get it straight from the coconut without sugar, ice and colour added. When you are ready, plain rice or *bubur* (rice porridge) is a good way to start. Avoid fried, spicy or heavy foods and dairy products for a while. After three days without relief, see a doctor.

INTESTINAL PARASITES:
It is estimated that 80–90% of all people on Java have intestinal parasites and these are easily

passed on by food handlers. Prevention is difficult, short of fasting, when away from luxury hotel restaurants and even these are not guaranteed. It's best to take care of parasites sooner rather than later by routinely taking a dose of anti-parasite medicine such as Kombatrin (available at all *apotik*) once a month during your stay and again when you get on the plane home. If you still have problems when you get back, even if only sporadic, have stool and blood tests. Left untreated, parasites can cause serious damage.

MOSQUITO-BORNE DISEASES:

Malaria is rare in Java (Ujung Kulon National Park is an exception) and Bali, but common elsewhere in Indonesia, with widespread chloroquine resistance. Nusa Tenggara, Maluku and Irian Jaya are particularly high-risk areas and the potentially fatal *faliparium* strain is common. Make sure you get good advice on prophylactic medications before coming, and take them religiously.

Symptoms are fever, cough, muscle aches and diarrhoea; if you fear you may have malaria, take your temperature each morning and evening and plot this on a chart. Temperature rises at 2- or 3-day intervals are sure indicators, so carry a thermometer and take your temperature morning and evening if you are concerned. Try to get a blood test at a clinic in the nearest town, but remember that parasites can only be detected when you are having an attack. Ask the clinic to identify the strain: if they tell you it is *faliparium*, take immediate western medical advice and keep hold of your blood smear. Malaria is rapidly and effectively cured with medication.

The other mosquito concern is dengue fever, spread by the afternoon-biting *Aedes aegypti*, especially at the beginning of the rainy season in November. There is no prophylaxis for dengue. Symptoms are headache, pain behind the eyes, high fever, muscle and joint pains and rash.

The first line of defence for both these diseases is to avoid getting bitten, as far as practical. In the early evening, when malaria-bearing mosquitos are most active, wear long sleeves and cover exposed skin with an insect repellent such as *Autan* or *Off*, which is sold in general stores. If your room is not well screened and mosquitos are prevalent, use a mosquito coil or, better still, sleep under a net (see previous advice about camping).

CUTS AND BITES:

Your skin will come into contact with more dirt and bacteria than it did back home, so wash your face and hands more often. Untreated bites or cuts can fester very quickly in the tropics, and staphilococcus infection is common. Cuts and bites should be taken seriously and cleaned with an antiseptic such as Betadine solution, available from any pharmacy *(apotik)* and most small shops (ask for *obat merah*). Once the wound is clean, antibiotic ointment (also available locally) should be applied and the cut kept covered. Repeat this ritual often. Areas of redness around the cut indicate infection and a doctor should be consulted. At the first sign of swelling it is advisable to take broad-spectrum antibiotics to prevent a really nasty infection.

The main problems result from scratches caused by rattan and other climbers and leech or tick bites. Keeping covered will minimize the risk of scratches. Leeches are a nuisance, especially in wet areas with large mammal populations. Birders, who often stand still, are particularly prone to leeches. Just pull leeches and ticks off firmly and sharply and apply Betadine; stories of their leaving their mandible embedded are grossly exaggerated. Centipedes and forest scorpions are another problem; they can give a nasty bite, which in some people may cause an allergic reaction. When camping, check shoes and pockets before putting clothes on and don't sit down on logs before checking them first. Indonesia has several poisonous snakes, but bites are rare. A snake disturbed on the ground will strike at the lower calf and ankle so, again, it is best to keep these parts of the body covered.

FUNGAL INFECTIONS:

These are the real bane of the bird-watcher and are likely to occur on the scalp, between the toes and fingers (*tinea* or athlete's foot), in the crotch, or on the skin (ringworm). To prevent fungal infections, wear loose fitting, natural-fibre clothes, wash frequently, dry yourself carefully afterwards and use a medicated talcum powder such as *Purol*. If you do get a fungal infection, wash the area daily with medicated soap, dry it with a clean towel and then apply an antifungal powder such as the widely available *Tinaderm*. Try to expose the infected area to sunlight as much as possible.

HEAT PROBLEMS:

Sunburn and heat exhaustion or even heat stroke frequently catch out the birder who arrives in Indonesia and goes straight out into the field without taking precautions. Wear a hat, use a sun-block (15+), drink plenty of non-alcoholic fluids and avoid salt deficiency by taking extra salt with your food. In West Indonesian cities isotonic canned drinks such as *100 plus* and *Pocari Sweat* are widely sold. Allowing your body to acclimatize and avoiding heavy exercise or excessive alcohol consumption for a few days will reduce the risks of suffering from heat exhaustion. The symptoms of heat exhaustion are fatigue, lethargy, headaches, giddiness and muscle cramps. Prickly heat, an itchy rash caused by perspiration trapped under the skin, affects some new arrivals. Keeping cool and using a medicated talc are the best means of relieving the problem until you acclimatize.

AIDS AND HEPATITIS B:
Surprise! Safe sex is also a good idea in Indonesia. AIDS is just beginning to surface, with a number of documented HIV positive cases recently. Another consideration is the Hepatitis B virus, which affects liver function. It is only sometimes curable and can be deadly. The prevalence of Hepatitis B in Indonesia is a cause of international concern over the possibilities for the spread of HIV virus, which is passed on in the same ways.

Medical Treatment
The Indonesian name for pharmacy is *apotik*, and a hospital is called *rumah sakit.* In smaller villages you will find only government clinics, called *Puskesmas,* which are not equipped to deal with anything serious. Fancier hotels often have doctors on call, or can recommend one. Misuse of antibiotics is still a concern in Indonesia. They should be used only for bacterial diseases, and then for at least 10 to 14 days in order to prevent the develoment of antibiotic-resistant strains of your affliction.

Indonesians don't feel they've had their money's worth from a doctor ($5) without getting an injection or antibiotics. Be sure it's really necessary. Ensure that syringes have never been used before. Even in the big cities outside Jakarta, emergency care leaves much to be desired. Your best bet in the event of a life-threatening emergency or accident is to get on the first plane to Jakarta or Singapore. Contact your embassy or consulate by telephone for assistance. Medevac airlifts are very expensive (around $26,000) and most embassies will recommend that you buy insurance to cover the cost of this when in Indonesia.

Health Kit
Birding will take you to remote places so it is wise to be prepared and to carry with you a basic medical kit. The key ingredients are listed below; they include items that may cause some people allergic reactions and some prescription drugs, so the advice is to discuss this with your doctor before leaving home. Most of the items can be bought at any *apotik* in Indonesia and many names are the same in English (international brand names). Local brand names are given where necessary.
Scissors
Tweezers (suitable for extracting thorns)
Thermometer
Plasters *Band-aid*
Antiseptic swabs
Antibiotic powder/*Sulfanilamicle*
Antiseptic solution *Betadine/obat merah*
Triangular bandage; long bandage
Cotton wool (*cotton*)/cotton buds
Broad-spectrum antibiotic *Amoxycillin*
Antihistamine cream/tablets
Malaria prophylaxis
Anti-fungal powder *Tinaderm*
Anti-fungal cream *Mycostatin*
Paracetamol *Panadol*
Water purification tablets
Small plastic bottle of 70% alcohol
Powerful pain killer
Anti-diarrhoea tablets
Condoms *Kondom*
Sunscreen

Keep pills and liquid medicines in small, unbreakable plastic bottles, clearly labelled.

Accommodation
Indonesia has an extraordinary range of accommodation, much of it good value for money. Most cities have a number of hotels offering air-conditioned rooms with TV, mini-bar, hot water, swimming pool and the like costing $100 a night and up, while at the other end of the scale, you can stay in a $2-a-night *losmen* room with communal squat toilet (buy your own toilet paper), a tub of water (*mandi*) with ladle for a bath, and a bunk with no towel or clean linen (bring your own). And there's just about everything in between: from decrepit colonial hill stations to luxurious new thatched-roof huts in the rice fields.

A whole hierarchy of lodgings and official terminology have been established by government decree. Theoretically, a "hotel" is an upmarket establishment catering for businessmen, middle to upper class travellers and tourists. A star rating (one to five stars) is applied according to the range of facilities. Smaller places with no stars and basic facilities are not referred to as hotels but as *losmen* (from the French *logement*), *wisma* (guesthouse) or *penginapan* (accommodation) and cater for the masses or for budget tourists. Large hotels add 21% government taxes to their rates, *losmen* 10%.

Prices and quality vary enormously. In the major cities that don't have many tourists, such as Jakarta, Surabaya and Medan, there is little choice in the middle ranges and you have to either pay a lot or settle for a room in a *losmen*.

In areas where there are a lot of tourists, such as Bali, you can get very comfortable and clean rooms with fan or air-conditioning for less than $20 a night. In small towns and remote areas, you don't have much choice and all accommodation tends to be very basic.

It's common to ask to see the room before checking in. Shop around before deciding, particularly if the hotel offers different rooms at different rates. Avoid carpeted rooms, especially without air-conditioning, as they are usually damp and this makes the room smell.

Staying in Villages

Officially, the Indonesian government requires that foreign visitors spending the night report to the local police. This is routinely handled by *losmen* and hotels, who send in a copy of the registration form you fill out when you check in. Carry photocopies of your passport, visa stamp and embarkation card to give to officials when venturing beyond conventional tourist areas. This saves time, and potential hassles, for you and your host.

Where there are no commercial lodgings, you can often rely on local hospitality. But when staying in a private home, keep in mind the need to inform the local authorities. One popular solution is to stay in the home of the local authority, the village head or *kepala desa*. He will be used to putting up visiting officials in his home and will probably be too polite to ask for payment, but a small contribution of Rp5–7,000 per person per night is expected. The polite way to do this is to give it to his wife on leaving, with the words *untuk beli gula* (to buy sugar). You will eat with the family and, in remoter areas especially, it is good to bring some contributions with you: coffee, sugar, cigarettes and perhaps rice are useful items. Note down their address and send prints of the photos you took of them.

Bathroom Etiquette

When staying in *losmen*, particularly when using communal facilities, don't climb in or drop your soap into the tub of water *(bak mandi)*. This is for storing clean water.

If you wish to use the native paper-free cleaning method, after using the toilet, scoop water with your right hand and clean with the left. This is the reason one only eats with the right hand—the left is regarded as unclean, for obvious reasons. Use soap and a fingernail brush (locals use a rock) for cleaning hands. Bring along your own towel and soap (although some places provide these if you ask).

Finding Your Way

Westerners are used to finding things using telephone directories, addresses, maps, and so on, but in Indonesia phone books are out-of-date and incomplete, addresses can be confusing and maps little understood. The way to find something, if you have a specific destination in mind, is to ask.

To ask for directions, it's better to have the name of a person and the name of the *kampung*. Thus "Bu Herlan, Mertadranan" is a better address for asking directions even though "Jalan Kaliwidas 14" is the mailing address. Knowing the language helps here but is not essential. Immediately clear answers are not common and you should be patient. You are likely to get a simple indication of direction without distance or specific instructions. The assumption is that you will be asking lots of people along the way.

Maps are useful tools for you, but introducing them into discussions with the Javanese will often confuse rather than clarify. Nevertheless, the Indonesians seem to have built-in compasses and can always tell you where north is. If you introduce a map into your discussion, they are likely to insist that the north arrow on the map be oriented to the north before beginning.

Food and Drink

Pay attention to the quantity of fluids you consume in a day (drinks with alcohol or caffeine count as a minus). The tap water in Indonesia is not potable and it should be brought to a full boil for 10 minutes at least before being considered safe. Use boiled or bottled water to brush your teeth. Most Indonesians themselves are fussy about drinking water so if you're offered a drink it is almost certainly guaranteed to be safe.

Most Indonesians do not feel they have eaten until they have eaten rice. This is accompanied by side dishes, often just a little piece of meat and some vegetables with a spicy sauce. Other common items include *tahu* (tofu), *tempe* (soya-bean cake) and salted fish. The Javanese also love crispy fried tapioca crackers flavoured with prawns (*krupuk*) to accompany a meal.

No meal is complete without *sambal*—a fiery paste made from ground chili peppers with garlic, shallots, sugar and various other ingredients.

Cooking styles vary greatly from one region to another.

By western standards, food in Java is cheap. For $2, in most places, you can get a meal with bottled drink. Most people normally eat in restaurants only out of necessity (when they cannot eat at home). The major exception to this is the Indonesian Chinese, who are fond of restaurant banquets. Most Indonesians eat better at home than outside, and the range of dishes in restaurants is not great.

In most Javanese restaurants you will find a standard menu consisting of saté (skewered barbequed meat), *gado-gado* or *pecel* (boiled vegetables with spicy peanut sauce) and *soto* (vegetable soup with or without meat). Also found are some Chinese dishes like *bakmie goreng* (fried noodles), *bakmie kuah* (noodle soup) and *cap cay* (stir-fried vegetables).

In most towns on Java, you can also find a number of Chinese restaurants on the main street. Standard dishes, in addition to the *bakmie* and *cap cay* mentioned above, are sweet and sour whole fish (*gurame asem manis*), beef with Chinese greens (*kailan/ caisim ca sapi*), and prawns sautéed in butter (*udang goreng mentega*). Any one of these with a plate of vegetables (*cap cay*) and rice makes a delightful meal.

Javanese-style fried chicken (*ayam goreng*) is common and very tasty—cuts of meat stewed in coconut cream, coriander and other spices and then quick-fried to give it a crispy coating. Then there is the ubiquitous *nasi goreng* (fried rice), which is often eaten for breakfast with an egg on top. *Nasi goreng istimewa* comes with an egg on top.

Aside from this standard menu, there are restaurants everywhere in Indonesia that specialize in Padang food. Dishes from this region of West Sumatra are hot, spicy and salty (though in Central Java they tend also to be sweet). In a Padang restaurant you will be served a number of curries and meats, some-

times as many as 15 or 20 different types, all on small plates brought to your table. (Waiters gauge their skill by the number of dishes they can carry at once). You are charged at the end of the meal only for what you eat; the rest is taken back to the counter at the front.

Street Stalls (*Warung*)

Restaurant kitchens do not necessarily have healthier food preparation procedures than roadside *warung*. The important thing at a *warung* is to see what's going on and make a judgement as to whether or not the cooks inspire confidence. *Warung* rarely have a running water supply, so always beware.

The food is laid out on the table and you point to what you want to eat. Your first portion probably won't fill you up, so a second portion is ordered by saying *"Tambah separuh"* (I'll have another half portion, please). But only the price is halved. The amount of food is more like three-quarters. Finish off with a banana and say *"Sudah"* (I've had plenty and would like to pay now please). At this point the seller will total up the prices of what she served you and ask you how many *krupuk* and *tempe*, etc, you added; so keep track. The total will come to between Rp1,000 and Rp3,000 (45c to $1.20).

Vegetarianism

Say *"saya tidak makan daging"* (I don't eat meat) or alter menu items by saying something like *"tidak pakai ayam"* (without chicken) or *"tidak pakai daging"* (without meat). Dietary restrictions are very acceptable and common in Indonesia due to the various religious and spiritual practices involving food. However, finding food that truly has no animal products is a problem. Often meals which appear to be made exclusively of vegetables will have a chunk of beef in them to add that certain oomph.

Some recommendations are *gudangan*, which is made with a variety of fresh green vegetables with roasted spicy grated coconut sprinkled on it, and *gado-gado* and *pecel*, which is cold cooked vegetable salad with peanut sauce. *Tempe* and *tahu* are excellent sources of protein and can be prepared in an astonishing variety of ways.

Bird-watching Tips

Forest Birding

For birders used to temperate habitats, finding birds in the Indonesian rainforest can seem a daunting prospect. The massive, multidimensional structure, enormous leaves and dim light all conspire to keep birds well hidden. To get good views, you need to hone your fieldcraft skills to the special challenges that rain forest presents—but this is what makes rainforest birding so satisfying.

Not all rain forests are full of birds—the nutrient-poor forests on limestone and ultrabasic soils that cover large areas of Sulawesi and North Maluku, and the extensive peat swamp forests of Sumatra and Kalimantan, hold relatively few species. Lowland forests on sedimentary soils or hill forests on rich, volcanic soils support the highest bird densities—and therefore the best bird-watching. Submontane forest, at around 1,000 m, can be especially species-rich, as here there is an overlap between lowland and montane species.

It is natural to focus on pristine forest and head deep into the interior, but actually the most productive areas are often forest edge, selectively logged and, especially, newly logged forest because these areas are more open and allow you to look up into the forest canopy. Trees tend to fruit when under stress from disturbance, and this attracts fruit-eating species. However, although you may amass a long species-list in disturbed forest, it may not include the few specialist species that cannot tolerate such disturbance.

The golden rule for successful forest birding is to wear dull colours. Walking around in bright T-shirts (white is the worst) severely handicaps your ability to approach unnoticed, and Caucasian birders should remember that white arms and legs are similarly conspicuous. Wearing long-sleeved shirts and trousers will also help you to avoid scratches and bites.

Vary your birding approaches, search different components of the habitat, and—once you get to know an area—try to be in the right place at the right time. Generally, the hour before dawn is when owls and frogmouths call most, and first light is the best time to see ground thrushes. The early morning activity drops off quite quickly, 2–3 hours after dawn; sometimes there is a brief resumption in the late morning, but the next significant period of activity is not until late afternoon, when birds are preparing to roost.

A favourite topic of discussion among rainforest birders is the merits of walking quickly or slowly along the trail. Walking slowly and quietly means you will pick up more calls and movement and, because you will not be sweating with exertion, your concentration will be better. But striding out and covering ground will increase the number of mixed species flocks you encounter and improve your chances of seeing thinly-distributed species. It also offers the likelihood of surprising some of the forest's real gems—pittas, pheasants and rail-babblers—feeding out on the trail. Obviously, the best strategy is to vary your pace, but to spend more time covering ground quickly when you first arrive at sites, as this will enable you to identify places to return to and work more intensively.

Birds concentrate around particular features in the forest—fruiting and flowering trees are the best known. Look on the ground for telltale mounds of rotting figs signifying a fruiting tree above. If it is in a position where you can see comfortably into the canopy, just sit and watch; over a few hours probably every type of fruiteater—pigeons, hornbills, barbets—will pay it a visit. The same goes for flowering trees and nectar-drinkers. Fruiting bushes and shrubs along river banks or forest edges are another magnet for fruiteaters, particularly bulbuls, and, in the dry season, small pools on forest streams are good spots to stake out at midday when birds come down to drink or bathe. Midday is also the time to find a vantage point—a clearing or ridge top with a view over the forest—to scan for raptors. In any forest you will come across gaps where a rainforest giant has come crashing to the ground—because of wind, lightning strike or just old age—smashing an opening. Struggle through the debris and onto the fallen trunk; the pocket of still, sunlit air above is full of flies and dragonflies and these attract tree-swifts, flycatchers and falconets, which survey the gap from an exposed perch on a broken branch. Patches of forest that have died off, because of fire or flooding, are always good for woodpeckers.

Finally, if you are one of those lucky birders with the ability to mimic bird calls, make full use of your talent. Many species (notably babblers, pittas and trogons) are relatively easy to imitate and the real owner of the call is very likely to approach to investigate. Knowing the birds and habitats is what it is all about, and your fellow bird-watchers will always have additional tips for finding a particular species. A little background research—talking to people or reading the specialist trip-reports that circulate in birding circles (see Further Reading)—always pays dividends.

Tape Play-back

In Indonesia's forests, 80% of birds are located by their call, so learning the calls of common or target species will add greatly to your success in seeing them. The songs and calls of a selection of Indonesian birds are available on a few commercially produced tapes and CDs, or on tapes produced privately by birders. Some birders, and especially bird tour leaders, swear by tape-playback as the best technique for being sure of seeing several forest species.

However, there is some debate about the ethics of tape-playback: a recording represents a super-dominant intruder, so repeated playing could disrupt breeding or may even cause the bird to abandon its territory. One incident of play-back will not harm the bird; the problem arises when the same territory holder repeatedly suffers this stress as can happen at popular birding sites.

The principle of tape-playback is simple: a recording of the call is played, either to a bird heard calling or in likely-looking habitat. The territory-holder thinks there is an intruder and comes out to investigate. A pre-recorded passage is played or, if you do not have a recording or do not know the identity of the calling bird, its call is recorded directly and then played back.

Although simple in principle, using this technique requires practice and good equipment. The key is a good-quality directional microphone; Sennheiser is the most popular. If you just want to call the bird out, you can get away with a moderate-quality, recording walkman with a built-in speaker—as long as

the speaker is sufficiently loud. If you want good quality recordings that can be duplicated or deposited in wildlife sound archives, such as the British Library of Wildlife Sounds (BLOWS), a professional-quality recorder is required. Sony Walkman Professional or Marantz are the recommended brands. The Sony Datman, which records on digital analogue tape, gives the ultimate quality in sound recording, but there are concerns that the complicated electronics may not be able to withstand the high humidity in Indonesia for prolonged periods. All these professional-quality recorders require extension speakers and, although the results can be impressive, many birders cannot cope with the wires and hassle.

Caring for Equipment

Any birder's equipment list represents a serious financial outlay and conditions in Indonesia are tough on equipment, so spare the extra expense and trouble to care for your equipment properly. Tropical downpours and high humidity, especially at night, can result in problems with camera electronics and the dreaded fungus streaks on lenses. In the field always carry strong, air-tight plastic bags to stow your equipment when the heavens open, and put everything in airtight bags with silica gel when not in use. Knocks—and dust accumulated while travelling—are other hazards: use a strong, good-quality camera bag or, better still, one of the air- and watertight plastic cases (Pelican) used by divers. If you use the latter, however, make sure you open the valve when flying: the different air pressures can impound your lenses.

Film

With regard to the choice of film, the jury is still out. If you wish to publish or use your photos in presentations, use a positive slide film. Some bird photographers still prefer Kodachrome 64 ASA and 200 ASA, although mailing off the rolls for processing is a nuisance. 200 ASA is really too soft and grainy for enlargements, so try to stick to 64 or 100 ASA. Fujichrome has improved dramatically over the years, and many professionals now choose the 50 or 100 ASA Velvia/Sensia. 100 and 200 ASA Velvia/Sensia stored in refrigerators can now be bought at virtually any camera stores in the main cities in western Indonesia, but do not bank on finding it in the east. Slides can be processed in under two days in most big cities west of Ujung Pandang, but processing quality is variable. Ekta in Jakarta (see Practicalities) offers professional processing.

Getting Great Results

If you are after good bird pictures, forget about birding at the same time: many have tried to do both simultaneously and failed. Just pick one area and stay there for several days—or weeks—and get to know the area and birds well. In Indonesia a good rule of thumb is not to approach the birds—let them come to you. Conceal yourself near a food source in the cool and bright morning sun; it could be a fruiting or flowering tree or a muddy beach with a retreating tide. Streams and pools are good places at midday, when birds come down to bathe. Remember, birds are creatures of habit and will come back to the same spot and do the same thing day after day. Some Indonesian parks have hides and watchtowers, but generally you have to be prepared to find your own favourite spots.

Think also about why you are taking the photos. Is it for purely personal interest, or do you, like most photographers, get particular satisfaction from seeing the results of your work published? Editors require razor-sharp, perfectly exposed images. The growing popularity of photographic field-guides means that there is a thriving market for the classic, full-frame or centre-shot bird but, increasingly, editors of magazines and guidebooks are looking for more creativity, and photos that capture the essence of the place as well as the bird. Resist the temptation to get the bird as large as possible in the picture. Can you get an interesting angle—a low-angle shot of a wader against an expanse of mud and clear blue sky? a kingfisher surveying an expanse of forest? When you get a collection of photos together, even if it is only small, it is sure to be valuable: editors and photo agencies are crying out for better coverage of Indonesian natural history. There are still so many birds that have not yet been photographed in the wild—there is still so much to be done in Indonesia.

–Bas van Balen, Paul Jepson
& Morten Strange

PERIPLUS LANGUAGE GUIDES

Everyday Indonesian

ISBN: 0-945971-58-3

Knowing a few simple phrases of Indonesian opens up an entirely new, more fulfiling travel experience. Indonesians love it if you can communicate in their language, and in only a few short hours this book allows you to do just that!

Everyday Indonesian is designed specifically for the visitor to begin communicating effectively from the very first day. Essential vocabulary and phrases are given in order of importance, and the bilingual dictionary contains 2,000 commonly-used words. Extensive notes on grammer, etiquette, body language and culture will make your visit go a lot more smoothly.

Distributed by:

Berkeley Books Pte. Ltd. (Singapore & Malaysia)
5 Little Road, #08-01, Singapore 536983   Tel: (65) 280 3320 Fax: (65) 280 6290

C.V. Java Books (Indonesia)
Kelapa Gading Kirana, Blok A-14 No. 17, Jakarta 14240 Tel: (62-21) 451 5351 Fax: (62-21) 453 4987

Indonesian Language Primer

Personal Pronouns
I *saya*
we *kita* (inclusive), *kami* (exclusive)
you *anda* (formal), *saudara* (brother, sister), *kamu* (for friends and children)
he/she *dia* they *mereka*

Forms of Address
Father/Mr *Bapak* ("*Pak*")
Mother/Mrs *Ibu* ("*Bu*")
Elder brother *Abang* ("*Bang*" or "*Bung*")
      Mas (in Java only)
Elder sister *Mbak*
Younger brother/sister *Adik* ("*Dik*")

Note: These terms are used not just within the family, but generally in polite speech.

Basic Questions
How? *Bagaimana?*
How much/many? *Berapa?*
What? *Apa?*
What's this? *Apa ini?*
Who? *Siapa?*
Who's that? *Siapa itu?*
What is your name? *Siapa namanya ?*
When? *Kapan?*
Where? *Mana?*
Which? *Yang mana?*
Why? *Kenapa?*

Useful Words
yes *ya*   no, not *tidak, bukan*

Note: *Tidak* is used with verbs or adverbs; *bukan* with nouns.

and *dan*   better *lebih baik*
with *dengan*   worse *kurang baik*
for *untuk*   this/these *ini*
good *bagus*   that/those *itu*
fine *baik*   same *sama*
more *lebih*   different *lain*
less *kurang*   here *di sini*
there *di sana*

Civilities
Welcome *Selamat datang*
Good morning (7–11 am) *Selamat pagi*
Good midday (11 am–3 pm) *Selamat siang*
Good afternoon (3–7 pm) *Selamat sore*
Goodnight (after dark) *Selamat malam*
Goodbye (to one leaving) *Selamat jalan*
Goodbye (to one staying) *Selamat tinggal*

Note: *Selamat* is a word from Arabic meaning "May your time (or action) be blessed".

How are you? *Apa kabar?*
I am fine *Kabar baik*
Thank you *Terima kasih*
You're welcome *Kembali*
Same to you *Sama sama*
Pardon me *Ma'af*
Excuse me *Permisi*
(when leaving a conversation, etc).

Numbers
1	*satu*	6	*enam*
2	*dua*	7	*tujuh*
3	*tiga*	8	*delapan*
4	*empat*	9	*sembilan*
5	*lima*	10	*sepuluh*
11	*seblas*	100	*seratus*
12	*dua belas*	600	*enam ratus*
13	*tiga belas*	1,000	*seribu*
20	*dua puluh*	3,000	*tiga ribu*
50	*lima puluh*	10,000	*sepuluh ribu*
73	*tujuh puluh tiga*		

1,000,000 *satu juta*
2,000,000 *dua juta*
half *setengah*
first *pertama*   third *ketiga*
second *kedua*   fourth *ke'empat*

Time
minute *menit*   Sunday *Hari Minggu*
hour *jam*   Monday *Hari Senin*
day *hari*   Tuesday *Hari Selasa*
week *minggu*   Wednesday *Hari Rabu*
month *bulan*   Thursday *Hari Kamis*
year *tahun*   Friday *Hari Jum'at*
today *hari ini*   Saturday *Hari Sabtu*
tomorrow *besok*
yesterday *kemarin*
later *nanti*
What time is it? *Jam berapa?*
(It is) eight thirty. *Jam setengah sembilan.*
     (Literally: "half nine")
How many hours? *Berapa jam?*
When did you arrive? *Kapan datang?*
Four days ago. *Empat hari yang lalu.*
When are you leaving?
     Kapan berangkat?
In a short while. *Sebentar lagi.*

Basic Vocabulary

to be, have	*ada*	correct	*betul*
to be able, can	*bisa*	wrong	*salah*
to buy	*beli*	big	*besar*
to know	*tahu*	small	*kecil*
to get	*dapat*	pretty	*cantik*
to need	*perlu*	slow	*pelan*
to want	*mau*	fast	*cepat*
to go	*pergi*	stop	*berhenti*
to wait	*tunggu*	old	*tua, lama*
at	*di*	new	*baru*
to	*ke*	far	*jauh*
if	*kalau*	near	*dekat*
empty	*kosong*		
crowded, noisy	*ramai*		
only	*hanya, saja*		
then	*lalu, kemudian*		

Small Talk

Where are you from? *Dari mana?*
I'm from the UK. *Saya dari Inggris.*
How old are you? *Umurnya berapa?*
I'm 31 years old.
    Umur saya tiga pulu satu tahun.
Are you married? *Sudah kawin belum?*
Yes, I am. *Yah, sudah.* Not yet. *Belum.*
Do you have children? *Sudah punya anak?*
What is your religion? *Agama apa?* (it is inadvisable to answer that you have none)
Where are you going? *Mau ke mana?*
I'm just taking a walk. *Jalan-jalan saja.*
Please come in. *Silahkan masuk.*
I don't understand. *Saya tidak mengerti.*
I can't speak Indonesian.
    Saya tidak bisa bicara Bahasa Indonesia.
Please, speak slowly.
    Tolong berbicara pelan-pelan.

Hotels

Where's a *losmen? Di mana ada losmen?*
cheap *losmen losmen yang murah*
good hotel *hotel sangat baik*

Please take me to... *Tolong antar saya ke...*
Are there any empty rooms?
    Ada kamar kosong?
Sorry there aren't any. *Ma'af, tidak ada.*
How much for one night?
    Berapa untuk satu malam?
One room for two of us.
    Dua orang, satu kamar.
I'd like to stay for 3 days.
    Saya mau tinggal tiga hari.
Here's the key to your room.
    Ini kunci kamar.
Please call a taxi. *Tolong panggil taksi.*
Please wash these clothes.
    Tolong cucikan pakaian ini.

Restaurants

I want coffee, not tea.
    Saya mau kopi, bukan teh.
Without sugar, with sugar, with a little sugar
    tampa gula, pakai gula, dengan sedikit gula
May I see the menu?
    Boleh saya lihat daftar makanan?
I want to wash my hands.
    Saya mau cuci tangan.
Where is the toilet? *Di mana kamar kecil?*
fish, squid, goat, beef
    ikan, cumi, kambing, sapi
salty, sour, sweet, spicy, bitter
    asin, asam, manis, pedas, pedas

Directions

north	*utara*	west	*barat*
south	*selatan*	east	*timur*
right	*kanan*	left	*kiri*
near	*dekat*	far	*jauh*
inside	*di dalam*	outside	*di luar*

I am looking for this address/village.
    Saya cari alamat ini/kampung or desa ini.
How far is it? *Berapa jauh dari sini?*

Pronunciation and Grammar

Vowels

a	As in father
e	Three forms:
	1) Schwa, like the
	2) Like é in touché
	3) Short e; as in bet
i	Usually like long e (as in Bali); when bounded by consonants, like short i (hit).
o	Long o, like go
u	Long u, like you
ai	Long i, like crime
au	Like ow in owl

Consonants

c	Always like **ch** in **ch**urch
g	Always hard, like **g**uard
h	Usually soft, almost un-pronounced. It is hard between like vowels, e.g. *ma**h**al* (expensive).
k	Like **k** in **k**ind; at end of word, unvoiced stop.
kh	Like **k**ind, but harder
r	Rolled, like Spanish **r**
ng	Soft, like fli**ng**
ngg	Hard, like ti**ng**le
ny	Like **ny** in So**ny**a

Grammar

Grammatically, Indonesian is in many ways far simpler than English. There are no articles (a, an, the). The verb form "to be" is usually not used. There is no ending for plurals; sometimes the word is doubled, but often number comes from context. And Indonesian verbs are not conjugated. Tense is communicated by context or with specific words for time.

Indonesian for Birders

Explaining What You are Doing

Bird-watching will be a new concept for most of the Indonesian people you meet, so a few phrases of explanation will come in useful. Be prepared, though, for a few laughs as you explain, for *burung* (bird) is a common slang word for the male genitalia and in the Sundanese language of West Java it means crazy in the head!

I enjoy watching birds.
Saya senang mengamati burung.
I do not want to catch birds.
Saya tidak mau menangkap burung-burung.
I do not want to buy birds.
Saya tidak mau membeli burung.
I am not a researcher.
Saya bukan peneliti burung.
I bird-watch for a hobby.
Mengamati burung adalah hobi saya.

Talking about Birds

Armed with the names of bird families, colours and a few descriptive words it is surprisingly simple to talk about birds, especially if you show pictures in your field guide. This can bring a whole new dimension to your Indonesian bird-watching experience.

Names

The following set of family names are in widespread usage across the archipelago. If you wish to talk about a specific species, simply describe it. For example, Great-billed Parrot, *Burung Nuri yang paruh besar dan merah*, is the parrot with the big red bill.

Seabirds *burung laut*
Ducks *bebek, itik*
Shorebirds *burung pantai*
Egrets, herons and storks *bangau, kuntul*
Birds of prey *elang, alap-alap*
Rails *ayam ayaman*
Junglefowl *ayam hutan*
Owls *burung hantu*
Nightbirds *burung malam*
Megapodes, maleo *burung gosong*
Swallows and swiftlets *walet, layang-layang*
Hornbills *rangkok, enggang*
Imperial Pigeons *burung pombo, pergam*

Green pigeons *punai*
Woodpeckers *pelatuk*
Kingfishers *raja udang*
Parrots *burung nuri yang, betet, bayan,*
kakatua Lories *perkici*
Orioles *kepodang*
Drongos *srigunting*
Bulbuls *kutilang*
Starlings *jalak*
Sunbirds *sesap madu*
Finches and munias *emprit, pipit, bondol*
Birds-of-paradise *cendrawasih*
Crows *gaga*

Parts of a Bird

head	*kepala*
back	*punggung*
belly	*perut*
wing	*sayap*
tail	*ekor*
legs/feet	*kaki*
bill	*paruh*
eye	*mata*
crest	*jambul*
feather	*bulu*
wing-bar	*garis sayap*

Other Terms

male	*jantan*
female	*betina*
immature	*anak*
adult	*dewasa*
egg	*telur*
nest	*sarang*
hole	*lubang*
fly	*terbang*
dive (into water)	*menyelam*
dive (in the air)	*menukik*
to look for prey	*cari manksa*
binoculars	*keker(an), teropong*
telescope	*teropong*
tripod	*kaki tiga*
tape recorder	*tip*
cassette tape	*kaset*
nesting ground	*tempat bersarang*
roost place	*tempat tidur*
display area	*tempat bermain*
breeding season	*musim kawin, musim berbiak*

Note: Indonesians use the word *ekor* when talking about numbers of birds (or animals). How many did you see? *lima ekor* = five tail. Also, if a bird flushes, the word *lari* (to run or flee) is often used instead of fly.

Habitats and Landscape Features

primary forest	*hutan asli*
rain forest	*hutan tropis*
monsoon forest	*hutan musim*
mangrove	*hutan bakau*
wetland	*lahan basah*
swamp	*rawa*
agricultural land	*lahan pertanian*
ricefields	*sawah*
gardens	*kebun*
sea	*laut*
beach	*pantai*
river	*sungai, kali*
tree	*pohon*
branch	*cabang*
leaf	*daun*
island	*pulau*
estuary	*muara*
bay	*teluk*
cliff	*tebing*
peninsula	*semenanjung*
mountain	*gunung*
hill	*bukit*
waterfall	*air terjun*

Other

surfaced road	*jalan aspal*
stone road	*jalan batu*
trail	*jalan setapak*
shelter	*pondok*
cage	*sangkar*
snare	*jerat*
net	*jaring*
birdlime	*pulut*

Below are a few ideas you may want to use when asking questions and pointing to a picture in a fieldguide:

Have you seen this bird in this area?
Apa anda sudah pernah lihat burung ini di dearah ini?
What is this bird called?
Burung ini namanya apa?
Is this bird common here?
Burung ini terdapat banyak disini?
Where does this bird live?
Burung ini hidup dimana?
Can you take me to the place to see this bird?
Apa anda bisa mengantar saya ke tempat burung ini?
What does this bird eat?
Burung ini makan apa?

Where does this bird nest?
Burung ini membuat sarang di mana?
Where does this bird roost?
Burung ini tidur dimana?

Making Arrangements for the Field

To enter the remoter reserves, you will have to make arrangements in the nearest village or with local PHPA staff. Here are a few useful phrases:

Where is the village head's house?
Dimana rumahnya Pak Kepala Desa?
May I stay here?
Boleh saya menginap disini?
I would like to hire a guide.
Saya ingin menyewa seorang penyunjuk jalan.
What payment do you request for one day's guiding?
Bapak minta berapa upah sehari?
Have you been there before?
Bapak sudah pernah kesana?
Is there somewhere to stay in the forest?
Apa ada tempat untuk meninap di hutan?
Do we need a tent?
Apakah kita harus membawa tenda?
Can you bring cooking utensils?
Bapak bisa bawah peralatan untuk masak?
Must we buy cooking utensils before we go?
Apa kita harus membeli peralatan masuk sebelum berangkat?
How far is it to...?
Berapa jauh ke...?
Do we have to cross rivers?
Apa kita harus menyeberangi sungai?
Do we have to climb?
Apa kita harus menanjak?
Is the trail clearly marked along the way?
Apa ada tanda jelas sepanjang jalan?
I am looking for special birds.
Saya cari burung-burung khusus.
Please point out any bird you see to me.
Tolong menunjuk kepada saya setiap burung yang Bapak lihat.
Please do not be noisy on the trail.
Tolong jangan ribut kalau jalan.
Please walk behind me.
Tolong jalan di belakang saya.
We will be walking slowly because I want to stop and look at birds.
Kita akan jalan pelan-pelan karena saya ingin berhenti setiap kali ada burung.

–Bas van Balen & Paul Jepson

Java

Jakarta

Getting There

By air There are connections from all over the world with Jakarta's Soekarno-Hatta International Airport located 12 km northwest of the city. Taxi fare into town is $15; there is also a regular AC airport bus service to downtown for $2.

By sea Pelni passenger ferries visit Tanjung Priok docks from all parts of Indonesia (see route map on back flap). Non-Pelni boats also take passengers; contact them at the harbour master's office. There is also a 24-hr ferry service from Bakauheni, Sumatra, to Merak, *c.* 140 km west of Jakarta; journey time 2 hrs.

It is also possible to go by ferry from Batan and Bintan, the two Indonesian islands situated close to Singapore. Pelni services ply between these islands and Sumatra, as well as Jakarta and Surabaya.

Accommodation/Dining

There is a range of accommodation from the large international chains to the very inexpensive travellers' *losmen* on Jl Jaksa, in the city centre near Monas Square, but not much in the mid range for tourists. There is a very wide range of dining options: international standard (and price!) restaurants through to roadside food stalls.

For luxury hotels, try **Hotel Ciputra**, Ciputra Mall, ☎ 5606006, fax 5669655, near the Toll road with easy access to Soekarno-Hatta Airport; **Omni Batavia**, Jl Kali Besar 44–46, ☎ 6907926, fax 6904092. In North Jakarta in the centre of the old city: **Grand Hyatt**, Jl Thamrin, ☎ 3107400/7410, fax 334321, in the Plaza Indonesia Shopping Mall.

Along Jl Wahid Hasyim, near the Sarinah Department Store, there are three mid-price range hotels to choose from. All are simple, but centrally located and offer full facilities: **Arcadia Hotel**, (94 rms), ☎ 2300050, $80–85; **Hotel Cipta**, ☎ 4214700, $75–90; **Hotel Ibis Tamarind**, (125 rms) ☎ 3157706, $109.

At the cheaper end of the scale, one of the most popular and original guesthouses is

Wisma Delima, Jl Jaksa 5, fan and AC rms $9–20. A small café and travel infromation available. The **International Tator Hostel**, Jl Jaksa 37, is small, but very clean and newly renovated; some rooms with AC, $8–19. **PGI Guest House**, (Christian Guest House) at Jl Teuku Umar 17, ☎ 3909427, has a variety of rooms, well-maintained, simple and spacious. Location is residential and central.

Whatever your preference, Jakarta has it for eating—from roadside stalls to elegant European restaurants. You can sample regional dishes from all 27 of Indonesia's provinces or whallop down a Big Mac. **Senayan State House** is a chain of restaurants serving delicious *saté* and other local dishes, located at Jl Cokroaminoto, Jl Kegon Sirih and Jl Pakubuwono. For hot and spicy Padang food, **Natrabu** on Jl Salim 29, has won prizes for its food and its waiters' ability to carry 20 or more plates at one time. Inexpensive too. **Nelayan Garden** on Jl Gatot Subroto has great seafood, but is always crowded at lunchtime. Not to be missed is **Café Batavia**, located in Taman Fatahillah, north Jakarta. Serving superb Chinese food along with Indonesian and western fare; located in a restored 1805 2-storey building, with elegant atmosphere. Open 24 hrs.

Transport

Bus Very cheap but hot, cramped, crowded and dilapidated. Standard fare is about 15¢. Smaller Patas buses are slightly more expensive at 30¢, but less crowded and stop anywhere. City bus route maps are (sometimes) available at the Visitor Information Centre in Djakarta Theatre building on Jl Thamrin. Pickpockets and bag slashers are a common hazard on buses. If you are carrying expensive binoculars and cameras you will do much better to travel by taxi or hire a car.

Taxis Plentiful, and can be flagged down anywhere. Fares are fairly cheap by international standards. AC flagfall is Rp1,500, Rp550/km thereafter; make sure the meter is on. **Bluebird**, **Silver Bird** and **Gamya** all answer the same telephone numbers: 7981006, 7941234. Other 24-hr taxis ☎ **Express** 5709009, **Kosti**

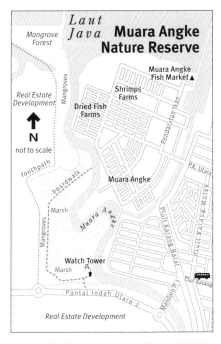

Jaya 780 1333, **Metropolitan** 672827, **Steady Safe** 3143333.

Car rental: Many companies now offer both chauffeur-driven (CD) cars with driver and gas included, as well as self-drive (SD) cars. CD daily rates (12 hrs) range from $60 (Kijang van) to $126 (Corolla sedan); SD daily rates include insurance minus $50 deductible, range from $47 (Kijang van) to $85 (Corolla sedan).
Avis, Jl Diponegoro 25. ☎ 314 2900.
Toyota Rent-A-Car, ☎ 5735757.
Bluebird, Mandarin Hotel, ☎ 3141307.
Hertz, ☎ 5505773.
Dynasty, ☎ 5856014.

General Information
Tourist Office Visitor Information Centre, Jakarta Theatre Building, Jl Thamrin 9. ☎ 3154094, 3142067; Soekarno-Hatta Airport, ☎ 550 7088.
Travel Agencies: **Boca Pirento**, ☎ 6682029 and **Vista Express Tours**, ☎ 336100.
PHPA Headquarters, Gedung Manggala Wanabakti, Jl Gatot Subroto, Jakarta. ☎ 5730311, 5730312. Another office is located at Jl Merkeka Selatan 8–9, Blok G, 21st Fl.
Post and Telkom Offices Small post offices and *wartel* are found throughout the city.
Foreign Exchange You can convert currency at major hotels and banks.
Health Malaria is not a problem in the city, but beware the daytime-biting mosquito that carries dengue fever.

Hospitals: **SOS Medika**, Jl Puri Sakti 10, Cipete, Central Jakarta. ☎ 750 6001 (emergency), 750 5980 (appointment). 24-hr outpatient clinic deals with emergencies.
Photography There are numerous 1-hr photo processing stores throughout the city Shops recommended by Jakarta's Photo Club and where slide film can be developed in 3–4 hrs are: **Standard Photo** at Jl Hang Lekir 10/20 and Jl Alaydrus 63 and **Kodak Color Lab**, Jl Wolter Monginsidi, Kebayoran. The Harco Plaza Building in Pasar Baru is the photography centre of Jakarta with over 30 shops selling new and second-hand cameras, accessories, printing supplies and offering repair services.

Around Jakarta

MUARA ANGKE
This once-rich wetland site has been drastically reduced in extent by housing and golf course development, and now only a 27-ha nature reserve survives. However, this marsh and its adjoining mangroves still offer good birding and are one of the easiest places to see the endangered Javan Coucal.

Key Species
Javan Coucal, Javan Plover, Milky Stork, Black-headed Ibis, Small Blue Kingfisher, Black-winged Starling, Watercock and a good site for crakes and *acrocephalus* warblers, passage terns and waders.

Getting There
By taxi Ask for Pondok Indah Kapuk estate ($7/Rp15,000 from Blok M).
By bus P37 Blok M–Muara Angke (Rp700); P6b Kampung Rambutan bus station–Muara Angke (Rp700); P46 Pulo Gadung–Muara Angke (Rp700); Metro 02 from Senen–Muara Karang (Rp400); Metro U30 Kota–Muara Angke (Rp400). Whichever bus you take, get off at the west end of Jl Pluit Karang. Look for the massive entrance arch to the Pondok Indah Kapuk estate; 20 m beyond this is a roundabout. Take the only exit, Jl Pantai Indah Utara 2, and walk along for 75 m. On the north side of the road you will see a sign for the reserve and a little bamboo bridge entrance.

General Information
A few metres across the bamboo bridge is a warden's post where you should report. Boats to Pulau Rambut can also be arranged here.

Immediately behind the post is a tall watchtower, which is the best place to scan from for Javan Coucal. A 1–2 km boardwalk follows the edge of the reserve (3 sides, excluding the river boundary). There is good birding from the boardwalk, especially along the western edge, which passes through a fragment of mangrove and nipa palm swamp. Unfortunately, despite frequent repairs, the boardwalk is always in a state of collapse. Be careful not to fall through it, and expect not to be able to get the whole way. On the western edge a rickety bamboo bridge crosses from the boardwalk to the bund surrounding the new housing development. Walk seaward (north) for 55 m to the coastal mangroves.

A path runs west along the back of the mangroves until it reaches the canalised Angke river. The best area of mangrove is on the other side of the river. The mud in front can be good for waders, and Milky Storks sometimes feed there. You may be lucky and find a boatman who will ferry you across. If not, you have to return to Jl Pantai Indah Utara 2 and walk west along this road for 1.5 km (past another roundabout) where a bridge crosses the river. The mangroves are a further 700 m down the side of the river. 500 m west along the path at the back of the mangroves is a freshwater lagoon and a stone breakwater, which gives access through the mangroves to the mud.

PULAU RAMBUT

One of the closer in-shore "Thousand Islands" of Jakarta Bay, the 45-ha Pulau Rambut is home to a large waterbird colony including Milky Storks, herons, egrets and ibises. Well-maintained trails enter the forest and a tall watchtower provides memorable viewing.

Key Species

Breeding and roosting Milky Stork, Purple and Grey Herons, Black-crowned Night-heron, Intermediate and Little Egrets, Little Cormorant, Glossy and Black-headed Ibises, White-bellied Sea-eagle, Pied Imperial Pigeon. Frigatebirds on the crossing.

Getting There

From Muara Angke arrange a boat charter at the warden's post. Expect to pay $70 for a 20+ seater, or $40 for a smaller vessel. The trip along the coast to Pulau Rambut takes 1.5 hrs.

A cheaper way to get there is to drive to Tanjung Pasir, at the back of the airport. The regular boats that ferry villagers across to the neighbouring Untung Jawa island will drop you at Pulau Rambut for $1.50 (20 mins). Arrange for a pick-up, too, for not later than 4.00 pm. Alternatively you can charter a boat ($30).

To reach Tanjung Pasir by **bus**: from Blok M to Kalideres bus station, getting off before Kalideres at Pasar Cengkareng. From there take a white *bemo* to Kampung Melayu (Rp500), then a further *bemo* to Dadap (Rp500), and finally at *bemo* (Rp500) to Tanjung Pasir.

General Information

A permit is required and may be obtained from SBKSDA, Jl Salemba Raya 16, Central Jakarta, ☎/fax 390 4402. To save waiting, fax them your permit request with your name and passport number the day before you want to collect it. This is a full-day excursion.

Researchers are allowed to stay on the island with a permit but there are no facilities on the island for visitors, so take all your own food and drink with you. PHPA has a guesthouse on nearby Untung Jawa island ($7/Rp14,000).

KEMAYORAN

This former airport is being rebuilt as a garden city but is not due for completion until well into the 21st century. It is the home of the Jakarta Fairgrounds. A 6-ha fragment of mangrove swamp has been retained next to a man-made lagoon. Its full name is Hutan Rawa Payau Baru Bandar Kemayoran. A board provides access to the marsh.

Key Species

Little Cormorant, Little and Cattle Egrets, Black-crowned Night-heron, Small Blue and Sacred Kingfishers, Great Tit, Racquet-tailed Treepie.

Getting There

By bus From Blok M take Metro Mini S610 to Pondok Labu (Rp400), then Kopaja 06 (Rp700) to the Jakarta Fairgrounds, Kemayoran district (Rp700).

By taxi From Kota Station to Kemayoran (near the golf course $3/Rp6,000). The guard will ask to see your permit.

General Information

A permit for a visit to Kemayoran is obtained from DP3KK, Jl Angkasa, Kemayoran, Jakarta 10610 (behind Pasar Baru). ☎ 421 7135; fax 424 1356. Permits are free of charge but insurance for each site is Rp500.

MONAS

The focal point of the city, Monas Square is home to the national monument, a 132-m obelisk with a small historical museum at its base. Garden birds such as Sooty-headed Bulbul, Bar-winged Prinia and Olive-backed Sunbird can be seen in the surrounding parkland, and impressive numbers of White-bellied Swiftlets coming in to roost circle round the monument at dusk.

Getting There

On foot Monas is in the city centre close to Gambir railway station; ask for directions.
By bus PPD 70, PPD 12 or P1 from Blok M towards Kota. Get off at Monas.

General Information

Very popular with Jakartans, so best avoided on Sundays and public holidays. Elevator to the top costs Rp2,000; museum entrance Rp500. Open every day 8.00 am–5.00 pm.

RAGUNAN ZOO

Located in the south of the city just outside the outer ring road, this zoo houses 3,600 birds and animals. The grounds are quite leafy and good for wild birds. Red-breasted Parakeet and Orange-headed Thrush are regularly seen, and even Chestnut-winged Cuckoo has been recorded.

Getting There

By taxi About $2.50 from Blok M. Ask for *Kebun Binatang Ragunan.*
By bus Metro Mini S77 from Blok M to Kebun Binatang (Rp400). From Pasar Minggu by Kopaja S68 (Rp400).

General Information

The zoo is open daily 8.00 am–6.00 pm, admission Rp1,500. There are plenty of food stalls and informal restaurants in the grounds.

TAMAN BURUNG

The *Taman Burung* (Bird Park) is part of *Taman Mini Indonesia Indah (TMII)* (Beautiful Indonesia in Miniature), a theme park featuring the varied cultural and artistic traditions of the country. The bird park design is based on Wallace's Line, and two massive domes house birds of east and west Indonesia. A great place to brush up your identification skills and to photograph birds.

Getting There

TMII is located 3–4 km south of Jakarta just off the Jagowari toll road; take a taxi or a S15A

angkot from Ragunan/Pasar Minggu (Rp700).

General Information

Open daily 8.00 am–5.00 pm, general admission Rp2,000, and a further Rp2,500 to enter the bird park.

Pulau Dua

Pulau Dua is a 30-ha mangrove and scrub-covered former island (now connected by fish ponds to the shore) in Banten Bay, north of Serang on the Jakarta–Merak toll road, just 1.5 hrs from Jakarta. Famous for its large breeding colony and roost of egrets and herons, Pulau Dua is reputed to be the only breeding colony of Glossy Ibis on Java. Fishing Cat is relatively easy to see. It is the best site for the endemic and very localised Javan White-eye.

Key Species

Main attraction is the large breeding colony and roost of Little and Intermediate Egrets, Glossy Ibis and cormorants. This is the best locality to find the rare and endemic Javan White-eye.

Other Wildlife

Fishing Cat is frequently seen.

Getting There

By car Take the Jakarta–Merak toll road west and leave it at the "Serang Timor" exit (about 75 km from Jakarta). After exiting, turn right onto the main road into Serang and take the third major turning on the right, signposted "Banten Luhur". After 1 km turn left at the t-junction and then quickly right in a small town. Continue north for 7 km, and just before a girder bridge (500 m before Banten), turn left over the railway and drive 5 km to the village of Sawah Luhur. Park under a big tree (called locally *Pohon Kapuk*) on the left. From here a trail winds through the fish ponds for 1.5 km (take left hand forks where there is a choice) to the edge of the mangroves of Pulau Dua island. It is a further 750 km along the trail to the PHPA post.
By public transport Take a bus to Serang from Kalideres bus terminal. From the bus terminal in Serang catch a *bemo* to Pasar Rawu (Rp 300). From here take a local bus (*angkot*) to Sawah Luhur; they run every hour (Rp600 for the 17 km journey). In Sawah Luhur, ask them to drop you at *Pohon Kapuk*.

General Information

No entry permit is needed. You can stay at the very basic PHPA post but make sure you take a mosquito net; better still, camp. Leave a tip ($5/Rp10,000) for staying. There are no cooking facilities or fresh water: carry in everything you need. If you park overnight expect to pay $5/Rp10,000 for someone to guard your car.

Ujung Kulon Nat Park

Undoubtedly Java's most famous national park, Ujung Kulon has recently become one of Indonesia's most accessible reserves. Over 240 bird species have been recorded, and it is the only place where Javan Rhino is still found.

Key Species

Grey-headed Fish-eagle, Green Junglefowl, Green Peafowl (cocks in July–September with full trains), Beach Thick-knee, Javan Owlet, Javan Frogmouth, Blue-throated Bee-eater, Rhinoceros Hornbill, Great Slaty Woodpecker, Black-banded Barbet, Large Wren-babbler, Grey-cheeked Tit-babbler, Temminck's and White-breasted Babblers, Asian Paradise-flycatcher, Crested Jay.

Seabirds can be seen on the boat journey to the peninsula, especially during rough weather in the rainy season.

Other Wildlife

Javan Rhino (you are unlikely to see one), Banteng, Leopard, Asian Wild Dog, Palm Civet and Mongoose. Crocodiles in the swamps of the Nyiur and Cigenter rivers; Green Turtles on the west beaches. If you travel there by boat, dolphins, Whale Sharks and other marine animals are possible.

Getting There

By bus Buses leave Kalideres bus station, West Jakarta, for Labuan via Serang and Pandeglang every 30 min from 6.00 am to 9.00 pm, becoming less frequent in the evening; the journey takes 3–4 hrs. Do not take buses that go via Cilegon. There are also 6 buses a day between 8.00 am and 6.00 pm from Bandung via Bogor; these take about 5 hrs on the old back road (partly in very poor condition) via Rangkasbitung and Pandeglang.

From Labuan it is 90 km by road to Tamanjaya. Cars can be chartered in Labuan (4WD essential in the rainy season). Minibuses cost

Rp4,500 from the corner of Jl Sudirman/Stasiun to Sumur, then take an *ojek* (motorbike taxi) for the last 20 km to Tamanjaya (Rp5,000 pp + pack).

By sea The boat trip from Labuan to Peucang or Handeuleum Islands takes 1–5 hrs depending on whether you take the speedboat ($750) or the wooden boat ($350.) Obviously you need to be in quite a large group to make this worthwhile, or be lucky in getting a spare seat on someone else's booking. Call PT Wanawisata (see below) for more information. Boats can also be arranged through PHPA in Labuan. Call in advance: sometimes there is only one a week. During the rainy season, Nov–Mar, stormy weather may delay sea travel.

Accommodation/Dining

In **Labuan** try **Rawayana Hotel**, Jl Perintis Kemerdekaan, 300 m south of the PHPA office. 25 rms: $12.50 with fan; $25AC.

At **Tamanjaya** there is very simple accommodation—a guest-house (4 cottages: $10S, $15D) and a homestay (2 rms: $5S, $7.50D including breakfast.)

Handeuleum Island Guesthouse, 4 economy rms: $15D, $20.00 T, max 10 people.

Peucang Island Flora A Lodge 6 "superior" units with AC; **Flora B Lodge** 10 standard units with AC; **Fauna Lodge** 6 economy rms ($30–80.00 plus 15% tax). Restaurant serving Indonesian and European meals and basic supplies. This is the only food available on the peninsula, so take all your own provisions if staying at other sites. The package tours usually stay on these two islands. Reserve through PT Wanawisata (see opposite).

There are numerous free **campsites and basic shelters** in the park. Water is always available from rivers or wells, but be boiled for drinking.

General Information

The best time to visit is Mar–Oct. Malaria is prevalent in the park, so do not forget antimalarial pills.

Check in at the PHPA office: **Kantor Taman Nasional Ujung Kulon,** Jl Perintis Kemerdekaan 51, Caringin, Labuan 42264, Pandeglang, Jawa Barat. ☎ 0253-81731; open Mon–Fri, where boats can be booked. Park entrance fee Rp2,000, insurance Rp2,500; both renewable. PHPA guides and porters cost $5 a day; clients provide all meals for themselves, guides and porters. If you decide to do the trek to Cidaon/Peucang Island mentioned in the main article, you must discuss your return options before leaving Labuan.

At Labuan, Budi Marwanto and Aat Hidayat are both good for general information. In the park look out for Djarkasih; he is based on Peucang Island but can be contacted at Labuan when on leave.

PT Wanawisata Alamhayati, Gedung Manggala Wanabhakti Blok IV, Lantai II, Wing-A, Jl Gatot Subroto, Senayan, Jakarta 10270 (☎ 571 0392 ext. 5253) manages the island accommodation and boat travel and can provide information on trails. There are also Wanawisata offices in Labuan and Tamanjaya.

A full-colour guide book, *Ujung Kulon: Indonesia's National Park*, written by Margaret Clarborough, who has done several years' work in the park, is recommended.

Carita Beach

The patch of lowland rain forest along the trail to the Curug Gendang waterfalls is an increasingly popular destination for bird-watchers as it offers the best chances to see most of Java's lowland endemics along a very accessible trail. About 125 birds have been recorded here, with undoubtedly more to be added.

Key Species
Javan Hawk-eagle, Red-billed Malkoha, Javan Owlet, Brown Boobook, Javan Frogmouth, Javan Kingfisher, Black-crested Bulbul, Grey-cheeked Tit-babbler, White-breasted Babbler, Violet-tailed Sunbird, Crested Jay.

Other Wildlife
Javan Leaf Monkey, land tortoises.

Getting There
The turn off and entrance gate to the forest (where there are cheap *losmen*) are about 10 km north of Labuan on the coast road.

Accommodation/Dining
There are plenty of hotels, from 5-star to cheap *penginapan,* along the road between Cilegon and Labuan. There are also many food stalls and restaurants, though most may be closed on quiet weekdays. **Rumah Makan Diminati**, on the main road north of the forest entrance, has good food and cold beer.

General Information
The forest is managed as a *hutan wisata* (recreation forest) by the Perhutani Forestry Department. Entrance Rp1,500. Best time to visit Mar–Sep.

Bogor Botanic Gdns

These world-famous gardens are located in the centre of Bogor, a rapidly growing city of 300,000 people, 60 km south of Jakarta and famous for its record-breaking thunder-storms—300 have been recorded in a single year. Lying at an altitude of 260 m, the carefully laid-out gardens cover 87 ha and are one of the world's great biological treasure troves, with a collection of 400 palms, 5,000 trees and 3,000 orchid varieties.

Key species
Grey-cheeked Green Pigeon, Black-naped Fruit-dove, Blue-eared Kingfisher, Orange-headed Thrush, Yellow-throated Hanging-parrot, Plain Flowerpecker, Javan Munia, Spotted Wood-owl. In Oct and Nov look out for passage migrants.

Other Wildlife
Flying Foxes, monitor lizards. Banded Linsang is a possibility just before dusk.

Getting There
Bogor lies on the Jakarta–Bandung route, and is about 1 hr south of Jakarta on the Jagowari toll road.

By car Turn right at the end of the toll road (sometimes only left turns are permitted and you will have to do a U-turn); make an anti-clockwise circuit of the Botanic Gardens to the entrance, and park (Rp500) by the taxi stand in front of the Zoological Museum.

By bus The bus from Kampung Rambutan bus terminal in east Jakarta costs about 50¢ or 85¢ with AC. From Bogor's Baranangsiang bus station, it is best to walk the 500 m along the west side of the gardens. Turn left out of the bus station and then left again.

By train Express trains (*c.* 50 min) leave from Gambir Station in Jakarta at 7.33 am, 10.44 am, 2.20 pm and 4.46 pm ($1.00), plus two VIP (AC) trains at 9.33 am and 4.33 pm ($1.75). The hourly slow trains cost about 50¢. From the station entrance on Jl Raya Permag, turn left and take a No 7 *bemo* (Rp250) to the Botanic Gardens entrance on Jl Juanda opposite Plaza Bogor.

Accommodation/Dining
There is a wide range of accommodation in Bogor. Among the most convenient for the Botanic Gardens are:

Firman Pensione, 15 rms and 4-bed dormitory, Jl Paledang 48. ☎ 232246. Basic but convenient, friendly *losmen*, nice atmosphere. Superb view of Mt Salak from 1st floor balcony. Breakfast, tea and coffee included. $6-17D (S "negotiable"), dormitory $3.

Pangrango, 73 rms, Jl Pangrango 23. ☎ 328670; fax 314060. Bogor's largest hotel, situated in a pleasant, leafy part of town just off Jl Pajajaran. Restaurant, pool, tv, mini-bar. "Mini" $22 (no hot water), $40–45D, $65VIP.

Wisma Ramayana, 24 rms, Jl Juanda 54. ☎ 320364. Popular travellers' *losmen*, close to the Botanic Gardens entrance. Including breakfast, $10–21 (family).

Losmen Puri Bali, Jl Peledang 50, is where the famous Dutch naturalist Andries Hoogerwerf and his family lived in 1946–47.

Jongko Ibu, Jl Juanda (opposite the Post Office). Inexpensive, buffet-style Sundanese food. Very popular with travellers and visiting scientists.

Bogor Plaza, Jl Suryakencana (opposite entrance to Botanical Gardens). Food hall on top floor of multi-storey shopping centre. Plenty of choice with a range of mini-restaurants offering different cuisines, ices, juice bar. Probably the best budget choice for lunch after visiting the Botanic Gardens.

Delima, Jl Suryakencana (opposite Bogor Plaza). Also convenient for Botanic Gardens. Small restaurant with giftshop area selling carvings, batik and puppets.

Requests to stay in the Indonesian Institute of Sciences' guesthouse in the gardens can be made by writing in advance to Jl Juanda 18, PO Box 208, Bogor 16002.

General Information

The Botanic Gardens open every day 8.00 am–5.00 pm. $1 weekdays, 50¢ Sun and holidays. Cars $2.50, no cars admitted Sun and holidays.

The Zoological Museum (open 8 am–4 pm daily, 25¢) near the entrance to the gardens has a large collection of stuffed birds in dusty dioramas. The main skin collection is housed in the Ornithology Department, which is reached through a service entrance on the left of the Post Office on Jl Juanda. The collection is open only to *bone fide* researchers.

Gede/Pangrango National Park

Established in 1889 as the Cibodas reserve, this is one of the oldest tropical forest reserves on Earth, and there is an extensive body of scientific literature on the forest

and its wildlife. The national park protects 15,000 ha of mountain rain forest that covers the twin volcanoes of Gede and Pangrango.

The 600-ha Cibodas Botanic Gardens, with their collection of trees from around the world, adjoins the park's northern boundary. Together, the park and gardens constitute one of Asia's premier bird-watching sites, over 700 species of birds having been recorded there, including 25 species endemic to Java.

Key Species

Javan Hawk-eagle, Javan Scopsowl, Salvadori's Nightjar, Chestnut-bellied Partridge, Horsfield's Woodcock, Volcano Swiftlet, Pink-headed Fruit-dove, Blue-tailed Trogon, Spotted Crocias, White-bibbed Babbler, Sunda Blue Robin, and Sunda, Siberian and Island Thrushes.

Other Wildlife

Javan Gibbon, Javan and Ebony Leaf Monkeys, Long-tailed Macaque and Malay Stink-badger.

Getting There

Cibodas is 105 km southeast of Jakarta, 45 km southeast of Bogor and 84 km west of Bandung.

By car Take the Jagowari toll road from Jakarta or Bogor to its end at Cisarua (Rp4,000 from Jakarta, Rp500 from Bogor). Turn left at the lights on the road to Puncak and Bandung. 7 km over the summit of the Puncak pass turn right at a big, red signpost to Cibodas Golf Park. After about 3 km the road ends at the Botanic Garden gates. Park at the National Park headquarters just before the gates.

By bus From Jakarta take a Cianjur bus from Kampung Rambutan bus station and get off at the Cibodas turn just after California Fried Chicken, then catch a blue minibus to the park entrance (Rp300). From Bogor, minibuses to Cianjur leave from the bus station opposite the toll road. The journey takes 1–2 hrs (Rp1,500). Taxis from the rank outside Bogor Botanic Gardens charge $50 for a day trip to Cibodas; this is ridiculously expensive.

Accommodation/Dining

There are several "homestays" in the village, 400 m below the park entrance. **Fredy's Homestay** is popular with birders and keeps a bird log. Best to phone beforehand in the holiday season. 4 rms, ☎ (0255) 515473. $7.50–10D including breakfast. Dinner $3.

Cibodas Youth Hostel (ask for Pondok Pemuda). On the left by the market entrance gate. ☎ (0255) 512807. A 20-person dormitory, $2.50S, also a 2-rm bungalow, $12.50 rm.

Cibodas Botanic Gardens guesthouse. 6 rms. It is delightful to stay in the gardens, though the guest-house is rather basic and run-down. Bookings in advance (☎ 0255 512233) or try your luck mid-week. $15D. No restaurant or facilities.

Higher-standard accommodation is located back on the main road.

Summit Panghegar, (accommodates 112 in twin, double-bed rms) Jl Sindanglaya Raya 180, Pacet, Puncak. ☎ (0255) 511335; fax 512785. Hotel, villa and lodge accommodation: $75S–$100 villa suite. The best hotel to be found in the area.

Bukit Raya Permai, (179 rms) Jl Raya Cipanas, Sindanglaya, Cipanas. ☎ (0255) 512505, 512994; fax 512995. (Reservations can also be made in Jakarta: ☎ (021) 345 1991; fax 344 6093.) $40S weekdays–$190 for 6-bed bungalow on public holidays. This is a large, popular, resort-type hotel on 3 sites; however, it is nicely situated in a deep, wooded valley.

Simple meals are available in the several *warung* along the Cibodas market street, where drinks, biscuits and rolls can be bought for lunch on the mountain. For trekkers on the mountain, stock up beforehand.

General Information

Jun–Oct are the driest months; tropical downpours are usual Nov–May. The park can be very busy at weekends and on public holidays. Dawn is 5.30 am, and first light is the best time to see speciality species such as ground-thrushes and shortwings; dusk is at 6.00 pm.

Permits are obtained at the entrance, $2.50 per day. Foreigners are sometimes required to show passports. If you want to make an early start, buy your ticket the night before.

Park Management Office: Wisma Cinta Alam, Jl Raya Cibodas, PO Box 3, Sdl Cipanas, ☎ (0255) 512776.

Cibodas Botanic Gardens (☎ 0255 512233) are open 7 am–6 pm every day; Mon–Sat Rp2,200, Sun and holidays Rp1,200 (adults and children).

Trails are well marked and guides are not necessary. See map in the main article for trails, distances, walking times and any other information you may need.

A detailed, English-language guidebook to the path as far as the Cibeureum falls is available from the ticket office ($5); a more general park guide is also available. *Mt. Gede/Pangrango National Park: Information Book Series* Vols I (Cibodas to Cibeureum

trail guide) and II (general information), by Keith Harris.

Tangkuban Perahu Nature Reserve

The 2,076 m Tangkuban volcano dominates the northern side of the Bandung basin. A surfaced road winds right to the edge of the crater. This spectacular "drive-in" volcano is a popular tourist spot—with souvenir stalls and restaurants, but it is not difficult to slip off along one of the trails for some pleasant birding.

Key Species
This is the easiest place in Java to see the high-altitude specialities—Volcano Swiftlet and Island Thrush—and the forest birding is good.

Getting There
From Bandung drive north 16 km to the old Dutch resort town of Lembang. From here the Subang road skirts the eastern flanks of the volcano; a gate marking the entrance to the reserve is about 9 km from Subang. A surfaced road leads to the crater.

General Information
At the crater follow the trail anti-clockwise round the rim. 500 m below the crater is a big car park with restaurants. Across the road from the car park a trail leads 1 km through excellent forest to a second, smaller crater.

Pangandaran National Park

Though not as wild as many other reserves and parks in Java, Pangandaran, on the south coast at the border between West and Central Java provinces, offers an easy introduction to rainforest jungle.

Key Species
Frigatebirds, Green Junglefowl, Asian Pied Hornbill, Scaly-crowned Babbler.

Other Wildlife
Silvered Leaf Monkey, Long-tailed Macaque, Flying Lemur, semi-wild Banteng, Rusa Deer, Mouse-deer and Giant Squirrel. The huge *Rafflesia* flowers occasionally.

Getting There
Buses leave regularly from Jakarta, Semarang

and Yogyakarta to Pangandaran; they all take 9.5–11.5 hrs.

By train/bus Take the Bandung–Yogyakarta Express as far as Banjar (about 4 hrs) then change to bus for the last 50 km.

By car from Jakarta (400 km) the route is Bandung, Garut, Tasikmalaya, Ciamis, Banjar, then south to Pangandaran.

Accommodation/Dining

There are many hotels, *losmen*, homestays, foodstalls and restaurants in the village on the isthmus, and several very basic but attractively situated PHPA bungalows across the bay in the Forest Conservation Park at Karang Nini, on the east headland (ask at the PHPA office in town).

Five km out of town on the west beach **Delta Gecko** is recommended for friendly service, though it is not the easiest place to find. It has an inexpensive vegetarian restaurant, library, art studio and small shop, and offers a Poste Restante service. Located at Sindang Laut RT07/02, Cikembulan, Pangandaran. Postal address: PO Box 50, Kantor Pos, Pangandaran 46396, West Java. (No ☎/fax c/o Telkom Office.) 26 rms plus 18-bed dormitory. $3.5 dormitory, $5S, $6–15D, all prices include breakfast, coffee, tea, coconuts and bicycles. Take the bus beyond Pangandaran to Jl Pamugaran crossroads and walk towards the beach.

General Information

There is a charge (Rp1,000 per person, Rp6,700/sedan, Rp32,000/minibus) to enter Pangandaran village.

Guides can be hired to take you around the public part of the reserve, or you can join an organized jungle walking group, arranged by any of the travel firms in town.

PHPA Office, Jl Kidang Pananjung 266, Pangandaran 46396. ☎ (0265) 39041.

Post Office, ☎ (0265) 639284.

Telkom Office, ☎ (0265) 639333; fax 639003.

Segara Anakan

This large mangrove area, with its vast tidal mud-flat area, is unique in Java. Though not particularly rich in different species, the area holds some rare species in considerable numbers.

Key Species

Lesser Adjutant, Milky Stork, Javan Coucal, Ruddy and Stork-billed Kingfishers, Long-billed Spiderhunter, Copper-throated Sunbird.

Other Wildlife

Silvered Leaf Monkey, Long-tailed Macaque. Otters are often encountered along more remote creeks; freshwater dolphins and Dugongs have been reported but seem to have disappeared with the siltation of the estuaries.

Getting There

From Kalipucang, east of Pangandaran, there are passenger ferries to Cilacap (4 hrs, Rp1,500) at 7.00 am, 8.00 am, 12.00 pm and 1.00 pm, although boats are sometimes cancelled. A car ferry is also planned, starting from Majingklak. There are bus connections from Cilacap to the major towns of Central Java.

Accommodation/Dining

There is no accommodation inside the area, except for some huts and shelters owned by the forestry department, and private houses in the villages. If you stay overnight in Cilacap (it is not somewhere to hang around) there is accommodation ranging from $3–50.

Surabaya

Surabaya, Java's second-largest city, is the starting point for trips to the environmental centre at Trawas and the heronries of Ujung Pankah on the Solo Delta. The eastern national parks—Baluran, Alas Purwo and Meru Betiri—can be reached either from Surabaya or from Bali.

Getting There

Garuda runs 14 shuttle flights a day from Jakarta: from 6 am to 8.30 pm; 2 direct flights a day from Singapore, several direct flights daily from Ujung Pandang and Denpasar, and daily from Yogyakarta. Sempati flies from Taipei, Kuala Lumpur, Penang, Perth and Singapore as well as the same domestic destinations as Garuda. The taxi from Juanda Airport ,15 km into the city, costs $5.

Air-conditioned express trains depart nightly from Jakarta via Yogyakarta and Solo or Semarang and arrive early in the morning: Bima–Gubeng dep. 4.00 pm arr. Gubeng Station 5.30 am, costs $35 for all classes; and Argo Bromo dep. 8.00 pm arr. 5.00 am Pasar Turi Station) $50 all classes.

Night buses and public intercity buses arrive at Purabaya (also called Bungurasih).

The terminal is about 15 km south of downtown. From here you can take city buses that crisscross the city for Rp450 (more for the AC buses). You may prefer to take a taxi.

Accommodation/Dining

There are some inexpensive places as well as the likes of the **Hyatt Regency**. **Hotel Remaja** is the best value and the budget favourite is **Bamboe Denn**.

Bamboe Denn, Jl Ketabang Kali 6A. ☎ 544-0333. The travellers' favourite, cramped but friendly. 20 bed dorm, $3–4 bed; 7 rooms, $4S, $7D, $8T.

Hyatt Regency, Jl Basuki Rakhmat 124–128. ☎ 5311234; fax 5321508. 511 rooms. This is where many of the best restaurants and a number of airline offices can be found. From $220.

Remaja, Jl Embong Kenongo 12. ☎ 534 1359, 531 0045; fax 531 0009. 19 rooms. Almost always full. Call ahead. The best bet in Surabaya with AC rooms from $30S to $37D. Surabaya is full of restaurants of all descriptions; take your pick.

Transport

Garuda, Hyatt Regency, Jl Basuki Rahmad 124–128. ☎ 526321, 511234; fax 526322. Jl Tunjungan 29. ☎ 515590–1; fax 42324; Juanda Airport, ☎ 866 7513/4.

Merpati, Jl Raya Domo 111. ☎ 588111; Juanda Airport, ☎ 866 7513, 866 7607.

Sempati, Hyatt Regency, Jl Basuki Rahmad 124–128. ☎ 547 0381; fax 531 6746; Jl May Jend Sungkono, Kompleks Wonokitri Blok 5–10, ☎ 571612.

Bouraq, Jl Jend. Sudirman 70. ☎ 42383. Other airlines have offices at the Hyatt Regency, ☎ 531 1234.

Pelni, Jl Pahlawan 12. ☎ 21694; fax 21043.

Bus Bus company offices are mostly along Jl Arjuna.

Car hire Private cars (*plat hitam/taksi gelap*) can be hired from the parking lots of the larger hotels for $17/hr (2-hr minimum).

Taxi Zebra, ☎ 531 5555, 531 2233; **Merpati**, ☎ 531 5033, 531 5234; **Star**, ☎ 828 0228.

City buses and *bemo* are Rp450.

Becak are limited to short trips within areas bounded by the larger streets from which they are banned.

General Information

Tourist Office Juanda Airport. ☎ 841 7161, 841 1542 ext 603; Jl Pemuda 118. ☎ 532 4499; Jl Darmo Kali 35. ☎ 537 5448/9.

Travel Agencies: **Pacto Ltd**, Taman Hi-

buran Rakyat (THR), Surabaya Mall, Jl Kusuma Bangsa 15. ☎ 5345776, and at the Hyatt Regency ☎ 532 6385, 531 1234; **Orient Express**, Jl Pang. Sudirman 62. ☎ 545 6888, 545 6666.

SBKSDA (PHPA) Office, Jl Kutisari Selatan XIII/39, PO Box 29, Surabaya 60401. ☎ 60401.

Main Post Office, Jl Kebonrojo 10. ☎ 535 2499.

Main Telkom Office, Jl Garuda 4.

Foreign exchange: **Bank BCA**, Jl Raya Darmo 5. ☎ 571003-4.

Hospitals: **Rumah Sakit Katolik St. Vincentius A. Paulo** (RSK), Jl Raya Diponegoro 51. ☎ 577 4142, 537 7562.

Trawas

The PPLH (Pusat Pendidikan Lingkungan Hidup (Environmental Education Centre) at Seloliman was established in 1990 on the foothills of Mt Pananggungan and designed in traditional Javanese style.

Key Species

Javan Hawk-eagle, Javan Kingfisher, grey forms of Black-headed Bulbul, Black-crested Bulbul, Thick-billed Flowerpecker, Violet-tailed Sunbird.

Other Wildlife

Red forms of Silvered Leaf Monkey; good views of Flying Fox roost.

Getting There

From Surabaya:

By bus (About 3 hrs) From Pasar Turi train station take a bus to Joyoboyo terminal (Rp400), then change buses to Bungurasih terminal (Rp400). From Gubeng train station direct to Bungur Asih by minibus Rp400. From Bungur Asih take a Surabaya–Malang bus as far as Pandaan (Rp1,000); Pandaan-Trawas by colt (Rp1,000); Trawas to the Centre by *ojek* (Rp2,000). Alternatively, from Bungur Asih leave the Malang bus at Japanan (Rp800); take the Japanan–Mojokerto colt as far as Ngoro (Rp500); Ngoro to the Centre by *ojek* (Rp2,000).

From Malang, take a bus to Pandaan, then as above.

By car Surabaya south to Japanan, then west to Ngoro. From Ngoro ask directions south to PPLH, desa Seloliman. About 1.5 hrs. The Centre will also arrange transport from Surabaya at $45 for 7–8 people. See Surabaya representative's address below.

Accommodation/Dining

To book accommodation, contact the representative in Surabaya: PPLH Surabaya, Jl Bratang Gede 116, Surabaya 60245. ☎ (031) 5614493. Office hrs only.

Two guest -houses: for 6, $30 a night; for 10, $38. Bungalows (8) range from $15 a night for 1 person on weekdays to $25 a night for 3–4 people on weekends and public holidays. Dormitory, sleeps 60: $1.25 per person. Meals cost $1–4. There is also a small, reasonably-priced coffee shop.

General Information

The Centre hosts school classes, discussion groups and so on. A library with books and magazines on mainly environmental and biological topics is housed above the office and open for visitors (good for rainy afternoons). There is electricity but no telephone at the Centre (the nearest phone is in Trawas). Climbing Mt Pananggungan takes about 5 hrs up, 3 hrs down; water should be taken along.

Solo Delta

The large heronry of Ujung Pangkah is located on the Solo river delta north of Surabaya. Like the well-vegetated fish ponds and mangrove area along the coast, the mud-flats have a rich birdlife, especially of northern migratory shorebirds.

Key Species

Oriental Darter, Rufous Night-heron, Glossy Ibis, Black-headed Ibis, Asian Dowitcher, Javan Coucal, Javan White-eye, Asian Golden Weaver.

Getting There

Minibuses leave from Jembatan Merah (Surabaya) to Sedayu (Rp1,500). From Sedayu take an *ojek* (about Rp2,500) to the guard's house at "Suaka Burung". The whole trip takes about 2 hrs.

By car Take the road north from Surabaya to Gresik and Sedayu, then continue north to Pangkahkulon and watch for the sign to "Suaka Burung".

Accommodation/Dining

There is no formal accommodation and only very basic eating, however the village head can make arrangements for you to stay overnight in very simple accommodation. Offer Rp10,000.

General Information

The heronry is a gazetted bird sanctuary and is supervised by the local government and PHPA. However, it is sufficient to report to the guard; the breeding colony is located at walking distance from his house. If you are a keen birder, you should certainly get out to the vast area of mud-flats. Motor boats can be chartered (Rp 20–30,000 for a trip of several hours; remember to take food for the boatman, too). The mouths of the Lembaan and Bedahanturi rivers are particularly good for shorebirds.

Baluran National Pk

Lying in the dry, northeastern extremity of Java and only a short journey from Bali, Baluran offers probably the best site in Indonesia to see Green Peafowl and Green Junglefowl, as well as African-type savannahs and large herds of grazing mammals.

Key Species

Green Peafowl, Green Junglefowl, White-bellied and Great Slaty Woodpeckers, Banded Pitta and Java Sparrow (still a few left but they are disappearing fast).

Other Wildlife

An internationally important population of Banteng (one of three largest in the world) and probably the island's largest population of the endemic Javan Deer (the peak of the rutting season is July). Barking Deer, Flying Fox, Leopard (including "Black Panthers"), Asiatic Wild Dog, and the scarce, red-coloured form of the Ebony Leaf Monkey.

Getting There

By bus From Ketapang (the Bali–Java ferry terminal and location of Banyuwangi Baru railway station) about 30 km south of Baluran, catch the public bus to Surabaya (they leave every 30 min or so) and get off at the park gate at Batangan (Rp 700, ask for Baluran). Alternatively, negotiate with a minibus (*bemo* or *lin*) driver to take you directly to Baluran (Bekol or Bama).

From Surabaya, do not go all the way to Ketapang or Banyuwangi but get the bus to drop you at Batangan (again, ask for Baluran.) To get into Bekol or Bama from Batangan, take a motorbike taxi (*ojek*) ($2.50/person) or hire a minibus from the house next to the park gate (negotiable but likely to be about $6–7.50).

Accommodation/Dining

Visitors to Baluran have the choice of staying at either Bekol or Bama. At Bekol there is an old, two-storey, stone-built guest-house (*pasanggrahan*) at $3S and a small bungalow (*wisma tamu*) at $5S. At Bama there are bungalows and a guest-house, also at $3S. There is no electricity at either place unless more than ten guests are staying (very rare) in which case the guards are allowed to start the generator. Food is not normally available in Baluran so visitors should bring their own (buy it in Galian/Bajulmati, a village about 3 km from the gate), but it is sometimes possible to arrange for the wife of one of the guards to cook. If you book accommodation at Bekol in advance through the park management office at Banyuwangi (see right), it can all be arranged for you. It is also possible to arrange for guards or *ojek* drivers to bring in a packed meal (*nasi bungkus*) from the local *warung*.

General Information

Avoid visiting Baluran at weekends (the chance of there being lots of noisy tourists is too high). The dry season (Aug–Nov) is the time of best visibility and easiest walking in Baluran; it is also the time when the large mammals are concentrated around the coastal water-holes and at Bekol. However, the early part of the wet season (Dec–Jan) is the best time to see the seed-eating birds (munias, Java Sparrow, etc). and the large herds of Banteng and Javan Deer on the grasslands north of Bekol. Green Peafowl and Green Junglefowl can be seen all year round but the peak of the peafowl breeding season is usually Nov/Dec.

Two nights is probably the minimum you will want to spend in the park; two full days would be better. Sunrise is usually about 4.45 am (West Indonesia time), sunset is generally about 5.30 pm (do not forget the hour's difference between Bali and Java).

Get your entrance ticket/permit ($1/person) from the gate at Batangan (there is no need to go to the office in Banyuwangi). Apart from the short coastal tracks there are six *c.*3-km, circular trails (unmissable, each marked with small carpark and large blue-and-white flower tubs!) off the Bekol-Batangan road and at the rangers' barracks at Bekol. Visitors wishing to explore very far from Bekol, Bama or the road have to take a park ranger (about $5/person for a *c.*5-hr walk; negotiate). **Baluran National Park** Management Office, Jl Jend. Ahmad Yani 108, Banyuwangi. ☎ (0333) 24119.

Alas Purwo National Park

Under the administration of Baluran National Park, Alas Purwo National Park, some 80 km to the south, is a little known and densely forested peninsula at the southeastern corner of Java. Probably more famous among surfing enthusiasts, the area also offers good birding and the chance to see turtles, Banteng and Asiatic Wild Dogs.

Key Species

Green Peafowl, Green Junglefowl, Banded Pitta, Javan Kingfisher, raptors and waders.

Other Wildlife

One of the largest populations of Banteng on Java and possibly the best place to see Asiatic Wild Dogs (which can sometimes be seen hunting the Banteng on Sadengan Feeding Ground.) Green, Leatherback, Hawksbill and Olive Ridley Turtles nest along the southern coast of the reserve.

Getting There

By bus From Banyuwangi's Brawijaya bus station take the Jember bus to Benculuk (Rp700) where you catch a minibus ("colt") to Tegaldlimo (about Rp1,000). At Tegaldlimo (a good place to buy food) arrange for a motorbike taxi (*ojek*) to take you to the Trianggulasi guest houses, stopping on the way at the reserve entrance at Pasaranyar, where you have to pay a $1 entrance fee. From Surabaya take the Banyuwangi bus that goes via Jember to Benculuk. Then as above.

Accommodation/Dining

Guest-house rooms ($3S) are available at Trianggulasi, about a 30-min drive from the entrance at Pasaranyar; visitors need to bring their own food as none is available in the reserve.

General Information

Avoid Alas Purwo at the weekends, particularly Sun, when hordes of beach-goers descend upon the place. Nov–Mar is the best time to see turtles laying eggs. Early morning and late afternoon/evening are the best times to visit Sadengan Feeding Ground. Allow a minimum of one night at Trianggulasi, which will allow you to visit Sadengan in the early morning and again in the late afternoon before leaving at dusk; two or more nights will allow you to explore the Segara Anak estuary and perhaps see some of the forested peninsula with one of the Reserve's guards as a guide. Sunrise and sunset are about 4.45–5.10 am and 5.30 pm respectively.

Visitors wishing to explore the peninsula are required to take a reserve ranger (the charge is negotiable but is likely to be about $6/person for a *c.*5-hr walk).

Sadengan Feeding Ground The 1-km track to the feeding grounds is about 500 m from Tianggulasi, back along the main Trianggulasi–Pasaranyar road. The turn-off on the right is signposted to Sadengan *(Lokasi Habitat Banteng)*. Approaching from Pasaranyar, turn off shortly after a small Hindu temple.

Marengan and Segara Anak The Marengan peninsula and Segara Anak backwater are most easily reached by following the signposted trail to Ngagelan from the Rawabenda guardpost on the main Trianggulasi-Pasaranyar road.

Meru Betiri National Park

The least visited of the "big three" sites at the eastern end of Java, Meru Betiri offers jungle trekking and turtle watching as well as the chance to see lowland forest birds.

Key Species

Lowland forest species including hornbills and 11 species of cuckoo.

Other Wildlife

Maybe a tiger if you are very lucky (but you had better take a photograph or nobody will believe you)! Banteng can also be seen, but Baluran and Blambangan are better sites. Green, Loggerhead, Hawksbill, Olive Ridley and Leatherback Turtles are all reported to nest along the coast (Nov–Mar is the best time to see them). The parasitic *Rafflesia zollingeriana* is a particularly notable plant (and it is apparently restricted to the Meru Betiri area).

Getting There

From the bus station in Banyuwangi take an *angkot* (minibus) to Jagag (Rp3,000, 1 hr). From Jagag catch a local bus to Sarongan on the edge of the park (Rp2,000, 1hr). At Sarongan either catch the daily truck for the 15-km journey along a deeply rutted track to Sukameda, or hire an *ojek* (Rp12,000).

Accommodation/Dining

There are two places to stay: **the plantation guest-house** at Sukamade, which charges $8 per person including three meals, or the **PHPA guest-house** behind the beach, a 3-km walk south through the plantations from Sukamade. The PHPA guest-house, although basic, is in a great location. You need to take your own food. Rp5,000 per night.

General Information

A permit is officially required from the PHPA office in Banyuwangi, but nobody bothers if you turn up without one.

Meru Betiri National Park Management Office, Kantor SBKSDA Jatim II, Jl Jawa 36, PO Box 182, Jember, East Java. ☎ (0331) 84710.

There are three main birding areas: two around Sukamade and one behind the beach. Short trails lead into the beach forest on either side of the PHPA guest-house, and there is a watchtower overlooking a small pool in the forest 100 m to the east. Behind (west of) Sukamade village two trails lead into the forest (ask for directions to the start). One is a 1.5-km, dead end up a hill. The other crosses the ridge and leads to a beach: this is a full day's hike there and back. The third area is at the northern end of the plantations along the Sukamade river valley. It is a 6–8 km walk to the natural vegetation so it may be best to hire an *ojek*. At the end of the plantations the track enters a bamboo grove and secondary forest and ends at the river after 500 m. Wade across the river. A trail follows the banks for a further kilometre through disturbed forest to an old watchtower, a good place to watch for raptors and birds of the forest edge.

–Bas van Balen, Margaret Clarbrough, Simon Hedges, Paul Jepson, Rosie Ounsted, Ria Saryanthi , with additional information from Nick Brickle, Russell Bright, Keith Harris, Daniel Philippe, Rudyanto, Kristina Sugiharto & Martin Tyson.

Bali

Bali's main beach resorts, Kuta, Sanur and Nusa Dua, catering for huge numbers of tourists, are located 20 km south of the provincial capital, Denpasar, and within 3–6 km of Bali's Nguruh Rai airport, which is becoming one of the main entry points to Indonesia.

Getting There

By air Flights from the Soekarno-Hatta International Airport in Jakarta are frequent, and if you land in Jakarta before 5 pm you can usually get a connection to Bali. (Although in peak season, these 90-min flights are almost always full. Book your flight all the way to Bali.) From the airport, hire a taxi to the place you intend to stay.

By train One can also take a train from Jakarta (slow, and a nightmare with scuba gear) which connects to Surabaya (12 hrs on Bima, $43 Executive; 8 hrs. on the new Express, $44 Executive class), then a train to Bayuwangi (4 hrs, $7.50 Business class), then a bus to and across the Ketapang, Java–Gilimanuk, Bali ferry ($3) and on to Denpasar (4 hrs, $2).

By long-distance bus Taking a night bus the entire way is probably a better option (24 hrs, Jakarta–Denpasar, $30.) From Ubung Terminal outside Denpasar, where you are dropped off, a minibus to the tourist triangle of Kuta–Sanur–Nusa Dua runs $3–5. All in all, best to arrive by plane.

By sea There are six ferries a day from Lembar on Lombok, $2.50–4 passenger, $25 car. There is also a high-speed (2 hr) catamaran service that departs Lembar 11.30 am and 5.00 pm, $17.50–25. Arrange these through your Lombok accommodation. Pelni's *Kelimutu*, *Dobonsolo*, *AWU* and *Tilongkabila* all stop in Bali on their various two-week routes.

Transport

Bouraq Jl Sudirman 7A, Denpasar, ☎223564.
Garuda Jl Melati 61, Denpasar, ☎ 235139.
Merpati Jl Melati 51, Denpasar, ☎ 235358.
Sempati Jl Diponegoro, Komplek Diponegoro Megah, Blok B/No. 27, ☎ 237343.

The following international airlines have offices in the Grand Bali Beach in Sanur,

288511. Direct phone lines are: Air France, ☎ 755523; Ansett Australia, ☎ 289636; Cathay Pacific, ☎ 753942; Continental-Micronesia, ☎ 287065/287774; Garuda, ☎ 288243; Japan Airlines and Japan Asia Airways, ☎ 287476/287577; Lufthansa, ☎ 286952; Malaysia Air Service, ☎ 288716/288511; Qantas, ☎ 288331; Sempati Air, ☎ 288824; Singapore Airlines, ☎ 287940; Thai International, ☎ 285071/3.

Wisti Sabha Building at the Airport houses: Air New Zealand, ☎ 756170/751011 ext. 1116; China Airlines, ☎ 754856/757298; EVA Air, ☎ 298935; KLM, ☎ 756127; Korean Air Lines, ☎ 754856/757298, fax: 757275; Royal Brunei, ☎ 757292.

Cars and minibuses There are numerous car hire offices. Rates go from as low as $15 excluding insurance per day for a Jimny up to $40 for a Kijang minibus. It's sometimes a good idea to ask at your hotel.

Motorcycle hire has become increasingly dangerous on Bali and is definitely not recommended for the inexperienced. Hire through car hire companies or personal contact. Check the bike over very carefully before agreeing to the hire.

Bus Bali is covered by a network of minibus routes and you can be dropped anywhere. You can also charter minibuses, but be prepared to haggle over the price ($30–40 a day, plus fuel). To travel between main tourist centres there are several useful, fixed-price shuttle bus services: **Perama** (based in Kuta, ☎ 751170) is recommended.

General Information

Regional Tourist Office, Komplek Niti Mandala, Jl Raya Puputan, Renon, Denpasar. ☎ (0361) 225649; fax 233475.

Travel Agencies There are many agencies around the Grand Bali Beach Hotel in Sanur. Among the most reputable are **Golden Bali Tour**, ☎ 226401, **Pacto**, ☎ 288511, **Rama Tours** and **Tunas Indonesia**, ☎ 284015. For airline tickets try **Vayatour** at Tanjung Bungkak, Denpasar.

PHPA Office Bali Barat NP, Kantor Pengelola Taman Nasional, Gilimanuk-Cecik Pos

Office, Bali Barat. ☎ (0333) 21312.
Photography: PT Modern Photo, opposite the gas station and Galael supermarket in Kuta, has the freshest film and best E-6 processing.

Sanur

Sanur has traditionally been the spot for luxurious seaside accommodation. Conveniently located near Denpasar on the main road up to the hills, Sanur is neither as frenetic as Kuta, nor as well-mannered as Nusa Dua; its main attraction is a white sand beach bordering a reef-sheltered lagoon. Sanur has a wide range of luxury and intermediate accommodations and a smaller range of budget *losmen*. There are waterbirds to be seen at the Suwung fishponds, by the Bypass road, and the beach at Merta Sari, and two delightful birding excursions, to Serangan and Nusa Penida islands, are recommended. The Nusa Dua decantation ponds (see Bali Bird tour) are also within easy reach.

Getting There
Simply drive out on the Bypass road to Kuta, the fishponds are on the left.

Around Sanur
MERTA SARI
A vast expanse of mud-flats, with mangroves and fishponds at the unspoilt, south end of Sanur beach.

Key Species
A good selection of shorebirds on the flats; in the mangroves Small Blue, Sacred and Collared Kingfishers, Brown-capped Woodpecker, Blue-tailed Bee-eater, Flyeater, Pied Fantail and Streaked Weaver.

Getting There
Head for the Travelodge off Jl Mertasari, which leads south at the junction of Jl Danau Poso and Jl Kesari in Blangjong. Carry on to the Mertasari temple and then walk down the beach to the mud-flats. For the mangroves and fishponds, walk west a few hundred metres along the beach.

SERANGAN ISLAND
A 72-ha island lying at the entrance to Benoa harbour. Known principally for its turtles and the important Sakenan temple, but also a great place for watching shorebirds and seabirds.

Key Species
Great, Lesser and, occasionally, Christmas Frigatebirds too. Herons, egrets and shorebirds.

Getting There
Dugout outriggers or more substantial craft can be hired almost anywhere along Sanur beach. Allow 3–4 hrs for the round trip; expect to pay $30 for the trip, more for larger craft. Alternatively, take a *bemo* to Suwung (Rp400), a boat-stage located off the Jl Ngurah Rai bypass. Either charter a boat for $10.00 or wait for the public boats costing Rp1–2,000.

NUSA PENIDA
A dry, sparsely populated island in the Lombok Strait to the east of Bali. A great place to get off the beaten track.

Key Species
White-tailed Tropicbird, White-faced Heron, Osprey, White-bellied Sea-eagle, Peregrine Falcon, Black-naped Fruit-dove, Green and Pied Imperial Pigeons, Yellow-crested Cockatoo, Edible-nest Swiftlet, White-shouldered Triller, Hair-crested Drongo, Red-chested Flowerpecker, Black-faced Munia.

Getting There & Around
Charter a 6-seat *jukung* from the beach north of the Bali Beach Hotel in Sanur, $28–38 for a 1-way crossing to Toyapakeh or Sampalan. Alternatively, hitch a ride on a motor-launch taking divers/surfers to Lembongan, or cruise over in luxury with pleasure boats sailing from Benoa Bay. For scheduled public transport take a bus or *bemo* to Kusamba, 10 km southeast of Klungkung, from where there is a regular *jukung* service. The 1.5 hr crossing costs $2.00.

Public transport around the island is sketchy and irregular. It may be best to walk, and sweat copiously. You can always get coconuts for refreshment!

Accommodation/Dining
Options are very limited. Try **Rumah Marzuki** in Toyapakeh and an adjoining *losmen* still under construction, $4 without breakfast.

In Sampalan there is a government-run *losmen*, $5 with basic breakfast.

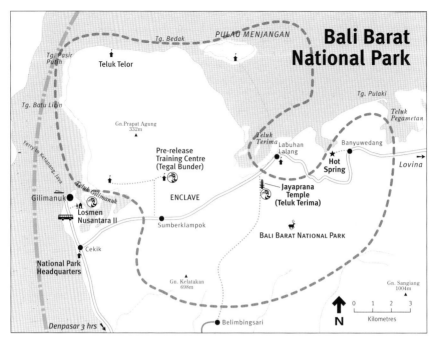

Bali Bird Tour

BEDUGUL

Accommodation/Dining

Ashram Guest House, Bar and restaurant. ☎ (0362) 22439. 27 rms. Own bakery. Rms $15–20D, new villas $35D including breakfast; also rooms in old schoolhouse, $7.50, no breakfast.

Bali Handara Kosaido Country Club, Pancasari. ☎ (0362) 22646. 37 rms. Fine setting overlooking Lake Buyan, adjacent to forest; walk from bar behind main wing and see barbets, thrushes etc. $90D–$350VIP. Includes **Kamandalu** restaurant, European/Indonesian/Japanese cuisine. Special order: *sushi*, also sensational value grilled pork and lamb chops; excellent sandwiches in bar.

Bedugul Hotel and restaurant, Lake Braten. ☎ (0362) 226593. Set in garden overlooking lake and backing on to forest. Good food. Watersports centre, noisy in the daytime with trippers and skiboats, OK in the evening. Cottages $30–35 (sleep 4); nice rooms in new wing $45 (2 double beds).

Lila Graha, Candikuning, Bedugul. ☎ (0368) 21446. 15 rms. Brilliant position in garden overlooking lake, up steep drive on left just before lake. Government-run: service variable,

but best value in town. Rooms quiet and very clean. $15–18D including breakfast.

Mutiara Sari Restaurant, Baturiti. On edge of valley before the steep climb to the pass, with honeyeaters in the garden. Chinese and European Cuisine. Specialties *susu tawar* (fresh, cool milk) or *susu manis* (fresh hot, sweetened milk), *ayam goreng* (fried chicken).

As well as those attached to hotels, there are several cheap restaurants around Candikuning market: **Rumah Makan Anda** is thoroughly recommended. Try also **Warung Unick** restaurant, Candikuning. Up a drive on the left past the lake. Medium priced, pleasant service. Recommended: Chicken Cordon Bleu and BBQ. Open for breakfast.

General Information

Bemos and buses from marketplace or lakeside, Rp1,000 to Singaraja, Rp3,000 to Gilimanuk. Boat rides on Lake Braten, $5–8 per hr. To see waterfowl on Lake Buyan: 2 km along south boundary road, stop near school, walk to lakeside on grassy track.

THE NORTH COAST

Accommodation/Dining

Apart from at Lovina (see the Periplus *Bali* guide), there is a limited choice of accommodation on the north coast. If you take the westerly route to the coast, the **Puri Lum-**

bung cottages at Munduk are a village/School of Tourism cooperative project that emphasizes environmental and cultural preservation.

If you take the road due north from Bedugul, you might try lunch at **Restaurant Segar** in Singaraja, an unpretentious Chinese restaurant.

Nusantara II Gilimanuk, opposite the ferry terminal and well off the road. $5 rm.

Pondok Sari Beach Bungalows and Restaurant, Pemuteran/Gerokgak. ☎/fax (0362) 92337. 20 rooms with open-air bathrooms, set in a beachside garden. 31 km before Gilimanuk and convenient for National Park. $12.50–22.50 +15% tax.

Pondok Wisata Asih homestay, Jl Jalak Putih, Gilimanuk. Off main road: fairly quiet. $6 rm, breakfast Rp3,000.

Puri Lumbung, Munduk. ☎/fax (0362) 92810/92514. 12 cottages, $43S, $50D including breakfast and tax. Also a **homestay**: 10 rms. $15S, $20D including private bath and breakfast. Excellent restaurant.

Puri Segara Cottages, next door to Pondok Sari and similarly priced. Family and single/double cottages. Lovely position.

Away from the hotels there are few dining opportunities. The best food in Gilimanuk—roast sucking pig and *nasi campur*—is available at **Rumah Makan Anita**, the last building on the right after the ferry terminal. You can also eat well at the little restaurant at Labuan Lalang. **Segar** restaurant, Jl Erlangga 37, Singaraja, has a wide range of medium-priced Chinese dishes.

BALI BARAT NAT PARK

The 17,500 ha Bali Barat National Park lies on the far western tip of Bali. Along the northern coast it protects the last areas of dry forest on the island, home of the remaining wild population of Bali Starling, which numbers just 35. The rest of the park has wetter forests. The park's main tourist attraction is the excellent wall of reefs around Menjangan Island. For birders the park is poorly served with trails, nevertheless the area offers an excellent mix of habitats, muddy shores, mangroves, dry forest and scrub, with wetter forests on the east of the north coast road, which bisects the park.

Key Species

Lesser Adjutant, Great-billed Heron, Malaysian Plover, Java Sparrow, Black-winged Starling, White-shouldered Triller. During the migration season shorebirds such as Oriental Plover and occasionally Great Knot; thousands of honey-buzzards and sparrow-hawks cross from East Java in the first two weeks of October.

Other Wildlife

There is fabulous snorkelling and diving off the coast of the National Park and from nearby **Pulau Menjangan**. Hundreds of species of coral, and a good variety of reef fish.

Getting There & Around

The park is 3 hrs by road from Denpasar and 2.5 hrs from Lovina. A charter from Kuta, Ubud or Lovina to the park will cost *c.* $45. There are numerous buses from Lovina and Ubung bus station, Denpasar, to Gilimanuk, the ferry head on Bali for East Java.

Bemo and horse-drawn carts ply the 1 km between Gilimanuk bus terminal and the harbour (Rp500/1000). There are plenty of public minibuses or *ojek* to ferry you along the road to the birding sites at Sumber Klampok, Labuhan Lalang and Banyuwedang.

General Information

The National Park office is at Cekik, 4 km from Gilimanuk and directly opposite the junction of the Gilimanuk–Denpasar and north coast roads. A permit to enter the park costs Rp2,500, and is available from both here and at Labuhan Lalang. An excellent guide is I Nyoman Lodiarta, a keen birder who speaks some English.

Seeing the Bali Starling

The last few birds are concentrated around the Teluk Kabar guard post on the north shore of the Parapat Agung peninsula. The best way to see them is to overlook their roosting area and watch them fly in at dusk. Access to this area is restricted and officially a letter of permission is required from PHPA in Jakarta (very difficult to obtain), but ask at the National Park HQ or Labuhan Lalang about the possibility of seeing the birds.

Gilimanuk Bay

A trail running northwest along the shore from Losman Nusantara II leads after 200 m to a dry bay covered with stunted mangroves; cross the bay to a grassy peninsula. From Sep to Nov this is a good place for Oriental Plover, and the inlet on the other side has waders in small numbers, among which are Great Knot and Grey-tailed Tattler. Along the walk look out for Savanna Nightjar, Black-winged Starling, Richard's Pipit and Asian Pied Starling.

Sumber Klampok

The village of Sumber Klampok is located mid-way between Cekik (Gilimanuk) and Labuhan Lalang. A track (with a barrier) on the north side of the road leads 1.5 km through fields to the National Park research centre and Bali Starling Pre-release Training Centre and captive breeding centre. The bushes around the complex are full of birds. Look for Green Junglefowl, Orange-breasted Green Pigeon, Racquet-tailed Treepie, Laced Woodpecker and Banded Pitta. In Apr–May and Sep–Oct migrant Yellow-rumped Flycatcher, Arctic Warbler and Oriental Cuckoo.

Labuhan Lalang

Labuhan Lalang is the main focus for park visitors as from here they can take a boat across for the snorkelling around Menjangan Island. Fixed-price boat charter is $30 for about 4 hrs, but you can probably arrange to share a 10-seater boat with other tourists. Snorkel and mask hire is $7.

The park staff also offer guided birding walks on the mainland for $7. The pleasant, 2-hr walk takes you southwest along the shore through the back of the mangroves, then across the road to the Jayaprana temple. Beyond the temple it drops down through scrubby forest to a river and then follows the river back to the road near Sumber Klampok. Birds to see are Buffy Fish-owl, Fulvous-chested Rhinomyias and Horsfield's Babbler. This is the place to look for migrating raptors.

Blimbing Sari to Labuhan Lalang trek

This rigorous, 7–8 hr trek can be arranged with the park guides. An early morning *bemo* charter takes you round to the microwave station on Mt Klatakan, near Belimbing Sari village, 5 km inland from Melaya on the Denpasar road. This is a good place to see Hill Myna, Rufous-bellied and Black Eagles and Chestnut-headed Bee-eater. The trail crosses two ridges (610 and 550 m) and then drops down a valley to Labuhan Lalang. Good chance of Wreathed Hornbill. A guide is essential and they ask $25 for this excursion.

Banyuwedang

Located 5 km west of Labuhan Lalang on the north coast road, this is a popular Hindu shrine and hot spring located 1 km down a side road. Trails lead out beyond the shrine to the coast, crossing dry river beds and passing through scrub. It is one of the best places to see Island Collared Dove, Small Minivet, Black-winged Starling and Java Sparrow.

Accommodation/Dining

If you have your own transport the nicest place to stay is **Pondok Sari Beach Bungalows and Restaurant**, Pemuteran/ Gerokgak, ☎/fax (03962) 92337. 20 rooms with open-air bathrooms ($12.50–22.50 +15% tax), set in a beachside garden and with private marine reserve. It is located 16 km east of Labuhan, 31 km from Gilimanuk on the northern road from Lovina.

Puri Segara Cottages, next door to Pondok Sari and similarly priced. Family and single/double cottages. Lovely position.

The only budget accommodation is available in Gilimanuk. We recommend **Nusantara II Gilimanuk**, 200 m up a track opposite the ferry terminal. Overlooks the bay and offers good, short bird walks to the northeast. Ideal for budget birders. $5 rm.

Pondok Wisata Asih Homestay, Jl Jalak Putih, Gilimanuk. Off main road: fairly quiet. $6 rm, breakfast Rp3,000.

There are few dining opportunities. The best food in Gilimanuk—roast sucking pig and *nasi campur*—is available at **Rumah Makan Anita**, the last building on the right after the ferry terminal. You can also eat quite well at the little restaurant at Labuan Lalang. **Restaurant Segar**, Jl Erlangga 37, Singaraja, has a wide range of medium-priced Chinese dishes.

Ubud

Ubud is a major tourist centre on account of its art and culture. There are numerous places to stay and eat, suiting all tastes and pockets.

THE BALI BIRD WALK

Bali Bird Walks take place at 9 am from the **Beggar's Bush** in Campuan, Ubud (next to the bridge), on Tue–Sun, or any other day by prior arrangement. It is best to book, either in person at Beggar's Bush or phone (0361 975009). Price $33 includes water while you walk, binoculars, lunch at Beggar's Bush, tea and coffee. Wear shorts, t-shirt, hat, walking shoes, and be prepared to get muddy and wet!

Also recommended viewing, about 3 km north of Ubud, is the heronry at Gunung Petulu. Here, in a village setting, nests and roosts a population of *c.*7,000 herons comprised of four species: Intermediate, Cattle and Little Egrets, and Javan Pond-heron.

–Victor Mason with additional information from *B van Balen, P Jepson & R Ounsted.*

Nusa Tenggara

LOMBOK

A great place for relaxing, enjoying the beaches and visiting temples and villages, Lombok has become Indonesia's new "in" tourist destination. Apart from on the slopes of Mt Rinjani, little natural vegetation remains and the island's bird fauna is very impoverished compared to that of its neighbours. There is good trekking and pleasant mountain birding in Rinjani National Park and this is well covered in all guides to the island.

SAPIT

On the mountain's eastern slopes, this pleasant area of forest (some degraded) mixed with shifting agriculture, is the island's only birding area.

Key Species

Chinese Goshawk, Black-naped Fruit-dove, White-shouldered Triller, Scaly-crowned Honeyeater, Lesser Shortwing, Mountain Leaf-warbler, Short-tailed Starling.

General Information

From Sapit a road leads uphill for 7 km to the start of the Air Panas ("hot springs") trail. The nicest thing to do is to charter a vehicle up ($2.5–5) and walk back, descending through degraded forest after 1–2 km. The sacred hot springs at Air Panas are surrounded by good primary forest through which there is a level trail.

Accommodation

"Harti Suci ("Pure heart") Homestay and Restaurant, in Sapit village, Pringgabaya is a small and simple *losmen*, but offers cool mountain air and spectacular views. Prices range from $7–25D per night.

KOMODO

Komodo is a beautiful island that offers great birding, as well as a chance to see the famous Komodo "dragons".

KOMODO NATIONAL PARK

The Komodo National Park, world famous as the home of the world's largest lizard, covers the 335 km by 15 km Komodo island and its slightly smaller neighbour, Rinca, as well as many smaller islands in between. The dry, lontar palm-studied landscapes set in sparkling blue seas create a delightful bird-watching setting. As well as Komodo Dragons and birds, there are fruit-bat roosts in the mangroves and some good snorkelling.

Key Species

One of the last strongholds of Yellow-crested Cockatoo; Orange-footed Scrubfowl are easy to see. Other notable species are: Great-billed Heron, Green Junglefowl, Beach Thick-knee, Green and Pied Imperial Pigeon, Nicobar Pigeon, Wallacean Cuckoo-shrike.

Other Wildlife

Komodo dragons, fruit bats in the mangroves at Pulau Kalong, superb corals at Pantai Merah. Feral horses, buffalo, and wild boar. Flying Fox roosts; green turtles, sharks and dolphins in surrounding seas.

Getting There

Reach Komodo by daily ferry from either Sape on Sumbawa (departs 8.00 am, 6 hrs, $4) or Labuhanbajo on Flores (departs 8.00 am, 4 hrs, $2). Transfer from ferry to shore by small boat ($1). You can also charter a boat from either of these ports: the longer and more dangerous trip from Sape costs $175–350 depending on the type and condition of the boat; from Labuhanbajo aim to pay $50–100.

Komodo's sister island, Rinca (which also has "dragons"), is reached by chartered boat from Labuhanbajo. Many hotels and travel agencies offer a day-trip package for $35 on a small fishing boat that can carry 8–10 people. The crossing takes 2 hrs.

Accommodation/Dining

On Komodo the **National Park Headquarters** at Loh Liang is the only accommodation on the island. Although it has 80 beds

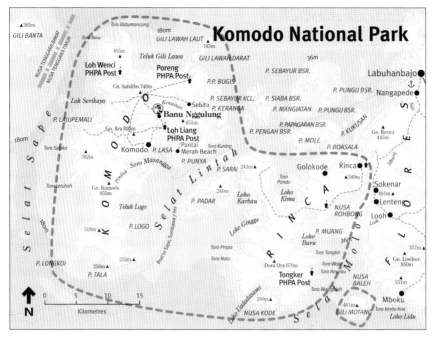

Komodo National Park

in shared cabins, in the peak season (June–August) it is often overcrowded and you may have to sleep on the floor, $4.50S, $7D. A canteen serves simple Indonesian meals and drinks.

On Rinca the National Park has similar accommodation (8 rms only) and a canteen at Loh Buaya.

General Information

The best time to visit is from Mar–May and Sep–Dec. The Park entrance fee is Rp2,000. Guides are compulsory for excursions. From Loh Liang to Banu Nggulung the cost is Rp3,000. Expect to pay $8–12 for longer trips.

FLORES

TRANS-FLORES HIGHWAY

The Trans-Flores highway winds some 700 km through the scenic mountains of the island, from Labuhanbajo in the west, to Larantuka on the island's eastern tip. Most of the road is paved, and it passes through all 5 of Flores's district capitals.

Labuhanbajo–Ruteng (126 km)	4 hrs
Ruteng–Bajawa (130 km)	4 hrs
Bajawa–Ende (126 km)	4 hrs
Ende–Moni (Keli Mutu) (52 km)	1.5 hrs
Moni–Maumere (96 km)	3 hrs
Maumere–Larantuka (137 km)	4 hrs

Transport

Public buses—cheap, reliable, and crowded—shuttle continuously back and forth along the highway. Most of the buses run during the day, although there are a few night expresses. No single bus makes the entire run; usually they are based in one district capital and just run to the next and back.

Chartering your own vehicle costs $40–60/day but allows you plenty of flexibility—essential for birding! Side-trips depend on the type of vehicle and the state of the roads. Check the state of the vehicle very carefully; many *bemos* are not fit for the out-of-town roads, nor are all the drivers competent. Remember that map distances often have little relevance to travel time.

Labuhanbajo

The little coastal town of Labuhanbajo is the main entry point to Flores for those travelling from Komodo or islands to the west.

Getting There

Daily ferries from Sape, Sumbawa, which stop at Komodo, arrive in the late afternoon. Hotel/*losmen* representatives meet the ferry, so simply walk to the *losmen* of your choice or be whisked to the out-of-town seaside hotels by boat. If you arrive by bus from Ruteng, you can be dropped where you want.

The Pelni ships *Binaiya*, *Tatamilau* and *Tilongkabila* each stop in at Labuhanbajo a total of 4 times each month on their respective 2-week routes.

The airport is a couple of kilometres out of town, $3 charter, 60¢ for a collective minibus. At present there are 6 flights a week to Labuhanbajo on the Kupang to Bima route; however the service is unreliable and often overbooked. Do not rely on getting a flight out: an "OK" ticket booked outside Labuhanbajo has no meaning.

Accommodation/Dining

Most places are geared to the low end of the budget travel market and are situated along the shore, a short walk from the harbour, though there are a few better quality hotels. **New Bajo Beach** The best in Labuanbajo, located about 1 km south of town, but with free transportation for guests. ☎ 41047, 41069. 16 very large rms, 10 cottages and a dining room in a nicely landscaped area with a beach. Tours can be arranged. Fan-cooled rms, $18S or D; AC rms $26S or D; cottages $16S or D. **Losmen Bajo Beach** is very popular with budget travellers. 25 rms, prices ranging from $3.50–6.50S to $5–9D. **Gardena** 8 cottages, a bit of a steep climb but worth it for the view from the restaurant. With enclosed facilities, $7.50S or D; shared facilities $5S or D.

Apart from the above accommodation, there are several beachside places, accessible only by (free) motorboat rides. See Periplus *East of Bali* guide for further details.

Restaurant Borobudur, next to the Gardena, and with a similarly wonderful "sundowner" view, serves the best food in town, including western-style fish and steaks. Also recommended is the **Losmen Bajo Beach**. Otherwise, try the **Nikmat** or the **Sunset Restaurant,** which serve Chinese and Indonesian food.

Transport

Merpati Jl Eltari, 1 km from town on the road to the airport. ☎ 41177.
Post Office On the main road along the shore, Jl Soekarno.
Ferry Office At the harbour at the north end of Jl Soekarno. Impossible to miss.
Car Hire at **Bajo Beach Hotel**, ☎ 41009, 41008.
Bus Local buses run up and down the main street. Your *losmen* will call one for you. Buses to Ruteng run 3 times daily ($3, 4–5 hrs). Charter minibus to Ruteng, $50–75. Night

buses direct to Ende, $7, 15 hrs.
Long-distance bus Several bus companies offer services to and from destinations to the west. **Langsung Indah** is reliable and comfortable. Fare for the 2-day, 1-night journey to/from Denpasar is $35. Book at your *losmen* or their kiosk at the harbour.

General Information

Tourist Office Jl Eltari, 300 m before the Merpati office.
Agency Tours: **Bajo Beach Hotel**, see above.
PHPA Office Komodo National Park Information Centre, Labuanbajo, Flores Barat, 86554 Labuanbajo. ☎ ✈0365) 40060.
Post Office Jl Soekarno near the Bajo Beach Hotel.

Foreign exchange is not available in Labuanbajo. Remember to stock up on malaria tablets as they are essential in this region; it is also advisable to carry a net.

Around Labuhanbajo

LAKE DOLAT

A marshy lake and buffalo wallow (approximately 6 km to the south of Labuhanbajo) attracts migratory waterfowl in the northern winter (Oct–Mar). At the height of the dry season (Jul–Sep) egrets and whistling ducks from surrounding areas concentrate at this rare area of fresh water.

Getting There

Few people in Labuhanbajo know where Lake Dolat is; an added confusion is that villagers along the way seem to know several areas as "Dolat". To be sure of getting there, take a guide from the National Park office. Alo Sahu knows the area and is a keen birder, but for 3 weeks every month he is based on Komodo.

Finding your own way there is a nice adventure and you will see plenty of open country birds, Black-winged Kites, Rainbow Bee-eaters, Singing Bush-larks and the like, along the way.

There are two ways of getting there. One is to charter a boat to take you down the coast to Nonganipa (about 30 min/$20 charter) and then walk inland asking along the way for Dolat. The locals do not consider it to be a lake, so your best bet is to ask for *Rawa* (swamp) Dolat or *Lahan Basah* (wetland) Dolat. The other option is to approach it by land. Take any *bemo* in the direction of Ruteng and ask to be dropped at

Cabang (branch) *ke kampung Nanganai*, which is 5 km out of town. There's a chicken farm on the right at the right place. Take the trail behind this farm over a small rise, then down through a bamboo grove to an area of paddies. Walk directly across the paddies for about 2 km until you come to a river with a village on the opposite bank. Wade the river then go through the village and carry on for about 3 km, asking at every opportunity for directions. It is best to head off in the early morning, take lunch and plenty of water, and approach it as a pleasant stroll which with luck will arrive at Lake Dolat.

POTAWANGKA

An area of pristine lowland forest, with exciting potential, easily accessible via the road which leads through to the village of Potawangka. Only recently discovered and no bird lists yet, the area has to be good and the villagers know Wallace's Hanging-parrot.

Getting There

Take any *bemo* in the direction of Ruteng and get off at a road junction on the left between Km Posts 10 and 11 from Labuanbajo. The side road leads 12 km to Potawangka village. After 1.5 km the road enters scrub and after a further 1 km you are into forest. Then it's forest all the way as the road climbs gently upwards to Potawangka.

PUARLDO TELKOM STATION

At the top of the pass between Labuhanbajo and the Lembang plains, this is the site for Flores Monarch and other endemic birds of the mid-altitude forests. A 300-m road leads off the main highway to the telegraph station, which is surrounded by forest. Simply bird along this road.

Getting There

The turning for the telegraph station is between Km Posts 33 and 34 if you are coming from Labuhanbajo, or 96 km from the direction of Ruteng. Take any bus running the Labuanbajo–Ruteng route and get off at the turning (but expect to pay the fare to the bus's destination).

For the return trip, all buses are likely to be packed to the gunnels, so you will probably have to hitch a lift on a passing truck. It is polite to to give the driver some *uang rokok* (cigarette money) for the ride.

Ruteng

The main town in the hills, Ruteng is the site of a major conservation and development project. It can be cold at this altitude, so it is worth taking warm clothing.

Getting There

By air The Merpati office is on a no-name dirt street in an area called Paukaba, near the Pertamina station (☎ 21147; airfield ☎ 21518). 6 direct weekly flights by 18-passenger planes to Kupang ($70); 6 weekly flights to Bima ($51, with connection to Bali) of which 2 stop at Labuhanbajo on the way ($25). There are frequent cancellations due to bad weather, but great scenery. The landing field is close to town. Some *losmen* send out cars to meet the planes. Otherwise, it's 60¢ for the short ride to town.

By bus There are several buses a day, all early morning departures. Labuhanbajo ($2), Bajawa ($2), Ende—a long, tough 9 hrs— ($3.50). The best bus line for the Ende run is Bis Agogo. The driver will drop you off at the *losmen* of your choice.

Accommodation/Dining

The highest priced rms have hot water—a godsend on cold mornings and evenings.

Dahlia, Jl Kartini 8, ☎ 21377. 27 rms, of which 6 VIP. Has hot water. A reasonable attached restaurant. Economy $4S, $5D; standard $9 S, D; VIP $18S or D.

Agung III, Jl Waeces ☎ 21080. New, best in town. An extension of the Agung I, with 21 pleasant rooms, lacking only hot water. Restaurant. $14S or D.

Sindha, Jl Kom. L. Yos Sudarso 28, ☎ 21197. 26 rms, 14 w/attached facilities. Good Indonesian and Chinese meals, $2.50–3. With attached facilities, $6.50–7S, $9–10D; w/shared facilities, $3.50S, $5D.

Manggarai, ☎ 21008. Quiet, with 10 large, airy rms. No restaurant. With attached facilities, $4S, $6D; w/shared facilities $2.50S, $4D.

It is best to eat at your *losmen*. The 5-table **Dunia Baru** serves simple Indonesian and Chinese dishes. There are several Padang style restaurants in the market area, of which the **Garuda** is the cleanest and best. The **Merlyn** near Hotel Dahlia has Chinese and western food.

Transport

Merpati, Jl Pau Kaba Kei Mbaumuku, ☎ 21147.

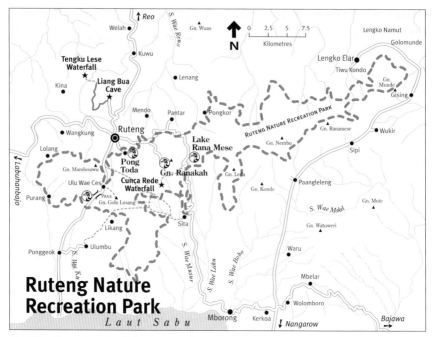

Ruteng Nature Recreation Park

Laut Sabu

Car Hire From **Hotel Dahlia**, $4.50 per hour, $60 for the day, same price for the run to Bajawa or Labuhanbajo. Alternatively, *bemos* can be chartered at the Ruteng bus terminal.

General Information
Agency Tours: **Astura Tours**, Jl A. Yani 14, ☎ 21795. This Jakarta-based company has an office in town to handle overland tours of Flores. Main office in Jakarta: Jl Soleh 36A, ☎ (021) 548 1879; fax (021) 530 0064.
Ruteng Nature Park Office (Kantor Taman Wisata Alam Ruteng) Satar Tacik, Ruteng, ☎ 21733, 21711. Ask for their booklet on birding in the area with bird lists for the sites mentioned below.
PHPA (SSKSDA), Jl Kathedral 1.
Foreign Exchange: **Bank**: **Rakyat Indonesia**, Jl Yos Sudarso, ☎ 21203, 21204.
Hospitals There is a Catholic mission hospital on the Labuhanbajo road and a government hospital in town (RSU).
Pharmacy: **Montang Rua Apotik**, Jl Yos Sudarso, ☎ 21259.
Souvenirs from **Tunas Jaya**, Jl Ranaka, ☎ 21815. This is also a weaving centre, with women working from 8.00 am to 5.00 pm. Nice local sarong-type cloth with distinctive Manggarai design ($33) along with ties, hats and purses with local motifs.
  A small handbook, *Birds of Ruteng Nature Recreation Park*, by Wendy King, is available from the office of the Biodiversity

Conservation Project on Jl Satar Tacik, Ruteng. It includes recommended walks, guide to bird families (with drawings) and a checklist.

Around Ruteng
Key Species
All the montane species, in particular Dark-backed Imperial Pigeon, Flores Scopsowl (a specimen recently collected near Lake Rana Mese), Russet-capped Tesia, Timor Leaf-warbler, Yellow-breasted Warbler, Flyeater, Brown-capped Fantail, Bare-throated Whistler, Mountain White-eye, Yellow-browed Dark-eye, Scaly-crowned Honeyeater.

GOLO LUSANG
7 km south of Ruteng on the road to Iteng, the 1,650 m pass between Mt Lika and Mt Watu Ndao is a fabulous place for an early morning symphony of Bare-throated Whistlers and views to the south coast and even across to Sumba.

Getting There
For an early start arrange a charter from your hotel the night before (Rp7,500); at other times take a *bemo* from the bus station in the direction of Ponggeok or Iteng (Rp1,000) and ask to be dropped off at the pass. To return to Ruteng flag down a passing *bemo* or truck (Rp1,000).

General Information

The forest on the south of the pass is less disturbed and to explore it simply wander down the road. Several wood-cutters' trails give access to the forest. An interesting trail enters to the southeast at Ulu Wae Ces, 1 km back down from the pass in the direction of Ruteng. The trail climbs upwards through a tunnel of shrubs and after 1 km enters secondary scrub and climbs steeply for a further 1 km to another pass. There is good forest over this pass and you reach a small meadow after another 1 km.

MT RANAKA

In 1987, this 2,140-m high mountain erupted, causing the telecommunications station to be relocated, but the 9-km access road is still open, providing visitors with the opportunity to walk or drive right up into the elfin forest that covers the higher slopes. This is a good place for pigeons and Chestnut-capped Thrush.

Getting There

This is the most accessible montane cloud forest on Flores. The turning is at Robo, at Km Post 9 along the road from Ruteng to Bajawa. The easiest way to get there is to charter a *bemo* from Ruteng to the top of Ranaka, $4 for a drop, $6 if it waits an hour and brings you back. Alternatively catch a public bus or *bemo* to Robo (Rp600) and make the strenuous, 9 km (2 hr) climb..

General Information

200 m back down the road from the top, a trail into the forest (opposite the km post) leads for 1 km through beautiful forest to the area that was devastated by the 1987 eruption. At km 7.6 on the left (coming down) is a turn to a small pond.

LAKE RANA MESE

Rana Mese, a small crater lake at 1,200 m located 22 km west of Ruteng on the Trans-Flores highway, supports waterbirds such as Sunda Teal, Pacific Black Duck and Little Pied Cormorant not found elsewhere in the area. The surrounding forest is good for Ruddy Cuckoo-dove, Sumba Cicadabird, Russet-capped Tesia, Russet-backed Rhinomyias and other forest birds.

Getting There

Take any public bus to Mborong from the terminal in Ruteng (Rp2,500) and get off at the park sign at Km Post 22. The lake is just a short walk down a stepped trail. Alternatively, take a *bemo* to Mano (Rp500) and walk the 6 km to Rana Mese. Flag down a vehicle to return to Ruteng.

General Information

To get into the forest, walk 100 m back along the road from the site sign board towards Ruteng and follow the small, unmarked footpath on the right towards the lake. The trail passes through good forest with a short, steep section leading down to the northern shore, which is very swampy.

PONG TODA

A pleasant 1.5-day walk into a beautiful ravine forested with old casuarina trees on the slopes of Mt Golo Dukol. The walk passes across open grass and shrub lands where you should see open-country birds such as Brown Quail, Golden-headed Cisticola, Red Avadavat and Five-coloured and Pale-headed Munias.

Getting There

Charter a car or a *bemo* to take you the 2 km from Ruteng to Leda, where the asphalt road turns to a dirt track. Walk west along this to the *Susteran* (nunnery). Looking west you will see the ravine and the footpath following the contour of the hill. Continue up the road for 1.5 km, cross a stream bed and walk across the grassy area until you reach a small footpath leading up to the left (south). This brings you along a gentle contour into the west side of the ravine. After about 1 km the path forks. Take the left-hand fork (which is actually a water system trail and pipeline), which leads into the casuarina forest. Here you should find, among other species, Dark-backed Imperial Pigeon, Great-billed Parrot, White-rumped Kingfisher, Little Minivet, Scaly-crowned Honeyeater and mixed bird flocks.

Kisol

An easy base for lowland forest birding. Kisol is a small village, 68 km from Ruteng, 9 km east of Mborong, on the road to Bajawa near the south coast. At Nangarawa, on the coast south of Kisol, there are patches of lowland forest and scrub; there is also a small estuary with mangroves, 10 km along a bad road passable to 4WD vehicles. Mt Poco Ndeki (Pacandeki) is a forested mountain south of Kisol, 45 min on foot.

Key Species

Most lowland species including Bonelli's Eagle, Orange-footed Scrubfowl, Green Junglefowl, Green Imperial Pigeon, Flores Green Pigeon, Great-billed Parrot, Red-cheeked Parrot, Moluccan and Wallace's Scopsowls, White-rumped Kingfisher, Elegant Pitta, Chestnut-capped Thrush, Asian Paradiseflycatcher, Black-naped and Spectacled Monarchs, Flame-breasted Sunbird, Yellow-spectacled White-eye, Thick-billed Darkeye, Flores Crow. In open country or on the south coast: Woolly-necked Stork, Changeable Hawk-eagle, Malaysian Plover, Beach Thick-knee, Lesser Whistling-duck.

Getting There

Take any Bajawa bus and get off at Kisol ($2). Alternatively charter a car for the 2-hr drive ($30).

Accommodation/Dining

It is possible to stay at the Catholic Seminary in Kisol, but get permission from its office near the cathedral before leaving Ruteng.

Otherwise there is the rather basic **Hotel Srie** in Mborang, which also has one restaurant attached, **Rumah Makan Minang Jaya**.

Bajawa

A lovely hill town set in splendid scenery and a popular tourist stopover on the Trans-Flores Highway. The birding is better at other sites, but the fascinating traditional villages of Bene and Luba, 12 km south of Bajawa, are well worth the diversion. The road down to these villages has good, open-country birding.

Accommodation/Dining

Korina, Jl A. Yani, ☎ 21162. 12 rooms, owned and operated by multi-lingual Pak Kornelis (he speaks English, Dutch and a little German) and his wife, Ibu Mariana. Pleasant and clean. Guides are available, and there is a restaurant close by. Rooms with enclosed facilities, $5.50S, $9D; with shared facilities, $4S, $6.50D.
Anggrek, Jl Haryono, ☎ 21172. 20 rms, attached restaurant next door. The rms and toilets very clean, pleasant; guides available. $7S or $9D.
Camellia, Jl A. Yani 82, ☎ 21458. Best restaurant in town. Some western dishes, along with lots of Chinese and Indonesian.

Riung

A small coastal town and delightful hang-out, due north of Bajawa. Best known for the excellent snorkelling on reefs around a group of islands just offshore in the bay and an immense fruit-bat colony in the mangroves surrounding one of the islands. For birders the main attraction is Great-billed Heron, which is easy to find along the shore. The dry monsoon forest on the hills immediately behind the town, as yet unexplored, is definitely worth checking out.

Getting There

There are 3–4 buses a day from Bajawa to Riung. The journey takes about 3 hrs and costs Rp4,000.

Accommodation

There are several homestays in Riung that offer pleasant, simple accommodation for around Rp20,000 full board. **Homestay Triana** is recommended. **Losmen Nur Ikhlas**, right on the shore, is quite popular, and the **Hotel Mandiri** has the best accommodation in town. This is a small town so just ask to be directed to the place of your choice.

General Information

PHPA Ask for Pak Niko (Nikodemus Manu) at Resor KSDA. He is knowledgeable about the area and will help arrange excursions.

The villagers have got themselves organized into a cooperative, *Himpunam Pramuwistata Indonesia*, which provides guides and manages trips out to the reefs. Expect to pay $7–10 for a guide and $25 for boat charter.

One or two small trading boats leave from Riung each week for Ujung Pandang via Tanahjampea (which has an endemic flycatcher). An adventurous (and cheap) way to link Nusa Tenggara and Sulawesi itineraries!

Ende

Ende is the largest town on Flores, situated on the south coast. After Maumere, it is the major transportation hub, and there is a port on either side of the small peninsula on which it is situated. The airport is near the town, and it is a 50m walk from the terminal to the main road, from where you can get a bus or *bemo* into town.

Accommodation/Dining

Dwi Putra, Jl Yos Sudarso 27–29. ☎ 21685. 46-room hotel. All rms w/attached facilities. Fan-cooled, $9.50S, $11D; AC rms $15S, $17D; VIP rms $43S, $54D. Huge restaurant with Indonesian, and seafood dishes. Post Office across the street.

Wisata, Jll Kelimutu 68. ☎ 21389. 30 rms. Restaurant, cold beer available. All rms large, with enclosed facilities, some with showers. The more expensive rms have AC. $4–15S, $6.50–26D. Good value.

Ikhlas, Jl A. Yani. ☎ 21695. 33 rms. This *losmen* is frequented by many travellers partially because the owner, Pak Jamal, speaks English and German and is the town's top source of travel information. Money changing and tours (including trekking) for individuals or small groups. Restaurant serves Indonesian and European food (50¢–$1.50). Rms w/attached facilities, $4S, $8D; w/shared facilities, $2–3D.

Merlyn, Jl Gatot Subroto, near the Losmen Ikhlas. ☎ 21667. Clean, has good Chinese seafood (85¢–$2.50). Near the old port, a series of adjacent mini-restaurants offer very inexpensive Indonesian dishes. Also in the downtown area, the **Istana Bambu** offers very good Chinese cooking and seafood: squid dishes start at $2, prawns at $3. Try the grilled lobster (if in season).

Transport

By bus Buses to Bajawa, Moni and Maumere are frequent, reliable, cheap and crowded. Going west (Labuhanbajo, Ruteng) the buses leave from Terminal Ndao, 2 km out of town on the road to Bajawa. For eastern destinations (Maumere) buses leave from Wolowono, 5 km from downtown. Regular *bemos* run between the town and terminals.

By sea The ferry leaves from Kupang every Saturday afternoon (16 hrs, overnight, $8–11) and for Waingapu every Tuesday afternoon (11 hrs, overnight, $6–8). Departures and the ticket office are at Pelabuhan Ipi. Tickets can be purchased one day ahead of departure.

Pelni's *Binaiya* stops in at Ende twice a month on its route between Waingapu (Sumba) and Kupang, and twice monthly between Kupang to Waingapu. The Pelni office is near the old port, Pelabuhan Ende, but the ships leave from the new port, Pelabuhan Ipi.

General Information

PHPA office, Jl Gatot Subroto, Km 3, ☎ 21754.

Moni and Keli Mutu

Most people go to Keli Mutu just to see the coloured lakes, but the walk back down from the lakes towards Moni village offers some good mountain birding including the "Flores Nightingale".

Key Species

Grey Goshawk, Rufous-bellied Eagle, Changeable Hawk-eagle, Green Junglefowl, Red-backed Buttonquail, Dark-backed Imperial Pigeon, Brown-capped Woodpecker, Snowy-browed and Little Pied Flycatchers, Black-naped Monarch, Common Golden Whistler, Helmeted Friarbird, Mountain White-eye. Check the vaccinium scrub at the top for Brown Quail, Blood-breasted Flowerpecker and Scaly-crowned Honeyeater.

Getting There

By bus Moni is about 7 hrs from Bajawa via Ende (2 hrs, 53 km from Ende) and 3.5 hrs (83 km) from Maumere. In Moni take a vehicle to the summit, eg the daily, pre-dawn truck laid on for tourists, $1.50; for 5–6 people, charter a jeep from Kelimutu Restaurant, $14 round trip; then walk back down (3 hrs).

General Information

There is easy access to habitats in the 700–1,600 m altitude range: casuarina and mountain forest near the summit, other habitats lower down. However, take great care around the lake and do not go alone: the ground is very unstable off the path. A tourist disappeared in 1995.

Around Moni

Other productive sites are the fig trees in Moni (Wallace's Scopsowl), woodland below the Sao Ria bungalows (Chestnut-backed Thrush, Rufous-chested Flycatcher and Wallacean Cuckoo-shrike), and tall, fruiting fig trees at altitudes up to 1,000 m (Flores Green Pigeon).

Accommodation/Dining

Accommodation is pretty limited. Most convenient and comfortable for this half-day trip is **Sao Ria Wisata Bungalow** on the Ende road, close to the Keli Mutu turning. 10 rms, $9S–$10D. **Watugana** is clean, friendly and offers lots of cultural and tour infomration. Of the homestays which have restaurants,

Daniel's is recommended for its excellent food, as is **Amina Moi**. **Kelimutu Restaurant** serves simple Indonesian food and a small selection of western fare.

General information
Telephone office At Kelimutu restaurant. **Car hire** At Kelimutu restaurant. Rates: Keli Mutu crater $15, Ende $25, Maumere $50. **Bus** There are regularly scheduled buses between Moni, Ende and Maumere (each $2). First one leaves at 8 am.

Mausambi

A pristine area of monsoon forest extending from the hills down to the sea where there is one of the last remaining bands of beach forest on Flores. Not yet really explored by birders, but Flores Crow has been seen here and there are plenty of lorikeets and pigeons.

Getting There
Mausambi is located 7 km west of Marole on the coast due north of Keli Mutu. The best way to visit this site is to charter a car and drop in here on the way from Maumere–Keli Mutu. By public transport bus-trucks leave from Ende, Detusoko (12 km before Keli Mutu) or Maumere 6–7 am daily; 3 hrs, Rp6,000 from Maumere. The buses return to their home-towns in the afternoon.

Maumere

Maumere, the principal town of East Flores, is best known for the spectacular diving and snorkelling to be found around the islands in Maumere Bay. The reefs were damaged by the 1993 earthquake and tidal wave but are now recovering well. For the birder there are two recommended day trips: to Pulau Besar, out in the bay, and Egon-Illimudu, a mountain 20 km east of town. Maumere is right on the Trans-Flores highway so there are frequent bus services from east and west. There are daily air connections with Ujung Pandang, Kupang, Bima and Bali, and connections to Surabaya and Jakarta.

Pelni's *Binaiya* stops in Maumere four times a month en route from Dili to Ujung Pandang and back.

Accommodation/Dining
Accommodation in Maumere is generally poor, with the exception of the pleasant **Hotel**

Wini Rai I on Jl Gajah Mada, ☎ 21388, 21239. 36 rms. $9S, 110D, standard, $15–18S, $16–20D AC. Or, try the **Bogor I**, Jl Wlamet Riyadi, ☎ 21191. 25 rms, $6.50 shared facilities, $9 private facilities, $11S, $17D AC.

Restaurant **Depot Bambu**, next door to the Wini Rai, serves good, cheap, Chinese food. The better restaurants, noted for their seafood, are **Sarinah** (☎ 21594) and **Stevani** (☎ 21273) on Jl Raya Centis, and **Golden Fish** (☎ 21667) on Jl Hasanuddin.

By far the best bet is to stay at one of the two dive resorts located 12–13 km east of Maumere on the road to Laruntuka. The **Sao Wisata**, Jl Sawista, ☎ 21555, fax 21666, is set up for dive packages. $20–35S, $30–40D fan; $55–65S, $60–70D AC. For birders the **Sea World Club**, Pondok Dunia Laut, PO Box 3, Jl Nai Roa, Km 13 (☎ 21570, fax 21102) may be better. It caters mainly for small-group tours, but is open to independent travellers. $10–25S, $25–30D fan; $25–30S, #30–35D AC.

Transport
Merpati, Jl Don Tomas, ☎ 21342. **Bouraq**, Jl Nong Miak, ☎ 21467. **Pelni** Lines, Jl Kol. S. Riyadi, ☎ 21355; fax 22020.

General Information
Tourism Office, Jl Wair Klau, ☎ 21489. **PHPA Office**, Jl Litbang 3, PO Box 147, ☎ 22009. Pak Dominggus Bolla, head of the office, is helpful and speaks a little English. They can help arrange trips to Pulau Besar and Egon-Illimudu. **Telkom Office**, Jl Soekarno Hatta, ☎ 21412. **Hospitals** Maumere's Catholic hospital, **RS St Elisabeth**, at Lele on the Ende road (turn south about 20 km from Maumere) is reputedly the best in eastern Indonesia. **Souvenirs** Art shop **Harapan Jaya**, ☎ 21227, art shop **Subur Jaya**, ☎ 21235, both on Jl Moa Toda.

Around Maumere
PULAU BESAR
This rugged, 3,000 ha island is by far the largest in Maumere Bay; it is about 25 km offshore (45 min by speedboat from Maumere or the dive clubs). The vegetation of coastal areas is cultivation and secondary growth, with patches of beach forest and mangroves. The interior is covered by semi-deciduous forest easily accessible along numerous trails that enter from coastal settlements.

Key Species

Bonelli's Eagle, Flores Green Pigeon and good range of forest and open country birds. Osprey, Brahminy Kite and White-bellied Sea-eagle around the coast.

Getting There

To reach the island, hire a boat from Sea World or Sao Wisata, or from the fishermen along the coast. The dive clubs charge well over $100 (although you may be able to get a dive group to drop you off). The fisherman charge around $75, but be careful of the sea-worthiness of their boats.

General Information

Even in the dry season (Apr–Oct) the seas can be choppy. You can stay overnight with the village head on the island, but bring your own food. The island is a nature reserve so you will need a permit, which you get from PHPA in Maumere, cost Rp7,500.

Egon-Illimudu

A volcanic peak with venting fumaroles approximately 25 km east of Maumere. The site's main interest is a rare example of pristine, moist eucalyptus woodland. Almost nothing is known about the birds of this habitat but it looks exciting.

Getting There

Probably best to charter a car, but also possible by public transport if you're willing to walk. Drive out past the dive clubs on the road east to Larantuka. Take the turning south between Km Posts 23 and 24 (from Maumere). After 5 km the asphalt turns to a dirt track and enters eucalyptus savannah and after another 2–3 km you reach pristine eucalyptus forest. The track continues upwards through forest and clearings for a further 8 km to the village of Bau Krengut, where there are great views of Mt Egon and the south coast.

Sumba

The island of Sumba is another birder's favourite with eight endemics—including a harnbill, fruit-dove and button-quail. However, it is also popular because of its amazing culture and spectacular landscape, so is a good destination for birders and non-birders alike.

Waingapu

Getting There

By air Waingapu is the capital of East Sumba district and the main entry point to the island. Merpati operates a circular route between Denpasar, Waingapu and Kupang, flying anti-clockwise (direct to Waingapu) on Wed, Fri and Sun; clockwise (Kupang) Mon, Thu and Sat. Bouraq has daily flights except Mon and Wed from Denpasar and flies Tue, Thu, Sat and Sun from Kupang. Each hotel meets the flights and provides free transport for the 4-km ride to town.

By sea Pelni's *Biaiya* ferry calls at Waingapu each week: one week on its way from Surabaya and Bima to Ende and Timor, Ujang Pandang and Balikpapan; the next week vice versa. There are also weekly overnight car ferries to Waingapu from Ende (Flores), usually Weds, but check locally on sailing times. Fare $5.50 economy, $6.50 VIP.

Accommodation/Dining

Merlin, Jl D.I. Panjaitan 25, ☎ 21490. 23 rms. $7S, $9D standard; $10.50S, $15D VIP; $21.50 suites with AC. Rooftop restaurant.
Hotel Sandlewood, Jl D.I. Panjaitan 23, ☎ 21887. 25 rms. $5.50–15S, #6.50–30D. Best restaurant in town.
Elvin, Jl Achmad Yani 73. ☎ 22097. 20+ rms. $5.50S, $6.50D economy; $6.50S, $8.50D standard, $10.50S, $13D AC.Restaurant.
Mini Indah, Jl Achmad Yani 27. Has cheap Indonesian food and is a good place to pick up *nasi bungkus* for packed lunches. **Warung Arema** and **Jawa Timur** serve good food. **Rajawali**, Jl Sutomo 9B, ☎ 61463, has good fried squid and shrimps, with billiard room.

Transport

Merpati, at Hotel Elim, Jl A. Yani, ☎ 21443, 21462.
Bouraq, Jl Yos Sudarso 57.
Pelni, Jl Hasanuddin 1, ☎ 21665; fax 21027.
Car and motorbike hire is arranged through hotels. Rates for car and driver are based on distance and average $40–60 for main destinations. Motorbike hire is $12 per day.
Local buses All out of town buses leave from the terminal near Sandlewood Hotel.

General Information

PHPA Office, Jl Gatot Subroto 10, Waingapu 87114, ☎ 21109. On the way in from the airport, 1 km before town. Ask for Pak Alex B. Ora, head of the office. He and his staff have been working with BirdLife for a number of years and have great knowledge of the island's forests and birds. Abdul Hair is a competent birder.

Post Office, Jl Sutomo 21. ☎ 21407.

Bank: **Rakyat Indonesia** changes money (US$ traveller's cheques).

Hospitals: **Rumah Sakit Umum (RSU)** Dr Umbu Ravameha, 2 km out of town on the road to Waikabubak; **Rumah Sakit Kristen Lindimara**, Jl Prof. Dr. W.Z. Yohennes 6, ☎ 21019, 21064, 21742.

Around Waingapu

WAINGAPU BAY

A few minutes walk from Waingapu town, the mud-flats and sandbars of Waingapu Bay attract good numbers of shorebirds during the migration months of Mar–May and late Jul–Oct. The variety of species is variable; careful scanning of the high water roost on a sandbar at the eastern end is sometimes rewarded with scarcer shorebird species.

Key Species

Far Eastern Curlew, Greater Sand-plover, Great Knot, Terek Sandpiper, Rufous-necked Stint. Broad-billed Sandpiper has also been recorded.

Getting There

Opposite the Police booth to left of the Merlin Hotel, take a track down the side of the mosque. Turn left at the asphalt road and walk for 400 m as far as a sharp right bend. Continue straight on along a dirt track for 100 m to a second asphalt road. Turn right and continue for 200 m to a sharp right-hand bend. Take a small path on the left across disused shrimp ponds to the beach.

PRIPAHAMANDAS (KILOMETER DUABELAS)

This steep-sided forest valley, the water catchment for Waingapu, offers a pleasant introduction to forest birding. Citron-crested race of Yellow-crested Cockatoo still occurs, Great-billed Parrot, Rainbow Lorikeet and Green Imperial Pigeon are all common.

Getting There

From Waingapu take any bus in the direction of Waikabubak and get off at Km 12 (you will have to pay the full Waikabubak fare); alter-natively hitch a ride or charter a vehicle from your hotel.

General Information

From Km 12 it is a 50-m walk to the top of the limestone escarpments and a lovely view into the valley. To descend into the valley bottom, there is a rough trail at Km 11. It is possible then to walk up the river and return via another trail, which joins the road at Km 15; however on this trail you have to climb a short rock face.

YUMBU MANGROVES

A beautiful band of mangroves, fronted by coral flats, 2 km down a track off the main Waingapu–Melolo Road. A lovely place to look for terns, Grey-tailed Tattler, and there's a possibility of Great-billed Heron.

Getting There

From Waingapu take the road east to Melolo. If travelling by bus ask for Jambatan Yumba and get off 3–4 km after passing through Watumbaka, just after a bridge (close to Km post 17).

General information

Follow a track on the left for 1.2 km to the back of the mangroves. The dry grasslands on either side of the track are where Sumba Button-quail has been seen. The track leads to a house, where there is a stream running through the mangroves. Wade along the stream to get to the coral flats.

Luku Melolo

A spectacular valley, with steep limestone escarpments protecting 7,800 ha of forest. On the eastern side of the valley a mosaic of forest and open grasslands that survives along the top of the escarpment is a great place to see many of Sumba's endemic birds.

Key Species

Peregrine Falcon, Short-toed Eagle, Sumba Hornbill, Citron-crested race of Yellow-crested Cockatoo, Sumba Green Pigeon, Sumba Cicadabird, Sumba Flycatcher, Sumba Brown Flycatcher, Red-headed Myzomela.

Getting There

Melolo village is 62 km (2 hrs) by road east of Waingapu. Buses leave the terminal about every hour (fare Rp5,000). The turning up to

Luku Melolo forest is the first on the right after the bridge in Melolo. Truck-buses are rare, and without your own transport you will have to rely on hitching on one of the infrequent vehicles for the 21 km, uphill drive to the forest.

General Information
Bird along the road from Km 21 to Km 25, with frequent excursions into the forest fragments and to the edge of the escarpment to look over the valley. At the small village of Paberaman-era (Km 25) a trail leads down to the river.

Mt Wangameti

Sumba's highest mountain supports the largest area of forest (40,000 ha) remaining on Sumba. It catches more rainfall than other areas of Sumba and is covered in evergreen forest, favoured habitat of the Red-naped Fruit-dove. Visitors can stay with the head of Wangameti village and hire a guide to explore the forest or climb the mountain.

Key Species
All Sumba's endemic species (except Sumba Buttonquail) and Red-naped Fruit-dove common. Eclectus and Great-billed Parrots, Sumba Cicadabird, Chestnut-backed Thrush, Tawny Grassbird and Russet-backed Rhinomyias.

Getting There
Wangameti village is about 65 km (3 hrs) south of Waingapu. From Waingapu drive west past the airport. 10 km from Waingapu take a turning on the right to Tana Rara, a further 49 km. Continuing along the road from Tana Rara to Kanangar, after 7 km you reach a rough track to Wangameti on the right. Larondja village, which abuts the forest, is 24 km along this track.

A car charter to Wangameti will cost $45. By public transport ask around for the Ende Manis truck at the terminal in Waingapu in the evening. This truck does a daily run up to the Wangameti area. If you are going by motorbike, be aware that petrol is often not available in Tana Rara or Kanagar, but you can arrange for Ende Manis to drop a jerry can of benzine at Wangameti.

General Information
Visitors can stay with a family in Larondja; they ask for Rp20,000 a night per person, including three basic meals. The village has a communal toilet block. Ask for Pak Umbu Tai

Maramba Hamu or Pak John when you arrive, and they will sort you out. The forest, which starts across a small river immediately behind the village, is criss-crossed with trails for collecting *loba* (the bark of a tree used in dyeing). The trek to the top of Wangameti is a relatively gentle climb and takes 3–4 hrs. Villagers ask Rp10,000 a day for guiding. The price for half day is the same because they lose a day's work.

Terimbang

A beautiful, unspoilt cove on the south coast, with a 1 km band of beach forest between the beach and fields around the village of Terim-bang. Forested escarpments rise inland from the villages. The area has yet to be birded properly, but looks to have great potential and may support all Sumba's endemics. As yet there is no accommodation; visitors camp on the beach. Fisherman will sell you fish to barbecue. Bring whatever else you need.

Key Species
Beach Thick-knees on the beach, Orange-footed Scrub-fowl and Rainbow Lorikeets, and the forest through which the road passes on the way is good for Cinnamon-banded Kingfisher, Citron-crested Cockatoo and Metallic Pigeon.

Getting There
Travelling west from Waingapu on the Waik-abubak road, turn left at Praipaha (47 km from Waingapu) on the road to Wahang and Tabundung. After a further 38 km, a turning on the right leads 8 km down to Terimbang. (The turning is in Kalala forest, a good area for Citron-crested Cockatoo). Buses leave the terminal in Waingapu each morning for Wahang, but you will need to walk the 8 km from the turning or wait for a lift on one of the very few vehicles going to Terimbang.

Terimbang and Wangameti are connected by a south coast road. From Wangameti return to Kanangar, then continue down to Manukangga on the south coast, turn west via Lalindi, Tabungdung and Wahang. This journey will take a full day by car or motorbike.

Manupeu

The beautiful, steep-sided Manupeu valley is dominated by the spectacular Matayangu waterfall and supports the highest known densities of Sumba Hornbill. It is an easy day trip by car from Waikabubak. The track to the valley passes through a mosaic of forest and grassland clearings. There is no accommodation in the area. The valley is known locally as a place of evil spirits, and several visitors who have camped in the valley have reported disturbing dreams.

Getting There
No public transport. A 1-day charter from Waikabubak will cost about $45. At Wailawa, 16 km from Waikabubak, turn south along an asphalt side road. The asphalt gives out after 10 km, 500 m before the forest edge. A 4WD can continue along a track for a further 3–4 km to the top of the valley, and a jeep track continues a further 5 km to the edge of the Manupeu valley. From there it is a 3-km walk down a steep trail into the valley bottom.

Waikabubak

Waikabubak, the capital town of West Sumba, is for most tourists the base for day trips to see traditional villages and megalithic tombs. The town has a beautiful traditional village on a small hill in its centre.

Getting There
The airport of West Sumba is at Tambulaka, a 1-hr drive to the northwest of the town. Merpati operates a Bima (Sumbawa)–Tambulaka–Waingapu service on Mon, Thu and Sat. Buses and taxis meet the flights. A half-hourly bus service connects Waingapu and Waikabubak. The 136-km journey takes 3.5 hrs and costs $4.

Accommodation
There is a variety of simple, but adequate *losmen*. The best is **Hotel Madang**, Jl Pemuda 4, ☎ 21197, 21292; fax 21634. 26 rms. Class 1: $17S, $20D; Class 2: $10S, $12D; Class 3: $8S, 12D; Economy: $5S, $7D. Restaurant and travel (car charter service). Other recommendations are **Hotel Artha**, Jl Veteran 11, ☎ 21112. 32 rms. Class 1: $18, Class 2: $14, Economy: $8.

General Information
Post Office, Jl Bhayangkara 1, ☎ 87211. **Foreign Eschange** None **Artshop/Souvenirs** On Jl Achmad Yani. **Hospitals**: **Rumah Sakit Lenemoripa**, Jl Eltari; **Rumah Sakit Umum**, Jl Adyaksa, ☎ 21021.

Poronumbu

This 900-ha forest fragment located close to Waikabubak supports most of Sumba's forest species including all the endemics. The forest covers a low ridge and the lower slopes are heavily disturbed, with maize fields eating into the forest edge.

Getting There
Take the road to Waibanga, northeast of Waikabubak. Just after Dokakaka church, 10 km from Waikabubak, take the track on the left to Dokakaka village (1 km). Continue along the track for a further 3 km to the forest edge. Trails enter the forest and climb the ridge. There are four *bemos* a day from Waikabubak terminal to Waibanga (Rp400 to the Dokakaka turning).

TIMOR

This 33,600 sq km island is the largest on Nusa Tenggara. Half its resident birds are of Asian origin, the other half of Australian origin.

Kupang

Kupang is the capital of Nusa Tenggara province. Sunrise is at 5 am and sunset at 5 pm.

Getting There
Downtown Kupang is 15 km from El Tari airport. Nusa Cenda University is 3 km from the airport and the government offices are located on a hill outside Kupang city centre. Merpati, Bouraq and Sempati have daily flights from Jakarta, and Merpati also flies from Denpasar and from Darwin, Australia. The taxi fare is $4 whatever the destination. Drivers receive commission from hotels, so do not believe your driver when he says your planned hotel is full. The harbour for ferries to and from Roti (daily), Ende and Waingapu is at Bolok, 14 km to the south of Kupang. *Bemos* meet the ferries; the fare to downtown Kupang is Rp600.

Accommodation/Dining
Kupang has one 3- and four 1-star hotels and a good range of less expensive accommodation. **Orchid Garden**, Jl Gunung Fatuleu 2. ☎ 21707, 32220; fax 31399. 40 rms. 3 stars. Swimming pool, television, restaurant with European, Chinese and Indonesian cuisine. $45S, $48D, $65 suite.

Clara's Hotel, Jl Pahlawan, about 1.5 km west of downtown towards Tenau harbour. ☎ 22580. 18 rms including spacious AC rooms. The bar-restaurant on the roof offers superb views of the bay. $11/person with free laundry and breakfast.

Wisma Susi, Jl Sumatra. ☎ 33421. 18 rms. Fan-cooled $6S, $8D; AC$10-14S, $13-23D. Rooms rather basic but sea-watching opportunities from 2nd and 3rd floors.

Losmen **Mariana** and **Pantai Timor** next door are bottom-range *losmen* of slightly better standard; **Pantai Timor** has a restaurant with a a good view of sea and sunset but very indifferent food.

Good Padang food is available at **Bundo Kanduang**, Jl Sudirman 49. **Teddy's Bar** (downtown right along the water.) ☎ 21142. Western food and well-stocked bar. **Depot Makan Palembang International**, Jl Sudirman 52. Good Chinese and Indonesian food. **Pondok Bambu** restaurant at King Stone Hotel, Jl Timor, 6 km east of downtown area. This is one of Kupang's best restaurants and is worth the trip out. Squid, prawn and crab dishes $2–2.50. Indonesian meals $1.50.

Transport

Merpati Jl Sudirman 21. ☎ 22654, 21121. Agent: Losmen Mariana (see above).

Bouraq Jl Sudirman 20A.☎ 21421, 31543.

Sempati Agent Wisma Susi (see above), ☎ 33421.

Pelni Lines Jl Pahlawan 3, opposite Fort Concordia. ☎ 21944.

Ferry Office Jl Cak. Doko 20. ☎ 21140.

Taxi Hire Try **Ford Taxi**. $3.50 per hr.

Local buses All out-of-town buses leave from Walikota/Oebobo terminal in the new eastern part of town.

General Information

Kupang Tourist Office, Jl Sukarno, near downtown bus terminal.

Provincial Tourist Office (Kantor Pariwisata) Jl Basuki Rahmat 1, ☎ 21540.

Travel Agencies: **Teddy's Bar** ☎ 21142. Teddy is almost always there and can arrange all sorts of excursions; **Pitoby Tour and Travel**, Jl Sudirman.

PHPA Office Jl Perintis Kemerdekaan, Walikota. ☎ 0380 31814.

Telecom Office Jl Urip Sumoharjo 11-13. ☎ 32101; fax 31001.

Foreign exchange: Visa and Mastercard. **Bank BCA**. Jl Sudirman 46A. ☎ 32801. Open 8.30 am–2 pm, weekdays; 8.30am–noon, Sat.

Health Malaria prophylaxis is essential in this region.

Hospitals: **Rumah Sakit Polisi** (Police Hospital) Jl Nanga 84. ☎ 21273. VIP rooms $20/day. Dr Hadi Sulisuyato speaks some English. **Doctors Internist**: Dr Iksan, Jl Sudirman. ☎ 21340. **Gynaecologist**: Dr Heru Tjahyone, Jl Sudirman. ☎ 22105.

Pharmacy: **Apotik Pelengkap**, Kompleks RSU. Open 24 hrs. ☎ 21356.

Souvenirs: **Dharma Bakti**, Jl Sumba 19–32, about 2 km east of downtown on the main coast road. Tremendous selection of handicrafts.

Baumata

A mixture of old forest trees, teak plantations and scrub behind the public swimming pool of Baumata, 9 km from Oesapa, which is where the main road to El Tari airport leaves the main Soe road (8.5 km from Kupang). Great spot to start birding, only half hour from Kupang with no shortage of transport.

Key Species

Exceptionally good for Red-rumped Myzomela, Streak-breasted Meliphagar and two friarbird species. Scrub behind teak plantation also supports White-bellied Bush-chat and Buff-banded Bushbird. Black-banded Flycatcher And Orange-banded Thrush also recorded. Elegant Pitta nests there in wet Season.

Getting There

Catch any *bemo* from Kupang going to Penfui, and ask for Baumata. From the airport turn off (3.5 km from Oesapa) it is only another 5.5 km uphill.

Bipolo

A small 50- ha remnant of lowland evergreen or swamp forest on the northeast end of Kupang bay. Numerous wood-cutter's trails and tracks dissect the forest providing easy access. In the dry season walk south along the sandy river bed, and you will eventually reach a vast area of paddies, mangroves and mudflats.

Key Species

All lowland forest species, but especially good for pigeons and parrots. Only known locality (since 1930s) for Timor Green Pigeon; also good for Pink-headed Imperial Pigeon, and Timor Black Pigeon. Only recent Timor locality for Great-billed Parrot; also good for Olive-headed and Rainbow Lorikeets and Olive-shouldered Parrot. Cinnamon-banded Kingfisher breeds; Elegant Pitta abundant during wet season. Timor Blue Flycatcher and Orange-banded Thrush common.

Getting There

Turn left off main Kupang–Soe road at Oelmasi, just past Km Post 38 (about 1 hr from Kupang). This asphalt road, which is in poor condition, eventually arrives at Pariti. About 14 km from the Oelmasi turn-off is the village of Bipolo. Follow the road through Bipolo to a bridge over the river bed. After the bridge the road passes through forest for about 1.5 km until it reaches the next hamlet, Taupkole. To reach the paddies and mangroves to the south, follow the edge of forest(along the creek bed on the eastern forest edge, or from Taupkole along the edge of the teak plantation). **By public transport** Buses to Parita leave from Walikota bus station in Kupang. The last bus back is between 6.30 and 7 pm. The fare to Oelmasi is Rp 2,500. A taxi charter from Kupang will cost $25, extra if he has to wait.

Accommodation

Check with the Sekretaris Desa Bipolo, who should be able to arrange for you to stay with a family. Take food with you as the area is poor.

Camplong

Camplong has a small (400 ha) recreation forest on the western end of the hills that dominate most of West Timor. The forest is semi-deciduous and quite disturbed, but still full of birds.

Key Species

Same as Bipolo, but much better for White-Bellied Bush-chat, especially at higher elevations, Flycatcher, and also Buff-banded Bushbird. Tricoloured Parrot-finch on the wetter southern forest fringe, near the Rusa Deer compound. In the wet season watch for Palaearctic raptors.

Getting There

Follow the main Kupang–Soe road. The forest starts just beyond the pool at Km Post 47 and continues up the meandering road to Km Post 50. Go as early in the morning as possible before traffic and horn tooting become

too bad. There are several trails providing access into the forest. The best strategy is to take a bus to the top of the escarpment (Km Post 50) where the teak plantation starts, and then walk slowly back down. All buses to Soe and beyond pass through Samplong; there is no shortage of them. Cost about Rp. 1,000.

Accommodation

The Catholic *wisma* **Oe Mat Honis** beside spring (*kolam*). Rp7,000 per night.

Soe

This small, pleasant town is the jumping-off point for trips to Mutis, Oel Bubek and other upland birding sites. There are numerous buses runing between Kupang and Soe. Note that the buses to Soe go from the Terminal Bis Oebobo. This is situated near Walikota on Jl El Tari (the road that goes to the airport). The fare is Rp4,250.

Accommodation

The best and newest is **Hotel Bahagia Dua**. $12 S. Attached restaurant. Other places are **Hotel Mahkota Plaza**, Jl Soeharto 11, ☎ 21168. $10 S; **Hotel Bahagia Dua**, Jl Gajah Madah 55, ☎ 21095; **Hotel Bahagia Satu**, Jl Diponegoro, ☎ 21015

Buat

A scenic area of rolling, grass–covered hills and evergreen forest remnants close to Soe at about 1,000 m above sea level.

Key Species

Similar to Camplong, but Spot-breasted Dark-eyes, Black-banded Flycatcher and Orange-banded Thrush much more abundant. The only recent (but unconfirmed) locality for Wetar Ground-dove and an undescribed owl. Yellow-eared Honeyeater and Metallic Pigeon abundant at times. Yellow-crested Cockatoo recorded.

Getting There

Everybody in Soe knows Buat, about 5 km to the northwest, where there is a swimming pool. It is easy to charter transport to Buat from any hotel is Soe for around Rp20,000 (for drop only).

The road passes through white gum-tree savannah and then enters a dense mahogany plantation. At the fork on the far (northern) edge of the plantation, turn right (the left fork goes to the swimming pool) and continue on an unsealed road past new forestry offices for about 1 km until you reach rolling, grass-covered hills and tiny forest remnants. Stop here and walk to the west, where a cliff appears rather suddenly (so take care) with a magnificent view of the forested valley. You can access the forest from several steep trails (best at the southern end of the cliff).

Gunung Mutis

A 10,000-ha nature reserve covering the beautiful eucalpytus forest around the base of Mt Mutis. The forest on the lower slopes is heavily grazed; the higher slopes (above 1,600m) are the best for birding. Officially a permit is required to visit, obtainable from the SBKSDA in Kupang.

Key Species
Timor Imperial Pigeon, Chestnut-backed, Sunda and Island Thrushes, Iris Lorikeet, Yellow-breasted Warbler, Pygmy Wren-babbler, Snowy-browed Flycatcher.

Getting There
Take the road from Soe to Kapan (20 km; 30 mins). Take the left-hand branch in Kapan and drive for a further hr (approx 35 km to Fatumenasi). A road is currently being constructed through the reserve to Nenas, 8 km distant. The good forest and birding start above Nenas. There are regular minibuses to Kapan and Fatumenasi from Soe.

Accommodation
It is possible to stay with villagers.

Oelnasi

A virtually unexplored, easily-accessible, large area of tall, semi-deciduous forest (450–550 m altitude), only 15 minutes west of Soe.

Key Species
Same as Camplong (although 200 m higher in elevation), but more birds to be seen, apparently. Good for pigeons/doves and raptors at times. Spot-breasted Dark-eye commoner.

Getting There
Take the main Kupang–Soe road to Km Post 95 (about 15 km from Soe) and look for a wooden-pole gate on the northern side of the road (on the left coming from Kupang) with caretaker's hut, opposite a stone wall. Obtain permission from the caretaker. Starting at the gate, a trail winds right through the middle of tall forest for at least 2 km, passing through several small grassy clearings, good for seeing aerial species and flying pigeons.

Oel Bubuk Forest

A tiny (less than 5 ha) remnant of lower montane (1,100 m above sea level) evergreen forest on the way from Soe to Kapan and Mt Mutis.

Key Species
Very similar to Buat, but easier to access. Chestnut-backed Thrush once recorded here (but Orange-banded more usual). Mountain White-eye and Blood-breasted Flowerpecker possible.

Getting There
Take the Soe–Kapan road. Stop at Km Post 14 from Soe, where the road passes through forest (for about 300 m). Most of the forest is on a steep hill on the right-hand (east) side of the road. A walking trail follows the southern edge, starting at a wooden-pole gate by the roadside. There are regular *bemos* from Soe, fare Rp500.

–Michele Bowe, Derek Holmes Margaret Kinnaird, Paul Jepson, Richard Noske, with additional information from Jan Colbridge, Alex B. Ora, Susanne Schmitt & Filip Verbalen.

Sumatra

Medan

Medan is the western gateway into Indonesia and the ideal starting point for a birding trek across the archipelago. The first stop on a birding itinerary is Berestagi, 66 km southwest of Medan. For full listings, see Periplus *Sumatra* guide.

Getting There
By air There are regular international flights to Medan's Polonia airport from Singapore, Kuala Lumpur, Penang and Amsterdam, as well as regular connections from Jakarta and other domestic airports. The airport is still in the middle of the city, and you can actually walk out of the airport entrance and get straight on to local transport. Airport taxis cost about $6.50.

By sea Hydrofoil services from Penang, Malaysia, to the main harbor at Belawan are available through most travel agencies. Pelni's *Bukit Guntang* operates on alternate weeks between Jakarta and Belawan.

By road ALS is the best bus service to and from Java or southerly points of Sumatra, however the Trans-Sumatran Highway still leaves much to be desired and delays due to repairs etc are common.

Accommodation/Dining
Novotel Soechi Medan, Jl Cirebon 76a, ☎ 561234; fax 572222.
Emerald Garden International, Jl K. L. Yos Sudarso 1, PO Box 2388, Medan 20235. ☎ 611888; fax 622888.
Hotel TiaraMedan, Jl Cut Mutiah, ☎ 523000, 538880; fax 510716.

Transport
Garuda, Tiara Convention Blg, Jl Cut Mutia, ☎ 538527, 538677; fax: 538502; and Dharma Deli Hotel, ☎ 516400. Ticketing office, Jl Letjen Suprapto 2, ☎ 516066.
Mandala, Jl Brigjend Katamso 37-E. ☎ 516379, 536999.
Merpati, Jl Brigjend Katamso 72/122. ☎ 514102.

Sempati, Tiara Convention Bldg, Jl Cut Mutia. ☎ 558870; fax 538477; also Dharma Deli Hotel ☎ 537900; Wisma BII ☎ 551612.
Thai International, Dharma Deli Hotel, Jl Balai Kota, ☎ 514483, 510541.
Pelni, Jl Kol. Sugiono 5–7, on the corner with Jl Cakrawati. ☎ 518533; fax 517474.
Jakarta-Lloyd, Jl A. Yani VI 3, ☎ 24690.
ALS, (long-distance buses) Jl Amaliun 24, ☎ 766685, 765938.
Smaller bus companies: **Pribumi** at Jl Sisingamangaraja terminal takes you to Berastagi.
Taxis You can pick these up along any main thoroughfare or at the Danau Toba, Surya, Tiara or Polonia Hotels; hourly rates are negotiated with the driver. Or try calling **Metax**, ☎ 524657; **Kostar**, ☎ 528181 (both metered). For out-of-town taxi charter try **Indah Taxi**, Jl Brigjend. Katamso 61, ☎ 516615.
Minibuses ply important routes around the city and average fares are 50 cents.
Motor Becak Average fare is 50 cents, plus 50 cents per km.
Car hire:National Car Rental ☎ 327011; fax 327153, $55–88 per day, $288–490 per week plus insurance and 10% tax; **Toyota Rent a Car**, Jl Sisingamangaraja 8, ☎ 741717; fax 712300, $45–70 per day including tax and insurance.

General Information
Provincial Tourist Office, Jl A. Yani 107. ☎/fax 538101.
Agency tours: **Pacto Travel,** Jl Brigjen Katamso 35-D. ☎ 513699, 510081.
BKSDA (PHPA) Office, Jl Sisingamangaraja No 14, PO Box 574. ☎ 722186.
Foreign Exchange: **Bank BCA**, Jl Diponegoro 15. ☎ 548800, 555800.
Post Office, Jl Bukit Barisan.
Telkom, Jl Prof. HM Yamin SH 13. ☎ 108.
Pharmacy: **Apotik Kimia Farma,** Jl Palang Merah, near the intersection with Jl Yani. Open 24 hours.
Hospitals Outpatient services can be had immediately and in most cases on a 24-hr basis at **Dewi Maya Hospital**, Jl Surakarta 2, ☎ 519291; **St Elizabeth Hospital**, Jl Imam

Bonjol/Jl Haji Misbah, ☎ 322455, 516951; **Rumah Sakit Herna**, Jl Mojopahit, ☎ 510766, 28935.

Photography: **Toko Solo,** Jl Arifin in Kampung Keling, or **Fuji Image Plaza** on Jl Gatot Subroto across from the Medan Fair for the best selection of colour print and slide film.

Gunung Leuser National Park

The massive Gunung Leuser National Park boasts the best lowland rainforest birding to be found in Indonesia. There are two areas where access inside the forest is relatively good. The park has received major financial support from the EU, and the Leuser Development Programme plans to further improve tourist access to the park.

Key Species
Many species of pheasants, hornbills, pittas, trogons, woodpeckers and kingfishers.

Other Wildlife
Tiger, Clouded Leopard, Sumatran Rhino, Tapir, Asian Elephant, Orang-utan and White-handed Gibbon. With the exception of the primates, all are very shy and only the determined with time to spare, or the very lucky, will be fortunate to see large mammals.

Getting There
Gurah lies at the southern main entrance of Gunung Leuser National Park immediately opposite the Ketambe Research Station, a distance of 35 km to the west of Kutacane, Southeast Aceh district, or about 250 km from Medan. If travelling by car from Medan, take the right fork in Kabanjahe (80 km from Medan) towards Tigabinanga. After Tigabinanga continue along the main road to Kutacane. On the left 3 km past Kutacane is the central office of Gunung Leuser National Park. The cost of hiring a car (eg a Kijang) from Medan to Kutacane is $90. The minibuses "Karo Indah", "Karsima" or "Degor Jaya" run directly from Medan to Kutacane. There our hourly departures from the Padang Bulan minibus station between 7 am to 6 pm. The journey takes 5–6 hours, costing Rp8,000.

For Gurah, take a minibus from the Kutacane terminal. Rp.2,000, journey time about 1.5 hrs. Last minibus for Gurah leaves Kutacane at 5 pm.

For a visit to Serakut and Soraya, the only current option is to go by rubber raft along the Alas River (see below).

Accommodation
The best place to stay is **Gurah Bungalow**, 300m beyond the recreation centre. It is situated within the forest so plenty of birds and mammals can be seen around the bungalows. $20 D. Has an attached restaurant and good

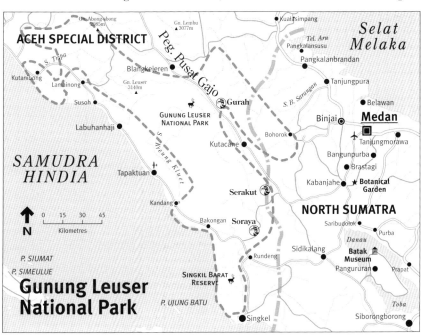

service and facilities.

In Balailutu village, 500 m before Gurah Recreation Centre, there are 4 basic guesthouses. The **Pondok Wisata** is the best. For Rp10,000 one can obtain a single cabin facility with a double bed and attached bathroom. Cabins without bathrooms are Rp 5,000. The guest-house's restaurant serves simple Indonesian fare for Rp1,500–2,500 per meal.

At the Gurah Recreation Centre there are PHPA cabins by the Alas river. The charge for staying at these is Rp5,000, but there are no bathroom or restaurant facilities.

General Information

For information about the Leuser Development Programme write to LDP, Jl Samanhudi No 12, Medan, Sumatra Utara. ☎ (061) 511061; fax (061) 570678.

Rafting packages of normally 3 days (longer trips can be negotiated) can be arranged directly at the "tour service" (Pondok Wisata) or Gurah Bungalow. Alternatively they can be arranged in Kutacane by contacting the tour service **Intu Alas** and at the **Rindu Alam Guest-house**. A 3-day package is $130 per person (minimum 2 person per rubber boat), inclusive of guide, life jacket, permit, insurance, accommodation in Serakut and Soraya, Indonesian food, and transport to the Situlen Estuary (40 km from Kutacane in the direction of Medan), which is where the raft trip starts.

The river journey from Situlen estuary to Serakut is 30 km and takes 4 hours, transversing several rather large rapids. The second day from Serakut to Soraya is 35 km and takes about 6–8 hours. On this stretch the rivers flows calmly and it is easy to bird from the raft. Day 3 can be spent around Soraya (longer if you arrange beforehand) and day 4, is a calm float for a distance of 20 km, taking 4–5 hours towards Desa Gelombang (disembarkation of the rafting trip).

Accommodation at Serakut, Soraya and Gelombang is in simple cabins built on stilts and furnished with mattresses and mosquito netting.

If you wish to return direct to Medan from Gelombang, there is a night bus, which goes via Berastagi (7 hours; Rp9,000).

Padang

Padang (population almost 500,000) is a clean and pleasant town with interesting Minang traditional-style buildings, good hotels, decent restaurants and competent travel agencies. The huge Kerinci Seblat National Park is 120 km south of the town.

Getting There

By Air There are frequent international connections with Singapore and Kuala Lumpur on **SilkAir**, **Garuda**, **Sempati** and **Pelangi**, and regular daily connections with Jakarta and Medan. Padang's Tabing international airport is 15 min north of the city on the road to Bukittinggi. The 6-km taxi ride into town costs $3–5; arrange it at the airport service counter. A *bemo* from the main road (200 m away) costs Rp300.

By sea Pelni's *KM Kerinci* and *Kambuna* leaves Jakarta's Tanjung Priok harbour every other Saturday morning arriving Sunday evening (36 hrs); 1st–4th class $100–46; "no class" tickets not recommended. The boat is always crowded.

By bus from Jakarta takes 2–3 days: $13–22; from Bandar Lampung 28 hrs, about $16.

Accommodation/Dining

The best and most expensive hotel is **Pangeran's Beach Hotel,** Jl Juanda 79 (on the way to the airport), ☎ 51333, 51618; fax 54613. Rooms from $55D; beachfront setting, pool, bar, good restaurant.

Femina Hotel, Jl Bagindo Aziz Chan 15, ☎ 21950, 22670; fax 34388. Best medium-priced hotel, conveniently situated for banks, post office etc. $7(S with fan) to $27(D with AC).

For budget travellers the best value hotels are on Jl Pemuda, opposite the bus terminal. Try the **Tiga Tiga**, ☎ 22173, Standard $10S–32D, VIP $20–25, or **Hang Tuah**, ☎ 26556/9, $5–10.

The very hot (*pedas*) and spicy food for which Padang is famous can be found throughout the city, though the best place to try it is probably **Simpang Raya** on Jl Bagindo Aziz Chan. For Chinese food, try the **Apollo** at Jl Cokroaminoto 36; seafood is recommended next door at No 34; **Nelayan Damar Plaza** shopping centre on Jl Pemuda has a rooftop cafeteria with good views. **Harum Manis** at Jl Niaga 213 serves excellent coffee.

Transport

Garuda/Merpati, Pangeran's Beach Hotel, Jl Juanda, ☎ 58489; fax 58488.
Mandala, Jl Pemuda 29, ☎ 32773.
Sempati, Pangeran's Beach Hotel, Jl Juanda 79, ☎ 51612; fax 55366.
Merpati, Natour Muara Hotel, Jl Gereja 34, ☎ 36501, 32010.

Pelangi, Jl Gereja 34, ☎ 38103; fax 38104.
SilkAir, Jl Hayam Wuruk 16, ☎ 38120/1; fax 38122
Pelni tickets are obtainable only at Jl Tanjung Priok 32, Teluk Bayur harbour, 7 km south of town, ☎ 61624; fax 62428. Early booking advised.
ANS long-distance buses, Jl Khatib Sulaiman, ☎ 26689, and near the terminal, ☎ 26214.
Safa Marwa bus company ☎ 30214; in Sungai Penuh,☎ (0748) 22376.
Car hire/taxis Safa Marwa Jl Pemuda 23B, ☎ 31851.

General Information

W Sumatra Provincial Tourist Office, Jl Jend Sudirman 43, ☎ 34232; fax 34231. Excellent city information leaflet and map.
Travel Agencies are numerous. Try **Tunas**, Jl Pondok 88c, ☎ 31661, 31668, fax 32806; **Natrubu**, Jl Pemuda 29, ☎ 37442, 33008, fax 23410; **Padang Citra Mandiri**, Jl Veteran 74, ☎ 21347.
PHPA Office, Jl Raden Saleh 4, ☎ 54136.
Main Post Office, Jl Aziz Chan 7. Mon–Thu 8-12 am, 1.30–4 pm; Fri, Sat 8–11.30 am only.
Main Telkom Office, Jl Ach. Dahlan. ☎ 50009.
Foreign Exchange: **Bank BCA**, Jl Agus Salim 10A, ☎ 32110-5, 32494.
Hospitals: **Jos Sudaso**, Jl Situjhu (private). **RS Dr M. Jamil**, Jl Perintis Kemerdekaan (public).

Kerinci-Seblat National Park

The massive and spectacular Kerinci-Seblat National Park in West Sumatra covers the large, fertile Kerinci valley, and is one of Asia's premier birding sites. The most popular base is the village of Keresik Tua at the foot of Mt Kerinci, at 3,800 m the highest peak west of Irian Jaya. The trail up the mountain takes you through a succession of habitats culminating in sub-alpine heath and bogs towards the summit, but it is at the lower altitudes that several of Sumatra's rarest endemics are regularly seen.

Other recommended birding sites in the vicinity are the Letter "W" waterfall and the Mt Tujuh trail, but other possibilities remain to be explored. Muaro Sako, on the road between Sungai Penuh, the main town in the valley, and Tapan, on the west coast, are good areas to see lower-altitude species.

Key Species

Bronze-tailed Peacock-pheasant, Salvadori's Pheasant, Red-billed Partridge, Horsfield's Woodcock, Waterfall Swift, Wreathed Hornbill, Fire-tufted Barbet, Orange-backed Woodpecker, Schneider's Pitta, Pink-headed Fruitdove, Blue-tailed Trogon, Blue-masked Leafbird, Sunda Laughing-thrush, Rusty-breasted Wren-babbler, Sumatran Cochoa, Sunda Treepie.

KERESIK TUA AREA

Getting There

By bus The village of Keresik Tua is at the northern end of the Kerinci Valley, 49 km before Sungai Penuh on the inland road from Padang. Anak Gunung, Gunung Kerinci and Safa Marwa bus companies operate night services from Padang to Sungai Penuh, via Keresik Tua, leaving the bus station on Jl Pemuda between 5.00 and 7.00 pm, and arriving at Keresik Tua at 2.00 or 3.00 am. It is advisable to book tickets ($3.50) in the morning from the company offices in the bus station. Safa Marwa also operates a tourist minibus which departs at 10 am, but you have to book a ticket ($8) at least two days in advance. It is not possible to buy return tickets in Keresik Tua, so you must either travel to Sungai Penuh or arrange a return pick-up with the driver. Better still, return via Muaro Sako (see below). Your hotel in Padang can easily arrange a taxi for the 5–6 hr journey to Keresik Tua; expect to pay $95.

Travelling overland from north or south Sumatra, take a bus along the Trans-Sumatran Highway as far as Bangko, 1,119 km south of Medan or 829 km north of Bandar Lampung. At Bangko leave the Trans-Sumatran and take a bus westwards to Sungai Penuh, a tortuous, nerve-shattering journey of *c.* 6 hrs, Rp4,000 ($2.00). From Sungai Penuh it is a further 1.5 hrs to Kersik Tua, departures 9.00 am, 11.00 am and 5.00 pm by local bus; $1.50.

Accommodation/Dining

Birders stay at **Homestay Keluarga Subandi** in Keresik Tua, located towards the south of the village, 50 m from the mosque and opposite the track through the tea plantation to Mt Kerinci. Pak Subandi keeps a bird log and speaks some English. $3.00 a night per person, $1.50 per meal. There are two *warung* in the village. Pak Subandi will not be too put out if you arrive on a 2 am bus, but it would be polite to send him a telegram beforehand via the Eco-Rural address (see overleaf). There are no phones in Keresik Tua.

General Information

Permits to enter the park can be obtained at the PHPA post halfway between Keresik Tua and the start of the Kerinci trail, or at Mt Tujuh. The main National Park office is SBKSDA Office Jambi, Jl Arief Rahman Hakim No 10, Jambi. ☎ (0741) 26451.

Management: Kompleks Perkantoran Pemuda Kerinci, Jl Arga Selebar Daun, Sungai Penuh, Kerinci Seblat, Jambi, ☎ (0748) 21692.

A village cooperative called Eco-Rural (Eco-cultural Travel Cooperative, Jl Raya Sungai Penuh-Muara Labuh, Desa Keresik Tua RT.V, Dusun III No. 19, Kayu Aro, Kerinci) organizes an excellent range of basic visitor services in the area. The cooperative has five homestays with a total of 20 rooms, provides guides ($10 per day), rents tents and sleeping bags ($2 per day), and will arrange transport around the area and back to Padang. All these services are arranged through your homestay owner.

May-August is the best time to visit.

MT KERINCI SUMMIT TRAIL

This is the trail where all the key species are seen. The start of the muddy and poorly maintained trail is a 5-km (50 min) walk up through tea and cinnamon plantations from Keresik Tua, but Pak Subandi will run you up on his motorbike for a small charge. From here it is a 9.5-hr climb to the summit of Mt Kerinci. There is a base camp *pondok* 40 minutes up the trail beyond the entrance archway, then shelters at approximately 2-hr intervals. People normally camp below the summit and make the final ascent for dawn. For birding there is no need to exert yourself as all the best birds are at lower altitudes and the trail between the entrance and the first *pondok* climbs gently. This stretch and the next 500 m are the best sections for birds, including Schneider's Pitta. After this it gets steep!

MT TUJUH TRAIL

This is a stiff, 2-hr climb up a ridge to the scenic, 100-ha Lake Tujuh. There are plenty of birds to be seen and the shelter by the lake is a wonderful place to camp. Ten km from Keresik Tua, in the direction of Padang, turn right in the village of Pelompek. After 2 km pass through the small village of Ulu Jarnih; 300 m further on is a PHPA post and the start of the trail. The first km climbs gently

through cinnamon plantations to a PHPA guest-house ($7 per night, no facilities), after which the trail becomes steep and very muddy.

LETTER "W" WATERFALL

Continuing on the Padang road from Pelompek, after 4 km you come to a small group of scruffy cafés, which mark the start, on the left, of the 200-m track to this magnificent waterfall surrounded by a small pocket of forest. This is the most reliable site for Blue-masked Leafbird and Waterfall Swift (at dusk).

LAKE BILIBIS

On the western flank of Mt Kerinci, "duck lake" sounds promising. The 3-ha lake, with its beautiful views of Kerinci, is charming, but the forest along the 2-km, leech-infested trail from the edge of the plantation was badly damaged by illegal logging in the 1980s and the birding is relatively poor. You will need a guide to find the start of the trail, which is a 1 hr 50-min (2-hr) walk from Keresik Tua.

LADEH PAYANG

Not yet on the birding map, this 100-ha swamp to the west of Mt Kerinci is said to be one of the best areas in the park to see tigers. The trail starts at Kebun Baru, a 18-km road and drivable track from Keresik Tua. It is said to be a 1.5-hr walk through cultivation to the edge of the forest and then 5.5 hrs through the forest to the swamp, where you can camp by a 3-storey watchtower. Lake Sakti is a further 2 hrs from the edge of the swamp.

Muaro Sako

If you have time to spare after visiting Mt Kerinci, a day at Muaro Sako could be very rewarding. The bird-watching is easy—you can see a wide range of birds, including half a dozen endemics, just by walking or driving along the scenic main road through the forest.

Key Species

Argus Pheasant, Helmeted Hornbill, Spot-necked and Cream-vented Bulbuls, Blue-masked Leafbird, Sumatran Drongo, Sumatran Treepie and Lesser Forktail.

Getting There

Muaro Sako is a village on the road between Sungai Penuh and Tapan. Buses leave Sungai Penuh for Tapan at 9.00 am and 5.00 pm. The 3-hr journey costs Rp2,000.

Accommodation/Dining

Facilities in Muaro Sako are very basic. Ask at the restaurant for a room (Rp4,000/night). The food does not come highly recommended. If you have your own transport, a long day-trip out of Sungai Penuh might be preferable.

General Information

For the best birding, simply walk back along the main road towards Sungai Penuh. The road winds through excellent forest, affording views of a wide range of species. Better still, leave the village early and hitch back up to the two *warung* about an hour out of Muaro Sako on the Sungai Penuh road. Then walk back down to the village (10–12 hrs).

Bandar Lampung

Bandar Lampung (often called Tanjung Karang) is the capital of Lampung Province. It is easily accessible from Jakarta, making excursions to Way Kambas and Bukit Barisan National Parks quite feasible for visitors to West Java.

Getting There

By air There are at least 6 daily Merpati flights between Bandar Lampung and Jakarta. Note that this flight departs from Jakarta's Halim Perdanakusuma airport, not Soekarno-Hatta. There is also a twice-weekly connection with Palembang. Bandar Lampung's Branti Airport is 25 km north of the city: take a taxi for $7 or a bus for $1.75.

By sea There are round-the-clock ferries to Merak, Java, from Bakauheni at Lampung's tip, 85 km south of Bandar Lampung. The ferry crossing takes less than 2 hrs and the fare is $12 for cars, $1 for passengers. There's also a jetfoil service to and from Jakarta, leaving Jakarta in the mornings and Bandar Lampung in the afternoons, at 2 pm. ☎ 31437 for more information, fare $15. Several door-to-door taxi companies do the Bandar Lampung–Jakarta trip, including ferry, faster than the bus services. **Dynasty Taxi** offers charters to Bakauheni and Jakarta, ☎ BL 45674/69, Jakarta 5680986, so does **Taxi SB90**, ☎ 31926, 31676, Jakarta 4721146. The fare is $12–14 per person. For a more leisurely voyage, Pelni's *Lawit* calls in every two weeks on its route between Jakarta and Padang.

By bus Bandar Lampung's main bus terminal is Rajabasa, 12 km from town, which can be reached by DAMRI service 2 from Jl Raden Intan, or by taxi. The *mikrolet* (*bemo*) station

is next door. All long-haul buses leave from Rajabasa, round the clock for Jakarta (fare $9) and other main towns.
By bus from Padang, 28 hrs, about $18.

Accommodation/Dining

There is quite a wide range of accommodation and some hotels have a great view over beautiful Lampung Bay.

Kenanga, Jl Kenanga, ☎ 481888; and **Wijaya** on Jl Seraya, ☎ 52163, both have the usual boxy rooms for $10.

Sriwijaya, Jl Kalimantan, ☎ 481046, has rooms for $11 and up.

Kurnia II, ☎ 52905, is a fairly new hotel. The plain rooms are clean; room with *mandi* and inefficient fan, $10 including breakfast.

Kurnia City, ☎ 62030, across the road is a little more expensive but offers a pool. $11–17. Both on Jl Raden Intan. Just along the road is **Andalas Hotel**, ☎ 61494, good AC rooms with *mandi* from $14.

Sheraton Inn Lampung is a low rise, resort style development set around a large pool. All facilities, including tennis and a gym. Rooms from $90. Jl Wolter Monginsidi 175, ☎ 486666; fax 486690.

Marcopolo has a superb location high on a hill with a large pool, open-air terrace café and bar, from which you can bird-watch over the bay. Good value from $17, $48 for a suite. Restaurant, AC and room service. Jl Dr Susilo, ☎ 62511; fax 54419.

Sahid Krakatau on Jl Yos Sudarso by the bay also has a swimming pool, restaurant, bar and full room facilities, rates from $33.

The **Pasar Mambo** night market has street stalls selling all local dishes including fresh Chinese seafood. The Sheraton's **Kebun Raya** serves great Indonesian food, and the **Marcopolo's Terrace Café** is a pleasant hang-out with birding potential. For Chinese food, try the **Golden Dragon** on Jl Yos Sudarso. **Cookies Corner** on Jl Kartini is a neat and tidy European-style café that serves chips, burgers and local favourites, toast and toasted sandwiches. There are Padang restaurants in abundance.

Transport

Merpati office. Jl Kartini 90, ☎ 63419, 63226.
Long distance bus ALS, Jl Raya Terminal Induk Rajabasa 24, ☎ 781090.

Bemo Local *bemos* do the usual about-town routes (double fare over the boundary).

Bus Larger DAMRI buses also serve the city and Rajabasa bus terminal.

Taxis can be chartered for about $4–5 per

hour; they wait in front of the Marcopolo Hotel.

Day **taxi** or **minibus charters** are available from hotels and travel agents, prices from $44.

General Information
Provincial Tourist Information Office Jl W.R. Supratman 39, Gunung Mas, Telukbetung, ☎ 482565.
PHPA Office, Jl Teuku Umar, ☎ 73177.
Hospitals: **Rumah Sakit Umum**, Jl Sriwijaya 15, ☎ 252373; **Rumah Sakit Imanuel**, Jl Soekarno Hatta, Sukarame, ☎ 704900.
Foreign Exchange Bank: **BCA**, Jl Yos Sudarso 100, ☎ 486205; fax: 486401.
Post Office Jl A. Dahlan 21, ☎ 261630.
Telkom Jl Majapahit 14, ☎ 252525.
Tour Agents: **Femmy Tours** on Jl W. Monginsidi 143, ☎ 492593, 485746, or **PT Sahid Tours** on Jl Yos Sudarso, ☎ 44022.

Way Kambas National Park

Way Kambas, on the east coast of Sumatra's Lampung Province, is one of Indonesia's best-known wildlife reserves. Tigers still roam the reserve, as do large herds of elephants. For the bird-watcher, the Way Kanan area is much preferred to the more generally visited Way Kambas, with its elephant training centre. The trails and canoe trips offer the opportunity to see a wide range of lowland forest birds and the possibility of seeing great rarities such as White-winged Duck and Storm's Stork.

Key Species
White-winged Duck, Storm's Stork, Large, Gould's and Sunda Frogmouths, Crested Fireback, Great Argus, Grey-headed Fish-eagle, Checker-throated Yellownape.

Other Wildlife
Siamang, Agile Gibbon, Banded and Silvered Leaf Monkeys, Elephant. Tiger and Tapir are present but very rarely seen.

Getting There
By car Way Kambas is 7–8 hrs by car and ferry from Jakarta. The turning east for Way Kambas off the Trans-Sumatran highway is signposted at Panjang, 4 km south of Bandar Lampung and 85 km north of Bakauheni harbour. Follow the road to Way Jepara and on

to Rajabasalama (92 km). In Rajabasalama turn right at the stone elephant; the park entrance is reached after 7 km, and Way Kanan after a further 13 km. Or take the Kota Bumi road north out of Bandar Lampung and follow the elephant signs.

By bus Direct buses, signed to Way Jepara, leave from Rajabasa bus station in Bandar Lampung; the last bus departs at 3 pm, but you should depart by lunchtime as the *ojek* drivers will not enter the park after dusk. The journey takes 3 hrs and costs $1.50. Get off at the stone elephant at Rajabasalama and hire an *ojek* for the 20-km journey to Way Kanan, $4.50.

From Bandar Lampung airport, which is on the northern Rajabasalama road, simply step out and flag down a Way Jepara bus. Alternatively you can take a taxi direct to Way Kanan ($25.00).

Accommodation/Dining
There is a 6-room guest house at Way Kanan. Quite basic, but clean sheets, $12.50D. You need to bring your own food but you can use the rangers' kitchen.

General Information
The dry season, May-Nov, is the best time to visit the wildlife reserve.

To obtain a permit, pay $2 at the park entrance, or get it in advance from PHPA in Bandar Lampung.

A rangers' cooperative organizes the Way Kanan facilities. The best bird guide is Apribadi, $7.50 a day. See map and main article for details of trails. Canoes can be hired for $12.50/day, full days only, and a speedboat for $80/day.

Bukit Barisan Selatan National Park

This 356,800-ha park covers the southern tip of the Barisan range and juts out as a spur into the Sunda Strait. It could act as a funnel for migratory passerines and raptors between August and October but this has never been checked out; the mosaic of scrub, forest and grassland around Bimbing looks particularly promising.

The whole park is below 700 m, making it an excellent place to see lowland forest specialities, and it boasts spectacular coastal scenery. The best birding excursion is the 4-day circular trek from Tambung across the southern tip to Belimbing, returning along a new track, which follows the coast. There is an alternative return route from Belimbing via the caves at Way Paya, which could be good.

In the northern part of the park there is a trail that leads into excellent forest and across the peninsula from the PHPA post at Sukaraja.

Key Species

Beach Thick-knee, Great Argus, Pink-necked Green Pigeon, Pied and Green Imperial Pigeons, Blue-crowned Hanging-parrot, Raffles Malkoha, Blue-banded Kingfisher, Rhinoceros Hornbill, Olive-backed Woodpecker, Black-and-yellow Broadbill, Rail Babbler, Short-tailed and Chestnut-rumped-Babblers, Purple-naped Sunbird, Black Magpie.

Getting There

The town to head for is Kota Agung. There are daily buses from Bandar Lampung; the journey time is approximately 4 hrs and the fare Rp2,500. If you fly to Bandar Lampung, taxis at the airport will drive you to Kota Agung for $40–45.

General Information

The National Park office is at Jl Raya Terbaya (☎ 0722 21064), this is 1.5 km before downtown Kota Agung on the main road from Lampung. Park entrance fee is Rp2,500. You are obliged to take a park guide to enter the park ($10/Rp20,000 per day).

THE SOUTHERN CIRCUIT

A daily ferry to Tampang leaves the quay at Kota Agung between 10.00 and 12.00 am. The crossing takes 4–6 hrs, depending how loaded the boat is. Fare Rp3,000. The transfer from the ferry to shore is by canoe through exhilarating surf. Make sure your equipment is in waterproof bags!

Buy your supplies in Kota Agung. There is a small PHPA post in Tampang, and visitors stay the night with Pak Salamat next door ($3.50/Rp7,500 per person). PHPA will arrange porters if you need them ($5/Rp10,000 a day per person). Pak Hasim knows the trails well. From Tampang it is a 6-hr birding walk (2-hr straight trek) to a good shelter at Duku Banyak. The forest here is excellent and it would be worth staying two nights. From Duku Banyak it is a 4-hr trek (but make a day of it) to the coast at Belimbing, site of a WW2 air field and a lighthouse. An ecotourism resort is being developed here by P.T. Nusantara (Rudy Schultz), next to the PHPA post. They are said to be welcoming to trekkers and you can stay here, in the PHPA post or camp. During bird migration months, especially, this area would be worth a couple of days.

A recommended side trip from Belimbing is the 3-hr trek north to the swiftlet caves at Way Paya. The trail follows the coast for 2 hrs before heading inland into the hills. It passes through excellent forest.

P.T. Nusantara has constructed a track along the south coast between Belimbing and Tampang. It passes through a mosaic of savannah and forest, and the birding is excellent. Take two days and camp at Lake Minjukut, reached after 5–6 hrs' walking. The next day is another 4–5 hr walk to Tambang Mas on the edge of the park. From here you can hire a boat for $15/Rp30,000 to take you round to Tambang, find an *ojek* or walk the last 12 km back to Tampang.

SUKARAJA

This is an area of hilly forest (still below 500 m) in the centre of the park. The birding is excellent. The base is the PHPA's Pos Sukaraja, close to the Kota Agung–Benkunat road, which bisects the park. The National Park office can arrange a jeep to take you up here for $25–30. The turning to the Sukaraja post is on the right, just after you pass the National Park boundary sign. It is a 20-min walk from the road through coffee plantations. Give at least Rp5,000 for staying at the post. The good forest starts 30 min to the west.

–Paul Jepson, Margaret Kinnaird, Rosie Ounsted, Dolly Priatna with additional information from *Nicholas Clark, Caroline Filby & John Riley.*

Kalimantan

Samarinda

Samarinda, the capital of East Kalimantan, is the main point of embarkation for boats up the Mahakam River and the starting point for trips to Kutai National Park. Samarinda is about 115 km north of Balikpapan, and 60 km from the sea upriver on the Mahakam.

Getting There
By air Bouraq flies 2–3 times and Pelita once daily from Balikpapan to Timindung Airport, which is on the north side of town; taxis to the downtown area cost $2.50.
By road You can also travel from Balikpapan by taxi (2–3 hrs, from $4 shared–$30 single) or public bus ($2 from the Batu Ampar Terminal, just outside Balikpapan).
By sea Weekly boats from Pare-Pare, Sulawesi (tickets from the Pelni office) arrive in Samarinda at the Pelni harbour (Jl Sudarso).

Accommodation/Dining
Aida, Jl Temenggung 4, near the Hidayah, ☎ 42572, 32412. 29 rms. Popular, good deal. All rms w/enclosed facilities. $11S, $12D; with AC $19S, D.
Bumi Senyiur, Jl P. Diponegoro 17–19. ☎ 41443; fax 38014. New, bungaglow-style. Restaurant (Japanese and Chinese food), pool, tennis court, travel agent. $65S, D; VIP rms $85S, D; VIP suite $300.
Hayani, Jl Pirus 17, ☎ 42653. 35 rms. In front of the Pirus. All rms with enclosed facilities $11S, D, new rooms $13S, D, with AC $27S, D.
Hidayah I, Jl Temenggung, ☎ 31408, fax 37761. 26 rms. Near Pasar Pagi in the downtown area. $11S, $12D, with AC $21S, D, VIP $26S, D.
Mesra International, Jl Pahlawan 1, ☎ 32772, fax 35453. 160 rms, all AC. Best hotel in town. All rms with AC, and colour TV. Fine, not too expensive restaurant, pool (non-guests Rp5,000/day), tennis court, fitness centre and golf, money exchange. Standard $65S–$68D, VIP $75S–$85D.

Pirus, Jl Pirus 20, ☎ 31462. 30 rms. Near downtown on a quiet street. $12S, D, with AC $30–31S, D.
A good variety of restaurants, all reasonably priced. Lots of bargain meals at food stalls. Not easy to find Western food, but try the Mesra Hotel's restaurant if you can't face another Indonesian or Chinese meal.
Lezat, Jl Mulawarman. Excellent Chinese restaurant. Various soups and lots of different dishes of frog, crab, chicken, pork, squid, fish, beef, oysters and shrimp, all about $4.50. Open 10 am to 11 pm.
Sudut Indah, Jl Imam Bonjol. Chinese dishes of chicken, shrimp, beef, fish, squid, crab and frog $2.75–$4. Steaks $3–$4. Indonesian dishes $1–$1.50. The AC here is welcome on a hot day.
Lesehan, Jl Pemuda. Javanese cooking, nice atmosphere sitting on floor mats, $1.50–$3.

Transport
Bouraq, Jl Mulawarman 24, ☎ 321105.
Pelita, Duta Miramar Travel Agency, Jl Sudirman 20, ☎ 43385, fax 35291.
Pelni, Jl Pelabuhan 1, Balikpapan. ☎ 24171, fax 22870.
Taxis: **Great Mahakam Travel** ☎ (0542) 23240 in Balikpapan; ☎ (0541) 38805 in Samarinda, for 3–7 passenger taxi. **Collective** sedan taxis leave from Jl Mulawarman, opposite the old Pinang Bahari market. For a chartered taxi, try either outside the better hotels or on Jl Mulawarman, or phone ☎ 31137.
Samarinda has a confusing array of bus, sedan taxi, and Kijang terminals.
Sungai Kijang Terminal Past the bridge over the Mahakam and near the Terminal Ferry. Most (but not all) of the vehicles to Balikpapan leave from here. Also, there are on average 8 Kijangs a day to Kota Bangun (3.5 hrs, $3); Kijangs to Bontang (3 hrs, $2.50).
Lempake Terminal About 6 km northeast of town. Buses to Bontang (3 hrs, $2); Kijangs to Bontang (3 hrs, $2.50), Sangatta (4 hrs, $10).
Boats See *Birding the Mahakam*.
Colt minibuses Rp400, to the ferry dock and bus terminal Rp600. Sedan taxis are found

outside the better hotels and charge $2–3 to in-town locations. They can be chartered for $4/hr, with a 2-hr minimum. Chartering a Colt is half this price, also with the 2-hr minimum. Or you can hire a motorcycle taxi for about Rp1,000.

General Information

Tourist Office, Jl Ade Irma Suryani I, ☎ 41669; fax 22111.
Travel Agency: PT. Duta Miramar Tours and Travel, Jl Jend. Sudirman 20. ☎ 43385; fax 35291. Offers 28 different tours in East Kalimantan. Depending on trip and number of persons: $45 for 1 day to $2,500 for 21 days.
PHPA Offices KanWil Kehutanan, Jl Rawa Indah (Jl M.T. Haryono = new name), ☎ 33766. SBKSDA, Jl Rawa Indah, ☎ 43556.
Main Post Office Jl Gajah Mada. Accepts only Giro cheques.
Main Telkom Office Jl Awang Long 8. ☎ 38502.
Foreign Exchange: Bank BCA, Jl Jend. Sudirman 30. ☎ 38900. Banks accept only US$ cash and US$ traveller's cheques.
Moneychanger Palapa Sakti, Jl Dermaga 52, ☎ 32156, accepts all major currencies and traveller's cheques.
Hospitals: Rumah Sakit Dirgahayu, Jl Merbabu 2, ☎ 42116; **Rumah Sakit Umum**, Jl A. Wahab Syahrani, Dr Sutomo, ☎ 38050.
Doctors An honest and good doctor is Dr Hengky Gosal (speaks English), who works at R.S. Dirgahayu but also has his own practice at Jl Agus Salim 3.
Souvenirs There are many souvenir shops along the Mahakam river in Samarinda, and in town. Most of the "old" souvenirs on sale are manufactured in front of the shops after hours.

Kutai National Park

One of Indonesia's first and largest reserves, Kutai offers excellent birding opportunities for twitchers, adventurers and the leisure tourist alike. More than 236 bird species have been recorded for the park.

Key Species

Rufous-bellied Eagle, Wallace's Hawk-eagle, Crested Partridge, Crested Fireback, Great Argus, Large Green Pigeon, Large Frogmouth, seven species of hornbill (notably Wrinkled), Blue-headed Pitta, Garnet Pitta, Bornean Wren-babbler, Bornean Bristlehead, Dusky Munia.

Other Wildlife

Proboscis Monkeys, Barking and Sambar Deer, Mouse-deer, Banteng, Clouded Leopard. Near Mentoko, you might see wild Orangutan, gibbons and leaf monkeys.

Getting There

Teluk Kaba From Samarinda take a taxi/Kijang (2–2.5 hours, $2.50) or bus (3 hrs, $2) to Bontang. Hire a boat from Bontang (Tanjung Limau harbour) to Teluk Kaba (1.5–2 hrs, $15).
Mentoko From Samarinda: take a bus all the way to Sangatta (4 hrs, $10). From Bontang: drive or take a bus north direct to Sangatta (about 2 hrs). From Teluk Kaba: walk 2–3 km back to the main road and take a bus to Sangatta (about 1 hr if the road is good). At Sangatta: a *ketinting* motor boat can be chartered upriver to Mentoko (2.5 hrs, $35). A rather more expensive way to travel is to take a boat all the way from Tanjung Limau to Mentoko (10 hrs for $50).

Accommodation/Dining

In Bontang the **Hotel Gembira** has AC, TV and hot water, and costs about $30 a night. At Sangatta try **Penginapan Haryono** or **Arfiah**. Teluk Kaba and Sangatta have field stations with limited space (Rp15,00 a day); information can be obtained at the National Park head office. Take along enough food.

General Information

The driest period is April to October. Before entering the park, visitors should report to the National Park office (Kantor Taman Nasional Kutai, Jl Mulawarman 236, Tromolpos 1, Bontang 75383, Kalimantan Timur, ☎ 0548 21191). The most accessible sites are Teluk Kaba and Mentoko, but hiking and camping are easy as the terrain is relatively flat. There is a 30-km jungle trail from Pinang (near Sangatta village) to Mentoko, and other trails lead from Teluk Kaba. Leeches are abundant at Mentoko during the rainy months; anti-leech socks are most effective, and better than repellents.

Tanjung Puting Reserve

Tanjung Puting Reserve in Central Kalimantan province covers 3,040 sq km of low-lying terrain characterised by blackwater rivers that flow into the Java Sea. The river mouths are bordered with nipa palm and mangrove swamps. In the remote centre of the reserve are "bird lakes", where thousands of herons and cormorants nest. There are seasonally inundated peat swamp forests, and heath forest on the drier ground. Most visitors come to see the orphaned Orang-utans at Camp Leakey, where there is a 200-m boardwalk and an extensive trail system. Over 220 species of bird have been recorded, including several species of hornbill and pheasant.

The park is best explored by boat from the coastal town of Kumai.

Key Species

Excellent range of rainforest and wetland species including: Storm's Stork, Blyth's Hawk-eagle, Lesser and Grey-headed Fish-eagles, Bulwer's Pheasant, Bay Owl, 7 species of hornbill, 10 species of woodpecker, Blue-headed Pitta, Black-and-white Bulbul and Rufous-tailed Shama.

Other Wildlife

Forty species of mammal including Western Tarsier, Proboscis Monkey, Agile Gibbon and Clouded Leopard.

Getting There

All-inclusive tours can be organised through Indonesia Expeditions, Jakarta.

A visit to the park starts at Pangkalanbun. There are daily flights from Jakarta, Pontianak and Banjarmasin. Taxis can be chartered from the airport to the coastal town of Kumai ($20). Alternatively, take a Colt from the market in nearby Sungai Arot to Kumai (Rp1,500, 30 min).

Pelni ships from Semarang and Surabaya call at Kumai every 2 weeks.

General Information

A *surat jalan* for the park is required from the police office in Pangkalanbun (you will need a photocopy of the photo-page of your passport and visa stamp). This must be handed to the PHPA office on Jl Idris (the coast road) in Kumai to get a park entrance permit. The PHPA office is open 8.00 am to 2.00 pm except Friday (8.00–11.00 am) and Saturday (8.00–12.00 am). Closed Sunday. The paperwork sometimes takes an hour. Local hotels will arrange the permit for a nominal charge. Entrance fee to the park is Rp2,500 and there is a $1–2 boat toll.

The PHPA office can arrange excursions; PHPA guide rate is Rp7,500 per day. There are also numerous travel agents in Kumai.

Rivers provide the major travel routes into the park. The most economical means is to take the daily public water taxi from Kumai upstream to Aspai (Rp3,500). Most visitors charter a longboat or *kelotok*. Hire charges are $35–40 per day.

The Baso family's *kelotok*, Garuda, is excellent value, offering food, accommodation, transport and guides for $35 a day. Their smaller *kelotok* sleeps 4–5; the large boat 8–10. A lovely, leisurely way to see the park, a night moored well away from settlements is an unforgettable experience. They are in high demand. To book write to Boat Garuda, Baso (Yatno), Jl Idris Rt. 6, No 507, Kumai Hulu 74181, Pangkalanbun, Kalimantan Tengah.

There are also speedboats for hire. They go about three times the speed of *kelotok*, but are not environmentally sensitive and prices are higher ($50–65+ per day).

The following agencies arrange packages to the park:

Banjarmasin: **Loksado**, ☎ 64833 and **Arjuna,** ☎ 58150.

Jakarta: **Ethanin Expresindo**, ☎ 421 6373, and **Indonesian Expeditions**, ☎ 570 0238, 570 3246; fax 570 1141.

An 80-page *Guide Book to Tanjung Puting National Park*, by Drs Galdikas and Shapiro, is published by Gramedia. It contains much useful information and a bird checklist.

Accommodation

Rimba Lodge is located on the Sekonyer river, just outside the park, and opposite the Tanjung Harapan post (near Sekonyer village). 35 rms. $30S, $55D. Canoes are available. Park permits can also be arranged here. Bookings, including package deals, can be made through the Blue Kecubung Hotel in Pangkalanbun (☎ 21211; fax: 21513).

To stay at the other accommodation, Camp Leakey, and Natai Lengkuas, prior booking and permission are required from the travel agent in Jakarta.

Recommended budget *losmen* in Kumai are **Losmen Kumara** (☎ 22062) $4–5, and **Losmen Cempaka** $3–4.

The Mahakam

Visitors can choose from several travel options: either join one of the many organized tours, which range from 2-day up to 3-week trips, or travel upriver independently by local transportation. Some stretches can be travelled by bus or car, but most of your time will be spent on one of the large boats that ply the river between Samarinda and Long Bangun. If you are in a hurry or want to visit remoter parts, it is best to charter a motorized canoe (*ketinting*). Flying directly to the Upper Mahakam above Long Bangun by small airplane is another option.

Key Species
White-shouldered Ibis upriver of Long Iram; Storm's Stork possible along the Ratah tributary. Lesser and Grey-headed Fish Eagles along the river. Wide variety of river and waterbirds.

Other Wildlife
Proboscis Monkey, Irrawaddy Dolphin, Estuarine and False Gharial Crocodiles, Monitor Lizards, freshwater turtles and dolphins.

Getting There
By boat From Samarinda the most common way to travel inland is on ordinary passenger boats leaving from the ferry landing (Pelabuhan Ferry) past the bridge, on the outskirts of town. Speedboats for 4–6 passengers can be chartered from the **Sapulidi Company**. All the boats heading upriver stop at Tenggarong, but many also stop at many other places beforehand, stretching the 45 km journey to Tenggarong to 4 hrs or more. Direct boats to Tenggarong leave from the Pasar Pagi dock (2–3 hrs, 50¢) and you can get there even faster on a chartered speedboat, good for 4–6 passengers (1 hr each way, $50 round trip).

Samarinda to Long Bagun takes 3 days and 2 nights in good conditions. Going upriver, boats spend a night at Data Bilang to avoid running into logs or sandbanks in the dark. $12. From Long Bagun to the Upper Mahakam past the rapids by chartered longboat: $750, or share one as far as Tiong Bu'u or Long Apari: $40. Tiong Bu'u back to Long Bagun $15–20.

If you want to go past the rapids, you need to come back by light plane. Try to get a seat on a MAF (Mission Aviation Fellowship) plane.

By bus to Kota Bangun: every 30 min from Jl Untung Surapati terminal. 2.5 hrs/$1.50.

By car from Melak to Tering (1 hr): $2.50.

By air DAS flies on Tuesdays and Thursdays to Datah Dawai, above the rapids: $29, max 5 passengers. Flights are regularly cancelled because of the poor condition of the Datah Dawai airstrip.

Accomodation/Dining
At Kota Bangun:
Penginapan Mukjizat Jl Mesjid Raya. Close to dock and bus terminal, nice view over river. $2.50S.
Penginapan Mekar, Jl Mesjid Raya. $2.50S.
Penginapan Marini, behind dock, close to Kepala Desa's office. $2.50S.
Sri Bagun Lodge, the last real hotel on the Mahakam. Tennis court, trips to nearby lakes. From $17.50S.

At Melak:
Penginapan Rahamat Abadi and **Bahagia** close to the dock; **Flamboyan** 100 m further upstream. All $2.50S.

At Long Iram:
Two *losmen:* one just above the dock (no name) and **Penginapan Wahtu** on Jl Soewondo.

At Datah Bilang:
Two *losmen:* one on the main street, close to the two *lamin.* One on the 1st floor of a floating *warung* owned by Pak Jamjam, $2.50S.

At Mura Ratah/Danumparoy:
No official *losmen* here. Report to the *kepala desa* and ask for Pak Dede, or Pak Atim and his wife, Ibu Sutra, who may be willing to provide accommodation. It would be right to pay $2.50 pp per night.

At Long Bagun:
Penginapan Uzman and **Artomoro**, both on the main street. $2.50S. Also tasty *nasi goreng* and *ayam goreng* at **Ayam Goreng Dimensi**, on the same street.

At Long Pahangai:
Two *losmen* on the main street, $2.50S.

At Long Lunuk:
One *losmen* with its own shop on the main street, or stay with Pak Lohat Bid and his family.

At Tiong Bu'u/Tiong Ohang:
Several *losmen* on both sides of the river, connected by a bridge. Usually $3.50S.

–Bas van Balen, Resit Sözer with additional information from *Raleigh Blouch, Paul Jepson & Kathy MacKinnon.*

Sulawesi

Ujung Pandang

Ujung Pandang is the capital and administrative centre of the province of South Sulawesi. It is the main point of entry for the south of the island and the base for a trip to Lake Tempe and the very popular Tana Toraja area. Ujung Pandang's Hasanuddin (International) Airport, the gateway to eastern Indonesia, is well connected to the rest of the archipelago.

Getting There

By air The airport is 25 km north of town on the road to Maros, 30 mins' drive. The half-hour taxi ride into town costs $6 or $8 AC, or you can walk 500 m to the main road and catch a *bemo* for $1 including luggage.

Garuda has 3 daily flights from Jakarta, $176.

Mandala has daily flights to Surabaya ($93), Jakarta ($152) and Ambon ($104).

Bouraq Daily flights to Palu and Gorontalo.

Sempati flies twice a week from Singapore (via Jakarta), 4 times a week from Kuala Lumpur and Perth (the latter via Jakarta), twice a week from Taipei (via Jakarta); two times daily from Jakarta, daily from Jayapura and Manado and Medan, twice daily from Surabaya and three times daily from Denpasar (via Surabaya).

Merpati Four flights daily to Surabaya ($100) and Jakarta ($164); twice daily to Ambon ($112) and Jayapura ($269); daily to Balikpapan ($72), Biak ($202), Bali ($76), Palu ($70) and Tana Toraja ($39).

By sea Five Pelni ships call at Ujung Pandang.on fixed schedules of 14 days.

By bus There is a daily bus service to and from all the major towns in South Sulawesi, however getting out of Ujung Pandang can be a hassle. Coaches and minibuses to other towns leave from terminal Pasar Daya at Km 15. Allow at least a half hour for the journey. First take a *bemo* (Rp150) or *becak* (Rp500–Rp1,000) to Sentral (the central *bemo* terminus) and from there a second *bemo* to Panaikan. From here, buses leave regularly throughout the day up to 7 pm.

Lima Express and **Litha & Co** are two of the better long-distance bus companies.

Accommodation/Dining

Ujung Pandang is expensive by Indonesian standards. At the lower end of the scale there are many cheap *penginapan* around the port area, but these are not recommended. Most of the larger hotels add 21% service and tax; smaller ones may add 10%.

Legend Hostel, Jl Jampea 5G (Jampea Plaza), ☎ 328203. 4 rms ($6) and 12 dormitory style bunk beds ($2.50). A place low-budget travellers can call their own. Clean, and the best value in town. Helpful staff who can arrange everything from trips to Toraja to sailing in a cargo *pinisi*.

Delia Orchid Park, Km 6, Jl Urip Sumohardjo, ☎ 442325. 22 rms. Contact in Ujung Pandang: Delia Florist and catering, Jl Bawakaraeng 57, ☎ 318219, 323967. Inconveniently located off the main road north out of Ujung Pandang (it's closer to the airport than to the harbour: make sure your driver knows the location!), but this place is a haven for orchid lovers. Also many other plants on the premises. Beautifully built and landscaped, all modern indoor facilities, very clean. $20–$40 S, D.

Makassar Golden, Jl Pasar Ikan 50–52, ☎ 314408; fax 320951; telex: 71290 MGHUP IA. Spectacularly situated on the waterfront in the centre of town, with views of the offshore islands. Coffee shop, bar and restaurants, swimming pool. Magnificent sunsets from the Toraja-style terrace restaurant. Free transport to the airport (with reservation). Major credit cards. $66–95S, $85–110D, $150–390 suite.

Victoria Panghegar, Jl Jend. Sudirman 24, ☎ 311863; fax 312468. 115 rms. Bar and restaurant, coffee shop, swimming pool. This luxurious, privately-owned hotel offers a range of services, from safety deposit boxes to chauffeur-driven cars. Free transport from airport and seaport upon request. Major credit cards accepted. $50–80S, $70–90D.

The main attraction of eating out in Ujung Pandang is the seafood: huge shrimps and lobsters, dark-skinned fish with delicate white flesh, and giant, juicy crabs. There is an enormous range of restaurants as well as several hundred metres of *warung* along the seafront.

Transport
Garuda, Jl Slamet Riyadi 6. ☎ 317704, 322543; fax 315719.
Bouraq, Jl Veteran Selatan 1, ☎ 83039.
Mandala, Jl HOS Tjokroaminoto 7C, ☎ 314451. Airport, ☎ 3326.
Sempati, Victoria Panghegar Hotel, Jl Jend. Sudirman 42. ☎ 311612; fax 319003 and Makassar Golden Hotel, Jl Pasar Ikan 50/52. ☎ 310690; fax 320951.
Merpati, Jl Gn. Bawakareang 109. ☎ 44271/2, 44274/5; fax 442480.
Pelni, Jl Jend. Sudirman 38. ☎ 331395; fax: 317964.
Long-distance bus: **Lima Express**, Jl Laiya 25. ☎ 315851, 315022; **Litha & Co.** Jl Gn. Merapi 160. ☎ 324847.
Hire car Self-drive cars and Toyota Land Cruisers are difficult to find, and expensive to rent. Taxis can be hired through most hotels for about $40/day: **Bosowa**, ☎ 311311, 328689 (blue cars); **Amal**, ☎ 313131, 313313 (white cars).
Becak Rp1,000–2,500.

General Information
Tourist Office, Jl A.P. Petta Rani. ☎ 443355; fax 443226.
SBKSDA (PHPA) Office, Jl Barang Baru 7, PO Box 1144, Ujung Pandang 90011,☎ 852709.
Agency Tours: **Limbunan Tours**, Jl Gn. Bawakaraeng 40–42 (Mailing address: PO Box 97), ☎ 323333, 316350; fax 314344, 314567. The only outfit with an on-line computer system linked with Garuda and Merpati: if it's humanly possible to book or confirm a flight, they can do it. Offices in Jayapura and Labuhanbajo, with plans to open one in Ambon. Tours offered include to Manado, Ambon, Banda, Irian Jaya, the Mahakam River in Kalimantan, Flores and Komodo. English-speaking guides.
Ramayana Satrya Tours, Jl Bulukunyi 9A (PO Box 107), ☎ 871791, 851114; fax 853665; branch offices in Maumere and Irian Jaya. Tours include bird-watching and other nature tours. English-speaking guides.
General Post Office, Jl Slamet Riyadi 10.
Telkom Office, Jl Balaikota 2 and Jl Jend. Sudirman.
Foreign exchange: **Bank BCA**, Jl Jend. A. Yani. Money changer **Haji La Tunrung** on Jl Monginsidi 42, just north of the fort, offers a similar rate to the banks, no service charge, ☎ 872910.
Hospitals: **Rumah Sakit Akademis** and **Rumah Sakit Stella Maris** are the best in Ujung Pandang; hospitals outside the capital offer only basic medical attention.
Surgeon Dr Louis Rajawane at the Rumah Sakit Akademis is highly regarded.
Pharmacy: **Kimia Farma**, Jl A. Yani. Open 24 hrs.
Souvenirs The main souvenir shopping streets are Jl Pasar Ikan, Jl Somba Opu (for gold and silver) and Jl Pasar Baru.

Lake Tempe

This shallow complex of lakes, with its intensive fishing industry, is a haven for large numbers of many waterbird species, especially in the man-made structures of floating vegetation (*bungka*) unique to this area. Halfway between the provincial capital of Ujung Pandang and crowd-pulling Tana Toraja, Tempe lies in the *Buginese* heartland and at the centre of the Sulawesi silk-weaving industry. While it is a must for the keen birder, everyone will find a half-day trip to the lakes delightful, as seeing birds is nowhere easier.

Key Species
Seasonally (usually Nov–Jan) up to 5,000+ Glossy Ibis, 10,000+ Garganey and tens of thousands of reed-warblers. Little Grebe, Little Pied Cormorant, Darter, Purple and Common Moorhens, Comb-crested Jacana, Yellow, Cinnamon and Black Bitterns, Black-crowned and Nankeen Night-herons, and Purple Heron; occasionally Milky Stork and Osprey.

Other Wildlife
Soa-soa, or Sail-fin Lizard, several species of Monitor Lizard, and Sulawesi's only aquatic tortoise, Asian Box Turtle.

Getting There
By car The 220-km journey from Ujung Pandang to Sengkang takes about 4 hrs; there are two major routes. The quicker is the coastal road which snakes along a narrow coastal plain to Pare-pare (2.5 hrs), from where you follow the major road to Tana Toraja that runs north of the lakes. After about an hour you reach a major junction; here you turn south to Sengkang (another 30 min).

A slower but more interesting alternative is via Camba. From Ujung Pandang follow the coastal road north to Maros (35 km), then head due east towards the wonderful karst landscape of Bantimurung (waterfalls and butterflies). At Bantimurung follow the road in the direction of Camba—it winds very slowly up the limestone escarpment, through a Nature Park (Camba) and offers great views. The scenic road from Camba to Soppeng (or Watansoppeng) is not as busy as the coastal road, taking about 2.5 hours; Soppeng–Sengkang is another 30 min.

By bus Alternatively, take a public bus to Parepare (2–3 hrs,) and from there a bus to Sengkang (another 1.5 hours). About $2.50.

Once in Sengkang it is easy to rent an outboard-powered *Buginese* longboat plus crew of two. Negotiate a price (usually per hr or half day, depending on what you want) beforehand—a half day will cost about $17–25, depending on your bargaining skills and the mood of your boatman. Best place to rent a boat is along the Walanae river, north of downtown Sengkang.

Accommodation/Dining

The **Apada Hotel and Restaurant** is run by members of the *Buginese* royal family of Sengkang. They can put on a traditional (and very stylish!) traditional *Buginese* feast.

Apada Hotel and Restaurant, Jl Durian 9, off Jl A. Yani, ☎ 21053. Restaurant speciality: traditional *Buginese* feast (about $8 pp, order in advance). $12–17D with AC.

Wisma Herawati, Jl A. Yani No. 22. ☎ 21082. Meals available if ordered in advance. $5–7D with fan.

Rumah Makan Romantis, Jl AP Petta Rani 2. Good food, cold beer, reasonable prices.

Rumah Makan Melati, Jl Kartini 54. Good food, inexpensive.

General Information

Best time to visit is Oct–Jan, when water levels are low. The fishing season peaks then, and it coincides with the arrival of migratory waterbirds such as Glossy Ibis and Garganey. As usual, early morning and late afternoon are best for trips on the lakes, not only because of the birds but because the heat of the sun can be a torment while sitting in a boat (none has a roof). Bring lots of water, sun cream and an umbrella (for sun and rain). Depending on what you want to see, you can spend 2–3 hrs on a quick look at the best spots, or 2–3 days if you want to tour all three lakes and see wildlife along the interconnecting streams. Guides are not necessary if water levels are high, but if they are low you will not find the

channels and it is generally wise to travel with a boatman. It is also useful that local boatmen know the rules regarding fishing nets and how to avoid snagging them. Be aware that the *bungka* are strictly off limits.

Palu

Lore Lindu National Park is about 50 km south of the city, so Palu acts as the main hopping-off point for the park.

Getting There

By air Merpati flies daily to Palu from Ujung Pandang. There are also flights from Jakarta, Bandung, Denpasar and Surabaya, calling first at Ujung Pandang. Bouraq has daily flights from Jakarta via Balikpapan, Manado, Gorontalo and Surabaya via Ujung Pandang. Taxis to and from the airport cost $7.50; you can also catch a *bemo* for the 20-km ride into town.

By bus There are no public buses direct from Ujung Pandang to Palu or Gorontalo; the journey entails a number of bus transfers. It is difficult to estimate the price of the journey, but what is certain is that the buses are old, dirty and often over-crowded.

By sea Shipping traffic to and from Palu comes out of Pantaloan Harbour, about 22 km north of town, beyond Tawaeli on the east coast of Palu Bay. Pelni calls once a week each way between Ujung Pandang and Balikpapan (Kalimantan), and twice a week between Ujung Pandang and Toli-Toli. Various smaller craft ply the coastal routes north and south.

Accommodation/Dining

Alam Raya, Jl Sis Aljufri 27. ☎ 21643. Economy $13, Standard $18, Deluxe $21, VIP $23.

Central Hotel, Jl Kartini 6, ☎ 21738; fax 23256. 50 rms. Part of large supermarket complex. Can be busy and noisy but very convenient with restaurant, supermarket and Telkom all in one complex. $17, Superior $24, VIP $34S or D.

Palu Golden, Jl Raden Saleh 1, ☎ 21126; fax 23230. 55 rms. Located next to the bay. Dirty beach, but good view from some rooms. The swimming pool is OK, but the restaurant is poor. $43–$54S, $54–$66D (try bargaining, especially for ground floor rooms).

Purnama Raya, Jl Wahidin 4 (below Hasanuddin shopping complex). ☎ 23646. Backpackers' haunt. $5–7. Good place to find local guides.

Rama Garden Hotel, Jl Monginsidi 81, ☎ 29500. $10–16S, $16–19.50D; VIP $19.50S, $24D.

Milano (in the Jl Hasanuddin shopping complex). Indonesian, Chinese and imitation western food. Prices reasonable. They have information on trekking tours and will help find local guides. Ask for Peter Meroniak, who speaks English.

For seafood, try **Taman Ria** and **Buluri Indah** on the road to Donggala and **Wisata Laut** and **Pondok Selero** on the Pantaloan road.

The best Chinese food in town is on Jl Raden Saleh at **Windy** restaurant, an un-signposted, unappealing house 50 m up the road from Palu Golden Hotel. A few tables and chairs, limited menu but excellent *mie goreng*.

Depot Marina on Jl Monginsidi is recommended for fast, cheap simple food. For outdoor food the night stalls on Jl Hasanuddin and Jl Sis Aljufri/Gaja Mada are good. Out of town you will find wonderful chicken dishes at Biromaru market (6 km on the road to Palolo) on Weds and Sats.

Transport

Merpati, Jl Mongonsidi 71. ☎ 21172, 23341.
Sempati, Central Hotel, Jl Kartini 6. ☎ 21612, 23833 (no flights from Palu).
Bouraq, Jl Mawar 10, ☎ 21195, 22995.
Pantaloan Harbour, ☎ 23815, 91027.
Pelni, Jl Gajah Mada 86. ☎ 21696; fax 23237.
Bemos (also called *taksi*) Rp350.
Metered taxi AC and reasonably priced. **Mutiara Taxi**, ☎ 28444; and **Taxi Puskud**, ☎ 52888.
Pony cart *Dokar* or *bendi* cost Rp300–1,500 depending on distance and whether shared.
Car hire For AC Kijangs try outside the Palu Golden, Central and Buana Hotels. Full-day charter in town $20–30; out of town $65 plus; this may or may not include driver's expenses (meals etc) and fuel. It depends on your negotiating skills. Also try at bus station for non-AC.
Travel agencies: **Wisata Gautama Pura** on Jl Sus Aljufri rents out a few shoddy minibuses, price varies. **Mahakam Motor**, on Jl Sunggai Malei 33, (☎ 22868) rents out 4WD, eg Toyota Landcruiser. $65 plus per day including driver.

General Information

Tourist Office, (Dinas Pariwisata Daerah) Jl Raja Moili 11, ☎/fax 26810 (400 m down the road from Palu Golden Hotel). Hardly brim-ming over with useful advice.

Travel Agency: **Wisata Gautama Putra**, Jl Sis Aljufri 10A, Komplex Palu Plaza, ☎ 52334, 51797. May be able to fix up trekking in Lore Lindu and elsewhere in the area.
Celebes Citra Wisata in the Hasanuddin shopping complex is good for tickets. ☎ 21374. For tourism advice try contacting Robert Hitchins, an Englishman who works in tourism in Central Sulawesi, ☎/fax: 29357.
PHPA Office, Jl S. Parman 9, ☎ 21260.
The Nature Conservancy, Jl. Towua 94, ☎/fax: 25280.
Post Office, Jl Mohammad Yamin.
Telkom Office, Jl Achmad Dahlan 7, ☎ 21004, 321304. There are several *warpostel* that stay open longer hours including the Pasifik Ocean, near the Palu Golden Hotel, and the Sentosa, near the Central Hotel.
Foreign Exchange Banks are open 8.00 am–3.00 pm Mon–Fri. Change traveller's cheques at **Bank EXIM**, Jl Hasanuddin. Mastercard/Visa withdrawals at **Bank Dana-mon**, Jl Hasanuddin. The only banknotes you can exchange are US$, and they must be in perfect condition.
Hospitals: **Budi Agung**, Jl Maluku (below Masomba market/bus terminal); **Balai Keselamatan** ("B.K."—Salvation Army) on Jl Woodward.
Pharmacy Kimia Farma, Jl Monginsidi 69, ☎ 21134.

Lore Lindu National Park

The 200,000 ha Lore Lindu National Park in the north of central Sulawesi is one of Asia's premier birding destinations—it is possible to see 80% of Sulawesi's 96 endemic bird species in a visit of 4–5 days. The park covers the Lindu, Besoa, Bada and Napu Valleys—famous for their ancient megaliths—and the mountain ridges in between. Birders tend to head for the higher ground where most of the endemics are found, and the most popular base is Kamarora at the northern edge of the park on the road to the Napu Valley. For those wishing to really get to know the park, an extensive system of trails links the different valleys, although bird densities seem lower in the southern parts of the park.

Key Species

Many of Sulawesi's endemics can be seen at Tangkoko and Dumoga-Bone; what sets Lore

Lindu apart is the easy access to high altitude forests which have a distinct set of endemics. Birds like: Malia, Sulphur-bellied, Yellow-flanked and Maroon-backed Whistlers, White-eyed Myza, Streak-headed Darkeye and Fiery-browed Myna.

Other Wildlife
Both species of Sulawesi's endemic dwarf buffalo, or *anoa*. Black Macaques and Babirusa.

Getting There
Access to Lore Lindu is via Palu, the provincial capital of Central Sulawesi. You can get to the park by bus (from the main bus station—Masomba market terminal), or you can organise a 4-wheel drive vehicle and driver from one of the tourist agents in Palu.

Both have their disadvantages. If you go by bus, do not be surprised if the journey takes most of a day, as this road is probably the worst in the southern hemisphere. A 4WD vehicle, on the other hand, can be expensive. A good compromise is to hire transport for a day to take you to the pass at the Anaso turn-off (as high as a vehicle can go) and, after the day's birding, ask the driver to drop you at Kamarora on the way back. If you choose this option, start early from Palu, or you will get to the top too late for the early birds. Allow at least 4 hrs for this trip.

General Information
If trekking between the areas below, a guide is advised as trails are poorly way-marked. Horses or porters can be hired to carry packs. There are PHPA posts in most villages, the staff of which are welcoming to guests provided that you have park entry permits from the SKSDA office in Palu.

To get to the Napu Valley, take the direct public bus from Palu and stay at the *losmen* with restaurant; for the Bada Valley (Gintu), there is a MAF flight from Poso, then take a jeep to the homestays. Tentena (Poso) is a 2-day walk from Gimpu. To go to Saluki, take the direct bus from Palu, and walk one hour to the Maleo watchtowers. Toro is connected to Palu by a daily direct bus and you can stay at the PHPA post there. The Lindu Valley is accessible via public bus from Palu to Sidaunta; (where you can stay at the Homestay at the PHPA post) then continue by horse or foot.

Kamarora is the place to base yourself when visiting the park.

Accommodation/Dining
The very basic PHPA bungalows in Kamarora can accommodate up to 15 people; book in advance at PHPA Palu office, Jl Parman 9. ☎ 21260. No restaurant; bring your own food from Palu and make arrangements with the ranger's wife to cook it.

General Information
It is essential to get a permit for the park. Obtain it from the BKSDA office at Jl Mohammed Yamin (road known also as "Jalur Dua") before leaving Palu. ☎ 21106. Costs Rp1,500.

The best guide is Pak Rolex (Rolex Lameanda) who works for the PHPA office at Palu. Other SBKSDA staff may be available, or ask in Palu.

Manado

Manado is a thriving city of some 300,000, on a bay of the same name near the tip of Sulawesi's northern peninsula. See Periplus *Sulawesi* guide for full listings.

Getting There
By air Dr Sam Ratulangi Airport is 7 km outside of town, and taxi coupons to just about anywhere in Manado cost $3–4; or take an *oplet* or minibus from the main road for Rp250. Airport info ☎ 52117, 60865.

Bouraq has daily flights from Balikpapan ($119), Jakarta ($245), Palu ($82); and Ujung Pandang ($109); Ternate ($44); and twice weekly from Davao City, Philippines ($200 one-way, $400 RT; or $150 one-way, $262 RT with advance purchase).

Garuda flies daily from Jakarta ($246).

Merpati has daily flights from Jakarta and Ternate, twice a week from Jayapura, ($106); twice weekly from Palu ($83), once a week from Ambon.

Sempati flies daily from Balikpapan, from Jakarta via either Balikpapan or Ujung Pandang; Singapore via Jakarta and Ujung Pandang.

SilkAir has a 3.5 hr flight from Singapore costing about $400.

By bus Buses run to and from Malalayang Terminal, 7–8 km south of Manado. Get from there to the central Paal Dua terminal or Pasar 45 by *mikrolet*. Night buses to and from Gorontalo (12 hrs; $6 non-AC; $7.50 AC) and Palu (48 hrs; $16, non-AC; $22 AC).

By sea Several Pelni boats stop at Bitung, just across the peninsula from Manado. For information, contact the Manado office.

There are departures on local lines to Ternate and Ambon a couple of times a week. The Ambon run takes about 3 days with several stops along the way and costs $27, including very simple meals.

Transport
Bouraq, Jl Sarapung 27B, ☎ 62757, 62675.
Garuda, Jl Diponegoro 15, ☎ 52154, 64535; fax 62242.
Merpati, Jl Sudirman 132, ☎ 64027, 64028.
Sempati, Kawanua City Hotel, Jl Sam Ratulangi 1. ☎ 51612; fax 61205.
SilkAir, Jl Sarapung 5. ☎ 63744, 63844; fax 53841.
Pelni Lines, Jl Sam Ratulangi 7, ☎ 60908; fax 67737.
Minibuses/buses Oplet and Mikrolet, Rp250 flat-rate fare around town. Most routes converge at the terminal at Pasar 45, outside Jumbo Supermarket. Transfer to onward destinations from the endpoints of the *oplet/mikrolet* routes: Tuminting for Molas (dive centres); Paal Dua for Bitung and points east and northeast; Malalayang for points south, including connections with buses on the Trans-Sulawesi Highway.
Taxis: **Indra Kelana Taxi Company** ☎ 52033. Charter for $3 an hour, min 3 hrs; or negotiate inner-city price. **Dian Taksi** (☎ 62421) charges by the km and time.
Car rental Cars may be chartered from hotels, dive resorts or travel agencies.

Accommodation/Dining
Manado has a wide range of accommodation, from luxury hotels to budget *losmen*. The best hotels for birders are those that cater for divers, namely the dive resorts.
Particularly recommended are **Barracuda** which is right on the water, and **Murex**, which has lovely gardens.
Barracuda Office: Molas Beach—Dusun II. ☎ 54288, 54279; fax 64848. Located out of town in Molas. Restaurant offers best seafood around, especially outrageous sweet-and-sour crab. Excellent birding in surrounding mangroves, just off your balcony if you rent the bottom bungalows. $20S, $30D.
Manado Beach Hotel. 20 km south of Manado, just beyond Mokupa. Jl Raya Trans Sulawesi, Tasik Ria. ☎ 67001, 67005; fax 67007. Overpriced but on the water. Usually fairly empty, so it is worth bargaining hard for a room. $70–80S, $80–90D plus 17.5% tax and service.
Murex, Office: Jl Sudirman 28. ☎ 66280; fax 52116. About 25-min drive south of Manado.

A gem. Superior (AC) $35S, $40D; standard (AC) $30S, $35D; economy (fan) $25S, $30D.
Novotel, Jl Sam Ratulangi 22, ☎ 51245, 51174; fax: 63545. International standards, lots of watersports activities; environmental conservation projects.
Tourists should be aware that when they frequent most of the popular, traditional Minhasa restaurants they are encouraging the hunting of wild-caught animals, many of which are endemic and endangered. There are some great alternatives:
Barracuda see above.
Hilltop, Jl 17 Augustus, on a sidestreet, up the hill from the tourist office. Bland food, but perfect for a beer at sunset.
Surabaya Restaurant, Jl M. Hatta. Great selection of Javanese cooking and the best fresh avocado juice in town. Reasonably priced.
Xanadu, Jl Sam Ratulangi. Excellent Chinese food, though a bit pricey. Recommended for an evening out.

General Information
North Sulawesi Tourism Office. Hard to find, on a side street just off Jl 17 Agustus, ☎ 64299.
PHPA Office, Jl Babe Palar 68, ☎ 62688.
Travel Agencies: **Pandu Express**, Jl Sam Ratulangi 91, ☎ 51188; fax: 61487. **Pola Pelita**, Jl Sam Ratulangi 113, ☎ 52231; fax: 64520.
Metropole, Jl Sudirman 58, ☎ 51333.
Post Office, Jl Sam Ratulangi 23, 5 minutes walk south of Kawanua City Hotel.
Telkom Office, (Perum Tel), Jl Sam Ratulangi between the Kawanua Hotel and the Post Office (across the street). Open 24 hours.
Foreign Exchange: **Bank BCA**, Jl Dotu Lolong Lasut, ☎ 52778.
Hospitals The best in Manado is the **Pancaran Kasih**, Jl Sam Ratulangi.
Doctor Dr Batuna (who speaks excellent English). Dr Batuna owns Murex and is often there.
Photography The Minhasans like to look as white as possible and print photographs very light, so for natural colours ask the clerk for *cetak alami*.
P.T. Modern Photo Film Co. Jl Sam Ratulangi past Hotel Minhasa. Best in town: fresh film and good print production. The "one-day slide service" at **Angkasa Color Photo Service** is not recommended.
Souvenirs: **Dynasty Art Shop,** Jl Sam Ratulangi 187 has a good selection of antiques. Flexible prices.

Tangkoko/DuaSudara Nature Reserve

Three forested volcanoes form the core of this 8,800 ha reserve on the northernmost tip of Sulawesi. An open forest understorey makes for excellent viewing conditions at all levels in the canopy and on the ground, and an abundance of figs and other fruit trees results in high densities of fruit-eating birds and mammals. It is possible to bird coral flats, lowland forests and cloud forest on volcanic summits all in a day, but you will get more out of the trip if you allow at least 2 days.

Key Species

Forty-seven Sulawesi endemics including Red-billed and Sulawesi Hanging-parrots, Yellow-breasted and Golden-mantled Racquet-tails, Blue-backed Parrot and Yellow-and-green Lorikeet. Yellow-billed Malkoha, Hair-crested Drongo, Spot-tailed Goshawk, Red-knobbed and Tariotic Hornbills. If you travel by sea watch out for Lesser Frigatebird, Brown and Red-footed Boobies, Sooty Tern and several species of swallow.

Other Wildlife

Spectral Tarsier, a tiny, nocturnal primate; Bear Cuscus, a pouched mammal related to the kangaroo, that moves slowly through the canopy aided by a prehensile tail; black macaques.

Getting There

Reach Tangkoko by land or sea from Manado. **Buses** depart hourly from Paal II bus terminal for Bitung and Girian (Rp1,500). At Girian change to *mikrolet* or open-backed jeep (Rp1,500) to the village of Batuputih on the western boundary of the reserve.
Cars may be chartered from hotels, dive resorts or travel agencies. Barracuda Dive Resort in Molas provides a car and driver for $45 for a 1-way drop; more if you want the car to wait overnight. The travel agents on Jl Sam Ratulangi do packages to Tangkoko for about $50 a day.
By sea A more scenic way to visit Tangkoko/DuaSudara is by boat but this is only advisable from June to September when seas are calm. Boats can be chartered from Murex and Barracuda dive resorts ($60 or more) or from Bitung Port ($38 but it is best to negotiate).

Accommodation/Dining

There are 3 *losmen* in the village of Batuputih. **Mama Roos's Homestay** by the bridge is the oldest and most popular. Across the street is the **Landa-Linda Homestay**, and amidst the coconut palms, on the edge of the village, are a new homestay operated by Mama Roos and the **Tangkoko Ranger's Homestay**. All homestays charge $8–10 a night, including 3 spicy meals.

General Information

The best time to visit is May–October; it is hottest and most crowded in July and August. Plan on spending at least 2 full days in the reserve: one to climb to the top of Mt Tangkoko and 1 to explore the lowland forest and forest edges.

No permit is required, but you must report to PHPA at the reserve entrance. The entrance fee costs Rp750 a day, and you have to hire one guide ($5–8 per day) per group of 4 visitors (tips appreciated). The best bird guides are Tulende Wode and Denand Kakahue; both know Latin names and speak a little English. Several other guides, Nelman Kakahue, Sakar Tinungki, Yopi Manduos and Boli Lambaihang, can point out the endemics, though not much else.

There are many interesting walks in the Nature Reserve. These include a 6-km trail from the beach to the cloud forest on the rim of Tangkoko volcano. The trail climbs 1,100 m through all major habitats and provides opportunities to glimpse montane birds such as Fiery-browed Myna, Sulawesi Woodpecker, Sulawesi Drongo and Scaly-breasted Kingfisher. Pack a lunch and spend a full day on this trail.

There is a 4-km loop trail on gentle slopes that passes through secondary and primary forest. Along this trail are fruiting strangler figs that attract mynas, fruit doves and other fruit eating birds. The trail passes through several well known Red-knobbed Hornbill nest areas and kingfisher and Chestnut-backed Thrush territories.

A 12-km trail parallels the beach, although only the first 4 km are well maintained. The trail passes through grasslands, a good area for bee-eaters, White-shouldered Trillers and coucals; beach forest, where one frequently spots Slender-billed Cuckoo-dove, Sulawesi Black Pigeon and several kingfisher species; and secondary and primary forest, where White-bellied Sea-eagles and Sulawesi Hawk-eagles are known to nest.

Bogani Nani Wartabone National Park

The Bogani Nani Wartabone National Park, formerly Dumoga Bone, is one of the two biggest terrestrial national parks of Sulawesi encompassing 300,000 ha of rainforest from 50–2,000 m above sea level. Almost all of Sulawesi's 75 endemic species occur in the park.

Key Species
Endemic birds that are are common and conspicious in the park include: Sulawesi Serpenteagle, Spot-tailed Goshawk, Isabelline Waterhen, Sulawesi Black Pigeon, Golden-mantled Raquet-tail, Fiery-billed Malkoha, Great-billed Kingfisher, Red-knobbed Hornbill, Ashy Woodpecker, Pied Cuckoo-shrike, Sulawesi Babbler, Finch-billed and White-necked Mynas, Yellow-sided and Grey-sided Flowerpeckers. Others are more locally distributed but still relatively easy to observe, like Maleo and Purple-winged Roller.

Other Wildlife
Crested Black Macaques, Wild Boar and Spectral Tarsier can be found around the guest-house in Dulodou. Try the veranda of the guest-house in the evening with the lights on for bats and huge beetles and butterflies. In the forest keep an eye out for Bear and Dwarf Cuscus.

Getting There
The village of Dulodou, some 2 km from the park headquarters can be reached directly by bus from the Malalayang bus station in southwest Manado. If requested the bus might stop at the Kosinggolan dam, just behind Dulodou, from which it is less then 1 km to the offices (cross the small dam left and continue on this road). The Manado–Duloduo trip takes about 6 to 7 hours and costs about Rp8,000.

Another entrance of the park with a good access to the forest is Toraut. Small buses (*oplets*) go from Duloduo to Toraut (12 km; Rp1,500).

Accommodation/Dining
The headquarters in Dulodou include a guesthouse with two rooms for two people each. Food is available on request. One night including three meals costs about Rp20,000. Though more remote, the Toraut area offers sleeping facilities for quite large numbers.

General Information
Visitors have to register at the Dulodou or Toraut offices. A small fee has to be paid for insurance each day (about Rp1,000).

Entering the forest is allowed only with a park guide, none of whom speak any English. The guide fee is around Rp15,000 a day. A good birding trip from Dulodou is the track to the Matayangan village and Maleo nesting ground. This trip starts from the guest-house in Dulodou and takes about 8 hrs, including transportation to Duloduo from Matayangan village.

A nice trip in the Dumoga valley is a visit to the Maleo nesting ground of Tambun. Arrange transportation and a guide the day before, leave early to the village of Imandi ("market with bats"!) and go inland to Mokintop village, total costs between Rp10,000–30,000). Another possibility is leaving the night before and staying in the small guesthouse of Imandi (50 m next to the post office).

Less than two km before Mokintop is the Tambun Maleo nesting ground. Maleos are around between October and May. Be there early to see the birds. In Mokintop village Purple-winged Rollers are common.

The road from Imandi to Mokintop gives good opportunities for rails, herons and raptors, while the Dumoga valley in the west, which is not part of the park, is rich in herons, rails and waders.

Rainfall is generally evenly distributed throughout the year with relative wet periods from November to January and from March to May and dry spells from June to October and in February, although local patterns of rainfall show great differences.

An excellent, full-colour guidebook with some superb photographs, *North Sulawesi: A Natural History Guide*, by Dr Margaret Kinnaird, is available from the Wallacea Development Institute.

Sangihe Island

Sangihe is the largest of a group of 77 islands (47 inhabited) strewn between North Sulawesi and the Philippines. Sangihe is almost totally covered in mixed plantations but the island's four endemic species, Red-and-blue Lory, Sangihe Hanging-parrot, Elegant Sunbird and Caerulean Paradise-flycatcher, can be found in forest remnants surviving on two of the island's volcanoes, the active Mt Awu in the north and Tamako in the southwest. The paradise-flycatcher was thought to be extinct until a British expedition made a brief sighting of one on Mt Awu in 1995.

Getting There

Merpati flies 4 times a week from Manado to Naha airport, Tahuna, the main town on Sangihe. Alternatively, passenger ferries leave the harbour every other evening at 6.00 pm. Check on the blackboard at the harbour for sailing dates. Fare is $5 for the 12-hr journey; cabins can be rented from the crew for $7. *Bemos* meet the ferry to transport you to the other end of town, where accommodation is concentrated.

Accommodation

New Victory Veronica at Jl Raramenusa 16, ☎ 7111, is reputed to be the best in town. Also recommended is **Pengingapan Seda Hana** at Rp12,000 for full board. Visitors must report at the police station on Jl 17 Agustus.

Mount Awu

From the terminal take the bus to Talawid Atas (2–3 hrs, Rp3,000). Get off at the school, walk right along the road and pass a junction after 50 m. After a further 50 m the trail up the mountain starts on the left between two houses. Follow the trail upwards through plantations for 1 hr. It climbs a ridge with forest in the valley on either side and plantations along the ridge top. This trail continues for 3–4 hours but does not enter forest; however, you can see Sanghie Hanging-parrot and Red-and-blue Lory flying overhead and Elegant Sunbird in mixed flocks in the plantation trees. This is where the 1995 sighting of Caerulean Paradise-flycatcher was made. Stay with Pak Ali at the school house (Rp 10,000 a night for full board). He will also act as a guide for Rp10,000 a day.

Tamoko

Take the bus from Tahuna to Tamoko (5 hrs, Rp4,500). There are no *losmen* in Tamoko, so report to the *kepala desa* (village head) and ask him to find you somewhere to stay. From the market in Tamoko take another bus to Kentuhang (1 hr; Rp1,000). Get off at the end of the road, where it branches into two unsurfaced tracks that lead up to the crater rim. Take either track and climb steeply. After 2–3 hrs of secondary scrub the tracks enter forest. Red-and-blue Lory and Caerulean

Paradise-flycatcher have not been seen here yet, but Sangihe Hanging-parrot and Elegant Sunbird are easy, as are Blue-backed Parrot, Blue-tailed Imperial Pigeon, Hooded Pitta, Lilac-cheeked Kingfisher, Pied Cuckoo-shrike and Black-fronted White-eye.

–Marc Argeloo, Tim O'Brien, Wim Giesen, Margaret Kinnaird, Richard Noske with additional information from Sunarto, John Riley, William Wolmer, Duncan Melville & Robert Hitchins.

Maluku

Ambon City

Ambon City (population 284,000) on the 945 sq km island of the same name, is the capital of Maluku province and the starting point for trips to Seram and Banda. The wet season falls between May and August. For full listings see Periplus *Spice Islands* guide.

Getting There

Pattimura Airport is on Ambon Island's Hitu Peninsula, across the bay from Ambon City—37 km and 45 mins by road. A vehicle and passenger ferry runs every few minutes between Poka and Galala, where the bay narrows, which cuts the travelling distance in half. The airport taxis charge $9 for the trip. You can get to town more cheaply by taking public transport from the roadside in front of the airport to the ferry terminal at Poka. From Galala, the ferry terminal on the other side of the bay, shared taxis whisk passengers the remaining 6 km into town.

By Air Merpati, Sempati and Mandala all have daily flights from Jakarta or Bali, via Ujung Pandang. Bouraq flies twice a week from Davao, the Philippines. From Pattimura Airport Merpati and Bouraq have daily flights to Ternate and also connect with Biak and Jayapura in Irian Jaya.

Merpati flies to many small strips on the outlying islands, but services are often cancelled and getting a return booking can be difficult.

By Sea The Pelni cruise ships, *Dobonsolo*, *Rinjani*, *Kerinci* and *Ceremai* all call in at Ambon on their 14-day circuits. Forward schedules are difficult to come by but connections to or from Tual and Banda in Maluku, Fak-Fak (Irian Jaya) and Java, Bali, Sulawesi, Timor and Flores are all possible.

Accommodation/Dining

There is no really cheap accommodation on Ambon. The **Mutiara** is highly recommended, and on the budget side, try the **Beta** or the **Wisma Game**.

Ambon Manise, Jl Pasar Mardika 53A, ☎ 53888, 54888; fax 54492, 54493. 99 rooms, restaurant, swimming pool, tennis and squash courts, and money changer. $54–90 S/D, $7 for extra person. Ambon's only 3-star hotel.

Mutiara, Jl Raya Pattimura 12, ☎ 53075; fax 52171; telex 731234 TIARA IA AB. 31 rooms, all with TV and AC. Friendly and pleasant staff. Good restaurant and bar. Live music nightly. $48–54S, $54–60D.

Beta, Jl Wim Reawaru, ☎ 53463. 26 rooms. One of the best of the cheaper hotels. $7S, $8–10D.

Cenderawasih, Jl Tulukabessy, ☎ 52487. 18 rooms with TV. Restaurant. $23S, $30–36D.

Tirta Kencana, Jl Raya Amahusu, Amahusu, ☎ 51867. 20 rms. $40D, $45–55 VIP, $40 cottage. Located right on the shore 4 km south of Ambon City. Nice shore-side restaurant noted as the place where many of Indonesia's best crooners started their careers.

Wisma Game, Jl A. Yani, 17 rooms. One of the bettter, cheaper hotels. $5–8 fan; $10–18 AC.

Best eateries in town are:

Halim, Jl St. Hairun, ☎ 52177. Seafood, Chinese and Indonesian.

Yang-Yang, Jl Wim Reawaru 9c, ☎ 44992. Good Chinese food close to Hotel Beta.

For a traditional Chinese breakfast of strong coffee and *telur setengah matang* (half-boiled egg) **Rumah Kopi Sariwangi** on Jl A.M. Sariwangi is excellent.

Ambon Plaza is a glossy new shopping centre where you can buy just about anything. The 3rd floor **Kupu-kupu** coffee shop has a souvenir shop selling high quality locally made handicrafts. Kentucky and California Fried Chicken and a cafeteria are also located here.

Transport

Garuda/Merpati, Jl A. Yani 19, ☎ 52481, 42480; telex: 49154 MERPATI AI.

Sempati, Jl AM Sangaji 46C, ☎ 61612; fax 42451.

Bouraq, Jl Sultan Baabullah 19, ☎ 43143, 52314; fax 43143.

Mandala, Jl A. J. Patty No. 19, ☎ 42551; fax 42377.

For small plane charter: **SIL** (Paul Westland).

☎ 47751 and **Indoavia**, Jl A. Rhebok. ☎ 53866.
Pelni, Jl Pelabuhan 1, ☎ 52049; fax 53369.
For the small inshore cruisers that leave most evenings to islands in central Maluku, go to the old harbour (Pelabuhan Kepal Motor) and check on sailing times.
Taxi hire Cost about $3/hr, sometimes with a 2-hr minimum.
Local buses Crowded minibuses depart for all parts of the island from Batu Merah terminal, more often in the early morning and late afternoon. In-town *mikrolet* mostly depart from the Mardeka terminal. Fares run from Rp200 to nearby Galala (6 km) to Rp1,400 to Asilulu (70 km).
Becaks For short distances in town, a trip costs Rp350 to Rp1,500, depending on the distance and your bargaining ability.

General Information
Maluku Government Tourist Office, Jl Raya Pattimura, ☎ 52471. The "Kantor Parawisata" is on the ground floor of the governor's office (free city and island maps).
Agency tours
P.T. Daya Patal Tour and Travel, Jl Said Perintah SK II/27A.☎ 53529, 53344, 52498; fax 44709; telex: 73140 DPAB IA. A quality outfit: contact Hans Rijoly or Salomon.
BKSDA VII Office, Ir Erdie Suherdie (Head), Jl Kebun Cengkeh, Batu Merah Atas, Ambon 97128.
SBKSDA Office, Ir Minto Basuki (Head), Jl Pandan Kasturi, Tantui, Kotak Pos 1068 Ambon, ☎ 41189.
SBKSDA Maluku Office, Jl Laksda Leo Wattimena, Passo, ☎ 611033.
BirdLife International, Maluku Field Office, Jl Pandan Kasturi SK 43/3, Tantui. PO Box 1097,☎/fax: 54845.
Post Office, Jl Raya Pattimura, ☎ 52165; fax 54488.
Telkom Office, Jl JB Sitanala, Talaka, ☎ 54444, 56253; fax 54199.
Foreign exchange: **Bank BCA**, Jl Sultan Hairun 17, ☎ 44315.
Health centre: Kantor Kesehatan Wilayah (District Health Office). Jl Dewi Sartika, Karang Panjang, ☎ 52861, 42147; ☎ 56607. 3 doctors: Dr Krisna (clinic ☎ 52715), Dr Polanunu and Dr Ristianto (home ☎ 53411, 51526). Dr Ristianto speaks English.
Hospital Otto Kuyk, Jl Tantui. ☎ 52711, 52712, 52715.
Pharmacy Pelita Farma, Jl Setia Budi. ☎ 42014. Open 24 hrs.
Photography Master Photo, off Sempurna, Jl A.Y. Patty 40. In-store print processing. Stocks Fuji Sensia and Kodak Ektachrome 100 slide film. Fuji store in Ambon Plaza recommended for good, quick processing.

Around Ambon City

SIRIMAU
Just 6 km from town the 550 m Sirimau hill is tipped with a 1-ha patch of rain forest surrounding a sacred urn and stone stools, where once the Raja of Soya held meetings. The area is a tourist park, and the forest is a 15-min walk from the entrance gate at the end of the Soya road. Two trails wind through the forest.

Key Species
White-eyed Imperial Pigeon, Slender-billed Cuckoo-dove, Claret-breasted Fruit Dove, Common Paradise-kingfisher, Golden Bulbul, Island and Slaty Monarchs, Ashy Flowerpecker and Ambon Yellow White-eye.

Getting There
Take an orange *bemo* signed "Soya" from Mardeka bus station to the end of the line (Rp400.)

PASSO BAY
An easily accessible area of mangroves and mud-flats at the eastern end of Ambon Bay. At low tide good for egrets, cormorants, terns and migrant waders.

Getting There
From Mardeka bus station, take the red minibus to Hunut. Ask to get off 200 m after Taman Passo.

HILA
The forested hills behind Hila, on the north coast of Ambon, are full of parrots. This is the best birding site on Ambon and exploring it is a morning or full-day excursion.

Key Species
Gurney's Eagle, Lazuli Kingfisher, Claret-breasted Fruit-dove, Long-tailed Mountain-pigeon, Salmon-crested Cockatoo, Red Lory, Eclectus and Great-billed Parrots, Ambon Yellow White-eye.

Getting There
Hila is 42 km from Ambon City, where there are regular buses from Batu Merah bus station. The journey takes 70 min, costs Rp1,400.

Accommodation

Manuala Beach Hotel Desa Kaitetu, ☎ 61666. Pleasant beach-side place with attached restaurant. 20 rms. $12–17D. Book beforehand if going at a weekend.

General Information

The trail starts just before a bridge, 50 m to the east of Manuala Beach Hotel. Almost immediately the trail forks. Take the right-hand track and climb steeply for about 1 hr through clove plantations to a viewpoint overlooking a valley; continue on upwards for another hour to a field. Skirt round the bottom of this and continue on until a second field, which offers a spectacular view of the valley and is an excellent raptor and parrot-watching spot.

Manusela National Park

The rugged Manusela National Park on Seram vies with Halmahera as Maluku's premier birding destination on account of its many endemic species and unspoilt wilderness. Expedition-style trekking is required to enter the park, and the going is tough.

Key Species

Southern Cassowary, Blue-eared, Purple-naped and Moluccan Red Lories, Salmon-crested Cockatoo, Lazuli Kingfisher, Pale Cicadabird, Moluccan Thrush, Streak-breasted Fantail, Bicoloured and Grey-hooded Dark-eyes, Spectacled Honeyeater, Seram Friarbird, Long-crested Myna, Black-naped Oriole.

Getting There

Enter the National Park either from Mosso on the south coast or Wahai on the north coast. The trail from Mosso is unbelievably steep so it is best to start at Wahai.

For Wahai, there are a number of bus companies that leave from Ambon to Saka, on Seram's north coast. One is Annugrah, which leaves at 6.00 am from Jl Mesjid Jaya Al Fatah by the Alfatah Mosque. Buy your tickets the day before from the office in this street. Other buses leave from the Batuh Merah end of Mardeka bus terminal. The journey takes 8 hrs, and costs Rp20,000 including ferry. Public speedboats for the 2-hour journey along the coast from Saka to Wahai meet the buses; they arrive in Wahai between 5 and 6 pm (Rp8,500.)

If you wish to go to Mosso, the best way is to cross to Amahai on Seram from the small port of Telehu in northeast Ambon, then either charter a speedboat ($50, 8–10 people, 2 hrs) or catch the public ferry, *Lae-lae*: departures at 8.00 am and 1.00 pm ($7, 2 hrs.) Amahai to Mosso involves first a 4-hr bus ride to the district town of Tehoru (Rp 6,500), then either a 20-min chartered speedboat ride to Mosso ($25) or a 1-hr *pok-pok* (unsafe and wet motorised *prau*) journey.

Accommodation

In Mosso stay with the *kepala desa* (village head;) in Wahai, at **Losmen Sinar Indah**, $7, or $9 with meals. It is also possible to stay at the National Park Centre, but take your own food.

General Information

The National Park Centre at Sasa Ratu is about 10 km from Wahai on the road to Pasahari. There are regular buses from Wahai to Pasahari (Rp4–5,000.) There is good roadside birding along the road to Pasahari, which passes through forest for 10 km. Walk, or charter a *bemo* for Rp15,000/hr.

Ask the park staff to guide you along the trail to the nipa and mangrove swamps, a walk of 2 km north of the HQ; the guide will cost $5. At the harbour in Wahai, speed boats can be hired to take you along the coast to the same mangroves: $30–40 for half a day.

To go trekking in Manusela, report to Pak Edi at the National Park or (better) at his home in Wahai along with your permits, which you must get in Ambon City before departing, to arrange your trek. Also report in at the police station in Wahai. You need to take cooking equipment, food and, depending on your route, camping gear (*see p 189*); this can be bought in Wahai. Strong, worn-in walking boots are essential. Make sure also that you take a compass and rain gear. Expect to pay $7–10 per day for your guide, $5 per day per porter plus their food and cigarettes.

For routes see map on page 163. Approximate walking times between villages or over-night camps, not counting birding stops are:

Wahai to Wasa: 6–7 hrs, gentle up-hill walk, stay in village.

Wasa to Roho: 5–6 hrs, uphill walk, stay in village.

Roho to Wasa Mata: 3 hrs, steady uphill, stay in shelter.

Wasa Mata to Kanikeh: 4–5 hrs, over ridge, stay in village. (Roho to Kanikeh can be done in a day—it depends on how much time you want to spend birding).

Kanikeh to Selumena: 7 hrs. Initial 1.5-hr climb out of Kanikeh valley then a flat walk to Selumena, largely following river. Stay in village.

Selumena to Manusela: 3-4 hrs, undulating and muddy with river crossings, stay in village.

Manusela to Hatumete (south coast): A hell walk which can be done in 8 hrs, but more likely 12. Leave Manusela at first light and make the 1,200 m ascent to the summit as quickly as possible (3–3.5 hrs.) The almost 2,000 m descent is 5–6 hrs' solid walking. Be warned: the trail is dangerous—steep and slippery—in places. Stay in Sinar Hari, a small cluster of houses with spectacular views 2 hrs before Hatumete or Mosso.

Kobipoto to Solalama: 7 hrs, downhill, forest camp.

Solalama to Sola: 7 hrs, flattish but swampy, stay in village.

Sola to Wahai: A full day's walk on a track.

If you plan to climb towards Mt Binaya from Kanikeh, you should make a small offering before you go. The *adat* (customary) law of the area embraced the sudden arrival of hundreds of western Operation Raleigh venturers with the interpretation that they were returning to the homes of the ancestors and your guides will be fearful if you ascend the mountain without first making an offering to your own ancestors.

Ternate

The tiny island of Ternate, less than 10 km in diameter, and its similar sized neighbour, Tidore, were once the world's only source of cloves and in the past saw bloody conflicts between the Portuguese, Spanish, British and Dutch for control of the lucrative spice trade. Today Ternate, with a population of 50,000, is the second largest city in Maluku and, for birders, the hopping off place for Halmahera.

Getting There

There are daily Merpati flights to Ternate's Ba Ullah airport from Ambon and Manado, and Merpati flies once or twice a week to Galeha on Halmahera and other small airstrips in the region. From the airport, a taxi into town costs about $3.

Pelni's *Kerinci* stops in Ternate every 2 weeks on its way back to Ambon, Surabaya and Jakarta. The *Ceremai* stops in every week on its way between Jakarts, Ujung Pandang and Jayapura.

Accommodation/Dining

Nirwana, Jl Pahlawan Revolusi, ☎ 21787. 24 rms. $12S, $18D, $24VIP, is the best known hotel, but is now overpriced and dirty.

Neraca Golden, Jl Pah. Revolusi 30, ☎ 21668, 21327. 28 rooms, all AC, TV. Meals available. $28 standard, $40 VIP, $55 suite. Most of the better hotels have restaurants; the one at the **Neraca** has lovely views across to Tidore.

Several places in Ternate town serve good Indonesian and Chinese dishes for about $3 to $5 per meal, almost all have karaoke. Try:

Gamalama, Jl Pah. Revolusi, ☎ 21712. Indonesian.

Garuda, Jl Pah. Revolusi, ☎ 21090. Chinese, Indonesian.

La Bamba, Jl Bosoiri. Excellent Chinese cooking.

Pondok Katu, Jl Baranjangan, for all kinds of excellent fish, prepared in various ways.

Roda Baru, Jl Pah. Revolusi, ☎ 21513. Padang cooking.

Siola, Jl Stadion, ☎ 21377. Generally considered the best in town for seafood.

Transport

Merpati, PT Eterna Raya, Jl Bosoiri 81, ☎ 21314, 21648, 21649.

Bouraq, Jl Baabullah 96, ☎ 21042.

Pelni, Jl Jend. Ahmad Yani (in the harbour complex *Komplek Pelabuhan*), ☎ 24434; fax 21276.

Local passenger boats There are frequent passenger boats—often several a week—to Bitung, Tobelo, Bacan, Obi, Kayoa, Sanana and, once a week, direct to Manado. Boats travel mostly at night. For departure times check at the small offices at the entrance to the main harbour. Fares are according to distance, but all below $12. For about $2 you can rent a mattress and about $5 (after perhaps a bit of bargaining) should get you one of the crew's bunks for the night.

Speedboats Speedboat services to Sidangoli leave from a small jetty down an alley by the Garuda restaurant. Fare $4.50, or $30 to charter the boat. They leave when they are full.

Car Ferry Three departures a day to Sidangoli (Halmahera) from main harbour at 8.00 am, 12.00 am and 1.00 pm; returns 10.30 am, 1.30 pm and 4.30 pm. Fare $1 for 1-hr crossing.

Taxis All the hotels can arrange taxis for trips around Ternate. Expect to pay $30–40 for a charter.

Bemos There are plenty of *bemos* running around Ternate. Charter for $4 per hour from the *bemo* stand near the Nirwana.

General Information

Ternate Tourism Bureau Located in the Bupati's office complex on Jl Pah. Revolusi. Can help with most arrangements and can arrange an English-speaking guide (don't expect perfection) for $10 a day, plus expenses.

Foreign Exchange: Bank Expor-Impor or **BNI 46** for travellers' cheques or cash. Both banks are on Jl Pah. Revolusi.

Travel Agencies There are two travel agencies in town; neither is exceptional.

Indo Gama, Jl Jend. A. Yani 131 (next to Crysant Hotel), P.O. Box 21, ☎ 21288, 21681; fax 21580.

Pelita Express, Jl A. Yani, ☎ 21580.

Pak Haji Umar Ammari, a professional photographer, can set up tours for you and serve as your guide. He speaks English and Dutch and can be contacted at home: Jl Pah. Revolusi, Falajawa, Ternate. ☎ 21197.

SSKSDA (PHPA) Office, Jl Bandar Udara Babulah, PO Box 32, Ternate, ☎ 21525.

Post Office, Jl Pah. Revolusi, ☎ 22863, 21204.

Telkom Office, Jl Pah. Revolusi, ☎ 22213

Hospital: RS Umum, Jl Tanah Tinggi, ☎ 21281.

Around Ternate

LAKE TOLIRE BESAR

This stunning, emerald, crater lake surrounded by 50 m high cliffs is a wonderful birding hang-out. Sit on the high rim and scan the trees fringing the lake for White Cockatoo and Blue-capped Fruit-dove and the forested slopes of the Gamalama volcano for Gurney's Eagle. Watch Great-billed Parrots flying across and walk the trail round the crater rim looking for Dusky Scrubfowl, friarbirds and munias.

Getting There

The lake is almost halfway round the island from Ternate town and it is best to charter a *bemo* to get to it. From the road, it is a 15-min walk up through scrubby forest to the crater edge.

Halmahera

Most birders satisfy themselves with birding around Kali Batu Putih and Sidangoli mangroves, where virtually all the 24 species endemic to North Maluku can be found but, time and budget permitting, a 4–5 day trip to the standardwing lek at Labi Labi and Molluccan Scrubfowl nestground at Galela is recomended.

TANAH BATU PUTIH

This is an area of logged and disturbed forest in the hills leading out of Sidangoli, where most of Halmahera's speciality species can be seen during a 3–4 day visit. A basic birdwatchers' *losmen* is run by Demianus Bagali, usually known as Anu.

Key Species

Most species endemic to North Maluku including: Wallace's Standardwing, Paradise Crow, Ivory-breasted Pitta, Dusky Scrubfowl, Moluccan Owlet-nightjar, Gurney's Eagle, Halmahera Cuckoo-shrike. Invisible Rail was re-discovered by Anu in the nearby Akelolo sago swamp.

Accommodation

Anu's *losmen* burnt down in 1995. He is rebuilding it on the left of the road by the start of the logging trail (see above) $8 per night; $6 extra for three basic meals. Anu charges $12 per day for guiding.

Getting There

From the ferry terminal at Sidangoli take a *bemo* (Rp1,500) or *becak* (Rp 500) to Anu's brother's shop, Toko Mandiri, in Desa Domato, 1 km away. He will tell you where Anu is and run you up to Tanah Butu Putih for $4.50.

General Information

Anu knows the best sites to see each of the key species and they are also noted in the birders' logbook. There are three main trails: the first climbs a hill of good forest across the stream in the valley to the right of Anu's *losmen* and is the place to see Wallace's Standardwing, Ivory-breasted Pitta and Nicobar Pigeon. To the left of the main road, an old logging trail leading up the valley for several km is the most productive birding area. A summit, a 2-km walk up the main road, provides an excellent vantage point to watch for raptors at midday.

In Sidangoli, the Akelolo sago swamp, where Invisible Rail has recently been seen, should not be missed. The nicest way to get there is to hire a longboat from Sidangoli ($10–15) for the journey through the mangroves to the village of Akelolo. Good chance of Beach Kingfisher and plenty of Imperial Pigeons. Alternatively, the swamp can be reached on foot. It is a hot, 2-km walk along a trail on the right of the main road, 1 km out of Sidangoli. Exploring the swamp requires wading up to your knees in mud—and the rail only calls after heavy rain! You will need Anu to show you the best areas; do not forget to ask him to show you the Great-billed Heron nest tree.

LABI-LABI
This village is located on the east side of Kao Bay, and is the site of the most easily accessible display area of Wallace's Standardwing, which was filmed by the BBC for "Attenborough in Paradise" in 1995. The tree is in an area of limestone forest a 4-km trek from the village. There is a shelter in the forest and the villagers are organised with tarpaulin and cooking equipment to run a pleasant jungle camp.

Getting There
There is no public transport to this site and you will need Anu to take you there. Unfortunately the trip is currently expensive—$750 per group—because there are only two speedboats to hire for the 2-hr crossing. Anu has an arrangement with the village head that every visiting bird group will make a donation (included in the price) to pay for guarding the display area. If you get to Labi-labi independently, please support this system. The speedboats leave either from Kao or Toebelo.

Accommodation
In Kao accommodation is at **Losmen Dirgahayu** ($7.50.) In Tobelo there is a wider selection: **Pantai Indah** is the best ($9, $22 AC); try also **Alfra Mas** ($7.50–14) or **Melati** ($3.00,) both on Jl P. Revolusi.

GALALA
The extraordinary, 1.5-km nesting beach of the Mollucan Scrubfowl is located 4 km to the north of Galela. The scrubfowls fly in at night, so getting good views is difficult— just before dawn is best. The nest ground is managed in a traditional manner and birders should not go without a letter of introduction from either Anu or Pak Amir at the PHPA office in Tobelo. With this you will be able to stay in one of the small huts; bring your own food, candles and mosquito repellent

Banda Islands

The tiny Banda Islands are one of Indonesia's best get-away-from-it-all destinations. Fabulous diving and snorkelling and opportunities for other watersports such as wind-surfing, water-skiing and fishing, coupled with the island's fascinating history, attract increasing numbers of tourists, but the islands have not yet been spoilt by unsightly tourist developments. For the bird-watcher these islands

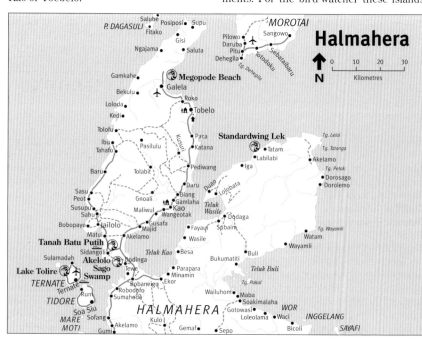

offer a few interesting small-island specialities and very good seabird-watching opportunities.

Getting There
By air Merpati fly from Ambon on Wed, Sat and Mon (fare $37). The 65-min flight leaves at 7 am. It is by 18-seater plane and the baggage limit is 10 kg, although this is not always strictly enforced. A *bemo* (one of the 12 motor vehicles on Banda) meets the plane for the 10-min drive to town. Attendants from Des Alwi's two hotels usually meet all arriving flights.
By sea The large Pelni passenger liner, *Rinjani,* stops in Banda every second Friday and the following Sunday, before heading on to Ujung Pandang, Surabaya, Jakarta and Dumai (Sumatra), and then back again on its 2-week route. Perintis lines offer deck passage at something like $3, but they can be slow and uncomfortable.

Accommodation/Dining
All accommodation on Banda tends to fill during October and the last 2 weeks of December—reserve ahead. The only two hotels in Bandaneira are owned by Des Alwi, who organises diving operations on the islands. There is a selection of homestays.

Des Alwi's two hotels have great shoreside locations. The staff are always friendly and helpful and can arrange boat excursions and the rental of diving or fishing equipment.
Maulana, Jl Pelabuhan. 27 rooms, all with toilets. $30S, $40D; bungalow $45. Add $5 for a sea-front room and $12 for full board.
Laguna Inn, Jl Pelabuhan. 8 rooms, all with toilets. Try to get a room with a good view of Gunung Api. $25S, $30D; $10 extra for full board.

For reservations of these two hotels, contact: **Hotel Maulana**, PO Box 3193, Jakarta, Indonesia. ☎ (021) 360372; fax 360308. In Banda: ☎ (0910) 21022, 21023; fax 21024.

Recommended *losmen* are:
Likes Homestay, just past Maulana Hotel. 6 rms, $4 including meals.
Rumah Budaya, Jl Nusantara. 4 rms, $9–14.
Delfika, Jl Nusantara. 8 rms, $9–14.
Selecta, Jl Nusantara. 7 rms, 2 with inside toilet. $8–12.
Note: Add 10% tax and service to the above.

Most people eat at their hotels; fresh *sushi* is a specialty of the **Maulana** (order a day ahead). Generally, fresh vegetables, eggs and other produce are often hard to come by or expensive. There is one sit-down restaurant in Bandaneira, the **Nusantara.** In the small market you can find fruit, such as soursop, jackfruit and limes, and snack foods such as fried fish.

General Information
The rainy season is from mid-June through August (southeast monsoon.) High winds (the west monsoon) can blow from mid-January to February (the east monsoon).
Foreign exchange There are no banks on Banda, so bring all the rupiahs you will need from Ambon.
Boat rentals The Maulana and the Laguna Inn, both on Jl Pelabuhan on Bandaneira, rent boats of various capacities:
Large vessel: Diesel-powered, for more than 10 passengers, $150/day, $25/hr.
Launch: Diesel-powered, 5–10 passengers, $100/day, $20/hr.
Speedboat: Gasoline-powered, 4 passengers, $110/day, $25/hr.
Manuk Island For the 2–3 day journey out to this island (about 120 km southeast of Banda) Indonesia's largest seabird colony, you will need the large vessel; they charge about $880 for this trip.
Lontar (Banda Besar) To reach Lontar Island, to see the nutmeg groves and Fort Hollandia, charter a boat from one of the hotels or from a free-lancer at the dock near the market.
The Maulana and the Laguna Inn can provide water-skiing ($25/hr) and windsurfing boards, $2/hr. If you want to go diving, again, the outfits are Des Alwi's hotels, the Maulana and the Laguna. A 2-tank, day's dive, including equipment rental, works out at about $80.

Yamdena (Tanimbar Islands)

Yamdena is well off the beaten track and has only been visited by a handful of birders, but beautiful, pristine, tropical ecosystems and 8 endemic species, including a megapode, cockatoo, two thrushes and two fantails, make Yamdena well worth a visit.

Getting There
Merpati flies "pioneer flights" (ie they are not obliged to operate them and frequently don't) twice a week, on Thursdays and Saturdays ($80.) Return flights can only be booked at the Harapan Indah Hotel in Saumlaki (Yamdena's capital.) There are many stories of people waiting days—even weeks—to get a seat out.

Pelni's *Tatamilau* calls in at Saumlaki from Tual on its way to and from Denpasar.

Accommodation/Dining

There are two adequate hotels, the **Harapan Indah** and **Pantai Indah**, both located on the main street in Saumlaki. They charge $8–10 per person per night, including three simple meals.

General Information

There is only one road, which runs along the southeast coastline. Arrange with your hotel for a vehicle and driver for the day (about $40) and simply drive up the road until you find promising looking places. About 20 km out of Saumlaki (there are no km marker posts) is a large chicken-rearing compound on the right. The birding is good if you walk north along the road from here and then explore along an old logging track leading into a forest grassland mosaic on the left after 500 m. 5 km past the compound the road crosses a large tidal channel. The tall forest to the south of the channel, on the east side of the road, is a good area for endemics, including Slaty-backed Thrush.

It is also worth hiring a speedboat to explore the western seaboard of Yamdena, but hire costs are high (at least $150 per day.) Island Whistler is quite easy to find on small islands at the entrance to Saumlaki Bay, and you should see Australian Pelican and Great-billed Heron. A great 2–3 day trip is to head up the western coast to the remote village of Matikan, which backs onto pristine monsoon forests, with a diversion along the way to explore the mangrove and swamp forests fringing the Salwassa Bay.

Kai Islands

The Kai Islands, Kai Kecil, Dullah (Tual) and Kai Besar, are not as bird rich as the Tanimbars, but nevertheless support 4 endemic species. Kai Coucal is common on all three islands, White-tailed Monarch and Great Kai White-eye are confined to Kai Besar, and Little Kai White-eye to Kai Kecil. The beaches are an added attraction: those on Kai Kecil are truly a vision of paradise.

However, the vegetation is mainly scrub and only a few patches of good forest remain. There is good forest to be found on Kai Besar and other islands in the group: Warbala and Manir.

Getting There

There are flights every day by either Merpati or Bouraq (most days both) to Kai Kecil. The flight takes 1 hr 20 mins and costs $100 one way. The airport is located at Langgur, on Kai Kecil, which is connected to Dullah Island by a bridge. Tual, the capital of Southeast Maluku, is on Dullah. Taxis ($7) meet the plane for the 20-min drive into Tual. Alternatively walk out to the main road and jump on a *bemo* for Rp300.

Accommodation/Dining

There are a few *losmen* in Tual. The **Hotel Mira** is adequate. Better, though, to stay at Ohoidertawun beach, a 30-min drive from Tual on the west coast of Kai Kecil. A Dutch couple runs the **Savana Cottages** ($10–15) at the east end of the village. The bay is huge, the beach just idyllic, and there is easy access to forest behind. Trails lead about 5 km into the forest and there are lots of scrubfowl mounds. Catch a bus from the new Langgur Terminal (Rp500) or charter a *bemo* ($3).

The stunning Pasar Panjang beach at Ohoillilir (also on the west coast) is popular with locals and back-packers alike. A group of beach cottages is located 500 m north of the village. The beach is 15 km from Tual; take a bus from the Langgur Terminal (Rp1,000).

General Information

Taman Anggrek, signposted on the right just before Dullah village, a short bus journey from Langgur Terminal, has a patch of forest surrounding a small lake. Kai Cicadabird and Little Kai White-eye have been seen here.

There is a nice patch of mangrove forest (at Ur), about 5 km outside Tual. From Tual take a *bemo* signed Ur. In Ur village ask directions to "Hutan Bakau". Wander around the bay and through the mangroves.

There is still good forest in the northern part of Kai Besar. The raja of Watlaar, on the northwestern shore, is a proponent of the role of traditional law in forest conservation. Ferries leave a small quay in Ohoiren (close to the bridge on the Langgur side) at 10.00 am and 12.00 am to Banda Eli on Kai Besar. From there catch a *bemo* to Yamtel on the east coast, from where longboats leave at 2 pm for the 3-hr journey up the coast (Rp6,000).

–Simon Badcock, Yusup Cahyadin, Paul Jepson, Michael Poulsen, with extra information from Julia Aglionby, Demianus Bagali, Nick Brickle, Russel Bright & Filip Verbelen.

Irian Jaya

Important Notes for travellers in Irian Jaya

As a foreigner wishing to move around Irian Jaya, it will be necessary to first obtain your *Surat Keterangan Jalan* or travelling permit. This travelling permit is issued by the Head of Police and lists the places that you are approved to visit. At airports in Irian Jaya, the Police usually check whether you have the correct travelling permit before they will allow you on the plane.

Even if you do manage to get on the plane without the permit, at your destination police will check the arrival of all foreigners and you will need to show the permit to them. Therefore, although it means spending an extra day in Jayapura to get the permit, you are strongly advised to do so, as this will significantly reduce your risk of hassles with authorities when travelling within the province.

Planes to Jayapura arrive in Sentani airport some 45 minutes from Jayapura town. You may need to travel into Jayapura itself to visit the police station. From the airport, an airport taxi will set you back Rp 35,000 for an air-conditioned minibus which will take you to wherever you want to go. Alternatively you can take a three stage regular taxi ride from the airport and you will share a smaller vehicle with around 20 other people. Using this means, you go from Sentani to Abepura (Rp800), from Abepura to Terminal Entrop (Rp400) and from Terminal Entrop to Jayapura centre (Rp400).

Travelling permits can be obtained at either the local level police station (POLRES) on Jl Achmad Yani (☎ 0967 34161), next to the Hotel Matoa, or from the regional level (POLDA) police station on Jl. Sam Ratulangi (☎ 0967 31834) opposite the Catholic church. At the time of writing, it appears that the POLRES station is a better bet to get permits to travel to remote places than the POLDA station which seem more circumspect, so try going to the POLRES station first.

When you arrive at the Police station head for the "Bagian Orang Asing" (Foreigners Section) and ask for a *Surat Keterangan Jalan*. At this stage you will need to state all the places you want to visit, so that the police can make one Travelling Permit for all your intended visits. It is best to list all your possible destinations (your flight is cancelled, the plane doesn't arrive?) you can still visit somewhere else. You will need to take with you half a dozen copies of your passport and your visa and take at least six copies of a passport sized photo of yourself. Once you get your permit, make several copies as you will need to leave a copy of it with the police in each the places you are visiting.

Bear in mind that the "Bagian Orang Asing" normally shuts on Saturdays and Sundays, so try to arrive in Jayapura when the following day is a week day, otherwise you will be hanging around Jayapura for the weekend. Also try to get the police station in the morning, as things shut up around two in the afternoon.

Manokwari

Getting There
By air Merpati flies to Manokwari from Biak daily ($41), and from Jayapura on Tues, Thu, Fri and Sat (7.00 am, $101). There may also be unscheduled flights. Do not rely on reservations confirmed by computer: Ensure that your name is on the handwritten list for the specific flight.

By sea Pelni's 2,000 passenger *Ciremai* and *Dobonsolo* and the 1,000 passenger *Tatamailau* call in at Manokwari between Sorong and Jayapura.

Accommodation/Dining
Hotel Mutiara, international standard, very new hotel owned by Merpati Airlines, Jl Yos Sudarso, ☎ 21777; fax 21152. From $30–65.
Hotel Arfak, Jl Brawijaya 8, ☎ 21293, 22607. 13 rms. Quiet, with a good view over the bay and the Arfak Mountains. $13–16 economy, $15–19 fan, $17–23 AC. All meals included.

Hotel Mokwam, Jl Merdeka, ☎ 21403. 12 large, clean rms. $24–27. An attached restaurant serves Indonesian and Chinese dishes, ($2.50–$4).

Losmen Apose, Jl Kotabaru, opposite the Merpati office. ☎ 21369. 9 rooms. Often full, so book ahead. Cheap and clean to boot! $5 fan, shared facilities; $10–12 AC, private facilities, exluding tax.

Hotel Maluku, Jl Sudirman. ☎ 21948. Clean, welcoming. $7–10 economy, $10–14 standard, $15–22 AC, including morning snack.

Hotel Mulia, Jl Yos Sudarso. ☎ 21320, 21328. 9 rooms. Very clean, in the heart of town. $11–15 fan, shared facilities; $16–23 AC, including morning and afternoon snack.

Transport

Merpati, Jl Kota Baru 39, ☎ 21133, 21153; airport, ☎ 21004.

Pelni, Jl Siliwangi 24, ☎ 21852; fax: 21284.

General Information

PHPA Office, See previous page.

Post Office, Jl Siliwang, branch office at Jl Yos Sudarso.

WWF, Jl Pertanian Wosi Dalam, PO Box 174, Manokwari 98312, ☎ 22493.

Foreign exchange: **Bank Expor-Impor**, Jl Jogyakarta 1. Mon–Fri 8am–3pm.

Souvenirs Toko Sumber Alam, Jl Sudirman 47; **Cinta Alam**, Jl Yos Sudarso; **Gallery Korwar**, Jl Pahlawan.

Arfak Mountains

The spectacular Arfak mountains, on the eastern corner of the Vogelkop peninsula rise steeply behind the coastal town of Manokwari. Dissected by roaring torrents and sheer, steep-sided valley gorges, trekking into the Arfaks takes stamina, but the effort is rewarded with sightings of some spectacular species only found in the mountains of the Vogelkop Peninsula.

Key Species

Wattled Brush-turkey, Vogelkop Whistler, Vogelkop Bowerbird, Long-tailed Paradigalla, Buff-tailed and Black Sicklebills, Arfak Astrapia, Western Parotia, Magnificent Bird-of-paradise.

Getting There

Manokwari to Mokwam

The Mission Aviation Fellowship (MAF) flies every week or two to Mokwam but more frequently to Minyambou, which is an easy few hours' walk from Mokwam. They will try to schedule a flight to suit your timing if given several days' notice, but it is very difficult to contact them other than in person; WWF or a travel agent may be able to help. The cost is very reasonable and depends on the total weight of the party and luggage. It is unlikely to exceed $50 a journey! Their hangar and operations are located on the far side of the airport; address is Kantor TEAM, Manokwari 98311, ☎ 21155.

Accommodation

There is virtually no accommodation or food in the Arfaks. However, the porters/guides are adept at building waterproof shelters so it is feasible to manage without a tent. At Mokwam it may be possible to stay in the WWF hut, if pre-arranged with WWF, a valuable source of information—and possibly assistance—in Manokwari.

General Information

The permit or *surat jalan* is most conveniently arranged in Jayapura (at Sentani Airport, at the police/immigration office just outside the terminal) or Biak. You may need an endorsement to travel outside Manokwari, so report to the local police on arrival.

Porters are easily hired in Mokwam to carry luggage, food and cooking utensils, all of which you should bring with you. Competent guides such as Seth Wongger, Vosim or Yafet can be found by asking around for them in the village. The guides can show you good birds around Mokwam, eg Long-tailed Paradigalla and Western Parotia on Siobri, and the spectacular bowers of Arfak Bowerbird.

Rain occurs most days throughout the year, especially in the afternoon and evening. It is warm/hot every day but can be quite cool at night on or near the ridge. There are a few leeches and mosquitos.

Batanta Island

Located off the western tip of the Vogelkop peninsula, this island is the only home of the—even by bird-of-paradise standards—extraordinary Wilson's Bird-of-paradise. Guides will take you to a lek, and in a visit of two days you should see other memorable and rare species such as Red Bird-of-paradise, Pheasant Pigeon, Rufous-bellied Kookaburra, Papuan Frogmouth, and Puff-backed Meliphaga. The overall species diversity is, however, much lower than on the mainland.

Getting There

At the jetty in Sorong, the regional capital of the Vogelkop Peninsula, served by daily flights from Ambon, Biak, Jayapura and Jakarta (via Ujung Pandang), find a boat to hire for the 3-day return trip to Batanta. Expect to pay around $300 for 3 days, including petrol. The crossing to Yenenes on Batanta takes 3–3.5 hrs, then it is a further 1.5 hrs east along the coast to Wai Lebed (a village of a dozen or so huts strung along the beach).

General Information

In Wai Lebed, ask for Anton Dai, who will guide you to the Wilson's Bird-of-paradise lek. The trail runs east along the shore to a small lodge that offers good accommodation. Here the forest meets the sea. The Red Birds-of-paradise are a few hundred metres inland in the lowland forest. The Wilson's lek is a tough, 1.5-hr walk up to a ridge on the flank of Mt Batanta. You have to start at dawn.

Jayapura

Jayapura is the capital of Irian Jaya province and serves as a relay point to Wamena in the Baliem Valley, and Merauke.

Getting There

By air There are daily Merpati flights from Ambon (via Timika, Biak), Denpasar (3–4 stops) daily, Surabaya (via Biak, Ujung Pandang), Jakarta 2–3 times daily (2–4 stops); Manado (3 stops), and Ujung Pandang twice daily (via Biak). Sempati also flies from most of these destinations, plus Taipei. All flights land at Sentani Airport, 32 km from Jayapura. Minibus-taxis into town cost $10, or walk 200 m to the main road and take a public minibus: to Abepura (40¢), then change buses to the Entrop terminal (20¢), then change again for Jayapura (40¢). It may be possible to get the *surat jalan* at the airport if you are just passing through and don't want to go into town.
By sea Pelni's passenger ships *Ciremai* and *Dobonsolo* call at Jayapura every 2 weeks.

Accommodation/Dining

Jayapura offers accommodation ranging from the 2-star **Matoa** down to budget *losmen*.
Matoa, Jl Ahmad Yani 14, ☎ 31633; fax: 31437; telex 76208 Matoa IA. Two stars; the only international standard hotel in town. All rooms with central AC, colour TV/video, mini-bar. $65S, $90D, $100+ suite with continental breakfast.
Triton, Jl Ahmad Yani 52; PO Box 33, ☎ 33218, 33171. 24 rms. Free airport taxi; colour TV/video, all rooms AC. Next to the Rasa Sayang Restaurant (steak, occasionally venison). $18–45.
Losmen Kartini, Jl Perintis 2, ☎ 31557. 12 rms, quite clean. With outside bath $5S, $9D; with attached bath, $12D. All w/simple breakfast.
Jaya Grill, Jl Koti 5, ☎ 34783. On the water, towards the main docks, enclosed and AC. 10.30 am–2.30 pm and 6.30 pm–10.30 pm. Seafood, chicken, frog, pork, $5–6; steaks (from Jakarta) $8–10; simple Chinese or Indonesian dishes $1.50–2.50; wide variety of booze; cold beer.

Losmen in Sentani all include simple breakfast, and will help with the police for your *surat jalan*, and transportation to the airport.
Mansapur Rani Guest House, 200 m from the terminal, Jl Jaboso 113, ☎ 91219. 20 rooms. $7 per person w/light breakfast.
Minang Jaya Just off the main road to Jayapura, past airport turnoff. ☎ 91067. 25 rooms. $9S, $15D w/fan and attached bath; $15S, $18D AC.
Sentani Inn, Jl Raya Sentani, 3 km from the airport on the main road to Jayapura, ☎ 99352. 16 rms. Clean; friendly staff. Breakfast included. $9S, $16D w/fan; $12S, $16D AC.

Transport

Garuda, Jl Percetakan 4–6, ☎ 36217/8; fax 31752.
Merpati, Jl A. Yani 15 Lantai I/21, next to the Hotel Matoa, ☎ 33111, 33227, telex 76143, 76299; airport ☎ 91167.
Sempati, Jl. Percetakan 17, ☎ 31612, fax 35290; airport ☎ 91612, fax 91636.
MAF The Missionary Aviation Fellowship office (a Protestant support airline) is next to the Sentani air terminal; no commercial flights to where either Garuda or Merpati flies. Officer: Wally Wiley, ☎ (0967) 171 (Sentani, by day), ☎ (0967) 178 (evenings). For charters, they can be contacted through the Missionary Fellowship office in Jayapura, located a bit past the Bank of Indonesia on the harbour road, PO Box 38, Jayapura, ☎ 21264; telex 76142. MAF's schedule is set according to the church's requirements, and they take into account the weights of passengers, including their luggage, with missionaries having first priority. For a special chartered flight, contact them several months ahead of time. Then confirm, 2 weeks prior.

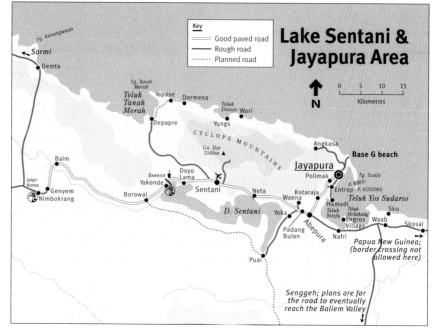

Lake Sentani & Jayapura Area

Key
Good paved road
Rough road
Planned road

N
0 5 10 15
Kilometres

Senggeh; plans are for
the road to eventually
reach the Baliem Valley

Papua New Guinea;
(border crossing not
allowed here)

Pelni, Jl Halmahera 1. ☎ 21270; fax 21370.
Taxis The taxi terminal is across the road from the Post Office ($10/hr).
Minibus At the taxi terminal across the road from the Post Office. 15¢–40¢ to nearby destinations.
Car hire Renting a minibus with driver locally runs $5–10/hr, with a day rate of about $50, or $60–$80 if further away than Lake Sentani. Be sure you notify your hotel ahead of time if you will need a taxi. There may not be one available for spur of the moment excursions.

General Information
Tourist Office, Jl Raya Abepura 17, Entrop, PO Box 2166, Jayapura, ☎ 32216, 34447, fax 31519.
Travel Agencies: Natrabu Tours and Travel, Jl Batukarang 1, Jayapura 99223, ☎ 35613. Has branches throughout Indonesia.
PHPA Office, Jl Tanjung Ria II, Base G, P O Box 545, Jayapura.
WWF, PO Box 1245, Jayapura 990112, ☎/fax 42765.
Post and Telkom Office, Jl Koti 3.
Foreign Exchange: **Bank expor-Impor**, Jl Ahmad Yani. 8.00 am–1.00 pm.
Hospitals There is a *Puskemas* (clinic) at Doc. 2. Dr Toni Pranato is the malaria and dengue specialist.
Doctors Dr Oey, reputedly the best doctor in the area is retired, but will still see pa-

tients. His office is on the highway half way between Jayapura and Sentani. ☎ 21789. He speaks English and German; his nurse (also his wife) speaks French. Hours: 5–9pm, Mon, Wed, Fri.
Dr Manapa, Jl Irian (near the cinema), ☎ 34465 (office), 33473 (home). Dr Manapa speaks English.
Souvenirs Souvenirs can be found at the Hotel Matoa shop, at the shop attached to the museum at Cendrawasih University and the Negeri Museum, and at the Perindustrian office in Abepura.

Biak and Supiori Islands

These two islands in Geelvink (Cenderawasih) Bay support 5 endemic species and another 3 shared only with neighbouring Numfor Island. This is reason enough to make the flight out from Jayapura or Sorong to Biak. The Indonesian government is making efforts to develop tourism on the island. Biak itself is largely deforested; neighbouring Supiori is a nature reserve, although the terrain makes for quite difficult walking.

Key Species
The endemics are Yellow-bibbed Fruit-dove, Biak Red Lory, Geelvink Pygmy Parrot, Biak

Coucal, Biak Paradise-kingfisher, Biak Monarch, Biak Flycatcher, Biak White-eye.

General Information

All but one of the 8 endemics can be found in an area of mixed degraded and primary forest on the far eastern tip of Biak. Charter a vehicle in Biak town to take you east along the southern coast road via Mokmer and Bosnik to Warafri (take a turning on the left just before the Barito Pacific base camp), about an hour's drive from Biak. Bird along the road or logging tracks.

In Supiori, the place to head for is the village of Korido on the southwest coast. Public boats leave from Biak town only erratically, so probably the best option is to hire a powered longboat for the trip. A bridge now connects Biak and Supiori. The section of road between Yemdoker and Korido is finished, but the section between Yemdoker and Sorendiveri is still under construction. You will need 2–3 days to stand a good chance of finding the endemics, and the 5-hr sea trip can be wet and is not totally safe. Expect to pay $75–100 for the 3-day charter. The Police Station in Korido will sort you out with basic accommodation. There is a steep trail into primary forest behind the village and trails running inland and parallel to the coast in both directions from Korido. A site for the intrepid only.

Wamena and the Baliem Valley

Getting There

Merpati has several daily flights from Jayapura to Wamena. They leave from 7 am–10.30 am and are usually in relatively large Fokker F-27s: 45 mins, $34. They are busy and sometimes cancelled due to bad weather, so it is important to book and confirm in advance.

(Note: The Baliem Valley is officially "dry", meaning no alcohol is allowed. Bag searches have loosened up, and there is some tolerance of small amounts for a tourist's personal use, but we still suggest you respect this rule.)

Accommodation/Dining

Other than the Hotel Jayawijaya, 3 km out of town, and Losmen La-uk in Jiwika, all the hotels/losmen are within walking distance of the airport. The best rooms are at the **Nayak Hotel**, just across the road from the airport.

Baliem Pilamo Hotel, Jl Trikora 114, ☎ 31043; fax 31798. 17 rms, all with indoor facilities. $24S, $33D standard; $42S–45D VIP. A new, clean hotel. Good restaurant serving shrimp or steak ($4), rice or noodle dishes ($1.50–2) or soup and vegetable dishes ($1–2).
Hotel Nayak, Jl Gatot Subroto 1, PO Box 1. Directly across from the airport, ☎ 31067. 12 rms with bath. The best rms in town.$18S, $23D.
Baliem Cottages, Jl Thamrin, PO Box 132, ☎ 31370. Some 600 m from the airport. 15 thatch-covered cottages, a bit run down but spacious. The restaurant is not always open. $18–23, $30 for family room.
Losmen Sjahrial Jaya, Jl Gatot Subroto 51. 23 double rooms with bath attached. $7S, $13D.

Most hotels/*losmen* serve meals, and there are food stalls around the market serving inexpensive Indonesian food. The **Sinta Prima**, on Jl Trikora, is the best restaurant in town, serving Chinese food and freshwater crayfish. Meals range from $2 to $5.

General Information

Agency tours **Chandra Nusantara Tours and Travel**, Jl Trikora 17 (next to the Sinta Prima Restaurant), PO Box 225, Wamena, ☎ 31293; fax 31299; telex 76102 CNTWMX IA. Or fax, in Jayapura: (967) 22318. This outfit is run by Sam Chandra, who is very experienced in taking people to the highlands.
Post Office, Jl Timor, is open Mon–Thu from 8.00 am to 2.00 pm; Fri to 11.00 am and Sat to 12.30 pm.
Telkom Office, Jl Thamrin 22. Open 24 hours.
Foreign exchange: **Bank Rakyat Indonesia**, Jl Trikora. Will change US$, A$, D.M. and French francs. They accept American Express, Bank of America, Thomas Cook's, Bank of Tokyo, and Visa Australia traveller's checks. Hours: Mon–Thu, 8.00 am to 12.30 pm; Fri to 11.30 am and Sat to 11.00 am.
Souvenirs You can find these at the Pasar Nayak market, in the "Souvenir Shop" across the road from the market. You will probably also be offered items while you are sitting in your hotel lobby or in a restaurant. (Note: Some items may be made with protected species, so look at them carefully. Feathers of any kind will alert a baggage inspector back home, as will lizard skin. Stick to the net bags and gourds if you are not sure.)

THE LAKE HABBEMA TREK

One of the world's classic birding treks, from the high alpine lake and marshes down through pine, moss and rain forest into the Baliem Valley. Truly amazing birds—see below—and a people and culture from another age. Not to be missed, and, as there is a road up to Lake Habbema, the birds can be enjoyed on a (mostly) downhill trail.

Key Species

Snow Mountain and Blue-breasted Quails, Swinhoe's Snipe, Orange-billed Lorikeet, Painted Tiger-parrot, Lorentz's Whistler, Sooty Honeyeater, Snow Mountain Munia, Archbold's Bowerbird, Macgregor's Bird-of-paradise, Brown Sicklebill, Splendid Astrapia, King of Saxony Bird-of-paradise.

Getting There

To get to Lake Habbema, charter a jeep (c. $30) for the 90-min drive up a new road.

General Information

The requisite *surat jalan* should be obtained, eg at Jayapura/Sentani (see above), before flying into Wamena. When you arrive in Wamena, the police check your passport and permit. The desk clerk at the hotel/*losmen* will ask for these, and will usually be able to send someone to the police station (which is just behind Pasar Nayak) to take care of this for you. Make sure that your permit is endorsed for Lake Habbema, if necessary.

Recommended birding guides are Khas Towonggan and Girian (Freddy) Koya; Freddy's brother Meles, Katyus Yikuru, and Nicolas Alva are good porters, while Libarck Logo (found through Hotel Baliem) has proved a good cook/guide. Daily rates are between Rp7,500 and Rp10,000. Don't forget that the porters' staple diet is sweet potato and you need to carry enough for them as well as for your party.

The trek runs up the Ibele Valley, from the village of the same name to Lake Habbema. It can be done in either direction and, although there is some satisfaction in walking up through the different habitats found with increasing altitude, and out into the alpine zone, it is hard not to resist taking the new road to "the top" at Lake Habbema and enjoying the birding while walking downhill.

There are no "official" places to stay or eat on the trail. It is possible to manage without a tent—by staying in the rather dilapidated "posts"—but it is helpful to have one available. Food has to be carried in, as only sweet potatoes andeggs, are available in the villages.

The first day is spent birding the alpine grasslands and marshes around Lake

Habbema (3,000 m), with a spectacular panorama across to the rugged, snow-capped peaks of the Snow (Jayawijaya) Mountains. Pos IV, a hut by the lake, is dilapidated and leaky. From the lake it is about a 2-hr walk over the pass (3,200 m) to Pos III, located in moss forest and the place to stay for the first night. The trail down the Ibele valley is not too steep, but can be very muddy and slippery.

Walking times (at an average birding pace) between places to stay are listed below. How long you take is entirely up to you.

Habbema to Pos III	1.5–2 hrs
Pos III to Yaubagema	3 hrs
Yaubagema to Dyela	3 hrs
Dyela to Ibele	5 hrs
Ibele to Beneme	2.5 hrs
Alternatively,	
Dyela to Depolo	3 hrs,
Depolo to Beneme	5 hrs.

At Beneme the cultivation starts. You can catch a bus (or truck) back to Wamena from either Ibele or Beneme (1.5 or 1 hr, Rp 5,500).

Rain is a possibility at any time but there is said to be a drier period from March–May, with July also relatively dry. The temperature is generally pleasant during the day but it can be cold at night, particularly at the higher altitudes.

Merauke

Merauke (population around 40,000) is the capital of Merauke regency in the far southeast corner of Irian Jaya—as far as you can get from Jakarta and still be in Indonesia. The telephone code is 0971.

Getting There

By air Only Merpati flies to Merauke—from Jayapura; daily, leaving very early from Sentani Airport. The taxi from Mopah Airport in Merauke to anywhere in town costs $3. When you arrive at Merauke you have to show your *surat jalan* to the police at the airport and also report to the main police station on Jl Raya Mandala. Make 10 copies of your *surat jalan* while you are in town to give to police and army posts in the park.

By sea Pelni's 960-berth *Tatamailau* ferry calls in at Merauke once a month; check the Pelni office in Jayapura for a schedule.

Accommodation/Dining

There are several hotels in town, the quality depending on how much you want to pay. Hotel prices are generally much higher than elsewhere in Indonesia.

Nirmala Hotel, Jl Raya Mandala 66, ☎ 21849. The biggest hotel in town with a restaurant (good Chinese/Indonesian food but no atmosphere). $10 fan, shared facilities; $15, no hot water; $27 AC, TV, hot water, includes breakfast and afternoon snack.

Megaria Hotel, Jl Raya Mandala 166, ☎ 21932. Also good quality. No restaurant but evening meals can be ordered from a choice of menus at reception. Class II $20S, $26D, Class I $30S, $36D. All rooms AC; prices include breakfast and tax.

Hotel Asmat, Jl Trikora 3, ☎ 21065. Class III $8S, $11D, $4 for extra bed. Class II $9S, $13D, $5 for extra bed. Class I (AC) $12S, $15D, $6 for extra bed. Prices include breakfast and tax.

Hotel Flora, Jl Raya Mandala 221, ☎ 21879. $20S, $23D. All rooms AC, prices include breakfast and tax.

Hotel Nikmat, Jl Biak, ☎ 21375. $15 with AC, $9 without. Prices include breakfast and tax. There are several restaurants offering a variety of Chinese and Indonesian food. Hygiene standards are high at the **Nirmala** (see above). Other good restaurants are the **Café Mandala** (Chinese) and **Rumah Makan Merapi Jaya** (Padang), both opposite the Nirmala Hotel. There is a traditional night - market on Jl Aru with food stalls offering a large range of cheap food and snacks.

Transport
Merpati, Jl Raya Mandala, ☎ 21242.
Pelni, Jl Sabang 318, ☎ 21591, fax 21631.
Car hire To charter a taxi (*bemo*) ask at your hotel or look out for an empty one going by and ask to charter. $5 per hour.
Bemo Called taxis, *bemos* cost Rp350 for any distance within the town.

General Information
Merauke Tourist Office Kantor Parawisata on Jl Brawijaya opposite the Bupati's office near the airport.
KSDA (PHPA) Office, Jl Garuda, out of town in Mopah Lama on the way to Wasur.
Foreign Exchange: **Bank Exim**, Jl Raya Mandala, ☎ 21333. Changes US$ only. Open weekdays only 8.00 am–3.00 pm.
Post Office, Jl Brawijaya, ☎ 21655.
Main Telkom Office, Jl Postel, ☎ 21602. Also smaller *wartel* next door to Nirmala Hotel on Jl Raya Mandala.
Hospital The *Rumah Sakit* (hospital) is next to Bank Exim (you will smell it before you see it). The hospital is small and under-equipped.

Don't get sick in Merauke. Take anti-malarials and bring your own medical supplies.
Souvenirs Two good shops sell Asmat carvings and local handicrafts. **Toko Ujung** opposite Toko Adil on Jl Raya Mandala and the smaller but sometimes better **Toko Sumber Alam** on Jl Ermasu. Both places have more stock out back.

Wasur National Park

The 413,000 ha Wasur National Park, located in the extreme southeast of Irian Jaya, bordering the Papua New Guinea border, is a veritable bird paradise and access is easy. The flat expanse of the vast Fly-Digul River delta is a mosaic of swamps, reedbeds and open savannah woodlands with denser forests along the rivers. In the dry season, literally thousands of waterbirds—many migrants from Australia—concentrate on the receding pools. There are mangroves and mudflats to search for shorebirds, and two species of bird-of-paradise in the denser forest.

Key Species
Southern Cassowary, Brolga Crane, Magpie Goose, Australian Bustard, Noisy Pitta, Rufous-bellied and Spangled Kookaburras. Recently, Crimson Finch, White-spotted and Grey-crowned Mannikins and Fly River Grassbird have all been recorded on the Irian side of the Fly River and are all new additions to the Indonesian bird list. Black Mannikin, present just a few km across the border in Papua New Guinea, has not yet been confirmed in Wasur National Park.

Other Wildlife
Sugar Glider, Striped Possum, Rusa Deer, Agile Wallaby and forest wallabies, bandicoots and cuscus.

Getting There
The best place to get information and help in arranging tours to the national park is the World Wide Fund for Nature office on Jl Brawijayaat Sepadem (ask for "*kantor way way eff*"), ☎ 22407. WWF are developing community tourism activities, including birding, in the park. Hiring a jeep is expensive unless you are in a group (around $75 a day, which includes driver/guide and fuel). It is cheaper and more pleasant to hire horses from the villagers. This creates less disturbance and provides a good vantage point for watching birds if you can hang on (the horses are very tame).

The WWF office will give you the price per day and can help you arrange a guide. The park entrance fee (pay at either Wasur or Ndalir KSDA posts) is Rp500 per person. Do not forget copies of your *surat jalan* for the police posts in the park.

For the Maro river trip, you ideally need two days. Arrange boat hire from the Kelapa Lima Maro river crossing just to the north of Merauke. Like jeep hire, it is more economical if there are several people sharing the expense. Prices could be from Rp150,000–200,000 per day including a boatman. Take all your own food.

Accommodation/Dining

There are guest-houses in four villages: Yanggandur and Soa (for Greater Bird-of-paradise), Onggaya (by the beach near Ndalir) and Soa (on the Maro river). These provide very simple accommodation, cooking equipment etc. Take your own food and water into the park.

General Information

The best time to visit is from August to December.

If you hire a jeep and driver for the 3-day trip described in the colour section, spend the first night at Tomerau village and the second at Ukra. Leave Ukra mid-morning to get to Rawa Biru by early afternoon. Ask the driver to meet you in Yanggandur and spend the rest of the afternoon (3–4 hrs) walking the track

up to Yanggandur. Spend the night here for a dawn sighting of Greater Bird-of-paradise. Leave Yanggandur mid-morning to allow time to look around Wasur village on the way back to town. If you only have 2 nights, go straight to Ukra on the first night (you can get there in one day if you rush) and Yanggandur on the second.

At the village of Soa, about 5–6 hours up river (depending on tide), arrange for a guide to take you in the monsoon forest nearby. Best chances to find the King Bird-of-Paradise will be early in the morning.

Be very wary of snakes in Wasur: there are some real nasties including Taipan and Death Adder. There is no snake bite serum available in Merauke, so watch where you tread.

–Michele Bowe, Margaret Cameron,
David Gibbs & Jon Hornbuckle.

Wasur National Park

Bird Clubs and Conservation Organisations

Bird Clubs and Societies

Oriental Bird Club, c/o The Lodge, Sandy, Bedfordshire, SG19 2DL, UK. Web-site: http://www.netlink.co.uk/users/aw/index.html

OBC aims to promote an interest in the birds of the Orient (Pakistan to China and south to Indonesia). The club has an international membership of some 2,000 conservationists, scientists and keen birders. Its twice-yearly *Bulletin* is packed with the latest news, colour photos and articles on birds and birding in the region; an annual journal, *Forktail*, publishes scientific papers on bird status and distribution. The club also runs a small grants programme. Membership is $25 per year ($15 for nationals living in the region).

Indonesia Ornithological Society, c/o PO Box 310/Boo, Bogor 16003, Indonesia.

The society's main activity is the publication of *Kukila*, the journal of Indonesian ornithology. Here you will find the most up-to-date information on new bird surveys of islands and reserves in Indonesia. Subscription to *Kukila* is $15 per year (surface mail).

Symbiose Bird-watching Club, Jl MI Ridwan Rais 91, Beji Timur, Depok, ☎ (021)16422.

The club evolved from a group of students from the Biology Department at the University of Indonesia. It aims to promote birdwatching in Indonesia, and members get together for regular birding trips around Jakarta.

Kutilang, c/o Ignatius Pramana Yudha. Jl Pandega Maharisi 9, Yogyakarta 55281. ☎ (0274) 565411; fax (0274) 565258.

Kutilang (the name means bulbul) conducts surveys and bird awareness activities in and around Yogyakarta.

A number of locally based bird clubs have guided visiting birders in the past. In addition to Symbiose and Kutilang (above) they include:
Yayasan Pribumi Alam Lestari (YPAL),

Jl Paledang 20, Cibeureum, Bandung, West Java. ☎ (0251) 670139.
Klub Indonesia Hijau (KIH), P O Box 1009/BOUT, Bogor 16010, West Java.
Konservasi Satwa Bagi Kehidupan (KSBK), Jl Margo Basuki 11 No 4, Jetis, Mulyo Agung, Day, Malang 65151.
Bali Bird Club, c/o Beggar's Bush Bar and Restaurant, Tjampuhan, Ubud.

There are more than 40 smaller, university-based bird groups in cities across Java and Bali. A directory is maintained by BirdLife.

International Conservation Agencies

The agencies below all work in collaboration with the government conservation agency (PHPA). Details of their field offices are contained in the site practicalities.

BirdLife International—Indonesia Programme, PO Box 310/Boo, Jl Achmad Yani 11, Bogor 16003. ☎ /fax: (0251) 333234; e-mail: birdlife@server.indo.net.id; Web-site: http://www.ke.rim.or.jp/~birdinfo/indonesia/

BirdLife has an active conservation programme in Indonesia. Focus regions for field projects are Nusa Tenggara and Maluku, but BirdLife ornithologists conduct status assessments of threatened birds throughout Indonesia and are compiling a directory of Important Bird Areas.

The Nature Conservancy (Jakarta), Jl Radio IV 5, Kebayoran Baru, Jakarta 12001 ☎ (021) 7206484; fax (021) 7245092.

TNC's Indonesia programme has a strong marine element and is assisting with the management of the marine environment in Komodo National Park. The NTMNC programme also has activities in the buffer zones of Lore Lindu National Park.

Wetlands International—Indonesia Programme (formerly Asian Wetlands Bureau), PO Box 254/Boo, Jl Arzimar III/17,

Bogor 16002. ☎ (0251) 312189; fax (0251) 325755; e-mail: wi-ip@server.indo.net.id; Website: http://www.sdn.or.id/wi-ip/wetlands.html

The focus of Wetlands International is the wise and sustainable management of Indonesia's extensive wetlands. As well as managing large integrated projects, Wetlands International monitors the status of waterbirds and publishes field guides and awareness materials.

Wildlife Conservation Society, Jl Ciremai 9, Bogor. ☎/fax (0251) 325664.

WCS focuses on developing a detailed scientific knowledge of wildlife and ecosystems to support their conservation. Until 1995 WCS studied the wildlife of the Tangkoko reserve in North Sulawesi. They have now shifted their emphasis to South Sumatra.

World Wide Fund for Nature—Indonesia Programme, PO Box 7928 JKSKM, Jl Pela 3, Gandara Utara, Jakarta 12001. ☎/fax (021) 739 5907; e-mail: wwf-ip@indo.net.id.

WWF has a large presence in Indonesia with separate protected area, species and marine programmes. It is assisting PHPA with management of some massive National Parks such as Kerinci-Seblat (Sumatra), Kayan-Manatarn (Kalimantan) and Lorentz (Irian Jaya).

Government Agencies

Directorate General for Forest Protection and Nature Conservation (PHPA), Ministry of Forestry, Gedung Manggala Wanabakti, Jl Gatot Subroto, Jakarta. ☎ (021) 5730311, 5730312; fax 5734818.

This is the headquarters of PHPA and the main contact address for information. The national parks department is still located at the old PHPA office at Jl Juanda 100, Bogor. ☎ (0251) 321104.

The PHPA is a department within the Ministry of Forestry responsible for managing all National Parks and Protected Areas. There are seven regional coordinating conservation offices (BKSDA), under these are the provincial offices (SBKSDA) and under these the district offices (SSKSDA). The older national parks have their own managment unit and a park director, the rest are managed by the SBKSDA.

Tourist provision in many national parks is still poor, and visitors may find frustrations with limited trail systems, information provision and poor facilities. If you have suggestions for improvements its is best to write to the Director General PHPA, Department Kehutanan, Gd Manggala Wanabakti Blok 1 Lt8, Jl Jenderal Gatot Subroto, Jakarta 10270. A positively written letter, stating what you liked and then suggesting improvements is the best approach.

Indonesian Institute of Sciences (LIPI), Puslitbang Biologi (Centre for Research and Development in Biology), Jl Juanda 18, PO Box 208, Bogor 16002. ☎ (0251) 321040; fax 325854. LIPI Jakarta HQ: ☎ (021) 5225711; fax 520 7226.

Co-ordinates all scientific research in Indonesia, and manages the national collections including the Zoology Museum (with an Ornithology Department) located across the road from the Bogor Botanic Gardens.

–Paul Jepson

About the Authors

Bas van Balen is one of the world's leading authorities on the birds of West Indonesia. His 15 years in the country have been devoted to pioneering bird surveys to support the creation of new reserves in the remaining rainforest wildernesses of Kalimantan and Sumatra. He is a staff member of the BirdLife International Indonesia Programme and is currently completing his doctoral thesis on Javan forest birds.

Simon Badcock is a geographer and social anthropologist. Based at the University of Adelaide, he is currently finalising has doctoral thesis study on the relationships between people and forests in the Manusela National Park, Seram. During three extensive periods of field work he has gained an unrivalled knowledge of the park and its people.

Michele Bowe is a conservation officer with the World Wide Fund for Nature—Indonesia Programme. For four years, she worked and lived among the people of Wasur

National Park, before moving to her present position as head of the WWF programme in Nusa Tengarra.

Margaret Cameron has been bird-watching for nearly 30 years all over Australia, and has visited Papua New Guinea four times and Irian Jaya twice. A retired librarian, and former President of the Royal Australasian Ornithologists Union, she proves that you do not have to be young to climb the trails of Irian Jaya in search of Birds-of-paradise!

Rene Dekker is Keeper of Ornithology at the Rijksmuseum voor Natuurlyke Historie, in Leiden. He is a leading expert on megapodes and studied the Maleo for his doctorate degree.

Wim Giesen was senior ecologist for six years with the Wetlands International—Indonesia Programme and has lived in South Sulawesi for two years. He is now based in Holland and works as a consultant, specialising in the conservation and wise use of wetlands.

Jon Hornbuckle is a retired steel industry executive, who now devotes himself full-time to ornithology. He spends much of his time in the Tropics, birding or participating in ornithological projects, in the Philippines, Papua New Guinea, Bolivia and Ecuador, as well as in Indonesia.

Paul Jepson, a past chairman of the Oriental Bird Club, heads the BirdLife International Indonesia Programme. He lives in West Java, but his conservation work regularly takes him to Sumatra and the far flung islands of Nusa Tenggara and Maluku, where he has gained unique insights into the country, its birds and conservation issues.

Ron Johnstone is Keeper of Ornithology at the West Australian Museum in Perth and participated in a series of joint zoological expeditions between the West Australian Museum and the National Museum in Bogor, Indonesia to the islands of Nusa Tenggara.

Margaret Kinnaird is a conservation biologist with the Wildlife Conservation Society. During five years in Tangkoko, Sulawesi, she and her husband Tim O'Brien conducted the first detailed studies of the ecology of Sulawesi's two endemic hornbills. They now live in West Java and have shifted their attentions to Bukit Barisan National Park in South Sumatra.

Victor Mason is a long-term resident of Ubud, Bali, and an avid birder. His Bali Bird Walks have become a big hit with tourists as much because of his entertaining and colourful character as of the beautiful birds and landscapes he so expertly introduces.

Yus Rusila Noor is head of the Fauna Unit at the Wetlands International-Indonesia Programme and is a leading expert on the conservation of Indonesian waterbirds.

Richard Noske is a senior lecturer in ecology at the Northern Territories University in Australia. Richard makes frequent visits to Indonesia—sometimes to pursue his ornithological research interest and at other times simply to indulge his passion for birding.

Daniel Philippe works in Jakarta as President-Director of an international company. As a keen amateur bird-watcher he has as his "local patch" the remnants of natural vegetation that survive in the metropolis. He takes every available opportunity to go birding in other parts of the archipelago.

Dolly Priatna is a biologist and bird-watcher working as a research assistant with the Leuser Development Programme. He has been conducting biodiversity surveys in Gunung Leuser National Park for the last seven years and has deep knowledge of the area and its birds.

Resit Sözer is a biologist based at the University of Amsterdam. He studied Javan Hawk-eagles for his masters degree. His first love has always been gamebirds and he is currently conducting surveys to learn more about the status and ecology of the Bornean Peacock-pheasant.

Checklist of the Birds of Indonesia

This checklist is based on *The Birds of Indonesia: a Checklist (Peter's sequence)* by Paul Andrew (see Further Reading). However many bird-watchers now base their world lists on the alternative classification of Sibley & Monroe (1990); under this classification the Indonesian list is 22 species larger. For a list of the differences in species limits between these two classifications, see Andrew (1992). The English and scientific names of each species are listed. The column headed "EX" signifies whether the species is endemic to Indonesia "E", to the island of Borneo "B", to New Guinea and satellite islands "P", or if the species is distributed to the west "<" or east ">" of Indonesia.

The column headed "ST" refers to the species's status in Indonesia. "R" signifies a resident, breeding species, "M" a visitor from either the northern or southern winters, "P" a passage visitor on migration and "V" an accidental or casual visitor.

The distribution columns show in which of the eight regions into which this guide is divided the species has been recorded. These are Java "J", Bali "B", Nusa Tenggara "T", Sumatra "S", Kalimantan "K", Sulawesi "C", Maluku "M" and Irian Jaya "I". For boundaries see the map on page 19–20. Boundaries of Maluku include some islands on the edge of the Sulawesi, Lesser Sunda and Irian Jaya faunal regions, and consequently the species list for this region is inflated. An island-by-island distribution list for Nusa Tenggara and Maluku can be found in *The Ecology of Nusa Tenggara and Maluku* (see Further Reading).

–Paul Jepson

Bird Names (Scientific Names)

Bird Names (Scientific Names)	EX	ST	J	B	T	S	K	C	M	I
Casuaridae: Cassowaries										
Dwarf Cassowary *Casuarius bennetti*		→ R								I
Southern Cassowary *Casuarius casuariu*		→ R							F	I
Northern Cassowary *Casuarius unappendiculatus*	P	R								I
Procellariidae: Petrels, Shearwaters										
Cape Petrel *Daption capense*		→ V							M	
Tahiti Petrel *Pterodroma rostrata*		← → V			T?				M	I
Barau's Petrel *Pterodroma baraui*		V								
Dark-rumped Petrel *Pterodroma phaeopygia*		← V							M	
Antarctic Prion *Pachyptila desolata*		→ V	J							
Bulwer's Petrel *Bulweria bulwerii*		← P	J	B	T	S		C	M	
Jouanin's Petrel *Bulweria fallax*		V				S				
Streaked Shearwater *Calonectris leucomelas*		← → M	J		T	S		C	M	I
Wedge-tailed Shearwater *Puffinus pacificus*		← → M	J	B	T	S		C	M	I
Flesh-footed Shearwater *Puffinus carneipes*		← → M				S				
Hydrobatidae: Storm-petrels										
Wilson's Storm-petrel *Oceanites oceanicus*		← → M	J	B	T	S		C	M	I
White-faced Storm-petrel *Pelagodroma marina*		→ V			T	S				
Swinhoe's Storm-petrel *Oceanodroma monorhis*		← P	J	B					M	
Matsudaira's Storm-petrel *Oceanodroma matsudairae*		→ P			T				M	
Podicepedidae: Grebes										
Black-throated Little Grebe *Tachybaptus novaehollandiae*		← → R	J	B	T			C	M	I
Red-throated Little Grebe *Tachybaptus ruficollis*		← → R	J	B	T	S		C	M	I
Great Crested Grebe *Podiceps cristatus*		← → V							M	
Phaethontidae: Tropicbirds										
Red-tailed Tropicbird *Phaethon rubricauda*		← → R	J		T	S			M	
White-tailed Tropicbird *Phaethon lepturus*		← → R	J	B	T	S	K	C	M	I
Fregatidae: Frigatebirds										
Great Frigatebird *Fregata minor*		← → M\R	J	B	T	S		C	M	I
Lesser Frigatebird *Fregata ariel*		← → M	J	B	T	S	K	C	M	I
Christmas Frigatebird *Fregata andrewsi*		← → M	J	B	T	S	K			
Phalacrocoracidae: Cormorants, Darters										
Great Cormorant *Phalacrocorax carbo*		← → M\R?				S			M	I
Little Black Cormorant *Phalacrocorax sulcirostris*		→ R	J	B	T	S	K	C	M	I
Little Pied Cormorant *Phalacrocorax melanoleucos*		→ R	J	B	T			C	M	I
Little Cormorant *Phalacrocorax niger*		← R				S	K			
Oriental Darter *Anhinga melanogaster*		← R	J	B	T	S	K	C	M	
Australian Darter *Anhinga novaehollandiae*		→ ?							M	I
Sulidae: Boobies										
Masked Booby *Sula dactylatra*		← → M\R?	J		T	S		C	M	I
Red-footed Booby *Sula sula*		← → M\R	J	B	T	S		C	M	I
Brown Booby *Sula leucogaster*		← → M\R	J	B	T	S		C	M	I
Abbott's Booby *Sula abbotti*		← M\R	J			S			M	I
Pelecanidae: Pelicans										
Great White Pelican *Pelecanus onocrotalus*		← V	J	B						
Spot-billed Pelican *Pelecanus philippensis*		← R?	J			S				
Australian Pelican *Pelecanus conspicillatus*		→ M	J	B	T			C	M	I
Ardeidae: Herons, Egrets, Night-herons, Bitterns										
Grey Heron *Ardea cinerea*		← R	J	B	T	S				
Pacific Heron *Ardea pacifica*		→ R								I

Bird Names (Scientific Names)	EX	ST	J	B	T	S	K	C	M	I
Great-billed Heron *Ardea sumatrana*	← →	R	J	B	T	S	K	C	M	I
Purple Heron *Ardea purpurea*	←	R	J	B	T	S	K	C	M	
Great Egret *Casmerodius albus*	← →	R\M	J	B	T	S	K	C	M	I
Pied Heron *Egretta picata*	→	R\M						C	M	I
Intermediate Egret *Egretta intermedia*	← →	R\M	J	B	T	S	K	C	M	I
White-faced Heron *Egretta novaehollandiae*	→	R\M		B	T			C	M	I
Little Egret *Egretta garzetta*	← →	R\M	J	B	T	S	K	C	M	I
Chinese Egret *Egretta eulophotes*	←	V	J			S	K	C		
Reef Egret *Egretta sacra*	← →	R	J	B	T	S	K	C	M	I
Cattle Egret *Bubulcus ibis*	← →	R\M	J	B	T	S	K	C	M	I
Chinese Pond-heron *Ardeola bacchus*	←	M				S	K			
Javan Pond-heron *Ardeola speciosa*	←	R	J	B	T	S	K	C		
Striated Heron *Butorides striatus*	← →	R	J	B	T	S	K	C	M	
Black-crowned Night-heron *Nycticorax nycticorax*	←	R\M	J	B	T	S	K	C		
Rufous Night-heron *Nycticorax caledonicus*	← →	R	J	B	T			C	M	I
Japanese Night-heron *Gorsachius goisagi*	←	V						C	M	
Malayan Night-heron *Gorsachius melanolophus*	←	R	J	B		S		C	M	
Forest Bittern *Zonerodius heliosylus*	P	R							M	I
Yellow Bittern *Ixobrychus sinensis*	← →	M\R	J	B	T	S	K	C	M	I
Schrenck's Bittern *Ixobrychus eurhythmus*	←	M	J			S	K	C	M	
Cinnamon Bittern *Ixobrychus cinnamomeus*	←	R	J	B	T	S	K	C	M	
Black Bittern *Ixobrychus flavicollis*	← →	R\M	J	B	T	S	K	C	M	I
Ciconiidae: Storks										
Milky Stork *Mycteria cinerea*	←	R	J	B	T	S		C		
Woolly-necked Stork *Ciconia episcopus*	←	R	J	B	T	S		C		
Storm's Stork *Ciconia stormi*	←	R				S	K			
Black-necked Stork *Ephippiorhynchus asiaticus*	← →	V	J						M	I
Lesser Adjutant *Leptoptilos javanicus*	←	R	J	B		S	K			
Threskiornithidae: Ibises, Spoonbills										
Glossy Ibis *Plegadis falcinellus*	← →	R\M	J	B	T	S	K	C	M	I
Black-headed Ibis *Threskiornis melanocephalus*	←	R\M				S				
Australian Ibis *Threskiornis molucca*	→	V							M	I
Straw-necked Ibis *Threskiornis spinicollis*	→	M							M	I
White-shouldered Ibis *Pseudibis papillosa*	←	R					K			
Royal Spoonbill *Platalea regia*	→	V	J	B	T			C	M	I
Accipitridae: Osprey, Bazas, Buzzards, Kites, Eagles, Harriers, Hawks										
Osprey *Pandion haliaetus*	← →	R\M	J	B	T	S	K	C	M	I
Jerdon's Baza *Aviceda jerdoni*	←	R\M				S	K	C	M	
Pacific Baza *Aviceda subcristata*	→	R			T			C	M	I
Black Baza *Aviceda leuphotes*	←	M	J			S				
Long-tailed Buzzard *Henicopernis longicauda*	P	R							M	I
Oriental Honey-buzzard *Pernis ptilorhynchus*	←	R\M	J	B	T	S	K	C	M	I
Barred Honey-buzzard *Pernis celebensis*	←	R						C	M	
Bat Hawk *Macheiramphus alcinus*	← P	R				S			M	
Black-winged Kite *Elanus caeruleus*	← P	R	J	B	T	S	K	C		I
Black Kite *Milvus migrans*	← →	R\M			T	S		C	M	I
Whistling Kite *Haliastur sphenurus*	→	R								I
Brahminy Kite *Haliastur indus*	← →	R	J	B	T	S	K	C	M	I
White-bellied Sea-eagle *Haliaeetus leucogaster*	←	R	J	B	T	S	K	C	M	I
Lesser Fish-eagle *Ichthyophaga humilis*	←	R				S	K	C		
Grey-headed Fish-eagle *Ichthyophaga ichthyaetus*	←	R	J			S	K	C		
Short-toed Eagle *Circaetus gallicus*	←	R	J	B	T					
Crested Serpent-eagle *Spilornis cheela*	←	R	J	B		S	K			
Sulawesi Serpent-eagle *Spilornis rufipectus*	E	R						C	M	
Spotted Harrier *Circus assimilis*	→	R\M			T			C	M	
Pied Harrier *Circus melanoleucos*	←	V					K			

Bird Names (Scientific Names)

Bird Names (Scientific Names)	EX	ST	J	B	T	S	K	C	M	I
Marsh Harrier *Circus aeruginosus*	←	M				S				I
Swamp Harrier *Circus approximans*	→	M								I
Crested Goshawk *Accipiter trivirgatus*	←	R	J	B		S	K			
Sulawesi Goshawk *Accipiter griseiceps*	E	R						C		
Shikra *Accipiter badius*	←	M				S				
Chinese Goshawk *Accipiter soloensis*	←	M	J	B	T	S	K	C	M	I
Spot-tailed Goshawk *Accipiter trinotatus*	E	R						C		
Brown Goshawk *Accipiter fasciatus*	→	R			T			C	M	I
Grey Goshawk *Accipiter novaehollandiae*	→	R			T				M	
Black-mantled Goshawk *Accipiter melanochlamys*	P	R							M	I
Moluccan Goshawk *Accipiter henicogrammus*	E	R							M	
Grey-headed Goshawk *Accipiter poliocephalus*	P	R							M	I
Japanese Sparrow-hawk *Accipiter gularis*	←	M	J	B	T	S	K	C		
Besra *Accipiter virgatus*	←	R	J	B	T	S	K			
Small Sparrow-hawk *Accipiter nanus*	E	R						C		
Collared Sparrow-hawk *Accipiter cirrhocephalus*	→	R								I
Rufous-necked Sparrow-hawk *Accipiter erythrauchen*	E	R							M	
Vinous-breasted Sparrow-hawk *Accipiter rhodogaster*	E	R						C	M	
Meyer's Goshawk *Accipiter meyerianus*	→	R							M	I
Chestnut-shouldered Goshawk *Accipiter buergersi*	P	R								I
Doria's Hawk *Accipiter doriae*	P	R								I
Rufous-winged Buzzard *Butastur liventer*	←	R	J					C		
Grey-faced Buzzard *Butastur indicus*	←	M\R	J	B	T	S			M	I
Common Buzzard *Buteo buteo*	←	M	J	B						
New Guinea Eagle *Harpyopsis novaeguineae*	P	R								I
Black Eagle *Ictinaetus malayensis*	←	R	J	B		S	K	C	M	
Spotted Eagle *Aquila clanga*	V					S				
Gurney's Eagle *Aquila gurneyi*	P	R							M	I
Wedge-tailed Eagle *Aquila audax*	→	R								I
Bonelli's Eagle *Hieraaetus fasciatus*	←	R			T				M	
Booted Eagle *Hieraaetus pennatus*	←	V	J	B						
Little Eagle *Hieraaetus morphnoides*	→	R							M	I
Changeable Hawk-eagle *Spizaetus cirrhatus*	←	R	J	B	T	S	K			
Javan Hawk-eagle *Spizaetus bartelsi*	E	R	J							
Sulawesi Hawk-eagle *Spizaetus lanceolatus*	E	R						C	M	
Blyth's Hawk-eagle *Spizaetus alboniger*	←	R				S	K			
Wallace's Hawk-eagle *Spizaetus nanus*	←	R				S	K			

Falconidae: Falcons, Kestrels, Hobbies

Bird Names (Scientific Names)	EX	ST	J	B	T	S	K	C	M	I
Black-thighed Falconet *Microhierax fringillarius*	←	R	J	B		S	K			
Brown Falcon *Falco berigora*	→	R								
Eurasian Kestrel *Falco tinnunculus*	←	M				S				
Spotted Kestrel *Falco moluccensis*	E	R	J	B	T		K	C	M	I
Australian Kestrel *Falco cenchroides*	→	V	J		T				M	I
Eurasian Hobby *Falco subbuteo*	←	R	J		T					
Oriental Hobby *Falco severus*	← →	R	J	B	T	S	K	C		
Australian Hobby *Falco longipennis*	→	R\M			T			C	M	
Peregrine Falcon *Falco peregrinus*	← →	R\M	J	B	T	S	K	C	M	I

Anatidae: Whistling-ducks, Swans, Pygmy Geese, Ducks

Bird Names (Scientific Names)	EX	ST	J	B	T	S	K	C	M	I
Magpie Goose *Anseranas semipalmata*	→	R								I
Spotted Whistling-duck *Dendrocygna guttata*	← →	R						C	M	I
Plumed Whistling-duck *Dendrocygna eytoni*	→	V								
Wandering Whistling-duck *Dendrocygna arcuata*	← →	R\M	J	B	T	S	K	C	M	I
Lesser Whistling-duck *Dendrocygna javanica*	←	R	J	B	T	S	K			
Black Swan *Cygnus atratus*	→	V								I
White-headed Shelduck *Tadorna radjah*	→	R			T				M	I
White-winged Duck *Cairina scutulata*	←	R	J			S				
Green Pygmy Goose *Nettapus pulchellus*	→	R			T			C	M	I

Bird Names (Scientific Names)

Bird Names (Scientific Names)	EX	ST	J	B	T	S	K	C	M	I
Cotton Pygmy Goose *Nettapus coromandelianus*	← →	R\M	J			S	K	C		
Salvadori's Teal *Anas waigiuensis*	P	R								I
Eurasian Wigeon *Anas penelope*	←	V						C		
Sunda Teal *Anas gibberifrons*	←	R		B	T	S	K	C	M	
Grey Teal *Anas gracilis*	→	R\M							M	I
Pacific Black Duck *Anas superciliosa*	→	R	J	B	T	S	K	C	M	I
Northern Pintail *Anas acuta*	← →	V	J							
Garganey *Anas querquedula*	← →	M	J	B	T	S	K	C	M	I
Australian Pochard *Aythya australis*	→	R?	J		T			C		I
Tufted Duck *Aythya fuligula*	←	V						C		

Megapodiidae: Scrubfowls, Brush-turkeys, Maleo

Bird Names (Scientific Names)	EX	ST	J	B	T	S	K	C	M	I
Philippine Scrubfowl *Megapodius cumingii*	←	R						C		
Sula Scrubfowl *Megapodius bernsteinii*	E	R						C	M	
Orange-footed Scrubfowl *Megapodius reinwardt*	→	R	J	B	T				M	I
Tanimbar Scrubfowl *Megapodius tenimberensis*	E	R							M	
Forsten's Megapode *Megapodius forstenii*	E	R							M	
Dusky Scrubfowl *Megapodius freycinet*	E	R							M	I
New Guinea Scrubfowl *Megapodius affinis*	P	R								I
Moluccan Scrubfowl *Eulipoa wallacei*	E	R							M	I
Red-billed Brush-turkey *Talegalla cuvieri*	E	R								I
Black-billed Brush-turkey *Talegalla fuscirostris*	P	R							M	I
Brown-collared Brush-turkey *Talegalla jobiensis*	P	R								I
Wattled Brush-turkey *Aepypodius arfakianus*	P	R								I
Waigeo Brush-turkey *Aepypodius bruijnii*	E	R								I
Maleo *Macrocephalon maleo*	E	R						C		

Phasianidae: Quails, Partridges, Junglefowls, Pheasants, Peafowl

Bird Names (Scientific Names)	EX	ST	J	B	T	S	K	C	M	I
Snow Mountain Quail *Anurophasis monorthonyx*	E	R								I
Long-billed Partridge *Rhizothera longirostris*	←	R				S	K			
Black Partridge *Melanoperdix nigra*	←	R				S	K			
Brown Quail *Coturnix australis*	→	R			T				M	I
Blue-breasted Quail *Coturnix chinensis*	← →	R	J	B	T	S	K	C	M	I
Grey-breasted Partridge *Arborophila orientalis*	←	R	J			S				
Chestnut-bellied Partridge *Arborophila javanica*	E	R	J							
Red-billed Partridge *Arborophila rubrirostris*	E	R				S				
Red-breasted Partridge *Arborophila hyperythra*	B	R					K			
Chestnut-necklaced Partridge *Tropicoperdix charltonii*	←	R				S				
Ferruginous Partridge *Caloperdix oculea*	←	R				S				
Crimson-headed Partridge *Haematortyx sanguiniceps*	B	R					K			
Crested Partridge *Rollulus rouloul*	←	R				S				
Hoogerwerf's Pheasant *Lophura hoogerwerfi*	E	R				S				
Salvadori's Pheasant *Lophura inornata*	E	R				S				
Crestless Fireback *Lophura erythrophthalma*	←	R				S				
Crested Fireback *Lophura ignita*	←	R				S				
Bulwer's Pheasant *Lophura bulweri*	B	R					K			
Red Junglefowl *Gallus gallus*	← F	R	J	B	F	S		F	F	
Green Junglefowl *Gallus varius*	E	R	J	B	T					
Bronze-tailed Peacock-pheasant *Polyplectron chalcurum*	E	R				S				
Bornean Peacock-pheasant *Polyplectron schleiermacheri*	B	R					K			
Green Peafowl *Pavo muticus*	←	R	J							

Turnicidae: Button-quails

Bird Names (Scientific Names)	EX	ST	J	B	T	S	K	C	M	I
Small Button-quail *Turnix sylvatica*	←	R	J	B						
Red-backed Button-quail *Turnix maculosa*	← →	R			T			C	M	I
Sumba Button-quail *Turnix everetti*	E	R			T					
Barred Button-quail *Turnix suscitator*	←	R	J	B	T	S		C		

Bird Names (Scientific Names)	Status		Distribution by Region							
	EX	ST	J	B	T	S	K	C	M	I

Gruidae: Brolga
☐ Brolga *Grus rubicunda* · · · → R · · · · · · · · · · I

Rallidae: Rails, Forest-rails, Crakes, Moorhens, Coots
☐ Lewin's Rail *Rallus pectoralis* · · · → R · · · T · · · I
☐ Slaty-breasted Rail *Gallirallus striatus* · · · ← R J B T S K C
☐ Buff-banded Rail *Gallirallus philippensis* · · · ←→ R\M? T C M I
☐ Barred Rail *Gallirallus torquatus* · · · ← R C M I
☐ Red-legged Crake *Rallina fasciata* · · · ←→ R\M J B T S M
☐ Slaty-legged Crake *Rallina eurizonoides* · · · ← M J S C M
☐ Red-necked Crake *Rallina tricolor* · · · → R?\M? T M I
☐ Chestnut Forest-rail *Rallicula rubra* · · · P R I
☐ White-striped Forest-rail *Rallicula leucospila* · · · E R I
☐ Mayr's Forest-rail *Rallicula mayri* · · · P R I
☐ Forbes's Forest-rail *Rallicula forbesi* · · · P R I
☐ Snoring Rail *Aramidopsis plateni* · · · E R C
☐ Blue-faced Rail *Gymnocrex rosenbergii* · · · E R C
☐ Bare-eyed Rail *Gymnocrex plumbeiventris* · · · → R M I
☐ Invisible Rail *Habroptila wallacii* · · · E R M
☐ New Guinea Flightless Rail *Megacrex inepta* · · · P R I
☐ Chestnut Rail *Eulabeornis castaneoventris* · · · → R M I
☐ Baillon's Crake *Porzana pusilla* · · · ←→ M\R? J B T S K C M I
☐ Ruddy-breasted Crake *Porzana fusca* · · · ← R\M J B T S K C
☐ Band-bellied Crake *Porzana paykullii* · · · ← M J S K C
☐ Spotless Crake *Porzana tabuensis* · · · ←→ R M I
☐ White-browed Crake *Poliolimnas cinerea* · · · ←→ R J B T S K C M I
☐ Common Bush-hen *Amaurornis olivacea* · · · ←→ R C I
☐ Isabelline Bush-hen *Amaurornis isabellina* · · · E R C
☐ White-breasted Waterhen *Amaurornis phoenicurus* · · · ← R B T S K C
☐ Watercock *Gallicrex cinerea* · · · ← M\R J B T S K C
☐ Dusky Moorhen *Gallinula tenebrosa* · · · → R T C M I
☐ Common Moorhen *Gallinula chloropus* · · · ← R J B T S K C
☐ Purple Swamphen *Porphyrio porphyrio* · · · ←→ R J B T S K C M I
☐ Common Coot *Fulica atra* · · · ←→ R J B T M I

Heliornithidae: Finfoots
☐ Masked Finfoot *Heliopais personata* · · · ← M? J S

Otididae: Bustards
☐ Australian Bustard *Ardeotis australis* · · · → R I

Jacanidae: Jacanas
☐ Comb-crested Jacana *Irediparra gallinacea* · · · → R T K C M I
☐ Pheasant-tailed Jacana *Hydrophasianus chirurgus* · · · ← M J B S K
☐ Bronze-winged Jacana *Metopidius indicus* · · · ← R J S

Rostratulidae: Painted Snipes
☐ Greater Painted Snipe *Rostratula benghalensis* · · · ←→ R J T S K

Haematopodidae: Oystercatchers
☐ Pied Oystercatcher *Haematopus longirostris* · · · → R M I

Charadriidae: Lapwings, Plovers, Dotterels
☐ Grey-headed Lapwing *Hoplopterus cinereus* · · · ← V C
☐ Red-wattled Lapwing *Hoplopterus indicus* · · · ← V S
☐ Javan Lapwing *Hoplopterus macropterus* · · · E E J
☐ Masked Lapwing *Hoplopterus miles* · · · → R\M M I
☐ Grey Plover *Pluvialis squatarola* · · · ←→ M\P J B T S K C M I
☐ Pacific Golden Plover *Pluvialis fulva* · · · ←→ M\P J B T S K C M I

Bird Names (Scientific Names)	Status EX	ST	J	B	T	S	K	C	M	I
Little Ringed Plover *Charadrius dubius*	← →	M\R?	J	B	T	S	K	C	M	I
Kentish Plover *Charadrius alexandrinus*	←	M	J	B	T	S	K		M	
Javan Plover *Charadrius javanicus*	E	R								
Red-capped Plover *Charadrius ruficapillus*	→	M	J		T					I
Malaysian Plover *Charadrius peronii*	←	R	J	B	T	S	K	C	M	
Long-billed Plover *Charadrius placidus*	←	V	J	B						
Lesser Sand-plover *Charadrius mongolus*	← →	M	J	B	T	S	K	C	M	I
Greater Sand-plover *Charadrius leschenaultii*	← →	M\P	J	B	T	S	K	C	M	I
Oriental Plover *Charadrius veredus*	← →	M	J	B	T	S	K	C	M	I
Red-kneed Dotterel *Erythrogonys cinctus*	→	R								
Scolopacidae: Curlews, Godwits, Snipes, Woodcocks, Sandpipers										
Little Curlew *Numenius minutus*	← →	P	J	B	T			C	M	I
Whimbrel *Numenius phaeopus*	← →	M	J	B	T	S	K	C	M	I
Eurasian Curlew *Numenius arquata*	←	M	J	B	T	S			M	
Far Eastern Curlew *Numenius madagascariensis*	← →	M\P	J	B	T	S	K	C	M	I
Black-tailed Godwit *Limosa limosa*	← →	M\P	J	B	T	S	K	C	M	I
Bar-tailed Godwit *Limosa lapponica*	← →	M	J	B	T	S	K	C	M	I
Common Redshank *Tringa totanus*	← →	M	J	B	T	S	K	C	M	I
Spotted Redshank *Tringa erythropus*	← →	V				S				
Marsh Sandpiper *Tringa stagnatilis*	← →	M	J	B	T	S	K	C	M	I
Common Greenshank *Tringa nebularia*	← →	M\P	J	B	T	S	K	C	M	I
Nordmann's Greenshank *Tringa guttifer*	←	M				S				
Lesser Yellowlegs *Tringa flavipes*		V				S				
Green Sandpiper *Tringa ochropus*	←	V	J	B		S	K	C		I
Wood Sandpiper *Tringa glareola*	← →	M\P	J	B	T	S	K	C	M	
Terek Sandpiper *Xenus cinereus*	← →	P\M	J	B	T	S	K	C	M	I
Common Sandpiper *Actitis hypoleucos*	← →	M\P	J	B	T	S	K	C	M	I
Grey-tailed Tattler *Heteroscelus brevipes*	← →	M\P	J	B	T	S	K	C	M	I
Wandering Tattler *Heteroscelus incanus*	→	V								I
Ruddy Turnstone *Arenaria interpres*	← →	M	J	B	T	S	K	C	M	I
Long-billed Dowitcher *Limnodromus scolopaceus*	P	V	J							
Asian Dowitcher *Limnodromus semipalmatus*	← →	M	J	B	T	S	K	C	M	I
Latham's Snipe *Gallinago hardwickii*	→	P?								I
Pintail Snipe *Gallinago stenura*	← →	M\R?	J	B	T	S	K	C	M	I
Swinhoe's Snipe *Gallinago megala*	← →	M\R?	J	B	T	S	K	C	M	I
Common Snipe *Gallinago gallinago*	←	M	J						M	
Horsfield's Woodcock *Scolopax saturata*	P	R	J							I
Sulawesi Woodcock *Scolopax celebensis*	E	R						C		
Moluccan Woodcock *Scolopax rochussenii*	E	R							M	
Great Knot *Calidris tenuirostris*	← →	M\P	J	B	T	S	K	C	M	I
Red Knot *Calidris canutus*	← →	P	J	B	T	S	K	C	M	I
Sanderling *Calidris alba*	← →	M	J	B	T	S	K	C	M	I
Rufous-necked Stint *Calidris ruficollis*	← →	P\M	J	B	T	S	K	C	M	I
Temminck's Stint *Calidris temminckii*	←	V					K			
Long-toed Stint *Calidris subminuta*	← →	P	J	B	T	S	K	S	M	I
Sharp-tailed Sandpiper *Calidris acuminata*	← →	ST	J	B	T	S	K	C	M	I
Curlew Sandpiper *Calidris ferruginea*	← →	P\M	J	B	T	S	K	C	M	I
Broad-billed Sandpiper *Limicola falcinellus*	← →	P			T	S	K	C	M	I
Ruff *Philomachus pugnax*	← →	V	J	B		S		C		
Recurvirostridae: Stilts										
White-headed Stilt *Himantopus leucocephalus*	← →	M\R	J	B	T	S	K	C	M	I
Phalaropodidae: Phalaropes										
Red-necked Phalarope *Phalaropus lobatus*	← →	M	J	B	T	S	K	C	M	I
Burhinidae: Thick-knees										
Bush Thick-knee *Burhinus magnirostris*	→	R								

Bird Names (Scientific Names)	EX	ST	J	B	T	S	K	C	M	I
☐ Beach Thick-knee *Esacus magnirostris*	← →	R	J	B	T	S	K	C	M	

Glareolidae: Pratincoles

Bird Names (Scientific Names)	EX	ST	J	B	T	S	K	C	M	I
☐ Australian Pratincole *Stiltia isabella*	→	M\R?	J	B	T	S	K	C	M	I
☐ Oriental Pratincole *Glareola maldivarum*	← →	M	J	B	T	S	K	C	M	I

Stercorariidae: Skuas, Jaegers

Bird Names (Scientific Names)	EX	ST	J	B	T	S	K	C	M	I
☐ South Polar Skua *Catharacta maccormicki*	← →	V				S				
☐ Pomarine Jaeger *Stercorarius pomarinus*	← →	M\P	J	B	T	S	K	C	M	I
☐ Arctic Jaeger *Stercorarius parasiticus*	→	P	J	B	T			C	M	
☐ Long-tailed Jaeger *Stercorarius longicaudus*	→	V	?	?	T					

Laridae: Gulls, Terns, Noddies

Bird Names (Scientific Names)	EX	ST	J	B	T	S	K	C	M	I
☐ Brown-headed Gull *Larus brunnicephalus*	←	V				S				
☐ Black-headed Gull *Larus ridibundus*	← →	M		B					M	I
☐ Sabine's Gull *Xema sabini*		V				S				
☐ Silver Gull *Larus novaehollandae*		V								
☐ Whiskered Tern *Chlidonias hybridus*	← →	M\P	J	B	T	S	K	C	M	I
☐ White-winged Tern *Chlidonias leucopterus*	← →	M	J	B	T	S	K	C	M	I
☐ Gull-billed Tern *Gelochelidon nilotica*	← →	M	J	B	T	S	K	C	M	I
☐ Caspian Tern *Hydroprogne caspia*	← →	M			T	S				I
☐ Common Tern *Sterna hirundo*	← →	M	J	B	T	S	K	C	M	I
☐ Roseate Tern *Sterna dougallii*	← →	M\R?	J	B		S	K		M	I
☐ Black-naped Tern *Sterna sumatrana*	← →	R	J	B	T	S	K	C	M	I
☐ Grey-backed Tern *Sterna lunata*	→	?							M	I
☐ Bridled Tern *Sterna anaethetus*	← →	R	J	B	T	S	K	C	M	I
☐ Sooty Tern *Sterna fuscata*	← →	M	J			S	K			
☐ Saunders' Tern *Sterna saundersi*	← →	M\R	J	B	T	S	K	C	M	I
☐ Great Crested Tern *Sterna bergii*	← →	M\R	J	B	T	S	K	C	M	I
☐ Lesser Crested Tern *Sterna bengalensis*	← →	M	J	B	T	S	K	C	M	I
☐ Chinese Crested Tern *Sterna bernsteini*	←	V							M	
☐ Brown Noddy *Anous stolidus*	← →	R	J		T	S	K	C	M	I
☐ Black Noddy *Anous minutus*	← →	V	J			S	K			I
☐ White Tern *Gygis alba*	← →	M	J		T	S			M	I

Columbidae: Green Pigeons, Fruit-doves, Imperial Pigeons, Doves, Crowned Pigeons

Bird Names (Scientific Names)	EX	ST	J	B	T	S	K	C	M	I
☐ Sunda Pin-tailed Pigeon *Treron oxyura*	E	R	J			S				
☐ Wedge-tailed Pigeon *Treron sphenura*	←	R	J		T	S				
☐ Large Green Pigeon *Treron capellei*	←	R	J			S	K			
☐ Pompadour Green Pigeon *Treron pompadora*	←	R							M	
☐ Thick-billed Green Pigeon *Treron curvirostra*	←	R	J			S	K			
☐ Grey-cheeked Green Pigeon *Treron griseicauda*	E	R	J	B				C	M	
☐ Sumba Green Pigeon *Treron teysmannii*	E	R			T					
☐ Flores Green Pigeon *Treron floris*	E	R			T					
☐ Timor Green Pigeon *Treron psittacea*	E	R			T					
☐ Cinnamon-headed Green Pigeon *Treron fulvicollis*	←	R				S	K			
☐ Little Green Pigeon *Treron olax*	←	R				S	K			
☐ Pink-necked Green Pigeon *Treron vernans*	←	R	J	B	T	S	K	C	M	
☐ Orange-breasted Green Pigeon *Treron bicincta*	←	R	J	B						
☐ Black-backed Fruit-dove *Ptilinopus cinctus*	E	R		B	T				M	
☐ Red-naped Fruit-dove *Ptilinopus dohertyi*	E	R			T					
☐ Pink-headed Fruit-dove *Ptilinopus porphyreus*	E	R	J	B		S				
☐ Red-eared Fruit-dove *Ptilinopus fischeri*	E	R						C		
☐ Jambu Fruit-dove *Ptilinopus jambu*	←	R	J			S	K			
☐ Maroon-chinned Fruit-dove *Ptilinopus subgularis*	E	R						C	M	
☐ Scarlet-breasted Fruit-dove *Ptilinopus bernsteinii*	E	R							M	
☐ Wompoo Fruit-dove *Ptilinopus magnificus*	→	R								I
☐ Pink spotted Fruit-dove *Ptilinopus perlatus*	P	R							M	I
☐ Ornate Fruit-dove *Ptilinopus ornatus*	P	R								I

Bird Names (Scientific Names)	Status		Distribution by Region							
	EX	ST	J	B	T	S	K	C	M	I
☐ Orange-fronted Fruit-dove *Ptilinopus aurantiifrons*	P	R							M	I
☐ Wallace's Fruit-dove *Ptilinopus wallacii*	E	R			T				M	I
☐ Superb Fruit-dove *Ptilinopus superbus*	→	R						C	M	I
☐ Rose-crowned Fruit-dove *Ptilinopus regina*	→	R			T				M	
☐ Coroneted Fruit-dove *Ptilinopus coronulatus*	P	R							M	I
☐ Beautiful Fruit-dove *Ptilinopus pulchellus*	P	R								I
☐ Blue-capped Fruit-dove *Ptilinopus monacha*	E	R							M	
☐ White-bibbed Fruit-dove *Ptilinopus rivoli*	→	R							M	I
☐ Yellow-bibbed Fruit-dove *Ptilinopus solomonensis*	→	R								I
☐ Claret-breasted Fruit-dove *Ptilinopus viridis*	→	R							M	I
☐ Orange-bellied Fruit-dove *Ptilinopus iozonus*	P	R							M	I
☐ Grey-headed Fruit-dove *Ptilinopus hyogastra*	E	R							M	
☐ Carunculated Fruit-dove *Ptilinopus granulifrons*	E	R							M	
☐ Black-naped Fruit-dove *Ptilinopus melanospila*	←	R	J	B	T	S	K	C	M	
☐ Dwarf Fruit-dove *Ptilinopus naina*	P	R								I
☐ White-bellied Imperial Pigeon *Ducula forsteni*	E	R						C	M	
☐ Grey-headed Imperial Pigeon *Ducula radiata*	E	R						C		
☐ Green Imperial Pigeon *Ducula aenea*	←	R	J	B	T	S	K	C	M	
☐ White-eyed Imperial Pigeon *Ducula perspicillata*	E	R							M	I
☐ Blue-tailed Imperial Pigeon *Ducula concinna*	E	R						C	M	I
☐ Spice Imperial Pigeon *Ducula myristicivora*	E	R							M	I
☐ Purple-tailed Imperial Pigeon *Ducula rufigaster*	P	R								I
☐ Cinnamon-bellied Imperial Pigeon *Ducula basilica*	E	R							M	
☐ Rufescent Imperial Pigeon *Ducula chalconota*	P	R								I
☐ Pink-headed Imperial Pigeon *Ducula rosacea*	E	R	J		T			C	M	
☐ Grey Imperial Pigeon *Ducula pickeringii*	←	R					K	C		
☐ Pinon's Imperial Pigeon *Ducula pinon*	P	R							M	I
☐ Collared Imperial Pigeon *Ducula mullerii*	P	R							M	I
☐ Zoe's Imperial Pigeon *Ducula zoeae*	P	R							M	I
☐ Mountain Imperial Pigeon *Ducula badia*	←	R	J			S	K			
☐ Dark-backed Imperial Pigeon *Ducula lacernulata*	E	R	J	B	T					
☐ Timor Imperial Pigeon *Ducula cineracea*	E	R			T				M	
☐ Pied Imperial Pigeon *Ducula bicolor*	←	R\M?	J	B	T	S	K	C	M	I
☐ White Imperial Pigeon *Ducula luctuosa*	E	R						C	M	
☐ Torresian Imperial Pigeon *Ducula spilorrhoa*	→	R							M	I
☐ Sombre Pigeon *Cryptophaps poecilorrhoa*	E	R						C		
☐ Papuan Mountain-pigeon *Gymnophaps albertisii*	→	R							M	I
☐ Long-tailed Mountain-pigeon *Gymnophaps mada*	E	R							M	
☐ Rock Pigeon *Columba livia*	← F	R	F	F	F	F	F	F	F	F
☐ Metallic Pigeon *Columba vitiensis*	←→	R			T		K	C	M	I
☐ Silvery Pigeon *Columba argentina*	←	R				S	K			
☐ Sulawesi Black Pigeon *Turacoena manadensis*	E	R						C	M	
☐ Timor Black Pigeon *Turacoena modesta*	E	R			T				M	
☐ Barred Cuckoo-dove *Macropygia unchall*	←	R	J		T	S				
☐ Slender-billed Cuckoo-dove *Macropygia amboinensis*	→	R	J	B	T	S		C	M	I
☐ Black-billed Cuckoo-dove *Macropygia nigrirostris*	→	R								I
☐ Little Cuckoo-dove *Macropygia ruficeps*	←	R	J	B	T	S	K			
☐ Great Cuckoo-dove *Reinwardtoena reinwardtii*	P	R							M	I
☐ Island Collared Dove *Streptopelia bitorquata*	←	R	J	B	T					
☐ Red Collared Dove *Streptopelia tranquebarica*	←	R	J					F		
☐ Spotted Dove *Streptopelia chinensis*	← F	R	J	B	T	S	K	F	F	
☐ Bar-shouldered Dove *Geopelia humeralis*	→	R								I
☐ Zebra Dove *Geopelia striata*	←	R	J	B	T	S	K	F	F	
☐ Barred Dove *Geopelia maugei*	E	R			T			F	F	
☐ Peaceful Dove *Geopelia placida*	→	R								I
☐ Emerald Dove *Chalcophaps indica*	←→	R	J	B	T	S	K	C	M	I
☐ Stephan's Dove *Chalcophaps stephani*	→	R						C	M	I
☐ New Guinea Bronzewing *Henicophaps albifrons*	P	R							M	I
☐ Cinnamon Ground-dove *Gallicolumba rufigula*	P	R							M	I

Bird Names (Scientific Names)	EX	ST	J	B	T	S	K	C	M	I
☐ Sulawesi Ground-dove *Gallicolumba tristigmata*	E	R						C		
☐ Bronze Ground-dove *Gallicolumba beccarii*	→	R								I
☐ White-bibbed Ground-dove *Gallicolumba jobiensis*	→	R								I
☐ Wetar Ground-dove *Gallicolumba hoedtii*	E	R			T				M	
☐ Thick-billed Ground Pigeon *Trugon terrestris*	P	R								I
☐ Pheasant Pigeon *Otidiphaps nobilis*	P	R							M	I
☐ Nicobar Pigeon *Caloenas nicobarica*	←→	R	J		T	S	K	C	M	I
☐ Western Crowned Pigeon *Goura cristata*	E	R						F		I
☐ Southern Crowned Pigeon *Goura scheepmakeri*	P	R								I
☐ Victoria Crowned Pigeon *Goura victoria*	P	R								I

Psittacidae: Lories, Lorikeets, Parrots, Cockatoos, Hanging-parrots

Bird Names (Scientific Names)	EX	ST	J	B	T	S	K	C	M	I
☐ Black Lory *Chalcopsitta atra*	E	R								I
☐ Yellow-streaked Lory *Chalcopsitta sintillata*	P	R							M	I
☐ Brown Lory *Chalcopsitta duivenbodei*	P	R								I
☐ Biak Red Lory *Eos cyanogenia*	E	R								I
☐ Blue-streaked Lory *Eos reticulata*	E	R			T				M	
☐ Violet-necked Lory *Eos squamata*	E	R							M	I
☐ Red-and-blue Lory *Eos histrio*	E	R						C		
☐ Moluccan Red Lory *Eos bornea*	E	R							M	
☐ Blue-eared Lory *Eos semilarvata*	E	R							M	
☐ Ornate Lorikeet *Trichoglossus ornatus*	E	R						C		
☐ Rainbow Lorikeet *Trichoglossus haematodus*	→	R	J	B	T			C	M	I
☐ Yellow-and-green Lorikeet *Trichoglossus flavoviridis*	E	R						C	M	
☐ Olive-headed Lorikeet *Trichoglossus euteles*	E	R			T				M	
☐ Iris Lorikeet *Psitteuteles iris*	E	R			T				M	
☐ Goldie's Lorikeet *Psitteuteles goldiei*	P	R								I
☐ Dusky Lory *Pseudeos fuscata*	P	R								I
☐ Black-capped Lory *Lorius lory*	P	R								I
☐ Purple-naped Lory *Lorius domicella*	E	R							M	
☐ Chattering Lory *Lorius garrulus*	E	R							M	
☐ Blue-fronted Lorikeet *Charmosyna toxopei*	E	R							M	
☐ Red-flanked Lorikeet *Charmosyna placentis*	→	R							M	I
☐ Red-fronted Lorikeet *Charmosyna rubronotata*	P	R								I
☐ Striated Lorikeet *Charmosyna multistriata*	P	R								I
☐ Pygmy Lorikeet *Charmosyna wilhelminae*	P	R								I
☐ Little Red Lorikeet *Charmosyna pulchella*	P	R								I
☐ Josephine's Lorikeet *Charmosyna josefinae*	P	R								I
☐ Papuan Lorikeet *Charmosyna papou*	P	R								I
☐ Plum-faced Lorikeet *Oreopsittacus arfaki*	P	R								I
☐ Yellow-billed Lorikeet *Neopsittacus musschenbroekii*	P	R								I
☐ Orange-billed Lorikeet *Neopsittacus pullicauda*	P	R								I
☐ Large Fig-parrot *Psittaculirostris desmarestii*	P	R								I
☐ Salvadori's Fig-parrot *Psittaculirostris salvadorii*	E	R								I
☐ Edwards's Fig-parrot *Psittaculirostris edwardsii*	P	R								I
☐ Orange-breasted Fig-parrot *Opopsitta gulielmitertii*	P	R							M	I
☐ Double-eyed Fig-parrot *Opopsitta diophthalma*	→	R							M	I
☐ Red-breasted Pygmy Parrot *Micropsitta bruijnii*	→	R							M	I
☐ Yellow-capped Pygmy Parrot *Micropsitta keiensis*	P	R							M	I
☐ Geelvink Pygmy Parrot *Micropsitta geelvinkiana*	E	R								I
☐ Buff-faced Pygmy Parrot *Micropsitta pusio*	P	R								I
☐ Palm Cockatoo *Probosciger aterrimus*	→	R							M	I
☐ Yellow-crested Cockatoo *Cacatua sulphurea*	E	R	J	B	T			C		
☐ Sulphur-crested Cockatoo *Cacatua galerita*	→	R							M	I
☐ Salmon-crested Cockatoo *Cacatua moluccensis*	E	R							M	
☐ White Cockatoo *Cacatua alba*	E	R							M	
☐ Tanimbar Corella *Cacatua goffini*	E	R							M	
☐ Little Corella *Cacatua sanguinea*	→	R								I
☐ Pesquet's Parrot *Psittrichas fulgidus*	P	R								I

Bird Names (Scientific Names)	EX	ST	J	B	T	S	K	C	M	I
Eclectus Parrot *Eclectus roratus*	→	R			T				M	I
Red-cheeked Parrot *Geoffroyus geoffroyi*	→	R			T				M	I
Blue-collared Parrot *Geoffroyus simplex*	P	R								I
Yellow-breasted Racquet-tail *Prioniturus flavicans*	E	R						C		
Golden-mantled Racquet-tail *Prioniturus platurus*	E	R						C	M	
Buru Racquet-tail *Prioniturus mada*	E	R							M	
Blue-naped Parrot *Tanygnathus lucionensis*	←	R					K	C		
Blue-backed Parrot *Tanygnathus sumatranus*	←	R						C		
Black-lored Parrot *Tanygnathus gramineus*	←	R							M	
Great-billed Parrot *Tanygnathus megalorynchos*	←	R		?	T			C	M	I
Red-breasted Parakeet *Psittacula alexandri*	←	R	J	B		S	K			
Long-tailed Parakeet *Psittacula longicauda*	←	R				S	K			
Olive-shouldered Parrot *Aprosmictus jonquillaceus*	E	R			T				M	
Red-winged Parrot *Aprosmictus erythropterus*	→	R								I
Moluccan King Parrot *Alisterus amboinensis*	E	R						C	M	I
Papuan King Parrot *Alisterus chloropterus*	P	R								I
Brehm's Tiger-parrot *Psittacella brehmii*	P	R								I
Painted Tiger-parrot *Psittacella picta*	P	R								I
Modest Tiger-parrot *Psittacella modesta*	P	R								I
Madarasz's Tiger-parrot *Psittacella madaraszi*	P	R								I
Blue-rumped Parrot *Psittinus cyanurus*	←	R				S	K			
Blue-crowned Hanging-parrot *Loriculus galgulus*	←	R	J			S	K			
Sulawesi Hanging-parrot *Loriculus stigmatus*	E	R						C		
Moluccan Hanging-parrot *Loriculus amabilis*	E	R						C	M	
Sangihe Hanging-parrot *Loriculus catamene*	E	R						C		
Papuan Hanging-parrot *Loriculus aurantiifrons*	P	R								I
Red-billed Hanging-parrot *Loriculus exilis*	E	R						C		
Wallace's Hanging-parrot *Loriculus flosculus*	E	R			T					
Yellow-throated Hanging-parrot *Loriculus pusillus*	E	R	J	B						

Cuculidae: Hawk-cuckoos, Cuckoos, Bronze Cuckoos, Koels, Malkohas, Coucals

Bird Names (Scientific Names)	EX	ST	J	B	T	S	K	C	M	I
Chestnut-winged Cuckoo *Clamator coromandus*	←	M	J	B		S	K	C		
Sulawesi Hawk-cuckoo *Cuculus crassirostris*	E	R						C		
Large Hawk-cuckoo *Cuculus sparverioides*	←	R\M	J	B		S	K	C		
Moustached Hawk-cuckoo *Cuculus vagans*	←	R	J			S	K			
Hodgson's Hawk-cuckoo *Cuculus fugax*	←	R\M	J	B		S	K	C	M	
Indian Cuckoo *Cuculus micropterus*	←	R\M	J			S	K	C	M	
Eurasian Cuckoo *Cuculus canorus*	←	V	J							
Oriental Cuckoo *Cuculus saturatus*	←→	R\M	J	B	T	S	K	C	M	I
Pallid Cuckoo *Cuculus pallidus*	→	V			T					I
Banded Bay Cuckoo *Cacomantis sonneratii*	←	R	J			S	K			
Plaintive Cuckoo *Cacomantis merulinus*	←	R	J			S	K	C		
Rusty-breasted Cuckoo *Cacomantis sepulcralis*	←	R	J	B	T	S	K	C	M	
Brush Cuckoo *Cacomantis variolosus*	←	R\M			T				M	I
Chestnut-breasted Cuckoo *Cacomantis castaneiventris*	→	R\M							M	I
Moluccan Cuckoo *Cacomantis heinrichi*	E	R							M	
Fan-tailed Cuckoo *Cacomantis flabelliformis*	→	R\M							M	I
Long-billed Cuckoo *Rhamphomantis megarhynchus*	P	R							M	I
Black-eared Cuckoo *Chrysococcyx osculans*	→	M							M	I
Asian Emerald Cuckoo *Chrysococcyx maculatus*	←	M				S				
Violet Cuckoo *Chrysococcyx xanthorhynchus*	←	R	J			S	K			
Horsfield's Bronze Cuckoo *Chrysococcyx basalis*	←→	M	J	B	T	S	K	C	M	I
Shining Bronze Cuckoo *Chrysococcyx lucidus*	→	M			T				M	I
Little Bronze Cuckoo *Chrysococcyx minutillus*	←→	R	J			S	K	C	M	I
Gould's Bronze Cuckoo *Chrysococcyx russatus*	←→	R			T		K	C		I
Green-cheeked Bronze Cuckoo *Chrysococcyx rufomerus*	E	R							M	
Pied Bronze Cuckoo *Chrysococcyx crassirostris*	E	R							M	
Rufous-throated Bronze Cuckoo *Chrysococcyx ruficollis*	P	R								I
White-eared Bronze Cuckoo *Chrysococcyx meyeri*	P	R								I

Bird Names (Scientific Names)	EX	ST	J	B	T	S	K	C	M	I
☐ White-crowned Koel *Caliechthrus leucolophus*	P	R								I
☐ Drongo Cuckoo *Surniculus lugubris*	←	R\M	J	B		S	K	C	M	
☐ Dwarf Koel *Microdynamis parva*	P	R								I
☐ Asian Koel *Eudynamys scolopacea*	←	R\M	J	B		S	K	C	M	
☐ Black-billed Koel *Eudynamys melanorhyncha*	E	R						C	M	
☐ Australian Koel *Eudynamys cyanocephala*	→	M			T				M	I
☐ Channel-billed Cuckoo *Scythrops novaehollandiae*	→	R\M			T			C	M	I
☐ Black-bellied Malkoha *Rhopodytes diardi*	←	R				S	K			
☐ Chestnut-bellied Malkoha *Rhopodytes sumatranus*	←	R				S	K			
☐ Green-billed Malkoha *Rhopodytes tristis*	←	R	J			S				
☐ Raffles's Malkoha *Rhinortha chlorophaea*	←	R				S	K			
☐ Red-billed Malkoha *Zanclostomus javanicus*	←	R	J			S	K			
☐ Yellow-billed Malkoha *Rhamphococcyx calyorhynchus*	E	R						C		
☐ Chestnut-breasted Malkoha *Rhamphococcyx curvirostris*	←	R	J	B		S	K			
☐ Sumatran Ground-cuckoo *Carpococcyx viridis*	E	R				S				
☐ Bornean Ground-cuckoo *Carpococcyx radiatus*	B	R					K			
☐ Goliath Coucal *Centropus goliath*	E	R							M	
☐ Greater Black Coucal *Centropus menbeki*	P	R							M	I
☐ Biak Coucal *Centropus chalybeus*	E	R								I
☐ Pheasant Coucal *Centropus phasianinus*	→	R			T					I
☐ Kai Coucal *Centropus spilopterus*	E	R							M	
☐ Lesser Black Coucal *Centropus bernsteini*	P	R								I
☐ Short-toed Coucal *Centropus rectunguis*	←	R				S	K			
☐ Greater Coucal *Centropus sinensis*	←	R	J	B		S	K			
☐ Javan Coucal *Centropus nigrorufus*	E	R	J							
☐ Lesser Coucal *Centropus bengalensis*	←	R	J	B	T	S	K	C	M	
☐ Bay Coucal *Centropus celebensis*	E	R						C		

Tytonidae: Owls, Grass-owls

Bird Names (Scientific Names)	EX	ST	J	B	T	S	K	C	M	I
☐ Barn Owl *Tyto alba*	←→	R	J	B	T	S		C	M	
☐ Sulawesi Owl *Tyto rosenbergii*	E	R						C		
☐ Minahassa Masked Owl *Tyto inexpectata*	E	R						C		
☐ Taliabu Masked Owl *Tyto nigrobrunnea*	E	R							M	
☐ Lesser Masked Owl *Tyto sororcula*	E	R			T				M	
☐ Australian Masked Owl *Tyto novaehollandiae*	→	R								I
☐ Greater Sooty Owl *Tyto tenebricosa*	→	R								I
☐ Eastern Grass-owl *Tyto capensis*	→	R?			T			C		I
☐ Oriental Bay Owl *Phodilus badius*	←	R	J	B		S	K			

Strigidae: Scopsowls, Owlets, Owls, Boobooks, Wood-owls

Bird Names (Scientific Names)	EX	ST	J	B	T	S	K	C	M	I
☐ White-fronted Scopsowl *Otus sagittatus*	←	R				S				
☐ Reddish Scopsowl *Otus rufescens*	←	R	J			S	K			
☐ Mountain Scopsowl *Otus spilocephalus*	←	R				S	K			
☐ Sulawesi Scopsowl *Otus manadensis*	E	R						C		
☐ Flores Scopsowl *Otus alfredi*	E	R			T					
☐ Javan Scopsowl *Otus angelinae*	E	R	J							
☐ Simeulue Scopsowl *Otus umbra*	E	R				S				
☐ Oriental Scopsowl *Otus sunia*	←	V				S				
☐ Moluccan Scopsowl *Otus magicus*	←	R			T	S		C	M	I
☐ Rajah's Scopsowl *Otus brookii*	B	R	J			S				
☐ Collared Scopsowl *Otus bakkamoena*	←	R	J	B		S	K			
☐ Mentawai Scopsowl *Otus mentawi*	E	R				S				
☐ Wallace's Scopsowl *Otus silvicola*	E	R			T					
☐ Barred Eagle-owl *Bubo sumatranus*	←	R	J	B		S	K			
☐ Buffy Fish-owl *Ketupa ketupu*	←	R	J	B		S	K			
☐ Collared Owlet *Glaucidium brodiei*	←	R				S	K			
☐ Javan Owlet *Glaucidium castanopterum*	E	R	J	?						
☐ Papuan Hawk-owl *Uroglaux dimorpha*	P	R								I
☐ Rufous Owl *Ninox rufa*	→	R							M	I

Bird Names (Scientific Names)	Status	Distribution by Region								
	EX	ST	J	B	T	S	K	C	M	I
☐ Barking Owl *Ninox connivens*	→	R							M	I
☐ Sumba Boobook *Ninox rudolfi*	E	R			T					
☐ Southern Boobook *Ninox novaeseelandiae*	→	R			T				M	
☐ Brown Boobook *Ninox scutulata*	←→	R\M	J	B	T	S	K	C	M	
☐ Ochre-bellied Boobook *Ninox ochracea*	E	R						C		
☐ Moluccan Boobook *Ninox squamipila*	E	R			T				M	
☐ Papuan Boobook *Ninox theomacha*	P	R								I
☐ Speckled Boobook *Ninox punctulata*	E	R						C		
☐ Spotted Wood-owl *Strix seloputo*	←	R	J							
☐ Brown Wood-owl *Strix leptogrammica*	←	R	J			S	K			
Podargidae: Frogmouths										
☐ Papuan Frogmouth *Podargus papuensis*	→	R							M	I
☐ Marbled Frogmouth *Podargus ocellatus*	→	R							M	I
☐ Large Frogmouth *Batrachostomus auritus*	←	R				S	K			
☐ Dulit Frogmouth *Batrachostomus harterti*	B	R					K			
☐ Gould's Frogmouth *Batrachostomus stellatus*	←	R				S	K			
☐ Pale-headed Frogmouth *Batrachostomus poliolophus*	B	R				S	K			
☐ Javan Frogmouth *Batrachostomus javensis*	←	R	J			S	K			
☐ Sunda Frogmouth *Batrachostomus cornutus*	B	R	J			S	K			
Aegothelidae: Owlet-nightjars										
☐ Moluccan Owlet-nightjar *Aegotheles crinifrons*	E	R							M	
☐ Feline Owlet-nightjar *Aegotheles insignis*	P	R								I
☐ Barred Owlet-nightjar *Aegotheles bennettii*	P	R							M	I.
☐ Wallace's Owlet-nightjar *Aegotheles wallacii*	P	R							M	I
☐ Mountain Owlet-nightjar *Aegotheles albertisi*	P	R								I
☐ Archbold's Owlet-nightjar *Aegotheles archboldi*	P	R								I
Caprimulgidae: Nightjars										
☐ Spotted Nightjar *Eurostopodus argus*	→	R							M	I
☐ White-throated Nightjar *Eurostopodus mystacalis*	→	M								I
☐ Diabolical Nightjar *Eurostopodus diabolicus*	E	R						C		
☐ Papuan Nightjar *Eurostopodus papuensis*	P	R								I
☐ Mountain Nightjar *Eurostopodus archboldi*	P	R								I
☐ Malaysian Eared Nightjar *Eurostopodus temminckii*	←	R				S	K			
☐ Great Eared Nightjar *Eurostopodus macrotis*	←	R				S		C	M	
☐ Grey Nightjar *Caprimulgus indicus*	←	R\M	J			S	K		M	I
☐ Large-tailed Nightjar *Caprimulgus macrurus*	←→	R	J	B	T	S	K	C	M	I
☐ Sulawesi Nightjar *Caprimulgus celebensis*	←	R						C		
☐ Savanna Nightjar *Caprimulgus affinis*	E	R	J	B	T	S	K	C	M	
☐ Bonaparte's Nightjar *Caprimulgus concretus*	B	R				S	K			
☐ Salvadori's Nightjar *Caprimulgus pulchellus*	E	R	J			S				
Apodidae: Swifts, Swiftlets, Needletails, Palm-swifts										
☐ Waterfall Swift *Hydrochous gigas*	←	R	J			S				
☐ Bare-legged Swiftlet *Aerodramus nuditarsus*	P	R								I
☐ Three-toed Swiftlet *Aerodramus papuensis*	P	R								I
☐ Volcano Swiftlet *Aerodramus vulcanorum*	E	R	J							
☐ Edible-nest Swiftlet *Aerodramus fuciphagus*	←	R	J	B	T	S	K	C		
☐ Uniform Swiftlet *Aerodramus vanikorensis*	←→	R						C	M	I
☐ Mossy-nest Swiftlet *Aerodramus salangana*	←	R	J	B		S	K			
☐ Mountain Swiftlet *Aerodramus hirundinaceus*	P	R								I
☐ Moluccan Swiftlet *Aerodramus infuscatus*	E	R						C	M	
☐ Black-nest Swiftlet *Aerodramus maximus*	←	R	J			S	K			
☐ White-bellied Swiftlet *Collocalia esculenta*	←→	R	J	B	T	S	K	C	M	I
☐ White-throated Needletail *Hirundapus caudacutus*	←→	P	J	B	T			C	M	I
☐ Silver-backed Needletail *Hirundapus cochinchinensis*	←	P	J	B		S				
☐ Brown-backed Needletail *Hirundapus giganteus*	←	R\M	J	B		S	K			

Bird Names (Scientific Names)	Status	Distribution by Region

	EX ..ST......J ....B ..T....S....K..C ...M ..I

☐ Purple Needletail *Hirundapus celebensis* ....← .....R ....C ....
☐ Silver-rumped Swift *Rhaphidura leucopygialis* ....← .....R ....J ....S ....K ....
☐ Papuan Needletail *Mearnsia novaeguineae* ....P ......R I
☐ Fork-tailed Swift *Apus pacificus* ....← →.....P ....J .....B....T.....S ....K....C ....M....I
☐ Little Swift *Apus affinis* ....← →.....R ....J .....B....T.....S ....K....C ....
☐ Asian Palm-swift *Cypsiurus balasiensis* ....← .....R ....J .....B....T.....S ....K....C ....

Hemiprocnidae: Tree-swifts
☐ Grey-rumped Tree-swift *Hemiprocne longipennis* ....← ....R ....J .....B....T.....S ....K....C ....M....
☐ Moustached Tree-swift *Hemiprocne mystacea* ....→ ....R ....M....I
☐ Whiskered Tree-swift *Hemiprocne comata* ....← ....R ....S ....K...........

Trogonidae: Trogons
☐ Blue-tailed Trogon *Harpactes reinwardtii* ....E ....R ....J ....S.................
☐ Red-naped Trogon *Harpactes kasumba* ....← ....R ....S ....K...........
☐ Diard's Trogon *Harpactes diardii* ....← ....R ....S ....K...........
☐ Whitehead's Trogon *Harpactes whiteheadi* ....B ....R ....K...........
☐ Cinnamon-rumped Trogon *Harpactes orrhophaeus* ....← ....R ....S ....K...........
☐ Scarlet-rumped Trogon *Harpactes duvaucelii* ....← ....R ....S ....K...........
☐ Orange-breasted Trogon *Harpactes oreskios* ....← ....R ....J ....S ....K...........
☐ Red-headed Trogon *Harpactes erythrocephalus* ....← ....R ....S ....

Alcedinidae: Kingfishers, Kookaburras
☐ Common Kingfisher *Alcedo atthis* ....← → ....M\R ....J ....B....T.....S ....K....C ....M....I
☐ Blue-eared Kingfisher *Alcedo meninting* ....← .....R ....J .....B....T.....S ....K....C ....M....
☐ Azure Kingfisher *Alcedo azurea* ....→ .....R ....M....I
☐ Blue-banded Kingfisher *Alcedo euryzona* ....← .....R ....J ....S ....K...........
☐ Small Blue Kingfisher *Alcedo coerulescens* ....E ....R ....J .....B....T....S...........
☐ Little Kingfisher *Alcedo pusilla* ....→ .....R ....M....I
☐ Variable Dwarf Kingfisher *Ceyx lepidus* ....← → ....R ....M....I
☐ Oriental Dwarf Kingfisher *Ceyx erithacus* ....R\M ....J .....B....T....S...........
☐ Sulawesi Dwarf Kingfisher *Ceyx fallax* ....E ....R ....C ....
☐ Stork-billed Kingfisher *Pelargopsis capensis* ....← .....R ....J .....B....T....S ....K...........
☐ Black-billed Kingfisher *Pelargopsis melanorhyncha* ....E ....R ....C ....M....
☐ Banded Kingfisher *Lacedo pulchella* ....← .....R ....S ....K...........
☐ Blue-winged Kookaburra *Dacelo leachii* ....→ ....R I
☐ Spangled Kookaburra *Dacelo tyro* ....P ....R ....M....I
☐ Rufous-bellied Kookaburra *Dacelo gaudichaud* ....P ....R ....M....I
☐ Shovel-billed Kingfisher *Clytoceyx rex* ....P ....R I
☐ Hook-billed Kingfisher *Melidora macrorrhina* ....P ....R I
☐ Lilac-cheeked Kingfisher *Cittura cyanotis* ....E ....R ....C ....
☐ Ruddy Kingfisher *Halcyon coromanda* ....← ....R\M ....J ....S ....K....C ....
☐ White-throated Kingfisher *Halcyon smyrnensis* ....← ....R ....S ....
☐ Black-capped Kingfisher *Halcyon pileata* ....← ....M ....J ....S ....K....C ....
☐ Javan Kingfisher *Halcyon cyanoventris* ....E ....R ....J .....B.................
☐ Blue-black Kingfisher *Halcyon nigrocyanea* ....P ....R I
☐ Blue-and-white Kingfisher *Halcyon diops* ....E ....R ....M....
☐ Lazuli Kingfisher *Halcyon lazuli* ....E ....R ....M....
☐ Forest Kingfisher *Halcyon macleayii* ....→ ....R\M ....T ....M....I
☐ Yellow-billed Kingfisher *Halcyon torotoro* ....→ ....R ....M....I
☐ Mountain Kingfisher *Halcyon megarhyncha* ....P ....R I
☐ Cinnamon-banded Kingfisher *Halcyon australasia* ....E ....R ....T ....M....
☐ Sacred Kingfisher *Halcyon sancta* ....→ ....M ....J .....B....T....S ....K....C ....M....I
☐ Sombre Kingfisher *Halcyon funebris* ....E ....R ....M....
☐ Collared Kingfisher *Halcyon chloris* ....← → ....R ....J .....B....T....S ....K....C ....M....I
☐ Beach Kingfisher *Halcyon saurophaga* ....→ ....R ....M....I
☐ White-rumped Kingfisher *Caridonax fulgidus* ....E ....R ....T ....
☐ Rufous-collared Kingfisher *Actenoides concretus* ....← ....R ....S ....
☐ Green-backed Kingfisher *Actenoides monachus* ....E ....R ....C ....

Bird Names (Scientific Names)

Bird Names (Scientific Names)	EX	ST	J	B	T	S	K	C	M	I
Scaly-breasted Kingfisher *Actenoides princeps*	E	R						C		
Common Paradise-kingfisher *Tanysiptera galatea*	P	R							M	I
Biak Paradise-kingfisher *Tanysiptera riedelii*	E	R								I
Kofiau Paradise-kingfisher *Tanysiptera ellioti*	E	R								I
Numfor Paradise-kingfisher *Tanysiptera carolinae*	E	R								I
Little Paradise-kingfisher *Tanysiptera hydrocharis*	P	R								I
Buff-breasted Paradise-kingfisher *Tanysiptera sylvia*	→	R								I
Red-breasted Paradise-kingfisher *Tanysiptera nympha*	P	R								I

Meropidae: Bee-eaters

Bird Names (Scientific Names)	EX	ST	J	B	T	S	K	C	M	I
Chestnut-headed Bee-eater *Merops leschenaulti*	←	R	J	B		S				
Blue-tailed Bee-eater *Merops philippinus*	←→	R	J	B	T	S	K	C		I
Rainbow Bee-eater *Merops ornatus*	→	M		B	T			C	M	I
Blue-throated Bee-eater *Merops viridis*	←	R\M	J			S	K			
Red-bearded Bee-eater *Nyctyornis amictus*	←	R				S	K			
Purple-bearded Bee-eater *Meropogon forsteni*	E	R						C		

Coraciidae: Rollers, Dollarbirds

Bird Names (Scientific Names)	EX	ST	J	B	T	S	K	C	M	I
Purple-winged Roller *Coracias temminckii*	E	R						C		
Common Dollarbird *Eurystomus orientalis*	←→	R\M	J	B	T	S	K	C	M	I
Purple Dollarbird *Eurystomus azureus*	E	R							M	

Upupidae: Hoopoe

Bird Names (Scientific Names)	EX	ST	J	B	T	S	K	C	M	I
Hoopoe *Upupa epops*	←	V				S				

Bucerotidae: Hornbills

Bird Names (Scientific Names)	EX	ST	J	B	T	S	K	C	M	I
White-crowned Hornbill *Berenicornis comatus*	←	R				S	K			
Bushy-crested Hornbill *Anorrhinus galeritus*	←	R				S	K			
Tarictic Hornbill *Penelopides exarhatus*	E	R						C		
Wrinkled Hornbill *Rhyticeros corrugatus*	←	R				S	K			
Red-knobbed Hornbill *Rhyticeros cassidix*	E	R						C		
Wreathed Hornbill *Rhyticeros undulatus*	←	R	J	B						
Plain-pouched Hornbill *Rhyticeros subruficollis*	←	R				S				
Blyth's Hornbill *Rhyticeros plicatus*	→	R							M	I
Sumba Hornbill *Rhyticeros everetti*	E	R			T					
Black Hornbill *Anthracoceros malayanus*	←	R				S	K			
Asian Pied Hornbill *Anthracoceros albirostris*	←	R	J	B		S	K			
Rhinoceros Hornbill *Buceros rhinoceros*	←	R	J			S	K			
Great Hornbill *Buceros bicornis*	←	R				S				
Helmeted Hornbill *Rhinoplax vigil*	←	R				S	K			

Capitonidae: Barbets

Bird Names (Scientific Names)	EX	ST	J	B	T	S	K	C	M	I
Fire-tufted Barbet *Psilopogon pyrolophus*	←	R				S				
Lineated Barbet *Megalaima lineata*	←	R	J	B						
Brown-throated Barbet *Megalaima corvina*	E	R	J							
Gold-whiskered Barbet *Megalaima chrysopogon*	←	R				S	K			
Red-crowned Barbet *Megalaima rafflesii*	←	R				S	K			
Red-throated Barbet *Megalaima mystacophanos*	←	R				S	K			
Black-banded Barbet *Megalaima javensis*	E	R	J							
Black-browed Barbet *Megalaima oorti*	←	R				S				
Mountain Barbet *Megalaima monticola*	B	R					K			
Yellow-crowned Barbet *Megalaima henricii*	←	R				S	K			
Orange-fronted Barbet *Megalaima armillaris*	E	R	J	B						
Golden-naped Barbet *Megalaima pulcherrima*	B	R					K			
Blue-eared Barbet *Megalaima australis*	←	R	J	B		S	K			
Black-throated Barbet *Megalaima eximia*	B	R					K			
Coppersmith Barbet *Megalaima haemacephala*	←	R	J	B		S	K			
Brown Barbet *Calorhamphus fuliginosus*	←	R				S	K			

Bird Names (Scientific Names)	EX	ST	J	B	T	S	K	C	M	I
Indicatoridae: Honeyguides										
Malaysian Honeyguide *Indicator archipelagicus*	←	R				S	K			
Picidae: Piculets, Woodpeckers										
Speckled Piculet *Picumnus innominatus*	←	R				S				
Rufous Piculet *Sasia abnormis*	←	R	J			S	K			
Rufous Woodpecker *Celeus brachyurus*	←	R	J			S	K			
Laced Woodpecker *Picus vittatus*	←	R	J	B		S				
Grey-faced Woodpecker *Picus canus*	←	R				S				
Greater Yellownape *Picus flavinucha*	←	R				S				
Checker-throated Yellownape *Picus mentalis*	←	R	J			S	K			
Lesser Yellownape *Picus chlorolophus*	←	R				S				
Crimson-winged Yellownape *Picus puniceus*	←	R	J			S	K			
Banded Woodpecker *Picus miniaceus*	←	R	J			S	K			
Common Goldenback *Dinopium javanense*	←	R	J	B		S	K			
Olive-backed Woodpecker *Dinopium rafflesii*	←	R				S	K			
Buff-rumped Woodpecker *Meiglyptes tristis*	←	R	J			S	K			
Buff-necked Woodpecker *Meiglyptes tukki*	←	R				S	K			
Great Slaty Woodpecker *Mulleripicus pulverulentus*	←	R				S	K			
Ashy Woodpecker *Mulleripicus fulvus*	E	R						C		
White-bellied Woodpecker *Dryocopus javensis*	←	R	J	B		S	K			
Fulvous-breasted Woodpecker *Dendrocopos macei*	←	R	J	B		S				
Grey-capped Woodpecker *Dendrocopos canicapillus*	←	R				S				
Brown-capped Woodpecker *Dendrocopos moluccensis*	←	R	J	B	T	S	K			
Sulawesi Woodpecker *Dendrocopos temminckii*	E	R						C		
Grey-and-buff Woodpecker *Hemicircus concretus*	←	R	J			S	K			
Maroon Woodpecker *Blythipicus rubiginosus*	←	R				S	K			
Orange-backed Woodpecker *Reinwardtipicus validus*	←	R				S	K			
Greater Goldenback *Chrysocolaptes lucidus*	←	R	J	B		S	K			
Eurylamidae: Broadbills										
Dusky Broadbill *Corydon sumatranus*	←	R				S	K			
Black-and-red Broadbill *Cymbirhynchus macrorhynchos*	←	R				S	K			
Banded Broadbill *Eurylaimus javanicus*	←	R	J			S	K			
Black-and-yellow Broadbill *Eurylaimus ochromalus*	←	R				S	K			
Silver-breasted Broadbill *Serilophus lunatus*	←	R				S				
Long-tailed Broadbill *Psarisomus dalhousiae*	←	R				S				
Green Broadbill *Calyptomena viridis*	←	R				S	K			
Hose's Broadbill *Calyptomena hosii*	B	R					K			
Pittidae: Pittas										
Schneider's Pitta *Pitta schneideri*	E	R				S				
Giant Pitta *Pitta caerulea*	←	R				S	K			
Banded Pitta *Pitta guajana*	←	R	J	B		S	K			
Red-bellied Pitta *Pitta erythrogaster*	← →	R\M						C	M	I
Blue-banded Pitta *Pitta arquata*	B	R					K			
Garnet Pitta *Pitta granatina*	←	R				S	K			
Black-crowned Pitta *Pitta venusta*	E	R				S				
Sula Pitta *Pitta doherty*	E	R							M	
Blue-headed Pitta *Pitta baudii*	B	R					K			
Hooded Pitta *Pitta sordida*	← P	RM	J			S	K	C	M	I
Fairy Pitta *Pitta nympha*		M?					K			
Ivory-breasted Pitta *Pitta maxima*	E	R							M	
Blue-winged Pitta *Pitta moluccensis*	←	M				S	K	C		
Mangrove Pitta *Pitta megarhyncha*	←	R					K			
Elegant Pitta *Pitta elegans*	E	R	J	B	T			C	M	
Noisy Pitta *Pitta versicolor*	→	R								I

APPENDIX

BIRDS CHECKLIST

294

Bird Names (Scientific Names)	Status		Distribution by Region							
	EX	ST	J	B	T	S	K	C	M	I
Alaudidae: Bush-larks										
☐ Singing Bush-lark *Mirafra javanica*	→	R	J	B	T		K			I
Hirundinidae: Martins, Swallows										
☐ Sand Martin *Riparia riparia*	← P	V					K			
☐ Barn Swallow *Hirundo rustica*	← →	M	J	B	T	S	K	C	M	I
☐ Pacific Swallow *Hirundo tahitica*	← →	R	J	B	T	S	K	C	M	I
☐ Red-rumped Swallow *Hirundo daurica*	← P	V				S				
☐ Striated Swallow *Hirundo striolata*	←	R	J	B	T	S			M	
☐ Tree Martin *Cecropis nigricans*	→	M			T				M	I
☐ Fairy Martin *Cecropis ariel*	→	V			T				M	I
☐ Asian Martin *Delichon dasypus*	←	M	J	B		S	K			
Motacillidae: Wagtails, Pipits										
☐ Forest Wagtail *Dendronanthus indicus*	←	M	J			S				
☐ Yellow Wagtail *Motacilla flava*	← →	M	J	B	T	S	K	C	M	I
☐ Grey Wagtail *Motacilla cinerea*	← →	R\M	J	B	T	S	K	C	M	I
☐ Richard's Pipit *Anthus novaeseelandiae*	← →	R	J	B	T	S	K	C	M	I
☐ Pechora Pipit *Anthus gustavi*	←	V			T			C	M	
☐ Red-throated Pipit *Anthus cervinus*	←	V					K	C		
☐ Alpine Pipit *Anthus gutturalis*	P	R								I
Campephagidae: Cuckoo-shrikes, Cicadabirds, Trillers, Minivets										
☐ Malaysian Cuckoo-shrike *Coracina javensis*	←	R	J							
☐ Wallacean Cuckoo-shrike *Coracina personata*	E	R			T				M	
☐ Black-faced Cuckoo-shrike *Coracina novaehollandiae*	→	R\M		B	T			C	M	I
☐ Buru Cuckoo-shrike *Coracina fortis*	E	R							M	
☐ Moluccan Cuckoo-shrike *Coracina atriceps*	E	R							M	
☐ Slaty Cuckoo-shrike *Coracina schistacea*	E	R						C	M	
☐ Stout-billed Cuckoo-shrike *Coracina caeruleogrisea*	P	R							M	I
☐ Caerulean Cuckoo-shrike *Coracina temminckii*	E	R						C		
☐ Sunda Cuckoo-shrike *Coracina larvata*	B	R	J			S	K			
☐ Bar-bellied Cuckoo-shrike *Coracina striata*	←	R	J			S	K			
☐ Pied Cuckoo-shrike *Coracina bicolor*	E	R						C		
☐ Yellow-eyed Cuckoo-shrike *Coracina lineata*	→	R							M	I
☐ Boyer's Cuckoo-shrike *Coracina boyeri*	P	R								I
☐ White-rumped Cuckoo-shrike *Coracina leucopygia*	E	R						C		
☐ White-bellied Cuckoo-shrike *Coracina papuensis*	→	R							M	I
☐ Hooded Cuckoo-shrike *Coracina longicauda*	P	R								I
☐ Halmahera Cuckoo-shrike *Coracina parvula*	E	R							M	
☐ Pygmy Cuckoo-shrike *Coracina abbotti*	E	R						C		
☐ Common Cicadabird *Coracina tenuirostris*	→	M\R			T			C	M	I
☐ Kai Cicadabird *Coracina dispar*	E	R							M	
☐ Sumba Cicadabird *Coracina dohertyi*	E	R			T					
☐ Sula Cicadabird *Coracina sula*	E	R							M	
☐ Sulawesi Cicadabird *Coracina morio*	E	R						C		
☐ Pale Cicadabird *Coracina ceramensis*	E	R							M	
☐ Black-shouldered Cicadabird *Coracina incerta*	P	R								I
☐ Grey-headed Cuckoo-shrike *Coracina schisticeps*	P	R								I
☐ Black Cuckoo-shrike *Coracina melas*	P	R							M	I
☐ Black-bellied Cuckoo-shrike *Coracina montana*	P	R								I
☐ Lesser Cuckoo-shrike *Coracina fimbriata*	←	R	J	B		S	K			
☐ Golden Cuckoo-shrike *Campochaera sloetii*	P	R								I
☐ Jeffery *Chlamydochaera jefferyi*	B	R					K			
☐ Pied Triller *Lalage nigra*	←	R	J			S	K			
☐ Sulawesi Triller *Lalage leucopygialis*	E	R						C	M	
☐ White-shouldered Triller *Lalage sueurii*	E	R\M?	J	B	T			C	M	
☐ Rufous-bellied Triller *Lalage aurea*	E	R							M	
☐ Black-browed Triller *Lalage atrovirens*	P	R							M	I

Bird Names (Scientific Names)

Bird Names (Scientific Names)	Status	Distribution by Region							
	EX...ST	J	B	T	S	K	C	M	I
☐ Varied Triller *Lalage leucomela*	→ ...R							M	I
☐ Ashy Minivet *Pericrocotus divaricatus*	← ...M				S	K	C		
☐ Small Minivet *Pericrocotus cinnamomeus*	← ...R	J	B			K			
☐ Fiery Minivet *Pericrocotus igneus*	← ...R				S	K			
☐ Little Minivet *Pericrocotus lansbergei*	E ...R			T					
☐ Grey-chinned Minivet *Pericrocotus solaris*	← ...R				S	K			
☐ Sunda Minivet *Pericrocotus miniatus*	E ...R	J			S				
☐ Scarlet Minivet *Pericrocotus flammeus*	← ...R	J	B	T	S	K			
☐ Bar-winged Hemipus *Hemipus picatus*	← ...R				S	K			
☐ Black-winged Hemipus *Hemipus hirundinaceus*	← ...R	J	B		S	K			
☐ Large Wood-shrike *Tephrodornis gularis*	← ...R	J			S	K			

Pycnonotidae: Bulbuls

Bird Names (Scientific Names)	Status	J	B	T	S	K	C	M	I
☐ Straw-headed Bulbul *Pycnonotus zeylanicus*	← ...R	J			S	K			
☐ Cream-striped Bulbul *Pycnonotus leucogrammicus*	E ...R				S				
☐ Spot-necked Bulbul *Pycnonotus tympanistrigus*	E ...R				S				
☐ Black-and-white Bulbul *Pycnonotus melanoleucos*	← ...R				S	K			
☐ Black-headed Bulbul *Pycnonotus atriceps*	← ...R	J	B		S	K			
☐ Black-crested Bulbul *Pycnonotus melanicterus*	← ...R	J	B		S	K			
☐ Scaly-breasted Bulbul *Pycnonotus squamatus*	← ...R	J			S	K			
☐ Grey-bellied Bulbul *Pycnonotus cyaniventris*	← ...R				S	K			
☐ Sooty-headed Bulbul *Pycnonotus aurigaster*	← ...R	J	B		F	F	F		F
☐ Puff-backed Bulbul *Pycnonotus eutilotus*	← ...R				S	K			
☐ Blue-wattled Bulbul *Pycnonotus nieuwenhuisii*	E ...R				S	K			
☐ Orange-spotted Bulbul *Pycnonotus bimaculatus*	E ...R	J	B		S				
☐ Flavescent Bulbul *Pycnonotus flavescens*	← ...R				S	K			
☐ Yellow-vented Bulbul *Pycnonotus goiavier*	← ...R	J	B	T	S	K	F		
☐ Olive-winged Bulbul *Pycnonotus plumosus*	← ...R	J			S	K			
☐ Cream-vented Bulbul *Pycnonotus simplex*	← ...R	J			S	K			
☐ Red-eyed Bulbul *Pycnonotus brunneus*	← ...R	J			S	K			
☐ Spectacled Bulbul *Pycnonotus erythropthalmos*	← ...R				S	K			
☐ Finsch's Bulbul *Criniger finschii*	← ...R				S	K			
☐ Ochraceous Bulbul *Criniger ochraceus*	← ...R				S	K			
☐ Grey-cheeked Bulbul *Criniger bres*	← ...R	J	B		S	K			
☐ Yellow-bellied Bulbul *Criniger phaeocephalus*	← ...R				S	K			
☐ Hook-billed Bulbul *Setornis criniger*	B ...R				S	K			
☐ Buff-vented Bulbul *Hypsipetes charlottae*	← ...R				S	K			
☐ Hairy-backed Bulbul *Hypsipetes criniger*	← ...R				S	K			
☐ Golden Bulbul *Hypsipetes affinis*	E ...R						C	M	
☐ Common Streaked Bulbul *Hypsipetes malaccensis*	← ...R				S	K			
☐ Sunda Streaked Bulbul *Hypsipetes virescens*	E ...R	J			S				
☐ Ashy Bulbul *Hypsipetes flavala*	← ...R				S	K			

Irenidae: Ioras, Leafbirds, Fairy Bluebirds

Bird Names (Scientific Names)	Status	J	B	T	S	K	C	M	I
☐ Common Iora *Aegithina tiphia*	← ...R	J	B		S	K			
☐ Green Iora *Aegithina viridissima*	← ...R				S	K			
☐ Greater Green Leafbird *Chloropsis sonnerati*	← ...R	J			S	K			
☐ Lesser Green Leafbird *Chloropsis cyanopogon*	← ...R				S	K			
☐ Blue-winged Leafbird *Chloropsis cochinchinensis*	← ...R	J			S	K			
☐ Golden-fronted Leafbird *Chloropsis aurifrons*	← ...R				S	K			
☐ Blue-masked Leafbird *Chloropsis venusta*	E ...R				S				
☐ Asian Fairy Bluebird *Irena puella*	← ...R	J			S	K			

Laniidae: Shrikes

Bird Names (Scientific Names)	Status	J	B	T	S	K	C	M	I
☐ Tiger Shrike *Lanius tigrinus*	← ...M	J	B		S	K	C		
☐ Brown Shrike *Lanius cristatus*	← ...M	J	B	T	S	K	C	M	I
☐ Long-tailed Shrike *Lanius schach*	← ...R	J	B	T	S	K		M	
☐ Bornean Bristlehead *Pityriasis gymnocephala*	B ...R					K			

Bird Names (Scientific Names)

Bird Names (Scientific Names)	Status	EX	ST	J	B	T	S	K	C	M	I

Turdidae: Shortwings, Forktails, Cochoas, Geomalia, Thrushes, Ground-robins

Bird Names (Scientific Names)	Status	EX	ST	J	B	T	S	K	C	M	I
☐ Great Shortwing *Heinrichia calligyna*	E		R						C		
☐ Lesser Shortwing *Brachypteryx leucophrys*	←		R	J	B	T	S				
☐ White-browed Shortwing *Brachypteryx montana*	←		R	J		T	S	K			
☐ Northern Scrub-robin *Drymodes superciliaris*	→		R							M	I
☐ Siberian Blue Robin *Luscinia cyane*	←		M				S	K			
☐ Oriental Magpie-robin *Copsychus saularis*	←		R	J	B		S	K			
☐ White-rumped Shama *Copsychus malabaricus*	←		R	J			S	K			
☐ White-browed Shama *Copsychus stricklandi*	B		R					K			
☐ Rufous-tailed Shama *Copsychus pyrropygus*	←		R				S	K			
☐ Sunda Blue Robin *Cinclidium diana*	E		R	J			S				
☐ Lesser Forktail *Enicurus velatus*	E		R	J			S				
☐ Chestnut-naped Forktail *Enicurus ruficapillus*	←		R				S	K			
☐ White-crowned Forktail *Enicurus leschenaulti*	←		R	J	B		S	K			
☐ Sumatran Cochoa *Cochoa beccarii*	E		R				S				
☐ Javan Cochoa *Cochoa azurea*	E		R	J							
☐ Common Stone-chat *Saxicola torquata*			V				S				
☐ Pied Bush-chat *Saxicola caprata*	←→		R		B	T			C	M	I
☐ White-bellied Bush-chat *Saxicola gutturalis*	E		R			T					
☐ Blue Rock-thrush *Monticola solitarius*	← P		M				S		C	M	
☐ Shiny Whistling-thrush *Myophonus melanurus*	E		R				S				
☐ Sunda Whistling-thrush *Myophonus glaucinus*	B		R	J	B		S	K			
☐ Blue Whistling-thrush *Myophonus caeruleus*	←		R	J			S				
☐ Geomalia *Geomalia heinrichi*	E		R						C		
☐ Slaty-backed Thrush *Zoothera schistacea*	E		R							M	
☐ Moluccan Thrush *Zoothera dumasi*	E		R							M	
☐ Chestnut-capped Thrush *Zoothera interpres*	←		R	J		T	S				
☐ Chestnut-backed Thrush *Zoothera dohertyi*	E		R			T					
☐ Red-backed Thrush *Zoothera erythronota*	E		R						C	M	
☐ Orange-banded Thrush *Zoothera peronii*	E		R			T				M	
☐ Orange-headed Thrush *Zoothera citrina*	←		R\M	J	B		S				
☐ Siberian Thrush *Zoothera sibirica*	←		M	J	B		S				
☐ Sunda Thrush *Zoothera andromedae*	←		R	J	B		S			M	
☐ Scaly Thrush *Zoothera dauma*	←		R	J	B	T	S				
☐ Fawn-breasted Thrush *Zoothera machiki*	E		R							M	
☐ Russet-tailed Thrush *Zoothera heinei*	→		R								I
☐ Greater Ground-robin *Amalocichla sclateriana*	P		R								I
☐ Lesser Ground-robin *Amalocichla incerta*	P		R								I
☐ Sulawesi Thrush *Cataponera turdoides*	E		R						C		
☐ Island Thrush *Turdus poliocephalus*	←→		R	J	B	T	S		C	M	I
☐ Eye-browed Thrush *Turdus obscurus*	←		M	J	B	T	S		C		

Orthonychidae: Logrunners, Jewel-babblers, Rail Babbler, Ifritas

Bird Names (Scientific Names)	Status	EX	ST	J	B	T	S	K	C	M	I
☐ Logrunner *Orthonyx temminckii*	→		R								I
☐ Papuan Whipbird *Androphobus viridis*	E		R								I
☐ Painted Quail-thrush *Cinclosoma ajax*	P		R								I
☐ Spotted Jewel-babbler *Ptilorrhoa leucosticta*	P		R								I
☐ Blue Jewel-babbler *Ptilorrhoa caerulescens*	P		R								I
☐ Chestnut-backed Jewel-babbler *Ptilorrhoa castanonota*	P		R								I
☐ Rail Babbler *Eupetes macrocerus*	←		R				S	K			
☐ Lesser Melampitta *Melampitta lugubris*	P		R								I
☐ Greater Melampitta *Melampitta gigantea*	P		R								I
☐ Blue-capped Ifrita *Ifrita kowaldi*	P		R								I

Timalidae: Babblers, Wren-babblers, Laughing-thrushes, Fulvettas, Crocias, Malia

Bird Names (Scientific Names)	Status	EX	ST	J	B	T	S	K	C	M	I
☐ Black-capped Babbler *Pellorneum capistratum*	←		R	J			S	K			
☐ Temminck's Babbler *Trichastoma tickelli*	←		R	J				K			
☐ Buttikofer's Babbler *Trichastoma buettikoferi*	E		R				S				
☐ Short-tailed Babbler *Trichastoma malaccense*	←		R				S	K			

Bird Names (Scientific Names)

Bird Names (Scientific Names)	EX	ST	J	B	T	S	K	C	M	I
☐ White-chested Babbler *Trichastoma rostratum*	←	R				S	K			
☐ Ferruginous Babbler *Trichastoma bicolor*	←	R				S	K			
☐ Horsfield's Babbler *Trichastoma sepiarium*	←	R	J	B		S	K			
☐ Sulawesi Babbler *Trichastoma celebense*	E	R						C		
☐ Abbott's Babbler *Trichastoma abbotti*	←	R	J			S	K			
☐ Black-browed Babbler *Trichastoma perspicillatum*	E	R					K			
☐ Moustached Babbler *Malacopteron magnirostre*	←	R				S	K			
☐ Sooty-capped Babbler *Malacopteron affine*	←	R				S	K			
☐ Scaly-crowned Babbler *Malacopteron cinereum*	←	R	J			S	K			
☐ Rufous-crowned Babbler *Malacopteron magnum*	←	R				S	K			
☐ Grey-breasted Babbler *Malacopteron albogulare*	←	R				S	K			
☐ Chestnut-backed Scimitar-babbler *Pomatorhinus montanus*	←	R	J	B		S	K			
☐ Rufous Babbler *Pomatostomus isidorei*	P	R								I
☐ Grey-crowned Babbler *Pomatostomus temporalis*	→	R								I
☐ Long-billed Wren-babbler *Rimator malacoptilus*	←	R				S				
☐ Bornean Wren-babbler *Ptilocichla leucogrammica*	B	R					K			
☐ Striped Wren-babbler *Kenopia striata*	←	R				S	K			
☐ Rusty-breasted Wren-babbler *Napothera rufipectus*	E	R				S				
☐ Black-throated Wren-babbler *Napothera atrigularis*	B	R					K			
☐ Large Wren-babbler *Napothera macrodactyla*	←	R	J			S				
☐ Marbled Wren-babbler *Napothera marmorata*	←	R				S				
☐ Mountain Wren-babbler *Napothera crassa*	B	R					K			
☐ Eye-browed Wren-babbler *Napothera epilepidota*	←	R	J			S	K			
☐ Pygmy Wren-babbler *Pnoepyga pusilla*	←	R	J		T	S				
☐ Rufous-fronted Babbler *Stachyris rufifrons*	←	R				S				
☐ Golden Babbler *Stachyris chrysaea*	←	R				S				
☐ White-breasted Babbler *Stachyris grammiceps*	E	R	J							
☐ Grey-throated Babbler *Stachyris nigriceps*	←	R				S	K			
☐ Grey-headed Babbler *Stachyris poliocephala*	←	R				S	K			
☐ Spot-necked Babbler *Stachyris striolata*	←	R				S				
☐ Chestnut-rumped Babbler *Stachyris maculata*	←	R				S	K			
☐ White-necked Babbler *Stachyris leucotis*	←	R				S	K			
☐ Black-throated Babbler *Stachyris nigricollis*	←	R				S	K			
☐ White-bibbed Babbler *Stachyris thoracica*	E	R	J							
☐ Chestnut-winged Babbler *Stachyris erythroptera*	←	R				S	K			
☐ Crescent-chested Babbler *Stachyris melanothorax*	E	R	J	B						
☐ Grey-cheeked Tit-babbler *Macronous flavicollis*	E	R	J							
☐ Striped Tit-babbler *Macronous gularis*	←	R	J			S	K			
☐ Fluffy-backed Tit-babbler *Macronous ptilosus*	←	R				S	K			
☐ Chestnut-capped Babbler *Timalia pileata*	←	R				S				
☐ Sunda Laughing-thrush *Garrulax palliatus*	B	R				S	K			
☐ Rufous-fronted Laughing-thrush *Garrulax rufifrons*	E	R	J							
☐ White-crested Laughing-thrush *Garrulax leucolophus*	←	R				S				
☐ Black Laughing-thrush *Garrulax lugubris*	←	R				S				
☐ Chestnut-capped Laughing-thrush *Garrulax mitratus*	←	R				S				
☐ Silver-eared Mesia *Leiothrix argentauris*	←	R				S				
☐ White-browed Shrike-babbler *Pteruthius flaviscapis*	←	R	J			S	K			
☐ Chestnut-fronted Shrike-babbler *Pteruthius aenobarbus*	←	R	J							
☐ Brown Fulvetta *Alcippe brunneicauda*	←	R				S	K			
☐ Javan Fulvetta *Alcippe pyrrhoptera*	E	R	J							
☐ Spotted Crocias *Crocias albonotatus*	E	R	J							
☐ Long-tailed Sibia *Heterophasia picaoides*	←	R				S				
☐ Chestnut-crested Yuhina *Yuhina everetti*	B	R					K			
☐ White-bellied Yuhina *Yuhina zantholeuca*	←	R				S	K			
☐ Malia *Malia grata*	E	R						C		

Sylviidae: Tesias, Stubtails, Warblers, Cisticolas, Prinias, Tailorbirds

Bird Names (Scientific Names)	EX	ST	J	B	T	S	K	C	M	I
☐ Javan Tesia *Tesia superciliaris*	E	R	J							
☐ Russet-capped Tesia *Tesia everetti*	E	R			T					

Bird Names (Scientific Names)

Bird Names (Scientific Names)	EX	ST	J	B	T	S	K	C	M	I
☐ Timor Stubtail *Urosphena subulata*	E	R			T				M	
☐ Bornean Stubtail *Urosphena whiteheadi*	B	R					K			
☐ Sunda Bush-warbler *Cettia vulcania*	←	R	J	B	T	S	K			
☐ Tanimbar Bush-warbler *Cettia carolinae*	E	R							M	
☐ Russet Bush-warbler *Bradypterus seebohmi*	←	R	J	B	T					
☐ Chestnut-backed Bush-warbler *Bradypterus castaneus*	E	R						C	M	
☐ Tawny Grassbird *Megalurus timoriensis*	←→	R			T			C	M	I
☐ Striated Grassbird *Megalurus palustris*	←	R	J	B						
☐ Little Grassbird *Megalurus gramineus*	→	R								I
☐ Buff-banded Bushbird *Buettikoferella bivittata*	E	R			T					
☐ Lanceolated Warbler *Locustella lanceolata*	←	M	J						M	
☐ Pallas's Warbler *Locustella certhiola*	←	M	J	B		S	K	C		
☐ Middendorff's Warbler *Locustella ochotensis*	←	V						C	M	
☐ Gray's Warbler *Locustella fasciolata*	← P	M						C	M	I
☐ Black-browed Reed-warbler *Acrocephalus bistrigiceps*	←	V				S				
☐ Clamorous Reed-warbler *Acrocephalus stentoreus*	←→	R	J		T		K	C	M	I
☐ Oriental Reed-warbler *Acrocephalus orientalis*	←	M	J	B	T	S	K	C	M	I
☐ Zitting Cisticola *Cisticola juncidis*	←→	R	J	B	T	S		C	M	I
☐ Golden-headed Cisticola *Cisticola exilis*	←→	R	J	B	T	S	K	C	M	I
☐ Brown Prinia *Prinia polychroa*	←	R	J							
☐ Hill Prinia *Prinia atrogularis*	←	R				S				
☐ Bar-winged Prinia *Prinia familiaris*	E	R	J	B		S				
☐ Yellow-bellied Prinia *Prinia flaviventris*	←	R	J			S	K			
☐ Plain Prinia *Prinia inornata*	E	R	J							
☐ Mountain Tailorbird *Orthotomus cuculatus*	←	R	J	B	T	S	K	C	M	
☐ Common Tailorbird *Orthotomus sutorius*	←	R	J							
☐ Dark-necked Tailorbird *Orthotomus atrogularis*	←	R				S	K			
☐ Rufous-tailed Tailorbird *Orthotomus sericeus*	←	R				S	K			
☐ Ashy Tailorbird *Orthotomus ruficeps*	←	R	J	B		S				
☐ Olive-backed Tailorbird *Orthotomus sepium*	E	R	J	?	T					
☐ Inornate Leaf-warbler *Phylloscopus inornatus*	←	M				S				
☐ Arctic Leaf-warbler *Phylloscopus borealis*	←→	M	J	B	T	S	K	C	M	
☐ Eastern Crowned Leaf-warbler *Phylloscopus coronatus*	←	M				S				
☐ Mountain Leaf-warbler *Phylloscopus trivirgatus*	←	R	J	B		S				
☐ Sulawesi Leaf-warbler *Phylloscopus sarasinorum*	E	R						C		
☐ Timor Leaf-warbler *Phylloscopus presbytes*	E	R			T					
☐ Island Leaf-warbler *Phylloscopus poliocephalus*	→	R							M	I
☐ Chestnut-crowned Warbler *Seicercus castaniceps*	←	R				S				
☐ Yellow-breasted Warbler *Seicercus montis*	←	R				S	K			
☐ White-rumped Warbler *Seicercus grammiceps*	E	R	J	B		S				
☐ Yellow-bellied Warbler *Abroscopus superciliaris*	←	R	J	B		S				

Muscicapidae: Flycatchers, Blue Flycatchers

Bird Names (Scientific Names)	EX	ST	J	B	T	S	K	C	M	I
☐ Streak-breasted Rhinomyias *Rhinomyias addita*	E	R							M	
☐ Russet-backed Rhinomyias *Rhinomyias oscillans*	E	R			T					
☐ Fulvous-chested Rhinomyias *Rhinomyias olivacea*	←	R	J	B		S				
☐ Grey-chested Rhinomyias *Rhinomyias umbratilis*	←	R				S	K			
☐ Rufous-tailed Rhinomyias *Rhinomyias ruficauda*	←	R				S				
☐ Henna-tailed Rhinomyias *Rhinomyias colonus*	E	R						C	M	
☐ Grey-streaked Flycatcher *Muscicapa griseisticta*	←	M			T	S		C	M	I
☐ Dark-sided Flycatcher *Muscicapa sibirica*	←	M	J			S	K			
☐ Asian Brown Flycatcher *Muscicapa dauurica*	←	R\M		B	T	S	K	C		
☐ Sumba Brown Flycatcher *Muscicapa segregata*	E	R			T					
☐ Ferruginous Flycatcher *Muscicapa ferruginea*	←	M				S				
☐ Verditer Flycatcher *Eumyias thalassina*	←	R				S	K			
☐ Island Flycatcher *Eumyias panayensis*	←	R						C	M	
☐ Indigo Flycatcher *Eumyias indigo*	B	R	J			S	K			
☐ Yellow-rumped Flycatcher *Ficedula zanthopygia*	←	M	J	B		S	K			
☐ Narcissus Flycatcher *Ficedula narcissina*	←	M					K			

Bird Names (Scientific Names)	Status		Distribution by Region							
	EX	ST	J	B	T	S	K	C	M	I
☐ Mugimaki Flycatcher *Ficedula mugimaki*	←	M	J	B		S	K	C	M	
☐ Rufous-browed Flycatcher *Ficedula solitaris*	←	R				S				
☐ Snowy-browed Flycatcher *Ficedula hyperythra*	←	R	J	B	T	S	K	C	M	
☐ Rufous-chested Flycatcher *Ficedula dumetoria*	←	R	J		T	S	K		M	
☐ Rufous-throated Flycatcher *Ficedula rufigula*	E	R						C		
☐ Cinnamon-chested Flycatcher *Ficedula buruensis*	E	R							M	
☐ Damar Flycatcher *Ficedula henrici*	E	R							M	
☐ Sumba Flycatcher *Ficedula harterti*	E	R			T					
☐ Lompobattang Flycatcher *Ficedula bonthaina*	E	R						C		
☐ Little Pied Flycatcher *Ficedula westermanni*	←	R	J	B	T	S	K	C	M	
☐ Black-banded Flycatcher *Ficedula timorensis*	E	R			T					
☐ Blue-and-white Flycatcher *Cyanoptila cyanomelana*	←	M	J			S	K			
☐ Large Niltava *Niltava grandis*	←	R				S				
☐ Rufous-vented Niltava *Niltava sumatrana*	←	R				S				
☐ Timor Blue Flycatcher *Cyornis hyacinthinus*	E	R			T				M	
☐ Blue-fronted Blue Flycatcher *Cyornis hoevelli*	E	R						C		
☐ Matinan Blue Flycatcher *Cyornis sanfordi*	E	R						C		
☐ Dark Blue Flycatcher *Cyornis concretus*	←	R				S	K			
☐ Rueck's Blue Flycatcher *Cyornis ruckii*	E	R								
☐ Pale Blue Flycatcher *Cyornis unicolor*	←	R	J			S	K			
☐ Hill Blue Flycatcher *Cyornis banyumas*	←	R	J				K			
☐ Bornean Blue Flycatcher *Cyornis superbus*	B	R					K			
☐ Sunda Blue Flycatcher *Cyornis caerulatus*	B	R				S	K			
☐ Malaysian Blue Flycatcher *Cyornis turcosus*	←	R				S	K			
☐ Tickell's Blue Flycatcher *Cyornis tickelliae*	←	R?				S	K			
☐ Mangrove Blue Flycatcher *Cyornis rufigastra*	←	R	J	B		S	K	C		
☐ Pygmy Blue Flycatcher *Muscicapella hodgsoni*	←	R				S	K			
☐ Grey-headed Flycatcher *Culicicapa ceylonensis*	←	R	J	B	T	S	K			
☐ Citrine Flycatcher *Culicicapa helianthea*	←	R						C	M	

Maluridae: Fairy Wrens

Bird Names (Scientific Names)	EX	ST	J	B	T	S	K	C	M	I
☐ Orange-crowned Fairy Wren *Clytomyias insignis*	P	R								I
☐ Wallace's Fairy Wren *Malurus wallacii*	P	R							M	I
☐ Broad-billed Fairy Wren *Malurus grayi*	P	R								I
☐ White-shouldered Fairy Wren *Malurus alboscapulatus*	P	R								I
☐ Emperor Fairy Wren *Malurus cyanocephalus*	P	R							M	I

Acanthizidae: Mouse-warblers, Scrub-wrens, Thornbills, Gerygones

Bird Names (Scientific Names)	EX	ST	J	B	T	S	K	C	M	I
☐ Rusty Mouse-warbler *Crateroscelis murina*	P	R							M	I
☐ Bicoloured Mouse-warbler *Crateroscelis nigrorufa*	P	R								I
☐ Mountain Mouse-warbler *Crateroscelis robusta*	P	R								I
☐ Beccari's Scrub-wren *Sericornis beccarii*	→	R							M	I
☐ Large Scrub-wren *Sericornis nouhuysi*	P	R							M	I
☐ Pale-billed Scrub-wren *Sericornis spilodera*	P	R							M	I
☐ Buff-faced Scrub-wren *Sericornis perspicillatus*	P	R								I
☐ Vogelkop Scrub-wren *Sericornis rufescens*	E	R								I
☐ Papuan Scrub-wren *Sericornis papuensis*	P	R							I	
☐ Grey-green Scrub-wren *Sericornis arfakianus*	P	R								I
☐ New Guinea Thornbill *Acanthiza murina*	P	R								I
☐ Grey Gerygone *Gerygone cinerea*	P	R								I
☐ Green-backed Gerygone *Gerygone chloronotus*	→	R							M	I
☐ Fairy Gerygone *Gerygone palpebrosa*	→	R							M	I
☐ Yellow-bellied Gerygone *Gerygone chrysogaster*	P	R							M	I
☐ Large-billed Gerygone *Gerygone magnirostris*	→	R							M	I
☐ Flyeater *Gerygone sulphurea*	←	R	J	B	T	S	K	C		
☐ Plain Gerygone *Gerygone inornata*	E	R			T				M	
☐ Rufous-sided Gerygone *Gerygone dorsalis*	E	R						C	M	
☐ Brown-breasted Gerygone *Gerygone ruficollis*	P	R								I
☐ Mangrove Gerygone *Gerygone levigaster*	→	R								I

Bird Names (Scientific Names)

Bird Names (Scientific Names)	EX	ST	J	B	T	S	K	C	M	I
Monarchidae: Monarchs, Boatbills, Fantails										
Rufous-winged Philentoma *Philentoma pyrhopterum*	←	R				S	K			
Maroon-breasted Philentoma *Philentoma velatum*	←	R	J			S	K			
Black-naped Monarch *Hypothymis azurea*	←	R	J	B	T	S	K	C	M	
Caerulean Paradise-flycatcher *Eutrichomyias rowleyi*	E	R						C		
Asian Paradise-flycatcher *Terpsiphone paradisi*	←	R	J		T	S	K			
Japanese Paradise-flycatcher *Terpsiphone atrocaudata*	←	V				S				
Philippine Paradise-flycatcher *Terpsiphone cinnamomea*	←	R						C		
Black Monarch *Monarcha axillaris*	P	R								I
Rufous Monarch *Monarcha rubiensis*	P	R								I
Island Monarch *Monarcha cinerascens*	→	R			T			C	M	I
Black-faced Monarch *Monarcha melanopsis*	→	M								I
Black-winged Monarch *Monarcha frater*	→	R\M								I
White-naped Monarch *Monarcha pileatus*	E	R							M	
Spot-winged Monarch *Monarcha guttulus*	P	R							M	I
Black-bibbed Monarch *Monarcha mundus*	E	R							M	
Flores Monarch *Monarcha sacerdotum*	E	R			T					
Spectacled Monarch *Monarcha trivirgatus*	→	R\M			T				M	I
White-tipped Monarch *Monarcha everetti*	E	R						C		
Black-chinned Monarch *Monarcha boanensis*	E	R							M	
Black-tipped Monarch *Monarcha loricatus*	E	R							M	
White-tailed Monarch *Monarcha leucurus*	E	R							M	
Kofiau Monarch *Monarcha julianae*	E	R								I
Hooded Monarch *Monarcha manadensis*	P	R								I
Biak Monarch *Monarcha brehmii*	E	R								I
Golden Monarch *Monarcha chrysomela*	→	R							M	I
Dark-grey Flycatcher *Myiagra galeata*	E	R							M	
Frilled Monarch *Arses telescophthalmus*	→	R								I
Rufous-collared Monarch *Arses insularis*	→	R								I
Biak Flycatcher *Myiagra atra*	E	R								I
Leaden Flycatcher *Myiagra rubecula*	→	R\M								I
Broad-billed Flycatcher *Myiagra ruficollis*	→	R			T			C	M	I
Satin Flycatcher *Myiagra cyanoleuca*	→	M								I
Restless Flycatcher *Myiagra inquieta*	→	R								I
Shining Flycatcher *Piezorhynchus alecto*	→	R							M	I
Yellow-breasted Boatbill *Machaerirhynchus flaviventer*	→	R							M	I
Black-breasted Boatbill *Machaerirhynchus nigripectus*	P	R								I
Lowland Peltops *Peltops blainvillii*	P	R								I
Mountain Peltops *Peltops montanus*	P	R							M	I
Rufous-tailed Fantail *Rhipidura phoenicura*	E	R	J							
White-throated Fantail *Rhipidura albicollis*	←	R				S	K			
White-bellied Fantail *Rhipidura euryura*	E	R	J							
Pied Fantail *Rhipidura javanica*	←	R	J	B	T	S	K			
Spotted Fantail *Rhipidura perlata*	←	R				S	K			
Willie-wagtail *Rhipidura leucophrys*	→	R							M	I
Northern Fantail *Rhipidura rufiventris*	→	R			T				M	I
Brown-capped Fantail *Rhipidura diluta*	E	R			T					
Cinnamon-tailed Fantail *Rhipidura fuscorufa*	E	R							M	
Friendly Fantail *Rhipidura albolimbata*	P	R								I
Chestnut-bellied Fantail *Rhipidura hyperythra*	P	R							M	I
Sooty Thicket-fantail *Rhipidura threnothorax*	P	R							M	I
Black Thicket-fantail *Rhipidura maculipectus*	P	R								I
White-bellied Thicket-fantail *Rhipidura leucothorax*	P	R								I
Black Fantail *Rhipidura atra*	P	R								I
Dimorphic Fantail *Rhipidura brachyrhyncha*	P	R								I
Streak-breasted Fantail *Rhipidura dedemi*	E	R							M	
Tawny-backed Fantail *Rhipidura superflua*	E	R							M	
Rusty-bellied Fantail *Rhipidura teysmanni*	E	R						C	M	
Long-tailed Fantail *Rhipidura opistherythra*	E	R							M	

Bird Names (Scientific Names)	EX	ST	R	J	B	T	S	K	C	M	I
☐ Rufous-backed Fantail *Rhipidura rufidorsa*		P	R								I
☐ Rufous Fantail *Rhipidura rufifrons*		→	R\M			T			C	M	I
☐ Mangrove Fantail *Rhipidura phasiana*		←→	R								I

Petroicidae: Australian Flycatchers, Australian Robins

Bird Names (Scientific Names)	EX	ST	R	J	B	T	S	K	C	M	I
☐ Torrent Flycatcher *Monachella muelleriana*		→	R								I
☐ Lemon-bellied Flycatcher *Microeca flavigaster*		→	R								I
☐ Golden-bellied Flycatcher *Microeca hemixantha*		E	R							M	
☐ Yellow-legged Flycatcher *Microeca griseoceps*		→	R							M	I
☐ Olive Flycatcher *Microeca flavovirescens*		P	R							M	I
☐ Canary Flycatcher *Microeca papuana*		P	R								I
☐ Garnet Robin *Eugerygone rubra*		P	R								I
☐ Alpine Robin *Petroica bivittata*		P	R								I
☐ Snow Mountain Robin *Petroica archboldi*		E	R								I
☐ White-faced Robin *Tregellasia leucops*		→	R								I
☐ Mangrove Robin *Peneoenanthe pulverulenta*		→	R							M	I
☐ Black-chinned Robin *Poecilodryas brachyura*		P	R								I
☐ Black-sided Robin *Poecilodryas hypoleuca*		P	R								I
☐ Banded Robin *Poecilodryas placens*		P	R								I
☐ Black-throated Robin *Poecilodryas albonotata*		P	R								I
☐ White-winged Robin *Peneothello sigillatus*		P	R								I
☐ Smoky Robin *Peneothello cryptoleucus*		E	R								I
☐ Blue-grey Robin *Peneothello cyanus*		P	R								I
☐ White-rumped Robin *Peneothello bimaculatus*		P	R								I
☐ Ashy Robin *Heteromyias albispecularis*		→	R								I
☐ Green-backed Robin *Pachycephalopsis hattamensis*		P	R								I
☐ White-eyed Robin *Pachycephalopsis poliosoma*		P	R								I

Pachycephalidae: Ploughbills, Whistlers, Shrike-thrushes, Pitohuis

Bird Names (Scientific Names)	EX	ST	R	J	B	T	S	K	C	M	I
☐ Wattled Ploughbill *Eulacestoma nigropectus*		P	R							M	I
☐ Goldenface *Pachycare flavogrisea*		P	R								I
☐ Mottled Whistler *Rhagologus leucostigma*		P	R								I
☐ Yellow-flanked Whistler *Hylocitrea bonensis*		E	R						C		
☐ Maroon-backed Whistler *Coracornis raveni*		E	R						C		
☐ Rufous-naped Whistler *Pachycephala rufinucha*		P	R								I
☐ Sooty Whistler *Pachycephala tenebrosa*		P	R								I
☐ Mangrove Whistler *Pachycephala grisola*		←	R	J	B	T	S	K			
☐ Island Whistler *Pachycephala phaionotus*		E	R							M	I
☐ Rusty Whistler *Pachycephala hyperythra*		P	R								I
☐ Bornean Whistler *Pachycephala hypoxantha*		B	R					K			
☐ Sulphur-bellied Whistler *Pachycephala sulfuriventer*		E	R						C		
☐ Vogelkop Whistler *Pachycephala meyeri*		E	R								I
☐ Sclater's Whistler *Pachycephala soror*		P	R								I
☐ Grey Whistler *Pachycephala simplex*		→	R							M	I
☐ Fawn-breasted Whistler *Pachycephala orpheus*		E	R			T					
☐ Common Golden Whistler *Pachycephala pectoralis*		→	R	J	B	T			C	M	I
☐ Mangrove Golden Whistler *Pachycephala melanura*		→	R								I
☐ Bare-throated Whistler *Pachycephala nudigula*		E	R			T					
☐ Lorentz's Whistler *Pachycephala lorentzi*		P	R								I
☐ Regent Whistler *Pachycephala schlegelii*		P	R								I
☐ Golden-backed Whistler *Pachycephala aurea*		P	R								I
☐ White-bellied Whistler *Pachycephala leucogastra*		P	R							M	I
☐ Drab Whistler *Pachycephala griseonota*		E	R							M	
☐ Black-headed Whistler *Pachycephala monacha*		P	R							M	I
☐ Little Shrike-thrush *Colluricincla megarhyncha*		→	R							M	I
☐ Grey Shrike-thrush *Colluricincla harmonica*		→	R								I
☐ Variable Pitohui *Pitohui kirhocephalus*		P	R							M	I
☐ Hooded Pitohui *Pitohui dichrous*		P	R								I
☐ White-bellied Pitohui *Pitohui incertus*		P	R								I

APPENDIX

Bird Names (Scientific Names)	Status		Distribution by Region							
	EX	ST	J	B	T	S	K	C	M	I
☐ Rusty Pitohui *Pitohui ferrugineus*	P	R							M	I
☐ Crested Pitohui *Pitohui cristatus*	P	R								I
☐ Black Pitohui *Pitohui nigrescens*	P	R								I

Aegithalidae: Pygmy Tit

	EX	ST	J	B	T	S	K	C	M	I
☐ Pygmy Tit *Psaltria exilis*	E	R	J							

Paridae: Tits

	EX	ST	J	B	T	S	K	C	M	I
☐ Great Tit *Parus major*	←	R	J	B	T	S	K			

Sittidae: Nuthatches, Sittellas

	EX	ST	J	B	T	S	K	C	M	I
☐ Velvet-fronted Nuthatch *Sitta frontalis*	←	R	J			S	K			
☐ Blue Nuthatch *Sitta azurea*	←	R	J			S				
☐ Papuan Sittella *Daphoenositta papuensis*	P	R								I
☐ Black Sittella *Daphoenositta miranda*	P	R								I

Climacteridae: Australian Treecreepers

	EX	ST	J	B	T	S	K	C	M	I
☐ Papuan Treecreeper *Cormobates placens*	P	R								I

Dicaedae: Berrypeckers, Flowerpeckers

	EX	ST	J	B	T	S	K	C	M	I
☐ Obscure Berrypecker *Melanocharis arfakiana*	P	R								I
☐ Black Berrypecker *Melanocharis nigra*	P	R							M	I
☐ Lemon-breasted Berrypecker *Melanocharis longicauda*	P	R								I
☐ Fan-tailed Berrypecker *Melanocharis versteri*	P	R								I
☐ Streaked Berrypecker *Melanocharis striativentris*	P	R								I
☐ Spotted Berrypecker *Rhamphocharis crassirostris*	P	R								I
☐ Yellow-breasted Flowerpecker *Prionochilus maculatus*	←	R				S	K			
☐ Crimson-breasted Flowerpecker *Prionochilus percussus*	←	R	J			S	K			
☐ Yellow-rumped Flowerpecker *Prionochilus xanthopygius*	B	R					K			
☐ Scarlet-breasted Flowerpecker *Prionochilus thoracicus*	←	R					K			
☐ Golden-rumped Flowerpecker *Dicaeum annae*	E	R			T					
☐ Thick-billed Flowerpecker *Dicaeum agile*	←	R	J	B	T	S				
☐ Brown-backed Flowerpecker *Dicaeum everetti*	←	R				S	K			
☐ Yellow-vented Flowerpecker *Dicaeum chrysorrheum*	←	R	J	B		S	K			
☐ Yellow-sided Flowerpecker *Dicaeum aureolimbatum*	E	R						C		
☐ Orange-bellied Flowerpecker *Dicaeum trigonostigma*	←	R	J	B		S	K			
☐ Plain Flowerpecker *Dicaeum concolor*	←	R	J	B		S	K			
☐ Crimson-crowned Flowerpecker *Dicaeum nehrkorni*	E	R						C		
☐ Ashy Flowerpecker *Dicaeum vulneratum*	E	R							M	
☐ Flame-breasted Flowerpecker *Dicaeum erythrothorax*	E	R							M	
☐ Papuan Flowerpecker *Dicaeum pectorale*	P	R								I
☐ Black-fronted Flowerpecker *Dicaeum igniferum*	E	R			T					
☐ Red-chested Flowerpecker *Dicaeum maugei*	E	R		B	T			C	M	
☐ Blood-breasted Flowerpecker *Dicaeum sanguinolentum*	E	R	J	B	T					
☐ Mistletoebird *Dicaeum hirundinaceum*	→	R			T				M	I
☐ Grey-sided Flowerpecker *Dicaeum celebicum*	E	R						C	M	
☐ Black-sided Flowerpecker *Dicaeum monticolum*	B	R					K			
☐ Buff-bellied Flowerpecker *Dicaeum ignipectus*	←	R				S				
☐ Scarlet-backed Flowerpecker *Dicaeum cruentatum*	←	R				S	K			
☐ Scarlet-headed Flowerpecker *Dicaeum trochileum*	E	R	J	B	T	S	K			
☐ Tit Berrypecker *Oreocharis arfaki*	P	R								I
☐ Crested Berrypecker *Paramythia montium*	P	R								I

Nectariniidae: Sunbirds, Spiderhunters

	EX	ST	J	B	T	S	K	C	M	I
☐ Plain Sunbird *Anthreptes simplex*	←	R				S	K			
☐ Brown-throated Sunbird *Anthreptes malacensis*	←	R	J	B	T	S	K	C	M	
☐ Red-throated Sunbird *Anthreptes rhodolaema*	←	R				S	K			
☐ Ruby-cheeked Sunbird *Anthreptes singalensis*	←	R	J			S	K			
☐ Purple-naped Sunbird *Hypogramma hypogrammicum*	←	R				S	K			

Bird Names (Scientific Names)

Bird Names (Scientific Names)	EX	ST	J	B	T	S	K	C	M	I
Purple-throated Sunbird *Nectarinia sperata*	←	R	J			S	K			
Black Sunbird *Nectarinia aspasia*	→	R						C	M	I
Copper-throated Sunbird *Nectarinia calcostetha*	←	R	J			S	K			
Olive-backed Sunbird *Nectarinia jugularis*	←→	R	J	B	T	S	K	C	M	I
Apricot-breasted Sunbird *Nectarinia buettikoferi*	E	R			T					
Flame-breasted Sunbird *Nectarinia solaris*	E	R			T				M	
Elegant Sunbird *Aethopyga duyvenbodei*	E	R						C		
White-flanked Sunbird *Aethopyga eximia*	E	R	J							
Crimson Sunbird *Aethopyga siparaja*	←	R	J			S	K	C		
Scarlet Sunbird *Aethopyga temminckii*	←	R				S	K			
Violet-tailed Sunbird *Aethopyga mystacalis*	E	R	J							
Little Spiderhunter *Arachnothera longirostra*	←	R	J	B						
Thick-billed Spiderhunter *Arachnothera crassirostris*	←	R				S	K			
Long-billed Spiderhunter *Arachnothera robusta*	←	R	J			S	K			
Spectacled Spiderhunter *Arachnothera flavigaster*	←	R				S	K			
Yellow-eared Spiderhunter *Arachnothera chrysogenys*	←	R	J			S	K			
Grey-breasted Spiderhunter *Arachnothera affinis*	←	R	J	B		S	K			
Bornean Spiderhunter *Arachnothera everetti*	B	R					K			
Whitehead's Spiderhunter *Arachnothera juliae*	B	R					K			

Zosteropidae: White-eyes, Blackeye

Bird Names (Scientific Names)	EX	ST	J	B	T	S	K	C	M	I
Oriental White-eye *Zosterops palpebrosus*	←	R	J	B	T	S	K			
Enggano White-eye *Zosterops salvadorii*	E	R				S				
Black-capped White-eye *Zosterops atricapilla*	B	R				S	K			
Everett's White-eye *Zosterops everetti*	←	R					K	C		
Mountain White-eye *Zosterops montanus*	←	R	J	B	T	S		C	M	
Yellow-spectacled White-eye *Zosterops wallacei*	E	R			T					
Javan White-eye *Zosterops flavus*	B	R	J				K			
Lemon-bellied White-eye *Zosterops chloris*	E	R	J	B	T	S	K	C	M	I
Ashy-bellied White-eye *Zosterops citrinellus*	→	R			T				M	
Pale-bellied White-eye *Zosterops consobrinorum*	E	R						C		
Great Kai White-eye *Zosterops grayi*	E	R							M	
Little Kai White-eye *Zosterops uropygialis*	E	R							M	
Lemon-throated White-eye *Zosterops anomalus*	E	R						C		
Cream-throated White-eye *Zosterops atriceps*	E	R							M	
Black-fronted White-eye *Zosterops atrifrons*	P	R						C	M	I
Biak White-eye *Zosterops mysorensis*	E	R								I
Dark-capped White-eye *Zosterops fuscicapilla*	P	R								I
Buru Yellow White-eye *Zosterops buruensis*	E	R							M	
Ambon Yellow White-eye *Zosterops kuehni*	E	R							M	
New Guinea White-eye *Zosterops novaeguineae*	P	R							M	I
Bicoloured Darkeye *Tephrozosterops stalkeri*	E	R							M	
Rufous-throated Darkeye *Madanga ruficollis*	E	R							M	
Grey-hooded Darkeye *Lophozosterops pinaiae*	E	R							M	
Streak-headed Darkeye *Lophozosterops squamiceps*	E	R						C		
Grey-throated Darkeye *Lophozosterops javanicus*	E	R	J	B						
Yellow-browed Darkeye *Lophozosterops superciliaris*	E	R			T					
Crested Darkeye *Lophozosterops dohertyi*	E	R			T					
Pygmy Darkeye *Oculocincta squamifrons*	B	R					K			
Spot-breasted Darkeye *Heleia muelleri*	E	R			T					
Thick-billed Darkeye *Heleia crassirostris*	E	R			T					
Blackeye *Chlorocharis emiliae*	B	R					K			

Meliphagidae: Straightbills, Longbills, Honeyeaters, Friarbirds

Bird Names (Scientific Names)	EX	ST	J	B	T	S	K	C	M	I
Olive Straightbill *Timeliopsis fulvigula*	P	R								I
Tawny Straightbill *Timeliopsis griseigula*	P	R								I
Long-billed Honeyeater *Melilestes megarhynchus*	P	R							M	I
Yellow-bellied Longbill *Toxorhamphus novaeguineae*	P	R							M	I
Slaty-chinned Longbill *Toxorhamphus poliopterus*	P	R								I

Bird Names (Scientific Names)	Status		Distribution by Region							
	EX	ST	J	B	T	S	K	C	M	I
☐ Pygmy Longbill *Oedistoma pygmaeum*	P	R								I
☐ Green-backed Honeyeater *Glycichaera fallax*	→	R							M	I
☐ Dwarf Longbill *Oedistoma iliolophum*	P	R								I
☐ Scaly-crowned Honeyeater *Lichmera lombokia*	E	R			T					
☐ Olive Honeyeater *Lichmera argentauris*	E	R							M	
☐ Brown Honeyeater *Lichmera indistincta*	→	R		B	T				M	I
☐ Silver-eared Honeyeater *Lichmera alboauricularis*	P	R								I
☐ White-tufted Honeyeater *Lichmera squamata*	E	R							M	
☐ Buru Honeyeater *Lichmera deningeri*	E	R							M	
☐ Spectacled Honeyeater *Lichmera monticola*	E	R							M	
☐ Yellow-eared Honeyeater *Lichmera flavicans*	E	R			T					
☐ Black-chested Honeyeater *Lichmera notabilis*	E	R							M	
☐ Drab Myzomela *Myzomela blasii*	E	R							M	
☐ Red-throated Myzomela *Myzomela eques*	→	R								I
☐ Dusky Myzomela *Myzomela obscura*	→	R							M	I
☐ Red Myzomela *Myzomela cruentata*	→	R								I
☐ Black Myzomela *Myzomela nigrita*	→	R								I
☐ Crimson-hooded Myzomela *Myzomela kuehni*	E	R							M	
☐ Red-headed Myzomela *Myzomela erythrocephala*	→	R			T				M	I
☐ Mountain Myzomela *Myzomela adolphinae*	P	R								I
☐ Crimson Myzomela *Myzomela dibapha*	→	R						C	M	
☐ Red-rumped Myzomela *Myzomela vulnerata*	E	R			T					
☐ Red-collared Myzomela *Myzomela rosenbergii*	P	R								I
☐ Spot-breasted Meliphaga *Meliphaga mimikae*	P	R								I
☐ Forest Meliphaga *Meliphaga montana*	P	R								I
☐ Mountain Meliphaga *Meliphaga orientalis*	P	R								I
☐ Scrub Meliphaga *Meliphaga albonotata*	P	R								I
☐ Puff-backed Meliphaga *Meliphaga aruensis*	P	R							M	I
☐ Mimic Meliphaga *Meliphaga analoga*	P	R							M	I
☐ Graceful Meliphaga *Meliphaga gracilis*	→	R							M	I
☐ Yellow-gaped Meliphaga *Meliphaga flavirictus*	P	R								I
☐ Streak-breasted Meliphaga *Meliphaga reticulata*	E	R			T					
☐ Tawny-breasted Honeyeater *Xanthotis chrysotis*	→	R							M	I
☐ Spotted Honeyeater *Xanthotis polygramma*	P	R								I
☐ Varied Honeyeater *Lichenostomus versicolor*	P	R								I
☐ Black-throated Honeyeater *Lichenostomus subfrenatus*	P	R								I
☐ Obscure Honeyeater *Lichenostomus obscurus*	P	R								I
☐ Orange-cheeked Honeyeater *Oreornis chrysogenys*	E	R								I
☐ White-throated Honeyeater *Melithreptus albogularis*	→	R								I
☐ Blue-faced Honeyeater *Entomyzon cyanotis*	→	R								I
☐ Plain Honeyeater *Pycnopygius ixoides*	P	R								I
☐ Marbled Honeyeater *Pycnopygius cinereus*	P	R								I
☐ Streak-headed Honeyeater *Pycnopygius stictocephalus*	P	R							M	I
☐ White-streaked Friarbird *Melitograis gilolensis*	E	R							M	
☐ Meyer's Friarbird *Philemon meyeri*	P	R								I
☐ Brass's Friarbird *Philemon brassi*	E	R								I
☐ Little Friarbird *Philemon citreogularis*	→	R							M	I
☐ Timor Friarbird *Philemon inornatus*	E	R			T					
☐ Dusky Friarbird *Philemon fuscicapillus*	E	R							M	
☐ Seram Friarbird *Philemon subcorniculatus*	E	R							M	
☐ Black-faced Friarbird *Philemon moluccensis*	E	R							M	
☐ Helmeted Friarbird *Philemon buceroides*	→	R			T				M	
☐ New Guinea Friarbird *Philemon novaeguineae*	→	R							M	I
☐ Noisy Friarbird *Philemon corniculatus*	→	R								I
☐ Leaden Honeyeater *Ptiloprora plumbea*	P	R								I
☐ Yellowish Honeyeater *Ptiloprora meekiana*	P	R								I
☐ Rufous-sided Honeyeater *Ptiloprora erythropleura*	E	R								I
☐ Rusty-backed Honeyeater *Ptiloprora mayri*	P	R								I
☐ Grey-streaked Honeyeater *Ptiloprora perstriata*	P	R								I

Bird Names (Scientific Names)

Bird Names (Scientific Names)	EX	ST	J	B	T	S	K	C	M	I
Sooty Honeyeater *Melionyx fuscus*	P	R								I
Short-bearded Honeyeater *Melionyx nouhuysi*	E	R								I
Cinnamon-browed Melidectes *Melidectes ochromelas*	P	R								I
Vogelkop Melidectes *Melidectes leucostephes*	E	R								I
Belford's Melidectes *Melidectes belfordi*	P	R								I
Yellow-browed Melidectes *Melidectes rufocrissalis*	P	R								I
Ornate Melidectes *Melidectes torquatus*	P	R								I
Western Smoky Honeyeater *Melipotes gymnops*	E	R								I
Common Smoky Honeyeater *Melipotes fumigatus*	P	R								I
Dark-eared Myza *Myza celebensis*	E	R						C		
White-eared Myza *Myza sarasinorum*	E	R						C		
Brown-backed Honeyeater *Ramsayornis modestus*	→	R							M	I
Rufous-banded Honeyeater *Conopophila albogularis*	→	R							M	I

Fringillidae: Serins

Bird Names (Scientific Names)	EX	ST	J	B	T	S	K	C	M	I
Sunda Serin *Serinus estherae*	←	R	J			S				

Estrildidae: Firetails, Parrot-finches, Munias, Sparrows

Bird Names (Scientific Names)	EX	ST	J	B	T	S	K	C	M	I
Red Avadavat *Amandava amandava*	←	R	J	B	T					
Mountain Firetail *Oreostruthus fuliginosus*	P	R								I
Crimson Finch *Neochmia phaeton*	→	R								I
Zebra Finch *Taeniopygia guttata*	→	R		B	T				M	
Tawny-breasted Parrot-finch *Erythrura hyperythra*	←	R	J		T		K			
Pin-tailed Parrot-finch *Erythrura prasina*	←	R				S	K			
Tricoloured Parrot-finch *Erythrura tricolor*	E	R			T				M	
Blue-faced Parrot-finch *Erythrura trichroa*	→	R						C	M	I
Papuan Parrot-finch *Erythrura papuana*	P	R								I
White-rumped Munia *Lonchura striata*	←	R				S				
Javan Munia *Lonchura leucogastroides*	E	R	J	B	T	S				
Dusky Munia *Lonchura fuscans*	B	R					K			
Black-faced Munia *Lonchura molucca*	E	R	J	B	T			C	M	
Scaly-breasted Munia *Lonchura punctulata*	← F	R	J	B	T	S	K	C	M	
White-bellied Munia *Lonchura leucogastra*	←	R	J			S	K			
Streak-headed Munia *Lonchura tristissima*	P	R								I
White-spotted Munia *Lonchura leucosticta*	P	R								I
Five-coloured Munia *Lonchura quinticolor*	E	R			T				M	
Chestnut Munia *Lonchura malacca*	←	R	J	B		S	K	C	M	
White-headed Munia *Lonchura maja*	←	R	J	B		S				
Pale-headed Munia *Lonchura pallida*	E	R			T			C	M	
Grand Munia *Lonchura grandis*	P	R								I
Grey-banded Munia *Lonchura vana*	E	R								I
Grey-crowned Munia *Lonchura nevermanni*	P	R								I
Hooded Munia *Lonchura spectabilis*	→	R								I
Chestnut-breasted Munia *Lonchura castaneothorax*	→	R								I
Black Munia *Lonchura stygia*	P	R								I
Black-breasted Munia *Lonchura teerinki*	E	R								I
Snow Mountain Munia *Lonchura montana*	P	R								I
Timor Sparrow *Padda fuscata*	E	R			T					
Java Sparrow *Padda oryzivora*	E	R	J	B	F	F	F	F	F	

Ploceidae: Tree Sparrow, Weavers

Bird Names (Scientific Names)	EX	ST	J	B	T	S	K	C	M	I
Tree Sparrow *Passer montanus*	← F	R	J	B	T	S	K	C	M	I
Asian Golden Weaver *Ploceus hypoxanthus*	←	R	J			S				
Streaked Weaver *Ploceus manyar*	←	R	J	B		S				
Baya Weaver *Ploceus philippinus*	←	R	J	B		S				

Estrillidae: Buntings

Bird Names (Scientific Names)	EX	ST	J	B	T	S	K	C	M	I
Black-faced Bunting *Emberiza spodocephala*	← →	V							M	

Bird Names (Scientific Names)

Bird Names (Scientific Names)	EX	ST	J	B	T	S	K	C	M	I
Sturnidae: Starlings, Mynas										
☐ Singing Starling *Aplonis cantoroides*	→	R							M	I
☐ Tanimbar Starling *Aplonis crassa*	E	R							M	
☐ Moluccan Starling *Aplonis mysolensis*	E	R						C	M	I
☐ Long-tailed Starling *Aplonis magna*	E	R								I
☐ Short-tailed Starling *Aplonis minor*	←	R	J	B	T			C	M	
☐ Asian Glossy Starling *Aplonis panayensis*	←	R	J	B		S	K	C		
☐ Metallic Starling *Aplonis metallica*	→	R\M			T				M	I
☐ Yellow-eyed Starling *Aplonis mystacea*	P	R								I
☐ Chestnut-cheeked Starling *Sturnus philippensis*		M					K	C	M	
☐ Purple-backed Starling *Sturnus sturninus*	←	M	J			S				
☐ Asian Pied Starling *Sturnus contra*	←	R	J	B		S				
☐ Black-winged Starling *Sturnus melanopterus*	E	R	J	B	T					
☐ Bali Starling *Leucopsar rothschildi*	E	R		B						
☐ Common Myna *Acridotheres tristis*	← F	R						F		
☐ White-vented Myna *Acridotheres javanicus*	←	R	J	B	F	F		C		
☐ Golden Myna *Mino anais*	P	R								I
☐ Yellow-faced Myna *Mino dumontii*	→	R							M	I
☐ Short-crested Myna *Basilornis celebensis*	E	R						C		
☐ Helmeted Myna *Basilornis galeatus*	E	R						C	M	
☐ Long-crested Myna *Basilornis corythaix*	E	R							M	
☐ White-necked Myna *Streptocitta albicollis*	E	R						C		
☐ Bare-eyed Myna *Streptocitta albertinae*	E	R						C	M	
☐ Hill Myna *Gracula religiosa*	←	R	J	B	T	S	K			
☐ Fiery-browed Myna *Enodes erythrophris*	E	R						C		
☐ Finch-billed Myna *Scissirostrum dubium*	E	R						C		
Oriolidae: Orioles, Figbirds										
☐ Brown Oriole *Oriolus szalayi*	P	R								I
☐ Dusky Oriole *Oriolus phaeochromus*	E	R							M	
☐ Seram Oriole *Oriolus forsteni*	E	R							M	
☐ Black-faced Oriole *Oriolus bouroensis*	E	R							M	
☐ Timor Oriole *Oriolus melanotis*	E	R			T				M	
☐ Olive-backed Oriole *Oriolus sagittatus*	→	M							M	I
☐ Yellow Oriole *Oriolus flavocinctus*	→	R							M	I
☐ Dark-throated Oriole *Oriolus xanthonotus*	←	R	J			S	K			
☐ Black-naped Oriole *Oriolus chinensis*	←	R	J	B	T	S	K	C		
☐ Black-hooded Oriole *Oriolus xanthornus*	←	M?				S	K			
☐ Black-and-crimson Oriole *Oriolus cruentus*	←	R	J			S	K			
☐ Timor Figbird *Sphecotheres viridis*	E	R			T					
☐ Wetar Figbird *Sphecotheres hypoleucos*	E	R							M	
☐ Green Figbird *Sphecotheres vieilloti*	→	R							M	
Dicuridae: Drongos										
☐ Pygmy Drongo *Chaetorhynchus papuensis*	P	R								I
☐ Black Drongo *Dicrurus macrocercus*	←	R\M	J	B						
☐ Ashy Drongo *Dicrurus leucophaeus*	←	R	J	B	T	S	K			
☐ Crow-billed Drongo *Dicrurus annectans*	←	M	J			S	K			
☐ Bronzed Drongo *Dicrurus aeneus*	←	R				S	K			
☐ Lesser Racquet-tailed Drongo *Dicrurus remifer*	←	R	J			S				
☐ Sumatran Drongo *Dicrurus sumatranus*	E	R				S				
☐ Sulawesi Drongo *Dicrurus montanus*	E							C		
☐ Spangled Drongo *Dicrurus bracteatus*	→	R							M	I
☐ Wallacean Drongo *Dicrurus densus*	E				T				M	
☐ Hair-crested Drongo *Dicrurus hottentottus*	←	R	J	B		S	K	C	M	
☐ Greater Racquet-tailed Drongo *Dicrurus paradiseus*	←	R	J	B		S	K			
Grallinidae: Magpie-lark, Torrent-lark										
☐ Magpie-lark *Grallina cyanoleuca*	→	R			T				M	I

Bird Names (Scientific Names)	EX	ST	J	B	T	S	K	C	M	I
Torrent-lark *Grallina bruijni*	P	R								I
Artamidae: Wood-swallows										
White-breasted Wood-swallow *Artamus leucorynchus*	←→	R	J	B	T	S	K	C	M	I
Ivory-backed Wood-swallow *Artamus monachus*	E	R						C		
Great Wood-swallow *Artamus maximus*	P	R								I
Black-faced Wood-swallow *Artamus cinereus*	→	V			T				M	I
Cracticidae: Butcherbirds, Australian Magpie										
Black-backed Butcherbird *Cracticus mentalis*	→	R								I
Hooded Butcherbird *Cracticus cassicus*	P	R							M	I
Black Butcherbird *Cracticus quoyi*	→	R							M	I
Australian Magpie *Gymnorhina tibicen*	→	R								I
Ptilonorhynchidae: Catbirds, Bowerbirds										
White-eared Catbird *Ailuroedus buccoides*	P	R								I
Spotted Catbird *Ailuroedus melanotis*	→	R							M	I
Archbold's Bowerbird *Archboldia papuensis*	P	R								I
Vogelkop Bowerbird *Amblyornis inornatus*	E	R								I
Macgregor's Bowerbird *Amblyornis macgregoriae*	P	R								I
Golden-fronted Bowerbird *Amblyornis flavifrons*	E	R								I
Flame Bowerbird *Sericulus aureus*	P	R								I
Yellow-breasted Bowerbird *Chlamydera lauterbachi*	P	R								I
Fawn-breasted Bowerbird *Chlamydera cerviniventris*	→	R								I
Paradisaeidae: Birds-of-Paradise, Paradise Crow, Manucodes, Sicklebills, Parotias										
Loria's Bird-of-paradise *Loria loriae*	P	R								I
Yellow-breasted Bird-of-paradise *Loboparadisea sericea*	P	R								I
Crested Bird-of-paradise *Cnemophilus macgregorii*	P	R								I
Macgregor's Bird-of-paradise *Macgregoria pulchra*	P	R								I
Paradise Crow *Lycocorax pyrrhopterus*	E	R							M	
Glossy-mantled Manucode *Manucodia atra*	P	R							M	I
Jobi Manucode *Manucodia jobiensis*	P	R								I
Crinkle-collared Manucode *Manucodia chalybata*	P	R								I
Trumpet Manucode *Manucodia keraudrenii*	→	R							M	I
Magnificent Riflebird *Ptiloris magnificus*	→	R								I
Wallace's Standardwing *Semioptera wallacei*	E	R							M	
Twelve-wired Bird-of-paradise *Seleucidis melanoleuca*	P	R								I
Long-tailed Paradigalla *Paradigalla carunculata*	E	R								I
Short-tailed Paradigalla *Paradigalla brevicauda*	P	R								I
Buff-tailed Sicklebill *Epimachus albertisi*	P	R								I
Pale-billed Sicklebill *Epimachus bruijnii*	P	R								I
Black Sicklebill *Epimachus fastuosus*	P	R								I
Brown Sicklebill *Epimachus meyeri*	P	R								I
Arfak Astrapia *Astrapia nigra*	E	R								I
Splendid Astrapia *Astrapia splendidissima*	P	R								I
Superb Bird-of-paradise *Lophorina superba*	P	R								I
Western Parotia *Parotia sefilata*	E	R								I
Carola's Parotia *Parotia carolae*	P	R								I
King of Saxony Bird-of-paradise *Pteridophora alberti*	P	R								I
King Bird-of-paradise *Cicinnurus regius*	P	R							M	I
Magnificent Bird-of-paradise *Cicinnurus magnificus*	P	R								I
Wilson's Bird-of-paradise *Cicinnurus respublica*	E	R								I
Greater Bird-of-paradise *Paradisaea apoda*	P	R							M	I
Lesser Bird-of-paradise *Paradisaea minor*	P	R								I
Red Bird-of-paradise *Paradisaea rubra*	E	R								I
Corvidae: Jays, Magpies, Treepies, Crows										
Crested Jay *Platylophus galericulatus*	←	R	J			S	K			

Bird Names (Scientific Names)	EX	ST	J	B	T	S	K	C	M	I
☐ Black Magpie *Platysmurus leucopterus*	←	R				S	K			
☐ Common Green Magpie *Cissa chinensis*	←	R				S	K			
☐ Short-tailed Green Magpie *Cissa thalassina*	←	R	J							
☐ Sunda Treepie *Dendrocitta occipitalis*	B	R				S	K			
☐ Racquet-tailed Treepie *Crypsirina temia*	←	R	J	B			K			
☐ House Crow *Corvus splendens*	←→	R	J							
☐ Slender-billed Crow *Corvus enca*	←	R	J	B	T	S	K	C	M	
☐ Banggai Crow *Corvus unicolor*	E	R						C		
☐ Piping Crow *Corvus typicus*	E	R						C		
☐ Flores Crow *Corvus florensis*	E	R			T					
☐ Long-billed Crow *Corvus validus*	E	R							M	
☐ Brown-headed Crow *Corvus fuscicapillus*	E	R							M	I
☐ Grey Crow *Corvus tristis*	P	R								I
☐ Large-billed Crow *Corvus macrorhynchos*	←	R	J	B	T	S	K		M	
☐ Torresian Crow *Corvus orru*	→	R							M	I

PERIPLUS LANGUAGE GUIDES

These handy pocket dictionaries are a must for travelers to Indonesia and Malaysia. Each book contains the 2,000 most commonly used words and is bidirectional, giving definitions from the language to English and vice versa.

Further Reading

Field Guides

Along with your travel guide, a field identification guide is essential baggage. MacKinnon's guide covering west Indonesia, and Beehler's to New Guinea (covering Irian Jaya of course) are both excellent. Wallacea, the central part of Indonesia, is not yet covered by a field guide, but one is in preparation by Coates and Bishop and, all being well, will be published by 1998. King and Smythies are now older texts but contain much additional information.

MacKinnon, J & Phillipps, K., 1993, *A Field Guide to the Birds of Borneo, Sumatra, Java and Bali*. Oxford University Press.

Beehler, B.M., Pratt, T.K. & Zimmerman, D.A., 1986. *Birds of New Guinea*. Princeton University Press, Princeton, NJ.

King, B.F., Woodcock, M. & Dickinson, E.C., 1975, *A Field Guide to the Birds of South-east Asia*. Collins, London.

Smythies, B.E., 1981, *The Birds of Borneo* (3rd ed), The Sabah Society and the Malayan Nature Society, Kula Lumpur.

Pocket Guides

The following attractive little guides are aimed more at the general reader describing and illustrating a selection of the species from the area. Derek Holmes' Sulawesi guide is a must for anyone visiting the area as it is currently the only book in which you will find quality illustrations of many of the island's endemics.

Francis, C.M. (comp from Smythies), 1984, *Pocket Guide to the Birds of Borneo*. The Sabah Society with World Wildlife Fund, Malaysia.

Holmes, D.A. & Ash, S., 1989, *The Birds of Java and Bali*. Oxford University Press (Images of Asia series), Singapore.

Holmes, D.A. & Ash, S., 1990, *The Birds of Sumatra and Kalimantan*. Oxford University Press (Images of Asia series), Singapore.

Holmes, D & Phillipps, K., 1996, *The Birds of Sulawesi*. Oxford University Press (Images of Asia series), Singapore.

Mason, V. & Jarvis, F., 1989, *Birds of Bali*. Periplus, Singapore.

Checklists

The following check-lists are essential for any serious student of Indonesian ornithology. They contain detailed distribution and status information and opinion on taxonomy. White & Bruce is a modern classic of ornithological scholarship and contains excellent overviews of biogeography, vegetation and exploration in the region. The OBC list is likely to become the standard for birders wishing to compare their tick-lists.

Andrew, P. 1992 *The Birds of Indonesia: A Checklist (Peter's sequence)*, Kukila Checklist No 1, Jakarta.

Inskipp, T. & Lindsey, N., 1996, *Checklist of the Birds of the Orient*. Oriental Bird Club: Cambridge.

Sibley, C.G. & Monroe, B.L. Jr., 1990, *Distribution and Taxonomy of Birds of the World*. Yale University Press, New Haven & London.

White, C. M .N. & Bruce, M. D., 1986, *The Birds of Wallacea (Sulawesi, the Moluccas & Lesser Sunda Islands)*, Indonesia. B.O.U Checklist No. 7. British Ornithologists' Union, London.

van Marle, J.G. & Voous, K., 1988, *The Birds of Sumatra, an Annotated Checklist*. British Ornithologists' Union Checklist No 10.

Bird Family Accounts and Guides

The increasing popularity of guides to bird families is providing birders with more detailed information and high quality illustrations of the species covered. Those listed below are particularly useful for some pretrip swotting-up to islands of Wallacea not yet covered by general field-guides. Ripley's *Rails of the World* is a large format luxury book, and Foreshaw's *Parrots of the World* is a massive tome. Those published since the 1980s are smaller format, but still too large and expensive to take with you on a trip.

Cooper, W. T. & Foreshaw, J. M., 1977, *The Birds of Paradise and Bower Birds*. Collins, Sydney.

Delcaour, J., 1951, *The Pheasants of the World*. Country Life Ltd, London.

Foreshaw, J. M., 1973, *Parrots of the World* (3rd ed 1989), Doubleday, New York.

Fry, C. H., Fry, K. & Harries, A., 1992, *Kingfishers, Bee-eaters and Rollers*. Christopher Helm/A & C Black, London.

Gilliard, T.E., 1969, *Birds of Paradise and Bower Birds*. Weidenfeld and Nicolson, London.

Goodwin, D., 1967, *Pigeons and Doves of the World*. British Museum, London

Harrison, P., 1983, *Seabirds: an Identification Guide*. Croom Helm/A.H. Reed, London.

Hayman, P., Marchant, J. & Prater, T., 1986, *Shorebirds: an Identification Guide to Waders of the World*. Croom Helm, London & Sydney.

Jones, N. J., Dekker, R. W. R. J. & Roselaar, C. S., 1995, *The Megapodes*. O.U.P, Oxford.

Kemp, A., 1995, *The Hornbills*. Oxford University Press.

Lambert, F & Woodcock, M., 1996, *Pittas, Broadbills and Asities*. Pica Press.

Ripley, J. H., 1977, *Rails of the World*. Fehely, Toronto.

General Ecology

These superb studies of the geography, species, habitats, and conservation issues of the region are fascinating reading for anyone wishing to acquire a deeper understanding of Indonesian ecology.

MacKinnon, K., Hatta, G., Halim, H. & Mangalik, A., 1996, *The Ecology of Kalimantan*. Periplus, Singapore.

Monk, K. A., 1996, *The Ecology of Nusa Tenggara and Maluku*. Periplus, Singapore.

Whitten, A. J., Sengili, D., Jazenul, A. & Nazaruddin, H., 1984 *The Ecology of Sumatra*. Yogyakarta Gajah Mandah University Press.

Whitten, A. J., Mustafa, M. & Henderson, G. S., 1988, *The Ecology of Sulawesi*. Yogyakarta Gajah Mandah University Press.

Whitten, A. J., Soeriaatmadja, R. E., & Affif, S, 1996, *The Ecology of Java and Bali*. Periplus, Singapore.

Edwards, I.D., MacDonald, A.A. & Procter, J., 1993, *Natural History of Seram, Maluku, Indonesia*. Andover, Intercept.

Exploration and Natural History

The tales of travel and adventure in past centuries provide hours of enjoyable reading and provide thought-provoking insights into pre-independence life in Indonesia. Several of those listed below are now out of print, but well worth tracking down through your library.

Beekman, E. M., 1981, *The Poison Tree; Selected Writings of Rumphius*.

Dunmore, J., 1969, *French Explorers in the Pacific. II. The Nineteenth Century*. Clarendon Press, Oxford.

Junge, G. C. A., 1954, *Ornithologisch ondersoek in de Indische archipel*. Ardea 41: 301-336.

Forbes, H., 1885, *A Naturalist's Wanderings in the Eastern Archipelago, a Narrative of Travel and Exploration from 1878 to 1883*. Sampson Low, London. (Newer editions available too).

Stresemann, E., 1975, *Ornithology. From Aristotle to the Present.* Harvard University Press, Cambridge.

Wallace, A. R., 1987 ed, *The Malay Archipelago*.Brash, Singapore.

Conservation

The conservation literature for Indonesia is extensive and diverse and mainly published in reports, often in the Indonesian language, and difficult to access outside Indonesia. The following are good overview publications in this field with a particular emphasis on birds.

Anon, 1993, *Biodiversity Action Plan for Indonesia.* Ministry of National Development and Planning, Jakarta.

Anon, 1995, *An Atlas of Biodiversity in Indonesia.* State Ministry of the Environment and KONPALINDO, Jakarta.

Collar, N.J., Crosby, M.J. & Stattersfield, A.J., 1994, *Birds to Watch 2: the World Checklist of Threatened Birds.* BirdLife International, Cambridge, U.K. (BirdLife Conservation Series No. 4).

Sujatnika, Jepson, P., Soehartono, T.R., Crosby, M.J., & Mardiastuti, A., 1995, *Conserving Indonesian Biodiversity: the Endemic Bird Area Approach.* PHPA/BirdLife International—Indonesia Programme, Jakarta.

FAO, 1982, *National Conservation Plan for Indonesia Vols I-VII.* Food and Agriculture Organisation of the United Nations, Bogor.

General

The BLOWS (British Library of Wildlife Sounds) archive is open to serious enquirers. They are pleased to receive recordings of species not yet in their collection and will provide lists of these for the areas you are visiting.

Wildlife Section of the British Library National Sound Archive (formerly BLOWS—British Library of Wildlife Sounds), 29 Exhibition Road, London SW7 2AS, UK. ☎ (44) 171 412 7402; fax (44) 171 412 7441; e-mail (Curator) richard.ranft@bl.uk

Index

Map Index